G000097407

Impediments to Trade in Services

The economic impact of barriers to world trade and investment in services has been thought impossible to measure. As a consequence, significant global policy initiatives such as the General Agreement on Trade in Services have been concluded in an information void. This book challenges the view that impediments to services trade cannot be quantified, detailing how these barriers can be measured and their significance estimated.

The book contains studies measuring impediments to trade and investment in a variety of sectors, including telecommunications, finance, shipping, education and air transport. The authors explain how the measures were calculated and show how the results could be used in sophisticated economic models. The final part of the book looks at current issues in services negotiations in the World Trade Organisation and the Asia Pacific Economic Cooperation forum.

The measurements and methods detailed in this work have clear relevance to policymaking on services liberalisation and could be used by both international and regional organisations in services negotiations. This work will consequently prove to be an extremely valuable addition to the literature of the field.

Christopher Findlay took up the position of Professor of Economics in the Asia Pacific School of Economics and Management at The Australian National University in October 1999. Prior to that he was Associate Professor of Economics at the University of Adelaide. His research is mainly on Australia's trade with Asia, particularly in the services sector.

Tony Warren is a principal consultant with the Network Economics Consulting Group in Canberra, where he provides economic and regulatory advice on trade practices issues to a range of transport and telecommunications companies in Australia, New Zealand and Southeast Asia. Dr Warren is also Visiting Fellow in the Asia Pacific School of Economics and Management at The Australian National University. His current research includes an international comparison of the impact of regulation on telecommunications pricing; and an analysis of the interaction of trade and competition policies in relation to service industries.

Routledge Studies in the Growth Economies of Asia

Impediments to Trade in Services

Measurement and policy implications

Edited by
Christopher Findlay and Tony Warren

London and New York

First published 2000
by Routledge
11 New Fetter Lane, London EC4P 4EE

Simultaneously published in the USA and Canada
by Routledge
29 West 35th Street, New York, NY 10001

Routledge is an imprint of the Taylor & Francis Group

Typeset in Garamond by Australia–Japan Research Centre, Canberra, Australia
Printed and bound in Great Britain by MPG Books Ltd, Bodmin

British Library Cataloguing in Publication Data
A catalogue record for this book is available from the British Library

Library of Congress Cataloging in Publication Data
Impediments to trade in services: measurement and policy implications / [edited by] Christopher Findlay and Tony Warren.
   p. cm.
  Includes bibliographical references and index.
  1. Service industries. 2. International trade. I. Findlay, Christopher C. (Christopher Charles) II. Warren, Tony, 1968–
HD9980.5.I52 2001
382'.45–de21   00-045765

ISBN 0-415-24090-5

Publisher's Note
This book has been prepared from camera-ready copy provided by the editors

Contents

Figures

Tables

Contributors

PAUL BELIN is currently working with the Productivity Commission, an Australian Government microeconomics research and advisory body. He has worked on a number of Commission inquiries including those on broadcasting regulation, international air services and the automotive industry. His research focuses on competition policy, industrial organisation and natural resource economics.

MALCOLM BOSWORTH is currently a Research Fellow at the Australia–Japan Research Centre, in The Australian National University's Asia Pacific School of Economics and Management. He has wide experience in trade and industry assistance measurement, including over 20 years at the Productivity Commission (and its predecessors). He is also a staff consultant for the World Trade Organisation, undertaking Trade Policy Reviews of member states.

ALESSANDRA COLECCHIA is an economist at the Organisation for Economic Cooperation and Development (OECD). She is currently examining the impact of information technologies and electronic commerce on productivity and economic performance. At the OECD she has also worked on the areas of trade policy, international trade in services, technology and skills.

PHILIPPA DEE is an Assistant Commissioner at the Productivity Commission. She has worked on a wide range of economic policy issues, evaluating Australia's policies on research and development, greenhouse gas, telecommunications and competition, and examining the effects of multilateral trade liberalisation. She was previously a Senior Research Fellow at The Australian National University and a research economist at the Kiel Institute of World Economics.

CHRISTOPHER FINDLAY took up the position of Professor of Economics in the Asia Pacific School of Economics and Management at The Australian National University in October 1999. Prior to that he was Associate Professor of Economics at the University of Adelaide. His research is mainly on Australia's trade with Asia, particularly in the services sector.

GERALDINE GENTLE has been analysing, developing and writing about microeconomic policy for many years with the Productivity Commission, where she is an Assistant Commissioner. She led the team on the international air services inquiry in 1998.

TENDAI GREGAN is the manager of the Wholesale Regulation and Analysis section at CitiPower and is responsible for research on Australia's electricity market. He was previously employed at National Electricity Market Management Company and at the Productivity Commission. His research interests include electricity market design, aviation policy and trade liberalisation.

ALEXIS HARDIN is a principal consultant with the Network Economics Consulting Group in Canberra, where she has been involved primarily in the Group's telecommunications work. This has included the preparation of reports on access pricing and competition, cost–benefit studies of regulatory policy changes and economic support in the development and assessment of cost proxy models. She has previously worked for the Productivity Commission, the Bureau of Industry Economics and the National Centre for Social and Economic Modelling.

LEANNE HOLMES is an economist at the Productivity Commission. She has previously held positions at the Australian Bureau of Agricultural and Resource Economics and The Australian National University. Her research has included trade policy, fisheries economics and energy economics.

MARTIN JOHNSON is an economist in the United States Department of Agriculture, where he conducts economic analysis of proposed anti-trust regulations and anti-trust cases. He was previously a research director at the Productivity Commission. His main research interests are industrial organisation and the analysis of competition policy for imperfectly competitive markets.

KALEESWARAN KALIRAJAN is a research economist at the Productivity Commission. He has contributed to Commission publications on international trade issues and has also examined the effects of tariff and non-tariff measures for trade between APEC (Asia Pacific Economic Cooperation) member economies.

JONG-SOON KANG is a Research Associate at The Australian National University's Asia Pacific School of Economics and Management and manages the University's International Economic Data Bank. Before joining the University, he worked at the POSCO Research Institute in Seoul and as steel industry specialist. His main research interests are the economics of industries and services especially in the Asia Pacific region.

STEVEN KEMP is a lecturer in microeconomics at the School of Economics and Finance at Curtin University in Perth, Western Australia. His research interests concern trade in education services, international students and economics education.

GREG McGUIRE is a senior research economist at the Productivity Commission. He has an extensive knowledge of issues involving international trade in services and restrictions on these services. He has contributed to a number of Commission publications on trade issues. Prior to joining the Commission, he was employed by the Australian Treasury and Finance Departments.

DUC NGUYEN-HONG is a research economist at the Productivity Commission. He has contributed to Commission publications covering trade and industry assistance issues.

MICHAEL SCHUELE is a research economist with the Productivity Commission. He has contributed to Commission publications covering barriers to services trade, APEC trade liberalisation and Australia's anti-dumping regime. He was previously employed by the Australian Bureau of Agricultural and Resource Economics and undertook research into issues related to fisheries and water resources.

TINA SMITH contributed to this book while she was a research economist at the Productivity Commission during the university summer vacation in 1998–99. She currently works as a graduate policy analyst with Australia's Department of the Treasury.

RICHARD SNAPE is Deputy Chairman of the Australian Productivity Commission, where he has presided on a number of major public inquiries, including broadcasting and international aviation. He is also Emeritus Professor of Economics at Monash University, having been professor there from 1971 to 1999. He has held visiting appointments at Stockholm University, the Graduate Institute for International Studies in Geneva and the Stockholm School of Economics. He was also previously at the World Bank in Washington.

SHERRY STEPHENSON is a Principal Trade Specialist with the Trade Unit of the Organisation of American States (OAS) in Washington DC and a member of the Trade Policy Forum of the Pacific Economic Cooperation Council (PECC). She was previously an advisor to the Ministry of Trade of the Government of Indonesia.

RAY TREWIN has been a Fellow in the Australia–Japan Research Centre at The Australian National University since 1992. Prior to that he was a senior officer in the Australian Bureau of Agricultural and Resource Economics from 1972. His main research interests are agricultural and resource economics, international trade, econometric modelling and policy analysis.

TONY WARREN is a principal consultant with the Network Economics Consulting Group in Canberra, where he provides economic and regulatory advice on trade practices issues to transport and telecommunications companies. He is also Visiting Fellow in the Asia Pacific School of Economics and Management at The Australian National University. His current research includes an international comparison of the impact of regulation on telecommunications pricing; and an analysis of the interaction of trade and competition policies in relation to service industries.

Foreword

This book's genesis lies in a shared concern among a number of Australian researchers about the lack of usable data on impediments to trade in services and the fact that global trade negotiations on services were occurring in an information vacuum.

In 1997 the Australian Research Council funded a joint project involving teams from The Australian National University (ANU), the University of Adelaide and the Australian Productivity Commission to address these concerns. This book is the product of that effort. We would like to thank the Australian Research Council for their generosity and ongoing support.

We would also like to thank Dr Philippa Dee, who led the Productivity Commission team. Dr Dee and her many colleagues enthusiastically supported this project, contributed many chapters to the book and have provided ongoing assistance for research in this field. We are looking forward to the next stage of our collaboration with the Commission examining the impact of domestic regulation on trade and investment in the services sector.

The ANU input was coordinated by the Australia–Japan Research Centre. We thank Professor Peter Drysdale, the Centre's Director, for his interest in the work and his backing for its completion. We are also grateful for the critical input and research effort of our colleagues at the Centre.

At the time the project began, Christopher Findlay was at the Department of Economics at the University of Adelaide. The Director of the Centre for International Economic Studies at Adelaide, Professor Kym Anderson, was a keen supporter of the project.

The work reported in this book has been tested at a number of workshops, seminars and presentations involving government officials and scholars from Australia and around the world. We are particularly grateful to participants in those events for their comments and their ongoing interest in the project. The work has also benefited from the comments of a number of officials involved in services negotiations in the World Trade Organisation and in the Asia Pacific Economic Cooperation process.

Finally, we would like to thank those involved in the book's production, especially Sarah Leeming, Minni Reis, Raelee Singh and Denise Ryan.

Christopher Findlay and Tony Warren
The Australian National University, May 2000

Abbreviations

AFTA	ASEAN Free Trade Agreement
AMS	aggregate measure of support
APEC	Asia Pacific Economic Cooperation
ASA	air service arrangements
ASEAN	Association of South East Asian Nations
CER	Closer Economic Relations agreement between Australia and New Zealand
CES	constant elasticity of substitution
CGE	computable general equilibrium
CPC	Central Product Classification
EU	European Union
FDI	foreign direct investment
GATS	General Agreement on Trade in Services
GATT	General Agreement on Tariffs and Trade
GDP	gross domestic product
GE	general equilibrium
GTAP	Global Trade Analysis Project
IAP	APEC individual action plan
ICAO	International Civil Aviation Organisation
IMF	International Monetary Fund
ISIC	International Standard Industrial Classification
ITU	International Telecommunications Union
IVANS	international value-added network services
MAST	measures affecting services trade
MIGA	Multilateral Investment Guarantee Agency
MFN	most favoured nation
MRA	mutual recognition agreement
MTS	maritime transport services
NAFTA	North American Free Trade Agreement
NGMTS	Negotiating Group on Maritime Transport Services
NT	national treatment
NTBs	non-tariff barriers
OAA	Osaka Action Agenda
OECD	Organisation for Economic Cooperation and Development

PECC	Pacific Economic Cooperation Council
PBTS	public basic telecommunications services
SOM	APEC Senior Officials Meeting
TRIMS	trade-related investment measures
UN	United Nations
UNCTAD	United Nations Conference on Trade and Development
UNESCO	United Nations Educational, Scientific and Cultural Organisation
UR	Uruguay Round
WTO	World Trade Organisation

1   Introduction

Christopher Findlay and Tony Warren

Studies of the measurement and impact of impediments to trade and investment in services are rare. Yet, for successful reform to take place, it is crucial that policies are transparent. Greater information, in terms of the detail of policy and the analysis of its effects, helps mobilise key countervailing interests against protectionist forces in domestic economies, aids political leaderships in constructing coalitions for reform and adds to the policymaker's confidence as strategies are designed and implemented. The urgency of work in this area has been increased by the focus on services in the in-built agenda of the World Trade Organisation (WTO) and by the increasing awareness of the need to drive reform in service industries so as to ensure rising standards of living around the globe. The research challenge addressed in this volume is to characterise, assess and then measure the economic impact of policies affecting services trade.

The barriers impeding trade in services are opaque, given the nature of the transactions involved. Some information is available – often in a qualitative form and from a diverse range of sources. This book shows how this sort of information can be combined into robust assessments of policy that prove to be powerful explanators of market outcomes. This opens up new opportunities to use these sorts of measures in the design of reform programs and in the international negotiations associated with their implementation.

This chapter reviews the nature of trade in services and the impediments involved, and spells out the case for greater transparency. A method is outlined for achieving that transparency and the chapter illustrates its application to a number of sectors. Related modelling issues are discussed and the chapter summarises the implications for the negotiating process.

WHAT ARE BARRIERS TO TRADE IN SERVICES?

Services transactions

A service is 'an economic activity that adds value either directly to another economic unit or to a good belonging to another economic unit'.[1] Consequently, services have as a defining feature the requirement for direct interaction between producers and consumers before the service can be rendered (Hirsch 1989).

This need for interaction influences how international transactions in services are conducted. If a producer in one economy can offer a service, then a consumer, resident in another country, must somehow interact with the producer to acquire it. Article I of the General Agreement on Trade in Services (GATS), substantially following Bhagwati (1984) and Sampson and Snape (1985), applied a four-part typology of how this meeting can occur internationally (also known as modes of supply):

- through cross-border communications in which neither the producer nor the consumer moves physically, interacting instead through a postal or a telecommunications network;
- through the movement of a consumer to a supplier's country of residence;
- through the movement of a commercial organisation to the consumer's country of residence; or
- through the movement of an individual service supplier to the consumer's country of residence.

Unfortunately, data are not available on the volume of trade in services according to each of these possible modes of supply. We need to examine standard trade and investment data to develop a clearer picture of international services transactions – and even these data are incomplete.[2] Furthermore, data on services transacted by the movement of labour are almost non-existent at an industry level. Chapter 2 in this book summarises the services trade and investment data that is available and highlights a number of features of the data, including the relatively rapid growth of services transactions. It is observed that for a sector once considered to be untradable, there has been a dramatic increase over the past decade in the proportion of total trade accounted for by services. This is true for both industrialised and developing economies. In some Pacific economies, the ratio of services trade to total trade is now over 30 per cent (Table 2A1).

WHY MEASURE BARRIERS TO TRADE IN SERVICES?

As international services transactions encompass foreign direct investment and the movement of labour, as well as traditional cross-border transactions, any policy that impedes service producers and consumers interacting through any of these channels (or modes of supply) is considered an impediment to trade.

Impediments to services trade come mostly in the form of non-tariff barriers (NTBs), reflecting the difficulties inherent in imposing tariffs directly upon either the service consumer or the service supplier as they interact across borders. NTBs are notoriously difficult to identify and measure. There have been very few systematic attempts to collect information on barriers to entry beyond the periodic trade reviews conducted by national trade negotiators.[3] No equivalent of the United Nations Conference on Trade and Development (UNCTAD) database on NTBs affecting tradable goods yet exists for the services sector.[4] As a consequence, very few studies have identified the barriers that exist or assessed the impact of these barriers on economic outcomes. This is concerning for several reasons.

At a policy development level, the lack of information on the extent and impact of impediments to trade in services undermines the liberalisation process. Evidence is available to suggest that service industries remain protected for the standard political economy reasons – protection is primarily afforded to uncompetitive industries that have significant political muscle (Warren 1996, 1997, 1998). For those involved in multilateral and regional negotiations, the evidence tends to confirm what many already suspect; negotiations on services encounter the same barriers to progress that are so familiar in negotiations on merchandise and agriculture. Powerful domestic interests limit the extent to which commitments to liberalisation will be made. If anything, the barriers to progress in services are even greater because of the relatively widespread involvement of the private sector in service provision and the public sector in service regulation.

Overcoming the forces of protection is never a trivial task and there is no simple solution.[5] However, it is generally considered useful in the domestic political process to make the costs of protection as transparent as possible. Not only does this help build coalitions of interest for liberalisation, it allows policymakers to have greater confidence in the implications of any decisions they may make.[6] The lack of information on impediments to trade and investment in services, and the consequent impact on the economy of these impediments, reduces the set of tools that policy reformers can use when pushing for liberalisation.

At a negotiating level, there is evidence that the desire for reciprocity has played a major part in determining the pattern of specific commitments made under the auspices of the GATS, as it has in other areas of the multilateral trade negotiations (Hoekman 1995; Warren 1996). It is generally accepted that in such a negotiating framework, multi-product negotiations (whereby concessions in one industry are traded for concessions in another) lead to more liberal outcomes by extending the set of industries over which concessions can be traded.[7] As Nau (1987) has argued:

> The across-the-board approach has clearly enjoyed the most success. It establishes politically salient overall goals early in negotiation while permitting great flexibility in subsequent negotiations to deal with individual products, sectors, barriers, or framework and institutional issues. By contrast, the product and sector approaches are, taken alone, unlikely to generate enough political interest and momentum to move negotiations forward at an early stage.

When dealing with NTBs, multi-product negotiations become technically much more difficult, as issues with the comparability of concessions arise (Olechowski 1987; Hoekman and Kostecki 1995). During the Uruguay Round, the problem of NTBs affecting agriculture was confronted directly with the development of the aggregate measure of support (AMS) and attempts to have this measure encompass all non-tariff and tariff barriers affecting agriculture (Croome 1995). Negotiators on services trade had no equivalent to the AMS, or even usable industry-level measures of impediments. During the Uruguay Round this may not have been too significant a problem, as negotiations seemed to have focused on developing the necessary framework and the specific commitments made by members appear overwhelmingly to have been examples of binding the status quo. However, as the new round of services negotiations approaches, the lack of information on impediments to services trade will undermine the potential for negotiated liberalisation.

HOW TO MEASURE BARRIERS TO TRADE IN SERVICES?

The measurement of impediments to trade in services involves a three-step process:

- First, available qualitative evidence that compares the way nations discriminate against potential entrants in various service industries is collected. This evidence is then transformed into a frequency-type index, with every attempt made to weight discriminatory policies by their economic significance.
- Second, the impact of the policies, as measured by the frequency indexes, is assessed against cross-national differences in domestic prices or domestic quantities, with the effect of other factors explaining these differences explicitly taken into account.
- Third, the measured impact of the frequency indexes (the coefficient) on prices or quantities is incorporated into a partial or general equilibrium model to assess the economy-wide impacts of the policies at issue. Where possible, partial equilibrium modelling is also undertaken to allow for the uncertain effects of liberalisation to be more clearly understood.

Chapters 4, 5, 10, 12, 14 and 15 provide examples of the first step of this method for measuring price impacts, generating frequency indexes of barriers to trade in services for various industries. Chapter 3 outlines a general approach to the second step of this method, giving particular attention to the identification of a benchmark against which price impacts can be assessed. Chapters 7, 11, and 13 use these frequency indexes for the telecommunications, financial services and maritime industries, respectively, to generate price-impact measures. Chapter 6 uses the frequency data on impediments to trade in telecommunications services to generate quantity-impact estimates. Chapter 8 presents an example of a partial equilibrium model and Chapter 16 discusses the challenges involved in the use of impact measures in general equilibrium models. The final three chapters of the volume examine policy issues.

Frequency measures

The measurement of NTBs using a frequency index involves:

- the collection of qualitative information on the impediments to trade; and
- the conversion of this qualitative information into a numerical index.

Collecting qualitative information has long proved an insurmountable hurdle in relation to services trade. To begin with, services trade issues were virtually ignored in policy and academic circles until the beginning of the Uruguay Round (Drake and Nicolaïdis 1992). It was not until the mid-1980s that any serious attempt was made to identify impediments to trade in services. Furthermore, the definition of what constitutes an impediment to trade in services continues to be a point of contention. For example, are prudential restrictions on offshore financial services firms or qualification requirements for foreign-trained doctors impediments to trade in services or legitimate regulatory instruments? Finally, it is a costly exercise to collect and verify the necessary information.

In relation to goods trade, significant efforts were made to bridge the information gap with the construction of such databases as the UNCTAD TRAINS NTM database. In relation to services, it was not until the end of the Uruguay Round that a significant international database on the incidence of NTBs became available. The requirement of the GATS that countries list in their individual schedules those sectors in which they were prepared to make commitments, and any specific barriers they wish to retain, produced the first systematic, if incomplete, database on impediments to trade in services.

The conversion of the qualitative information provided by the GATS schedules into a numerical index began with the pioneering work of Hoekman (1995) who developed a three-category weighting method as a means of assessing the extent of GATS commitments. Hoekman examined all GATS schedules and, for the purposes of assessment, allocated a number to each possible schedule entry (i.e. each possible commitment on market access or national treatment in each mode in each industry sub-sector). Specifically:

- Where a member has agreed to be bound without any caveats, a weight of 1 is allocated. A weight of 1 is also allocated in circumstances where a member declares that a particular mode of supply is 'unbound due to lack of technical feasibility', if other modes of supply are unrestricted. A common example of this situation is the cross-border supply of construction and related engineering services.
- Where a member has agreed to be bound but specific restrictions remain, a 0.5 weight is allocated. If a mode of supply is bound but specific reference

is made to the horizontal commitments, a weight of 0.5 is allocated. This is commonly the case for commitments on the movement of natural persons, where immigration constraints continue to apply.

- Where a member has explicitly exempted that particular entry from the operation of the GATS by recording an entry of 'unbound' or by simply failing to make any commitments at all, a weight of 0 is allocated.

Hoekman used these measures to quantify the extent of commitments (the greater the number, the more commitments made). However, other researchers quickly realised the potential to use this information to construct a frequency index of impediments to trade in services. The Pacific Economic Cooperation Council (1995), for example, utilised the Hoekman analysis to highlight the number of commitments that have not been made (the greater the number the more illiberal the economy).

Welcome as these first steps were, these studies have several key limitations, which were identified immediately by Hoekman (1995), the Pacific Economic Cooperation Council (1995) and others. They are also reviewed in this volume with respect to barriers to foreign investment in services by Hardin and Holmes in Chapter 4. There are two major concerns:

- First, the coverage of the GATS schedules. The positive-list approach adopted for the GATS schedules means that countries only schedule information in those industries where they agree these will be completely or partially bound. Unbound industries are assumed to be closed, but this may not always be the case. Many developing economies simply did not have available the detail required to meet the complexities of the scheduling process and so left many industries unbound, some of which may be quite open. There is also some anecdotal evidence to suggest that nations with liberal policies left some services unbound so as to maintain a retaliatory capability in future market access negotiations. Therefore, some industries that are recorded in the GATS-based indexes as impeded may be open, at least to suppliers from some economies.
- Second, the methodology does not distinguish between barriers in terms of their impact on the economy, with minor impediments receiving the same weighting as an almost complete refusal of access.

Work reported in this volume has attempted to develop, at a sectoral and modal level, a more complex weighting system than that used by Hoekman, and has sought to quantify differences in the effect of various partial commitments. More extensive databases have also been drawn upon to overcome some of the limitations with the information in the GATS schedules.

Better information sources

Several studies have sought to expand the dataset upon which the frequency indexes are based. To begin with, since the pioneering work of Hoekman, the content of the GATS schedules has been significantly expanded with the successful conclusion of the Agreement on Basic Telecommunications in February 1997 and the Agreement on Financial Services in December 1997. Marko (1998a) has updated the Hoekman-type frequency indexes on telecommunications so as to reflect the impact of the agreement that 69 nations signed. Marko finds that 58 per cent of the basic telecommunications services market in all of these countries is now covered by either partial or full GATS commitments.

At a cross-sectoral level, Hardin and Holmes, in Chapter 4, provide the most comprehensive attempt at a reformulated frequency measure. Their analysis of impediments to investment in selected service industries includes information from the Individual Action Plans (IAPs) produced by Asia Pacific Economic Cooperation (APEC) members. These documents have the advantage of being closer to a negative than a positive list of barriers to services trade, although they are still far from an exhaustive description of impediments. Applying their methodology to fifteen APEC economies, Hardin and Holmes find that communications and financial services tend to be subject to the most stringent FDI controls. Scores are particularly high for the communications sector because many economies impose ownership limits on telecommunications and broadcasting, and completely close postal services to foreign entry. The least restricted sectors include business and distribution services.

Moving beyond the GATS schedules, Warren, in work reported in Chapter 5, uses a 1997 survey by the International Telecommunications Union (ITU) to construct a set of policy indexes for 136 countries. These data have the distinct advantage of being drawn from a survey of actual policies, rather than inferring these policies from commitments made in trade negotiations. Five separate indexes are constructed, corresponding with the more important distinctions drawn in the GATS context, namely the differences between market access and national treatment, and between trade and investment. Data availability means that a distinction is made between access to mobile and fixed telecommunications markets only in relation to the market access restrictions on foreign investment.

In constructing these indexes, Warren incorporates not only data on economic policy but also economic variables, including a count of the number of firms actually competing in a market. A high degree of variation is found, reflecting the continuing resistance among many countries to the liberalisation of their telecommunications markets.

There are substantial impediments to trade in transport services. Those related to air transport are receiving increasing attention (e.g. in Warren et al. 1999), and in this volume we report some attempts to model the effects of policy reform. Kang and Findlay review changes in the regulation of the maritime sector in Chapter 9. In Chapter 10, McGuire, Schuele and Smith report on a technique for assessing impediments to trade in maritime services. The data on policy came from a variety of sources including a questionnaire developed by the WTO Negotiating Group on Maritime Services, GATS schedules, WTO Trade Policy Reviews, Office of the US Trade Representative information, OECD material and APEC IAPs. Separate indexes are developed to quantify restrictions on foreign suppliers of maritime services and on all suppliers.[8] The gap between the scores for these two types of entrants indicates the extent to which there is discrimination against foreign suppliers. Results reported for 35 economies in the Asia Pacific region, the United States and Europe show a large range in the degree of restrictiveness.[9] Chile, the Philippines, Thailand, Turkey and the United States treat foreign suppliers of services significantly less favourably than domestic firms.

Several frequency indexes of impediments to trade and investment in financial services have been produced, reflecting the pre-eminent position of this industry in the world economy. Previous work in this area includes papers by Mattoo (1998) and McGuire (1998). McGuire undertook a detailed analysis of the Australian financial services policy regime (both state and federal) in an effort to get a clearer picture of the barriers affecting financial services trade. Building upon this earlier research, in Chapter 12 McGuire and Schuele use a variety of sources to construct a set of indexes of impediments to trade in banking services. They differentiate between impediments relating to commercial presence and impediments on operations (raising funds and so on), and between impediments affecting foreign banks and impediments that affect all banks. Each of the inputs into the indexes are weighted to reflect the degree to which they are perceived to restrict access to the market.

Kemp, in Chapter 14, extends the methodology to a new sector when he examines impediments to trade and investment in education services. He identifies the various modes of delivery of this service, which include commercial presence, delivery from a home base, the movement of consumers, and the movement of teaching staff. This chapter reviews the sorts of barriers that tend to impede business in each mode and discusses methods to measure the significance of these barriers in various markets for Australian education services. Some of these methods are then illustrated using data and information on policy in the key markets.

In reviewing this research, it is increasingly apparent that the information necessary to construct frequency indexes of impediments to trade in services is available, although significant effort is often involved in collecting and collating the data. It is probable that over the next few years a database of impediments affecting most of the significant service industries will be constructed. Whether or not these data will be updated or simply remain as snapshots of policies at a particular period is difficult to anticipate.

Improved weighting techniques

The second major problem with the early frequency indexes of impediments to trade in services concerns the weighting of the qualitative information. Unweighted indexes treat all qualitative information equally. Consequently, a minor impediment to trade and investment such as a notification requirement receives the same score as a complete prohibition on entry. More recent indexes have sought to ameliorate this problem by weighting the qualitative information by its perceived economic importance.

Hardin and Holmes, in Chapter 4, seek to incorporate the relative economic impact of different policies into frequency data on the types of barriers affecting investment. Five types of barriers to foreign investment are identified. Weights are then developed within each of these categories on the basis of the perceived economic impact of each policy category. For example, they give a much greater weight to a policy that completely excludes foreign equity than to a policy that allows more than 50 per cent but less than 100 per cent foreign equity. Policies that limit investment in existing firms, but allow greenfields investment are given a lower weight that those policies that limit all investment.

In the construction of indexes of impediments to trade in tele-communications, Warren (see Chapter 5) also weights various inputs according to their perceived economic importance. For example, the actual number of competitors within an industry is given greater weighting, in a variable designed to capture market access, than the specific policies that governments have in place. Actual outcomes are seen as far more significant than policies which may or may not have been implemented.

The potential of frequency weighting systems, however, is most clearly demonstrated by an OECD pilot study on assessing barriers to trade in professional services (see Chapter 15). Colecchia's approach involves a series of questions within a flowchart, mimicking the questions that a service provider would ask when seeking to enter a foreign market. For example:

- 'can I physically access the market?' (market access);
- 'if I can access the market, am I then allowed to practice and to what extent?' (rights of practice);
- 'can I provide services as an independent firm?' (rights of establishment); and
- 'if I am required to practice in partnership with a local entity, what limitations does this place on me?'.

Scores are attributed to each answer and a detailed weighting system is proposed, whereby different constraints are deemed to have very different effects. Accountancy services in four countries (Australia, the United Kingdom, France and the United States) are examined. The United Kingdom is found to be the most liberal of the four countries, while the United States has the highest barriers.

The extent to which these more sensitive weighting systems can be generalised to other industries is not yet clear. However, the scope for further refinement of weighting techniques appears to be significant. It is hoped that the information generated by the price- and quantity-impact analyses illustrated in other chapters will allow for more formalised assessments of the economic impact of various policies, which in turn can be used to construct weights for future frequency indexes.

Partial-impact measures

Having identified and systematised the various cross-national differences in policy, it is possible in some industries to estimate the impact of these differences on core economic outcomes such as prices and consumption. This is necessary if more of the benefits from measurement are to be achieved.

The available research on the measurement of NTBs affecting goods trade provides a useful starting point on how to proceed in this regard. In their extensive review of the literature, Deardorff and Stern (1985) identify two broad methods of quantifying the economic impact of NTBs:

- *price-impact measures* that examine the impact of NTBs on domestic prices by comparing them with world prices; and
- *quantity-impact measures* that compare an estimate of trade volumes in the absence of NTBs with actual trade volumes.

These types of price and quantity-impact measures have been considered impossible to replicate in relation to service industries on grounds of data availability. A world price for many service industries is indeterminate. Similarly, the lack of systematic bilateral services trade data and the highly aggregated nature of the current account data limit the potential for traditional quantity-impact models.

As a consequence of these data concerns, it is necessary to identify alternative benchmarks against which to compare actual prices and quantities. Here the market power analysis associated with competition policy or anti-trust regulation is instructive. The aim of such analysis is to compare actual market outcomes with those that would be expected to prevail if the market were competitive (Areeda et al. 1995).

Price-impact measures

The theory underlying the price-impact approach is that if the market had no impediments to entry then it would be relatively competitive and prices would be expected to approach a firm's long-run marginal cost – defined as the cost of keeping a particular firm operating in the long run.[10] If there are impediments, however, there will be a wedge between price and marginal cost. Not only the margin over costs but also costs themselves might be affected. Costs might be higher because low-cost suppliers are excluded from the market or because protected firms are not operating at their lowest possible cost levels. For all these reasons – the margin effect, the cost difference effect and the cost reduction effect – prices observed in the presence of impediments may exceed those in their absence. The steps involved in the measurement of the price impact of services sector impediments are spelt out in Chapter 4 of this volume.

Trewin, in Chapter 7, uses econometric techniques to explain the observed differences in costs between telecommunications carriers in different economies. He divides cost differences between network characteristics and policy variables. These results are derived from an estimation of frontier cost functions from which efficiency measures can also be derived. Trewin tests for the impact of different types of policy variables (including measures referred to here such as the Marko and Warren measures). He also finds significant differences between economies of different income levels in the ways in which quality and policy variables affect costs. Another important contribution of this chapter is its illustration of how the relevant weights given to elements of the policy measures can be determined statistically. These results could also be used for further modelling of the impacts of various regulatory policies.

In Chapter 11, Kang seeks to explain the variation in transport costs due to the variations in the policy regime for maritime services. The chapter reports some econometric tests using data derived from the Global Trade Analysis Project (GTAP) database and using the policy measure reported in Chapter 10.

Kalirajan et al., in Chapter 13, examine the price–cost margins (or the net interest margins) of 694 national and state commercial banks in 27 economies. Using a two-stage econometric technique they were able to isolate the specific impact the trade restrictiveness indexes developed by McGuire and Schuele had on this margin, while correcting for the factors that influence the size of the buffer that banks need to manage their cash flow. The estimated impacts for Indonesia, Malaysia and the Philippines are the highest of the 27 economies, with the net interest margins at least 45 per cent higher than they would be in the absence of restrictions on trade in banking services. For the more industrialised countries, restrictions are less, resulting in smaller net interest margin increases.

Quantity-impact measures

Recently, several telecommunications studies have sought to examine the impact of barriers to entry, focusing upon the quantity of mobile telecommunications services consumed within an economy – rather than the quantity traded – and comparing this with international benchmarks (Ralph and Ludwig 1997; Ergas et al. 1998) The aim is to quantify the comparative impact of restrictions on telecommunications consumption, controlling for other explanatory variables. Restrictions on competition are modelled directly by counting the number of mobile operators in each country at each period.

In Chapter 6, Warren develops these earlier studies by extending the analysis from mobile telephony to include the fixed network services, measured in terms of the number of mainlines per hundred people. Warren expands the policy variable beyond a simple count of the number of operators (fixed and mobile) to include the ITU-derived indexes of telecommunications policies discussed above.

MODELLING

There are three main limitations with the price and quantity-impact estimates listed above. First, the mechanism by which the predicted reductions in price or increases in quantity occur is not clear. Does liberalisation affect economic outcomes through competition effects (reduced market power), cost-reduction effects (increased efficiency) or cost-differential effects (reduced input prices)? The second limitation with the price and quantity-impact estimates is that they fail to give a picture of the welfare implications from reform, including impacts on consumer and producer welfare. Third, even these techniques obviously fail to capture important intersectoral effects. What impact does the liberalisation of a particular service industry have on the economy as a whole? To overcome these limitations it is necessary to undertake further economic modelling.

Partial equilibrium methods

Air transport markets illustrate the scope to use partial equilibrium modelling methods to unpack the effects of liberalisation. There are various options for reform of international air transport where market access is often severely curtailed by a series of bilateral agreements.[11] Possible reform strategies include:

- liberalisation that permits the entry of further domestic suppliers without changing conditions of access for foreign suppliers;
- liberalisation that permits the commercial establishment by foreign carriers; and
- liberalisation that permits the further entry by foreign carriers from their home base (e.g. by those currently excluded or restricted under the terms of the bilateral agreements).

As noted above and in Elek et al. (1999), liberalisation can impact on prices and/or quantities as a consequence of three different effects:

- Competition effects, which refer to the reduction in market power that occurs through the removal of barriers to entry and the increase in the number of suppliers. Mark-ups over costs are expected to be reduced because of this effect.
- Cost-reducing effects, which come from two sources in the case of air transport. First, the greater intensity of competition in the markets affected leads suppliers to operate closer to their frontier levels of costs. Second, the relaxation of constraints otherwise imposed by the bilateral system facilitates the creation of networks, including new hubs. With greater

freedom than previously, and therefore more choice, airlines could be expected to achieve further cost reductions. This second set of effects therefore involves airlines moving closer to the minimum attainable levels of costs, given the input prices they pay.

- Cost-difference effects, which arise because of differences in input prices faced by airlines based in different locations. Airlines from different countries can deliver services to a particular market at varying costs. Some countries are likely, in other words, to have a comparative advantage in the provision of these services.

It is possible to identify these effects specifically by building on estimates of cost functions for air transport services. Results on the distance to the frontier of a particular airline, for example, and on the differences between frontiers of particular airlines can be used in partial equilibrium modelling to identify the effects of reform discussed above. An example of this approach is reported in Chapter 8. The model used here concentrates on supply and demand in air transport markets alone, but includes a series of markets over which airlines are likely to construct networks, captures networking choices explicitly and incorporates forms of imperfect competition which make explicit the determination of mark-ups over costs.

The second major limitation with price or quantity-impact measures is that they are unable to capture the impact of liberalisation on consumer and producer welfare. Airlines and consumers will be affected by reform in different ways. The impact of reform on consumers is relatively simple to describe – they gain from all three effects described above. The impact on airlines is more complex. The competition effects reduce airline profits, but their losses are offset by cost reductions. The main airlines to benefit from reform are likely to be the carriers with a comparative advantage in the provision of the service. Although, in the context of a market in which airlines provide differentiated services, even airlines that are relatively high-cost suppliers may see substantial gains from the scope to redesign their networks. Partial equilibrium modelling can be used to estimate the relative size of these effects on consumers and producers and also the scale of the net benefits, that is, the difference between consumer gains and airline gains or losses.

In summary, partial equilibrium modelling can be used to deal with the first two limitations of the price and quantity-impact assessments of the impact of reform, namely the unpacking of the origins of the effects identified and their impacts on consumer and producer welfare in relevant markets. But, by definition, the partial equilibrium methods fail to capture the intersectoral effects.

General equilibrium issues

The third major limitation with price- or quantity-impact measures is that they do not quantify the impact of liberalisation on the wider economy. To do this requires the incorporation of these measures into general equilibrium models such as a modified GTAP model (Hertel 1997) capturing the structure of service industries. This will allow policymakers to quantify the economy-wide costs of maintaining policies designed to exclude rival domestic and foreign firms from their services markets.

Hoekman and Primo Braga (1997) review some of the general equilibrium models. An important point they make is that since services are inputs into the production of most industries, an inefficient services sector can be very costly to the economy as a whole.[12] They note that if a country reformed its tariff structure – even reducing rates to zero – but did not include the services sector in the liberalisation process, then distortions would still remain and resource allocation would be affected. This point has usually been ignored in modelling work.

Modelling work has been constrained, however, by the lack of data on the impact of policies that restrict services trade and investment. Some attempts have been made to convert frequency measures into tariff equivalents and then simulate the effects of reductions in barriers. One such study by Brown et al. (1996) found that the welfare gains from Uruguay Round cuts in industrial tariffs would have been three times higher if services barriers had also been cut by 25 per cent.

Dee, Holmes and Hardin, in Chapter 16, review previous general equilibrium (GE) modelling work in more detail and note some of the challenges involved in capturing in this framework the important features of services trade liberalisation. They discuss the ways in which the various measures outlined above can be converted into tax equivalents for use in GE modelling. They note in particular the importance of:

- Distinguishing between services supplied by substitute modes, that is by local firms, by foreign-owned firms operating from a local base and by foreign firms operating from their home base (these are the same three modes of entry which were used as illustrations of reform in the discussion of the application of modelling methods to the air transport market).
- Identifying the different impacts of impediments in terms of effects on restrictions on ongoing operations and those on establishment (both of which may apply to local and foreign-owned firms, and may apply differentially to foreign-owned firms depending on how they want to access the market).
- Determining the distribution between local and foreign interests of any rents created.
- Capturing the possibility of perverse welfare effects from liberalisation that could occur when service that is subject to a tax in the initial equilibrium experiences a fall in output as a result of liberalisation (i.e. the consequence of the removal of the tax on close-substitute forms of delivery). The existence of these perverse effects supports the case for a broad program of reform in terms of sectoral coverage as well as modes of delivery.

Dee, Holmes and Hardin also discuss how these features can be incorporated into a GE model. Its results will, for the first time, allow for a complete assessment of the economy-wide impacts of services liberalisation and, conversely, will highlight the ongoing costs to economies of maintaining protection.

APPROACHES TO REFORM

The last three chapters of the volume review alternative approaches to reform.

Stephenson, in Chapter 17, compares differences between formal regional arrangements. She presents comparative information on the treatment of services transactions in the ASEAN Framework Agreement on Services, the Closer Economic Relations Agreement between Australia and New Zealand, the two free trade agreements involving Chile (one with Canada and one with Mexico) and the North American Free Trade Agreement.

Findlay and Warren, in Chapter 18, review the approach to services liberalisation used in the Asia Pacific Economic Cooperation (APEC) forum. They review the APEC methodology and discuss three ways in which the APEC process can contribute to liberalisation of the services sector, namely strengthening the capacity to implement unilateral action, constructing liberalising regional initiatives and complementing action at the global level.

Snape, in Chapter 19, comments on the issues in the application of rules to services at the global level. He compares the approach of the GATS with that of the GATT and comments on constraints on the application of the former. He discusses specific issues in relation to the GATS and its breadth of coverage and treatment of various modes of supply. There have been arguments that the GATS tried to do too much in terms of modes of delivery and coverage of barriers and that as a consequence it achieved too little in terms of obligations. Another view is that a bold approach to coverage was necessary since meaningful liberalisation in the services sector is not possible without including investment and without addressing all the barriers, including those now covered under the GATS definition of market access. It has also been observed that a wide scope in the negotiations on services helped mobilise interests in industrialised economies in the last round of negotiations, so much so that progress in other difficult areas was facilitated.

CONCLUSION

It is possible to construct weighting schemes to measure the effect of policy measures on international services transactions. These schemes reflect some expectation of the economic significance of the restrictions involved. Over time, as the extent of empirical work expands, the weights themselves may be determined endogenously. Policy measures constructed in this way are powerful explanators of market outcomes, especially when policy data from the GATS can be supplemented by data from industry sources. If market data are available, the significance of the policy measures can be tested in terms of their impact on market outcomes. Where market data are not available, outcomes can be inferred from the policy measures, given the confidence in this methodology based on its applications in other markets.

More explicit modelling in either a partial or general equilibrium framework is always desirable, although sometimes costly. These modelling methods can be used to make explicit the mechanisms by which policy choices affect market outcomes. Information of this sort is hidden in the single equation reduced-form approaches that are generally used in price or quantity-impact approaches. Modelling can also be used to derive simultaneously other impact measures, including welfare effects and redistributive effects.

The increased sophistication of the measurement techniques presented in this book has significant implications for the negotiating process. For the first time, measures of impediments to trade in services are becoming available which can be used as the focus for negotiations or for the documentation of commitments. This has a number of major consequences for international negotiations. It implies that:

- information will be available to help set priorities at the national level;
- commitments in global (and regional) talks can be codified more easily and therefore cross-sectoral negotiations can be facilitated;
- the constraint on the lack of incremental change – an inhibitor to reform because of the apparent all-or-nothing choices faced by negotiators – will be removed, since partial reform or sequencing will be more easily documented;
- a move to a negative-list approach to documenting commitments in any one sector will be facilitated by the greater information disclosures these techniques engender; and
- the difficulty that some economies have in being able to characterise their policy regimes and therefore participate meaningfully in the negotiations can be overcome again through the increased information disclosure that is a core result of these techniques.

The sets of measures and methodologies presented and reviewed here create new opportunities by introducing a new technology into the negotiating process that will make it easier to maintain the goal of a broad scope in the GATS without sacrificing obligations.

NOTES

An earlier version of this chapter was presented at the conference on Services 2000: New Directions in Services Trade Liberalisation, at the University Club, Washington DC, on 1–2 June 1999.

1   This definition is derived from the classic definition of services first proposed by Hill (1977).

2   See Stern and Hoekman (1987) for a discussion on the limitations of international data on services.

3   The problem with these reports or so-called 'black books' is that they are seldom comprehensive, simply reflecting the interests of exporters, and are usually based upon uncollaborated assertions from interested parties. Among the more widely distributed examples of these reports are the *National Trade Estimate Report on Foreign Trade Barriers*, produced by the Office of the US Trade Representative, and the European Commission's *1995 Report on US Barriers to Trade and Investment*.

4   Although, UNCTAD is currently developing its MAST (Measures Affecting Services Trade) database.

5   See the various contributions on this point in Williamson (1994).

6   On the usefulness of such information in reform, see Destler (1995), Garnaut (1994) and Corden (1994).

7   One of the major problems with the various post-Uruguay Round negotiations in services was that the sector-specific nature of the discussions limited the scope for successful bargaining.

8   Restrictions are grouped into two broad categories of those on commercial presence and 'other'. The former includes rules on forms of presence, investment in onshore service suppliers and permanent movement of people. The latter includes cabotage, port services, the UN Liner Code, treatment of conferences and temporary movement of people.

9   Brazil, Chile, India, Indonesia, Korea, Malaysia, the Philippines, Thailand and the United States are among the most restricted markets.

10   The excess of price over marginal cost as a proportion of price is known as the Lerner Index. See Lerner (1934).

11   For more details of the regulatory regime in international air transport markets, see Warren, Tamms and Findlay (1999).

12   There is also a literature on the importance of services intensity of production. Even though this ratio may be low in some developing countries, this could be because of the inefficiency of services supplied by arms-length transactions, which leads firms to undertake a higher provision of such services in-house. See Francois and Reinert (1996).

2 The services sector in output and in international trade

Jong-Soon Kang

INTRODUCTION

Until recently, trade in services was mostly ignored by international economists, reflecting a perception that services were non-tradable. This has never been accurate, since transportation and travel for instance have always been important economic activities. Since the early 1980s, furthermore, international services transactions expanded rapidly as new modes of supply such as electronic networks have materialised. In fact, services are now the fastest growing component of world investment and trade.

This chapter reviews the changing importance of services to national economies and the changing pattern of trade in services.

IDENTIFICATION OF SERVICES

A service can be defined as 'an economic activity that adds value either directly to another economic unit or to a good belonging to another economic unit' (Hill 1977). Consequently, services have as a defining feature the requirement for direct interaction between producers and consumers, or at least a consumer's assets, before the service can be rendered (Hirsch 1989). Three distinctions can usually be made between goods and services: production and consumption have to take place simultaneously; services cannot be stored; and services are intangible (Stern and Hoekman 1988). It seems clear from these definitions and from actual experience that services activities are both numerous and diverse in themselves and in the changes they effect in goods and persons.[1] In reality, however, it is often difficult to distinguish a service from a good, and it may not always be analytically meaningful or practical to separate them. It may also be quite difficult to distinguish goods from services at the industry level, depending particularly on the level of data aggregation (Stern and Hoekman 1988).

Services are provided by private companies, public enterprises or governments. In many cases there are no direct analogues that can be readily applied to value the provisions of services, for instance public services provided by governments such as education, medical care, public administration and national defence (Stern and Hoekman 1988). Input measures are commonly used to represent the value of services in these cases.

Identifying services or services sectors is also a confusing subject. Services can be classified according to different statistical or research purposes. While the national accounts system is useful for analysing the relative importance of the services sector to the national economy, the classification of services for the purpose of analysing international services trade can be found in a country's balance of payments accounts. Table 2.1 shows how services are dealt with in the national accounts and in the balance of payments.[2] Non-tradable services such as gas, electricity and water are excluded from balance of payments statistics. It could be argued that construction should be excluded from services due to intangibility of its output. In the national production statistics published in the World Bank's *World Development Indicators,* construction is excluded from services, together with gas, electricity and water, but the World Bank includes construction in its services trade statistics following the International Monetary Fund (IMF) balance of payments framework shown in Table 2.1.

Services are generally divided into two categories: factor services (interest, profits and dividends) and non-factor services (business, insurance and financial services). As shown in Table 2.1, most services statistics relate to transactions of non-factor services, even though some international organisations, such as the IMF, provide some data on trade in factor services.

Available data on services transactions show further shortcomings compared with those on manufacturing and merchandise. Only a limited number of industrialised countries collect and report services statistics at a relatively disaggregated level, while most developing countries only report data on commercial services, broken down roughly into transport, travel and other services (Hoekman 1996).[3] The IMF's *Balance of Payments Manual* is the prime source of cross-country data on services trade, but there are many weaknesses in terms of data coverage, consistency among reporting countries, concordance and comparability. Lack of disaggregation of data and difficulties in identifying trade by origin and destination are other problems in services statistics.[4]

SERVICES IN THE NATIONAL ECONOMY

In general, changes in industrial structure associated with economic growth occur in the following way: the primary sector's share of output falls while manufacturing and services tend to grow simultaneously until the primary sector becomes relatively insignificant. Once this point is reached, the share of services in output expands relative to the other two sectors.

Production

From 1980 to 1996, in all countries reported in Table 2.2, the services sector increased steadily in importance, while in most the shares of the agricultural

Table 2.1   Identification of services sectors

Balance of payments [a]	National accounts
1. Goods and services	1. Primary sector [b]
a. Goods	2. Manufacturing sector
b. *Services*	3. *Services sector*
	< Tradable services >
	Construction services
	Transportation services
	Travel services
	Communication services
	Insurance services
	Financial services
	Computer and information services
	Royalties and licence services
	Personal, cultural and recreational services
	Other services, private (including real estate)
	Government services
	< Non-tradable services >
	Electricity, Water, Gas,
	Ownership of dwellings
2. Income: investment income and	
compensation of employees	
3. Current Transfers	

Notes:
a   Balance of payments classification is from IMF 1993.
b   Primary sector includes agriculture, fisheries, forestry, mining and quarrying.

and manufacturing sectors declined. The share of services is greater in industrialised countries than those in the NIEs (newly industrialising economies) or developing countries. Leaving aside Hong Kong and Singapore, which are clearly special cases because they lack a primary sector, and Taiwan to a lesser extent, the services in total output are around or below 50 per cent of output in the NIEs and Asian developing countries. Services account for a greater share of industrialised countries' GDP at close to or above 70 per cent, with the exception of Japan at 60 per cent.

Among the developing economies, services were more important to South American countries than to Asian economies during the 1980s and 1990s, and they had relatively small agricultural sectors. In Argentina, Mexico and Uruguay, services were above 60 per cent of GDP in 1996, close to the levels of the industrialised countries.

Figure 2.1 shows that the importance of services in the national economy is positively associated with economic growth. In most developing countries in Asia, the share of services in the economy grew much faster than real GDP per capita, which was not the case in industrialised countries. Figure 2.1 together with Table 2.2 imply that as the economy matures, the growth rate

Table 2.2 Sectoral shares of value-added in GDP, selected economies, 1980–96 (per cent)

	Agriculture			Manufacturing			Services		
	1980	1990	1996[a]	1980	1990	1996[a]	1980	1990	1996[a]
Industrialised Pacific economies									
Australia	5.3	3.3	3.5	36.4	29.6	28.0	58.3	67.0	68.5
United States	2.5	2.0	1.7	33.5	27.7	25.8	64.0	70.3	72.5
New Zealand	10.7	6.8	8.3	31.2	26.0	25.1	58.1	67.2	66.6
Japan	3.7	2.5	1.9	41.9	41.2	38.0	54.4	56.3	60.0
Asian NIEs									
Korea	14.5	8.7	6.3	40.4	43.4	42.8	45.1	47.9	50.9
Taiwan	7.7	4.2	3.6	45.7	41.2	36.2	46.6	54.6	60.2
Hong Kong	0.8	0.3	0.1	31.7	25.3	16.0	67.5	74.5	83.8
Singapore	1.3	0.3	0.2	38.1	36.0	35.6	60.6	63.7	64.3
Developing Asian economies									
China	30.1	27.0	20.6	48.5	41.6	48.4	21.4	31.3	31.1
Philippines	25.1	21.9	21.4	38.8	34.5	31.7	36.1	43.6	46.9
Indonesia	24.0	19.4	16.3	41.7	39.1	42.7	34.3	41.5	41.0
Malaysia	21.9	18.7	12.8	37.8	40.3	46.2	40.3	40.9	41.0
Thailand	23.2	12.7	10.7	28.7	37.0	39.8	48.1	50.2	49.5
India	38.1	31.0	27.8	25.9	29.3	29.2	36.0	39.7	43.0
South America									
Argentina	6.4	8.1	6.0	41.2	36.0	30.7	52.4	55.9	63.3
Brazil	11.0	11.5[b]	14.0	43.8	38.9[b]	35.9	45.2	49.7[b]	50.0
Mexico	8.2	7.2	5.4	32.8	26.0	26.3	59.0	66.8	68.4
Uruguay	13.5	11.3	8.9	33.7	32.1	26.4	52.8	56.6	64.7
Venezuela	4.8	5.4	4.1	46.4	50.2	46.5	48.8	44.4	49.4
Europe									
France	4.2	3.4	2.4	33.7	29.2	26.5	62.0	67.4	71.1
Austria	4.4	3.1	1.5	35.9	32.2	30.5	59.8	64.7	67.9
Netherlands	3.5	4.0	3.1	32.2	28.9	27.1	64.3	67.1	69.8
Norway	3.7	3.2	2.5	35.4	31.2	29.9	60.9	65.6	67.7

Notes: Services in this table excludes construction, gas, electricity and water, but comprises not only wholesale and retail trade (including hotels and restaurants), transport, and government, financial, professional, and personal services (such as education, health care and real estate) but also imputed bank service charges, import duties and any statistical discrepancies noted by national compilers. Manufacturing includes manufacturing, mining, construction, electricity, water and gas. Value-added is the net output of a sector after adding up all outputs and subtracting intermediate inputs.

a 1995 data for Australia, Japan, Taiwan, Hong Kong, China, Indonesia and the European countries; 1993 data for the United States and New Zealand.

b 1991 data.

Source: World Bank, *World Development Indicators* (compiled from the International Economic Databank, Australian National University, Canberra. See <http://iedb.anu.edu.au> for more details).

Figure 2.1 Growth of income shares of services in association with GDP per
        capita, 1980–96

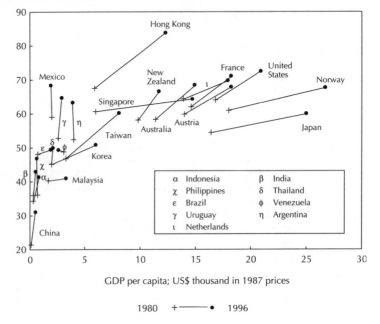

Share of service value added in GDP; %

GDP per capita; US$ thousand in 1987 prices

1980   +———•   1996

Notes: 1995 services data for Australia, Japan, Taiwan, Hong Kong, China, Indonesia, France,
Austria, the Netherlands and Norway; 1993 services data for the United States and New Zealand;
for a definition of services, see the notes in Table 2.2.

Source: World Bank, *World Development Indicators* (compiled from the International
Economic Databank, Australian National University, Canberra).

of the share of services in the national economy will slow but will continue
to grow and reach close to or above 70 per cent of GDP. Figure 2.2 shows
that in South American countries, the share of services in the economy
increased substantially even though their real GDP per capita did not grow
or even dropped during the period.

Employment

As economies grow, agriculture's share of employment declines steadily over
time and most of the labour that is released is employed in either the
manufacturing sector or the services sector. Table 2.3 presents data on the
evolution of employment by sector for selected economies. It is evident that
the share of employment in the services sector has increased markedly in all
the economies in the table but with varying degrees, according to their
development stages. In the industrialised countries and two of the advanced

Table 2.3 Sectoral shares of employment, selected economies, 1980–96
(per cent of total labour force)

	Agriculture			Manufacturing			Services[a]		
	1980[b]	1990[c]	1996[d]	1980[b]	1990[c]	1996[d]	1980[b]	1990[c]	1996[d]
Industrialised Pacific economies									
Australia	6.1	5.3	5.1	28.9	25.1	22.4	58.1	66.7	72.5
United States	3.4	2.8	2.8	30.8	26.3	24.1	63.0	70.3	73.1
New Zealand	11.2	10.4	9.5	32.6	24.9	24.8	56.2	64.8	65.8
Japan	10.2	7.0	5.5	34.7	33.4	33.4	52.9	56.9	61.1
Asian NIEs									
Korea	32.3	17.8	11.6	27.5	34.4	32.5	35.1	45.4	55.9
Hong Kong	1.3	0.9	0.4	49.7	36.8	25.7	48.9	62.3	73.9
Singapore	1.3	0.3	0.2	34.6	34.6	30.2	60.7	63.2	69.6
Developing Asian economies									
China	74.2	72.2	58.8	14.0	15.1	25.6	11.8	12.7	15.6
Philippines	52.3	45.8	41.7	15.1	15.3	16.6	32.6	38.9	41.6
Indonesia	57.8	55.2	44.0	12.1	13.6	18.1	30.1	31.2	37.9
Malaysia	40.8	27.3	19.4	18.8	23.1	32.2	40.5	49.5	48.4
Thailand	n.a.	62.1	50.1	n.a.	13.6	20.8	n.a.	21.3	29.1
India	69.5	64.0	n.a.	13.1	16.0	n.a.	17.4	20.0	n.a.
South America									
Argentina	13.0	12.2	1.5	33.7	32.4	24.6	53.4	55.5	73.9
Brazil	36.7	23.3	22.8	23.9	23.0	18.5	39.4	53.6	58.7
Mexico	36.3	27.9	22.5	29.1	23.8	22.5	34.6	48.3	55.1
Uruguay	16.6	14.3	4.8	28.1	27.2	26.7	55.2	58.6	68.6
Venezuela	14.7	11.8	13.2	28.7	26.7	23.6	55.6	60.0	63.2
Europe									
France	8.3	5.5	4.7	34.6	28.8	26.6	57.1	65.7	68.7
Austria	10.5	7.2	7.2	40.0	37.1	31.0	49.3	54.6	61.7
Netherlands	5.3	4.2	3.7	30.7	24.0	22.4	56.6	63.4	73.9
Norway	8.3	6.1	5.2	29.3	24.2	22.9	61.8	67.1	71.9

Notes:
a Services includes wholesale and retail trade and restaurants and hotels; transport, storage, and communications; finance, insurance, real estate, and business services; and community, social, and personal services (see the Notes in Table 2.2).
b 1979 data for Australia and the Netherlands.
c 1991 data for Singapore and Austria.
d 1995 data for Uruguay and Venezuela; 1994 data for France.
n.a. = 'not available'

Sources: World Bank, *World Development Indicators* (compiled from the International Economic Databank, Australian National University, Canberra); International Labour Organisation, *Yearbook of Labour Statistics*, 1998.

Asian NIEs – Hong Kong and Singapore – the services sector accounted for half or more of total employment in 1980. In the mid-1990s, services accounted for almost 70 per cent or above of total employment in all these economies except Japan and Austria. Agricultural employment in these countries has been relatively small and has continued to decline, accounting for less than 10 per cent of total employment in the 1990s. The share of manufacturing employment in total employment continued to decline throughout the 1980s and the 1990s.

In all the developing Asian countries except Malaysia, the agricultural sector accounted for a higher share of employment than the services sector, even in 1996. The share of the agricultural sector in employment declined relative to the services and manufacturing sectors in the 1980s and 1990s, but the speed of labour transfer from agriculture to services was much slower than in the industrialised economies. The Asian economies are in the rapid growth stage of development and the share of employment in the manufacturing sector also increased in the 1990s.

Services in the South American countries accounted for comparatively higher shares of employment, while agricultural shares were relatively small and continued to decline rapidly. The services sectors in South America accounted for between 55 and 75 per cent of total employment in 1996, much higher than in the Asian developing economies. This may be due to their relatively higher income levels, although their real GDP growth rates were very low (Figure 2.2).

The variation of services employment corresponds with real per capita income, reflecting the increased demand and specialisation associated with economic development. Given that the share of employment in agriculture can be expected to decline steadily over time as the economy grows, most of the labour that is released will have to be employed in the services sector unless labour-intensive technologies are used in manufacturing (Stern and Hoekman 1988). This partly explains why the share of both manufacturing and services employment increased in the 1980s and the 1990s in the Asian developing countries. In South America, however, the pattern of labour transfer looks similar to that in industrialised countries: agricultural and manufacturing employment both declined relative to services employment. This may be because manufacturing sectors in South America are less labour intensive than services sectors (see Table 2.4).

PRODUCTIVITY

The increasing share of the services sector in employment is not only associated with income growth but with the differential rates of productivity increase in commodity-producing sectors as compared with services (Stern and Hoekman 1988). Table 2.4 shows that the labour productivity in services increased in real terms in most economies except those in South America throughout the 1980s and the 1990s, although by not much more than in the manufacturing

Figure 2.2 Growth of employment shares of services in association with real GDP per capita, 1980–96

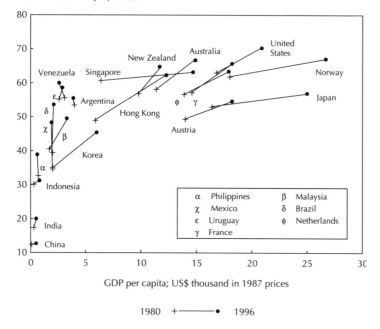

Share of services in employment; %

GDP per capita; US$ thousand in 1987 prices

1980 +————• 1996

Notes: 1979 employment data for Australia and the Netherlands; 1995 data for Uruguay and Venezuela; 1994 data for France; for a definition of services, see the notes in Table 2.3.

Sources: World Bank, *World Development Indicators* (compiled from the International Economic Databank, Australian National University, Canberra); International Labour Organisation, *Yearbook of Labour Statistics,* 1998.

sector. However, the level of labour productivity varied widely across countries at different stages of economic development. In industrialised countries, labour productivity in services was between US$25,000 and US$50,000 per worker in 1996. In Asian and South American developing countries, value-added per worker was relatively low at under US$10,000.

In developing Asia, except Malaysia and Thailand, value-added per worker was particularly low, not exceeding US$2,000. Although it has gradually increased, productivity in services has been lower than in the manufacturing sector. As the services sector is less capital intensive than the manufacturing sector, the labour that was released from the labour-intensive agricultural sector may have been attracted to services rather than to manufacturing. This suggests that productivity issues will be important to the future development of services, especially in the developing Asian economies.

Table 2.4   Sectoral value-added per worker, selected economies, 1980–96
(thousand US$ at 1987 prices)

	Agriculture			Manufacturing			Services[a]		
	1980[b]	1990[c]	1996[d]	1980[b]	1990[c]	1996[d]	1980[b]	1990[c]	1996[d]
Industrialised Pacific economies									
Australia	19.2	22.2	24.5	27.6	32.4	40.0	25.7	25.4	30.0
United States	16.3	28.4	32.5	33.4	42.3	49.4	37.9	38.7	40.5
New Zealand	12.7	16.9	17.9	19.6	23.4	28.5	27.3	23.4	26.1
Japan	13.2	15.4	16.7	39.7	56.2	57.8	35.1	42.7	44.2
Asian NIEs									
Korea	2.8	4.8	6.7	6.9	11.7	18.3	7.0	9.4	11.5
Hong Kong	9.5	6.3	8.8	9.8	15.0	20.8	21.2	27.0	40.5
Singapore	17.3	19.2	25.5	15.2	23.8	32.2	12.5	21.5	22.6
Developing Asian economies									
China	0.1	0.2	0.3	0.8	1.4	2.3	0.5	1.1	1.9
Philippines	0.8	0.7	0.8	4.7	3.5	3.5	1.9	1.7	1.8
Indonesia	0.4	0.5	0.6	2.6	3.4	3.8	1.7	1.6	2.0
Malaysia	2.2	3.6	4.7	7.7	9.9	11.2	5.7	5.2	7.3
Thailand	n.a.	0.5	0.7	n.a.	6.2	7.2	n.a.	5.3	5.9
India	0.3	0.4	n.a.	1.6	1.4	n.a.	1.1	1.6	n.a.
South America									
Argentina	6.1	6.7	6.7	12.3	9.2	19.2	14.0	8.3	9.9
Brazil	1.2	1.7	2.0	9.5	7.4	8.9	5.5	3.5	3.6
Mexico	1.4	1.4	1.7	7.5	7.9	8.5	9.3	5.7	5.0
Uruguay	5.2	5.3	22.0	8.9	7.0	8.0	5.7	4.9	6.1
Venezuela	3.2	3.3	3.0	12.6	16.5	14.2	8.8	5.9	6.1
Europe									
France	13.4	24.4	31.9	31.7	41.6	50.1	36.5	48.7	47.5
Austria	11.2	15.2	13.6	26.5	33.9	38.8	39.6	45.2	41.7
Netherlands	21.7	36.4	51.8	34.7	41.9	47.0	39.7	37.7	36.7
Norway	19.3	25.7	38.8	40.0	58.7	82.2	39.8	41.7	45.9

Notes:
a Services includes wholesale and retail trade; restaurants and hotels; transport, storage, and
   communications; finance, insurance, real estate, and business services; and community, social,
   and personal services (see the notes in Table 2.2).
b 1979 data for Australia and the Netherlands.
c 1991 data for Singapore and Austria.
d 1993 data for the US and New Zealand; 1994 data for France; and 1995 data for Australia,
   Japan, Hong Kong, China, Indonesia, Uruguay, Venezuela, and the European countries.
n.a. = 'not available'.

Source: World Bank, *World Development Indicators* (compiled from the International
Economic Databank, Australian National University, Canberra), Australian National University.

INTERNATIONAL TRADE IN SERVICES

International services trade will be shaped by a variety of economic forces, both domestic and international. Foremost among these will be the level of economic development. The share of services in national income and in total employment rises steadily as economies grow, therefore the share of services in international trade will also increase over time.

Commercial services include the tradable services defined in Table 2.1 except for government services. During the period 1985–97, the current dollar value of commercial services exports increased at an annual average rate of 10.9 per cent, faster than the average annual growth rate of goods exports of 9 per cent (Figure 2.3). In 1998 exports of commercial services decreased by 2.2 per cent, recording the first annual decline in dollar values since 1983. Exports of goods decreased by 2 per cent, the strongest drop since the early 1980s. The fall in world exports of goods and services may be partly due to the financial crisis in East Asia that started in 1997. Nevertheless, 1998 exports of both goods and services were still above 1996 levels.

Table 2.5 shows world exports of commercial services and their relative importance in GDP and in total exports of both goods and services for the period 1980–97. Exports of commercial services rose almost fourfold in nominal terms from US$366 billion in 1980 to US$1,318 billion in 1997. Exports of commercial services grew significantly faster than GDP and more rapidly than commodity exports. As a result, their share of GDP amounted to 4.6 per cent in 1997, while their share of total exports reached 19.4 per cent.

The changing share of services in total goods and services trade in major countries and regions is shown in Table A2.1.

Figure 2.3 Growth of world exports of goods and services, 1980–98

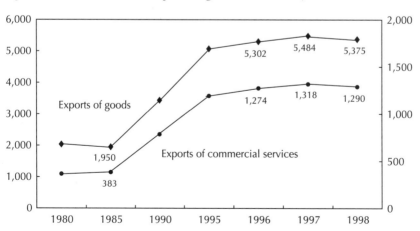

Sources: World Trade Organisation, *Annual Report*, 1998; International Economic Databank, Australian National University.

Table 2.5   Share of world exports of commercial services in GDP and exports of
goods and services, 1980–97

	1980	1990	1995	1997
Value (billion dollars)	365.7	784.3	1,192.8	1,318.0
Share in GDP (%)	3.4	3.7	4.3	4.6
Share in exports of goods and services (%)	15.2	18.6	19.0	19.4

Sources: World Bank, *World Development Indicators* (compiled from the International
Economic Databank, Australian National University, Canberra); International Labour
Organisation, *Yearbook of Labour Statistics*, 1998.

Trade in commercial services

Tables 2.6 and 2.7 show exports and imports of commercial services in major
countries and country groups and their relative importance in world trade in
services since 1980. The growth of world exports of commercial services was
particularly propelled by the growth within Asia. In the 1990s services exports
from Asia expanded far faster than the world average in the 1990s and many
economies in the region rapidly expanded their shares of the world total
(Table 2.6). Asian exports of services grew by 15 per cent per annum in the
period 1990–97 and Asia's share of world exports increased from 15 per cent
to 21 per cent during the same period. This performance was counterbalanced
by the performance of Western Europe, although this region still accounted
for nearly a half of world services exports in 1996. Services exports from
Western Europe dropped by 7.4 percentage points between 1990 and 1997.

Imports of commercial services have followed a similar pattern. Table 2.7
shows that developing economies in Asia and South America accounted for
a growing proportion of world services imports during the 1980s and the
1990s. Industrialised countries' shares fell in the 1990s. The East Asian
developing economies in particular rapidly increased their share of world
services imports. The combined share of two Asian NIEs, China and the
major ASEAN economies rose by 6.6 percentage points from 8.1 to 14.7 per
cent between 1990 and 1997. The combined share of North America, Western
Europe and Japan in world exports of commercial services dropped from 74
per cent in 1990 to 67 per cent in 1997.

A services trade specialisation index combining the export and import
figures of Tables 2.6 and 2.7 is constructed in Table 2.8. The index is net
trade divided by total trade in commercial services, with a negative number
representing a net importer.[5] Table 2.8 shows that degrees of specialisation
did not change dramatically in any part of the world throughout the 1980s
and the 1990s. Only Korea changed from a net importer to a net exporter of
services in 1998, while the Philippines turned from a net exporter to a net
importer. In general, Western European countries and the United States have

Table 2.6   World exports of commercial services by selected region and economy, 1980–98 (billion dollars and per cent)

	Value 1980	1990	1997	1998	Growth rate[a]	Share 1980	1990	1997
World	365.7	784.3	1318.0	1290.1	(9.0)	100	100	100
Asia	46.0	119.6	275.9	n.a.	(14.9)	12.6	15.2	20.9
Japan	18.8	41.4	68.1	60.8	(8.7)	5.1	5.3	5.2
China	n.a.	5.7	24.5	23.0	(27.3)	n.a.	0.7	1.9
NIEs	14.9	46.9	111.0	92.6	(15.4)	4.1	6.0	8.4
Korea	2.4	9.2	25.4	23.6	(18.6)	0.7	1.2	1.9
Taiwan	2.0	6.9	17.0	16.6	(16.1)	0.5	0.9	1.3
Hong Kong	5.8	18.1	38.2	34.2	(13.2)	1.6	2.3	2.9
Singapore	4.8	12.7	30.4	18.2	(15.6)	1.3	1.6	2.3
ASEAN (4)	3.6	15.4	52.4	35.4	(22.6)	1.0	2.0	4.0
Philippines	1.2	2.9	15.1	7.6	(31.7)	0.3	0.4	1.1
Indonesia	n.a.	2.5	6.8	4.1	(18.2)	n.a.	0.3	0.5
Malaysia	1.0	3.8	14.9	10.9	(25.7)	0.3	0.5	1.1
Thailand	1.4	6.3	15.6	12.8	(16.4)	0.4	0.8	1.2
Other Asia	4.0	7.0	12.5	n.a.	(10.2)	1.1	0.9	0.9
India	2.9	4.6	8.7	10.5	(11.1)	0.8	0.6	0.7
Oceania	4.8	12.9	22.3	n.a.	(9.6)	1.3	1.6	1.7
Australia	3.7	9.8	18.4	15.8	(11.0)	1.0	1.3	1.4
New Zealand	1.0	2.4	3.9	n.a.	(8.3)	0.3	0.3	0.3
North America	45.2	150.5	261.2	262.4	(9.6)	12.4	19.2	19.8
Canada	7.1	18.4	29.3	28.8	(8.1)	1.9	2.3	2.2
United States	38.1	132.2	231.9	233.6	(9.8)	10.4	16.9	17.6
South America	17.1	29.2	50.3	52.8	(9.5)	4.7	3.7	3.8
Brazil	1.7	3.7	6.8	8.0	(10.6)	0.5	0.5	0.5
Mexico	4.4	7.2	11.2	11.9	(7.6)	1.2	0.9	0.9
Western Europe	212.3	417.3	603.0	620.3	(6.3)	58.1	53.2	45.8
Austria	8.6	22.8	29.2	31.0	(4.3)	2.4	2.9	2.2
Benelux	28.2	54.8	82.0	82.9	(6.9)	7.7	7.0	6.2
France	42.2	66.3	80.3	78.6	(3.2)	11.5	8.5	6.1
Germany	25.8	51.6	74.7	75.7	(6.4)	7.0	6.6	5.7
Italy	18.8	48.7	71.7	70.1	(6.7)	5.1	6.2	5.4
Spain	11.5	27.6	43.6	48.0	(7.9)	3.1	3.5	3.3
United Kingdom	34.3	53.2	91.9	99.5	(9.6)	9.4	6.8	7.0
European Union (15)	191.1	370.6	535.9	549.9	(6.3)	52.3	47.3	40.7
Africa	12.7	18.6	27.5	25.8	(6.7)	3.5	2.4	2.1
Egypt	2.3	4.8	9.1	7.8	(11.2)	0.6	0.6	0.7
South Africa	2.9	3.4	4.9	4.2	(6.0)	0.8	0.4	0.4

Notes:
a Annual average growth rate for the period 1990–97.
n.a. = 'not available'.

Sources: World Trade Organisation, *Annual Report*, 1998; International Economic Databank, Australian National University.

Table 2.7   World imports of commercial services by selected region and economy, 1980–98 (billion dollars and per cent)

	Value 1980	1990	1997	1998	Growth rate[a]	Share 1980	1990	1997
World	397.2	816.1	1300.5	1290.7	(8.1)	100	100	100
Asia	62.2	162.4	335.2	n.a.	(12.8)	15.7	19.9	25.8
Japan	32.1	84.3	122.1	109.5	(6.4)	8.1	10.3	9.4
China	n.a.	4.1	30.1	28.6	(39.3)	n.a.	0.5	2.3
NIEs	11.9	43.6	95.8	87.0	(14.0)	3.0	5.3	7.4
Korea	3.1	10.1	29.0	23.0	(19.3)	0.8	1.2	2.2
Taiwan	2.6	13.9	24.1	23.3	(9.6)	0.6	1.7	1.9
Hong Kong	3.3	11.0	23.2	22.7	(13.2)	0.8	1.4	1.8
Singapore	2.9	8.6	19.4	18.0	(14.6)	0.7	1.1	1.5
ASEAN (4)	5.8	19.2	64.8	46.0	(22.5)	1.5	2.3	5.0
Philippines	1.3	1.7	14.1	10.0	(41.9)	0.3	0.2	1.1
Indonesia	n.a.	5.9	16.2	11.9	(18.4)	n.a.	0.7	1.2
Malaysia	2.9	5.4	17.4	11.9	(21.5)	0.7	0.7	1.3
Thailand	1.6	6.2	17.1	12.2	(18.6)	0.4	0.8	1.3
Other Asia	4.6	9.4	17.6	n.a.	(11.1)	1.2	1.2	1.4
India	2.9	5.9	12.3	13.7	(12.9)	0.7	0.7	0.9
Oceania	8.4	17.4	23.4	n.a.	(5.1)	2.1	2.1	1.8
Australia	6.3	13.4	18.4	16.7	(5.4)	1.6	1.6	1.4
New Zealand	1.7	3.3	4.9	n.a.	(7.1)	0.4	0.4	0.4
North America	39.0	125.4	188.4	196.3	(7.0)	9.8	15.4	14.5
Canada	10.1	27.5	35.9	34.8	(4.6)	2.5	3.4	2.8
United States	28.9	97.9	152.4	161.5	(7.7)	7.3	12.0	11.7
South America	28.3	34.3	64.7	67.3	(11.2)	7.1	4.2	5.0
Brazil	4.4	6.7	17.6	18.9	(17.4)	1.1	0.8	1.4
Mexico	6.3	10.1	11.8	12.7	(2.7)	1.6	1.2	0.9
Western Europe	189.1	395.7	559.6	581.9	(5.9)	47.6	48.5	43.0
Austria	5.7	14.1	28.4	28.7	(12.4)	1.4	1.7	2.2
Benelux	30.2	53.8	75.4	78.4	(5.8)	7.6	6.6	5.8
France	31.0	50.5	62.1	62.8	(3.5)	7.8	6.2	4.8
Germany	40.8	79.2	118.1	121.8	(6.9)	10.3	9.7	9.1
Italy	15.7	49.9	70.1	69.3	(5.9)	4.0	6.1	5.4
Spain	5.4	15.2	24.3	27.3	(8.1)	1.4	1.9	1.9
United Kingdom	25.2	44.6	71.3	76.1	(8.1)	6.4	5.5	5.5
European Union (15)	171.1	353.4	517.6	537.6	(6.6)	43.1	43.3	39.8
Africa	27.3	26.9	37.8	36.9	(5.8)	6.9	3.3	2.9
Egypt	2.2	3.3	5.8	5.7	(9.7)	0.6	0.4	0.4
South Africa	3.8	4.1	6.1	5.3	(6.7)	0.9	0.5	0.5

Notes:
a Annual average growth rate for the period 1990–97.
n.a. = 'not available'.

Sources: World Trade Organisation, *Annual Report*, 1998; International Economic Databank, Australian National University.

Table 2.8 Specialisation in commercial services trade by selected region and economy, 1980–98

	1980	1990	1997	1998
Asia	-0.15	-0.15	-0.10	-0.11
Japan	-0.26	-0.34	-0.28	-0.29
China	n.a.	0.17	-0.10	-0.11
NIEs	0.11	0.04	0.07	0.03
Korea	-0.13	-0.05	-0.07	0.01
Taiwan	-0.13	-0.33	-0.17	-0.17
Hong Kong	0.27	0.24	0.24	0.20
Singapore	0.25	0.19	0.22	0.01
ASEAN (4)	-0.23	-0.11	-0.11	-0.13
Philippines	-0.04	0.25	0.04	-0.13
Indonesia	n.a.	-0.41	-0.41	-0.49
Malaysia	-0.47	-0.18	-0.08	-0.04
Thailand	-0.08	0.01	-0.05	0.02
Other Asia	-0.07	-0.15	-0.17	n.a.
India	−0.01	-0.13	-0.17	-0.13
Oceania	-0.27	-0.15	-0.02	n.a.
Australia	-0.27	-0.15	0.00	-0.03
New Zealand	-0.28	-0.15	-0.11	-0.10
North America	0.07	0.09	0.16	0.14
Canada	-0.17	-0.20	-0.10	-0.09
United States	0.14	0.15	0.21	0.18
South America	-0.25	-0.08	-0.13	-0.12
Brazil	-0.45	-0.29	-0.44	-0.41
Mexico	-0.18	-0.16	-0.03	-0.03
Western Europe	0.06	0.03	0.04	0.03
Austria	0.20	0.23	0.01	0.04
Benelux	-0.03	0.01	0.04	0.03
France	0.15	0.14	0.13	0.11
Germany	-0.23	-0.21	-0.23	-0.23
Italy	0.09	-0.01	0.01	0.01
Spain	0.36	0.29	0.28	0.28
United Kingdom	0.15	0.09	0.13	0.13
European Union (15)	0.06	0.02	0.02	0.01
Africa	-0.37	-0.18	-0.16	-0.18
Egypt	0.03	0.18	0.22	0.15
South Africa	-0.13	-0.09	-0.11	-0.12

Notes: The specialisation index is calculated as (Export − Import) / (Export + Import). n.a. = 'not available'.

Sources: World Trade Organisation, *Annual Report*, 1998; International Economic Databank, Australian National University.

tended to export services, while developing regions have been net importers, except for the two city economies of Hong Kong and Singapore and for Egypt, which has important tourist attractions. Among the industrialised countries, Japan and Germany have been strong importers of services. Overall, industrialised countries have been responsible for most of the world's services transactions and have tended to export rather than import. In developing economies, with the exception of a few nations, both exports and imports of services have been growing but developing countries still tend to import services.

Trade by type of service activities

Tables 2.9 and 2.10 show the composition of world services trade by major type of activity in the main services trading countries in each region.[6] While the relative importance of different types of services activities varies across countries, depending on economic structure and stages of development, these tables depict a common trend. Although detailed breakdowns of services activities are very limited for most countries, three broadly defined non-factor services – transport, travel, and communication and information services – have accounted for 90 per cent of the world's exports and imports of services. Insurance and financial services transactions accounted for only 5 to 6 per cent of trade in the 1990s and in the category of royalties and licence fees, no country except the United States showed an export or import share above 10 per cent in the 1980s and the 1990s. The relative importance of travel services and royalty and licence fee transactions has gradually increased throughout the 1980s and 1990s, to the expense of transport services.

As in Article I of the GATS, Karsenty (1999) distinguished travel from other forms of services, in that it is generally supplied in the territory of one economy to consumers in other economies. Table 2.9 shows that travel services accounted for more than 50 per cent of total services exports in several developing countries that are regarded as attractive tourist destinations. In some developed countries with exceptional geographical conditions, such as Australia and New Zealand, or historic value, such as Austria and Spain, inbound tourism made up just under or above 50 per cent of services exports in 1996. While inbound tourism is determined by the country's abundance of tourism attractions, the level of travel imports (outbound tourism) is mainly determined by income. Table 2.10 shows that unlike the case of travel exports, shares of travel imports in total services imports do not deviate much from the world average, except for a few developing economies in East Asia.

Table 2.11 shows the shares of selected economies in the world in major international services transactions. The United States has been the largest single exporter and importer of all categories of services and has continued to strengthen its position in exports but to reduce its import shares in most services activities. In particular, the country received more than 45 per cent of the world's royalty and licence fees in 1996 but paid less than 15 per cent of fees.

Table 2.9 Composition of total services exports by major type of activity, selected economies, 1980–96 (per cent)

	Transport services			Travel services			Communications and information services[b]			Insurance and financial services			Royalty & licence fees		
	1980	1990	1996	1980	1990	1996	1980	1990	1996	1980	1990	1996	1980	1990	1996
World	33.4	24.9	23.6	25.6	31.9	32.5	33.8	31.8	32.7	3.0	6.4	6.2	3.3	4.1	4.9
Asia Pacific industrialised economies															
Australia	49.3	34.6	28.1	29.5	42.0	49.3	19.9	20.5	17.8	1.3	2.9	4.8	1.7	1.6	1.4
New Zealand	58.2	42.1	33.9	21.1	41.3	51.7	19.6	16.9	14.6	1.1	-0.2	-0.1	n.a.	n.a.	n.a.
Japan	62.9	39.2[a]	31.9	3.2	7.7[a]	6.0	32.4	53.6[a]	55.4	1.6	-0.4[a]	4.9	1.7	6.4[a]	9.9
Canada	34.1	22.0	20.3	34.2	33.1	31.1	31.7	44.9	48.6	n.a.	n.a.	n.a.	n.a.	n.a.	n.a.
US	29.9	25.8	20.4	22.3	32.7	34.2	44.6	38.1	41.1	3.2	3.4	4.3	14.9	11.3	12.8
Asian NIEs and developing economies															
Korea	33.5	33.0	36.9	7.8	28.2	18.2	53.1	35.2	41.8	5.6	3.6	3.2	0.1	0.3	0.7
Singapore	26.9	17.4	17.3	29.5	36.3	26.6	42.5	45.6	54.5	1.1	0.7	1.6	n.a.	n.a.	n.a.
China	n.a.	46.2	14.9	n.a.	29.7	49.5	n.a.	20.2	35.0	n.a.	3.9	9.7	n.a.	n.a.	n.a.
Philippines	14.2	7.6	2.9[b]	22.1	14.4	12.2[b]	63.6	77.6	84.3[b]	0.0	0.4	0.7[b]	0.0	0.0	0.0[b]
Indonesia	n.a.	2.8	n.a.	n.a.	86.5	95.9[b]	n.a.	10.7	4.1[b]	n.a.	n.a.	n.a.	n.a.	n.a.	n.a.
Malaysia	41.6	31.0	21.3[b]	28.0	43.6	35.2[b]	29.8	25.3	43.4[b]	0.6	0.1	0.1[b]	n.a.	n.a.	n.a.
Thailand	20.1	20.7	15.4	58.2	67.4	53.4	21.2	11.8	29.0	0.5	0.2	0.7	n.a.	n.a.	0.1
South America and Africa															
Brazil	46.8	35.8	42.4[b]	7.3	36.8	15.8[b]	38.1	24.3	25.3[b]	7.9	3.1	16.5[b]	0.7	0.3	0.5[b]
Mexico	9.7	11.0	13.0	69.7	68.3	63.6	10.4	16.6	8.1	10.2	4.1	7.5	0.5	0.9	1.1
Egypt	52.4	40.4	29.0	24.8	18.4	34.6	22.4	40.5	35.4	0.4	0.8	1.0	n.a.	n.a.	0.5
South Africa	41.8	32.6	27.0	47.1	51.6	52.3	2.5	5.9	11.0	8.6	10.0	9.6	0.6	1.5	1.6
Western Europe															
Austria	7.3	6.3	11.5	68.9	57.6	52.0	21.3	33.2	23.6	2.6	2.8	12.9	0.4	0.4	0.7
Belgium	32.7	25.8	26.1	14.1	13.1	17.7	48.6	44.0	41.8	4.7	17.1	14.4	1.4	2.4	1.9
France	24.2	21.3	22.8	19.0	26.5	31.9	53.4	37.7	36.2	3.4	14.5	9.1	1.1	1.7	2.1
Germany	26.6	22.5	23.3	15.1	20.4	20.8	57.4	50.3	48.9	0.8	6.7	7.0	1.8	3.0	3.9
Italy	23.9	20.7	21.6	46.7	33.1	42.9	22.9	40.9	28.1	6.5	5.4	7.3	0.5	2.1	0.5
Netherlands	51.5	43.4	41.0	13.1	13.4	13.3	34.3	42.5	44.2	1.2	0.7	1.4	2.4	3.5	4.8
Spain	25.9	17.0	15.2	60.0	66.5	62.3	11.6	12.2	18.8	2.4	4.3	3.6	0.3	0.3	0.5
UK	38.9	25.2	22.6	19.0	24.9	25.2	42.1	39.1	41.0	n.a.	10.8	11.2	3.1	4.5	6.0

Notes:
a 1991 figures.
b 1995 figures.
c World total is calculated from the sum of values reported by 211 individual economies listed in the original data source.
n.a. = 'not available'.

Source: World Bank, *World Development Indicators* (compiled from the International Economic Databank, Australian National University, Canberra).

Table 2.10 Composition of services imports by major type of activity, selected economies, 1980–96 (per cent)

	Transport services			Travel services			Communications and information services			Insurance and financial services			Royalty & licence fees		
	1980	1990	1996	1980	1990	1996	1980	1990	1996	1980	1990	1996	1980	1990	1996
World	37.6	30.0	27.9	23.8	28.9	30.3	31.0	28.9	31.7	3.7	6.0	5.0	1.9	3.2	3.7
Asia Pacific industrialised economies															
Australia	47.4	33.5	36.4	28.1	31.0	31.3	23.2	32.9	27.0	1.3	2.6	5.3	4.2	6.1	5.9
New Zealand	39.4	39.7	41.2	28.3	28.8	29.4	31.8	29.1	25.9	0.6	2.4	3.5	n.a.	n.a.	n.a.
Japan	52.2	30.5a	25.9	14.2	27.6a	28.5	31.3	40.5a	40.0	2.3	2.1a	3.8	4.1	7.0a	7.6
Canada	29.5	20.4	22.6	30.5	38.6	31.0	40.0	40.9	46.4	n.a.	n.a.	n.a.	n.a.	n.a.	n.a.
US	37.5	30.3	29.0	25.4	32.3	32.7	35.0	33.6	33.4	2.1	3.7	5.0	1.8	2.7	4.8
Asian NIEs and developing economies															
Korea	55.8	39.9	35.9	8.6	24.6	23.3	30.0	32.6	38.0	5.6	2.9	2.8	0.8	1.2	7.6
Singapore	38.3	40.6	33.8	11.4	20.9	32.5	46.1	29.5	28.3	4.3	9.0	5.3	n.a.	n.a.	n.a.
China	n.a.	74.6	45.7	n.a.	10.8	19.8	n.a.	12.5	33.5	n.a.	2.2	16.9	n.a.	n.a.	n.a.
Philippines	52.1	55.7	29.6b	7.4	6.4	6.1b	39.8	34.7	62.7b	0.8	3.4	1.6b	1.3	2.2	1.4b
Indonesia	n.a.	46.1	35.2b	n.a.	13.8	16.1b	n.a.	36.2	45.4b	n.a.	3.9	3.2b	n.a.	n.a.	n.a.
Malaysia	44.3	46.2	38.2b	24.5	26.4	16.0b	31.2	27.4	45.7b	n.a.	n.a.	n.a.	1.3	2.7	n.a.
Thailand	64.4	56.7	40.1	14.8	22.7	21.9	14.8	15.3	31.7	5.9	5.3	4.9	1.8	2.7	3.7
South America and Africa															
Brazil	56.5	39.8	42.6b	7.5	20.0	24.9b	35.0	37.8	23.3b	1.0	2.4	9.2b	0.8	0.7	3.9b
Mexico	28.2	24.3	38.6	47.0	53.5	31.3	16.3	16.2	19.0	8.5	6.0	8.9	2.7	3.7	3.3
Egypt	40.3	38.7	32.6	7.2	3.4	25.9	49.1	53.9	37.7	3.4	4.1	3.8	n.a.	n.a.	0.6
South Africa	48.4	47.6	46.7	20.3	26.7	27.5	20.0	15.8	17.0	11.3	9.9	8.8	5.3	3.1	4.4
Western Europe															
Austria	12.7	8.3	8.6	50.6	54.6	48.9	32.4	32.6	26.7	4.2	4.5	15.8	2.5	2.0	3.1
Belgium	29.7	22.7	22.3	25.7	20.6	28.3	39.5	42.3	38.4	5.2	14.4	11.0	3.6	5.0	3.5
France	28.4	28.7	28.6	18.7	20.2	24.3	48.1	32.4	35.8	4.8	18.7	11.3	3.2	2.7	3.6
Germany	25.1	21.5	19.3	41.2	39.6	39.7	33.2	33.3	38.5	0.6	5.7	2.6	3.4	4.5	4.6
Italy	43.8	28.5	35.0	11.8	20.6	23.4	31.3	41.2	33.1	13.1	9.7	8.5	2.8	3.9	1.5
Netherlands	43.9	37.8	30.2	26.6	24.4	25.2	27.1	37.2	41.7	2.4	0.9	2.9	3.5	5.8	6.2
Spain	38.6	29.2	28.4	21.5	26.5	20.2	34.6	38.3	44.4	5.4	6.0	7.1	3.0	6.4	5.8
UK	47.5	30.3	28.0	22.9	35.8	38.2	29.6	32.4	32.7	n.a.	1.4	1.2	3.3	6.0	5.3

Notes:
a 1991 figures.
b 1995 figures.
c World total is calculated from the sum of values reported by 211 individual economies listed in the original data source.
n.a. = not available'.
Source: World Bank, *World Development Indicators* (compiled from the International Economic Databank, Australian National University, Canberra).

Western Europe has been prominent in international services transactions. Eight Western European countries accounted for more than 75 per cent of the region's services transactions and more than 30 per cent of international transactions in transport, travel and communications services in the 1990s, even though shares were gradually declining. The region is also strong in exporting insurance and financial services: the eight nations accounted for over 51 per cent of the world total in 1996, which was down from 55 per cent in 1990. They also are important importers of insurance and financial services, accounting for about 40 per cent of the world total in 1996.

Although industrialised economies dominated international services trade, their combined share declined throughout the 1990s, as the importance of the rapidly industrialising countries grew. The developing East Asian economies of Korea, China, Singapore, the Philippines, Indonesia and Malaysia had an increasing combined share of both exports and imports of all types of services.[7] The rise in their import and export shares of communication and information services by more than 6 percentage points reflects the rapid recent growth of these services in the region.

Combining both export and import levels, Table 2.12 presents a trade specialisation index for services. Although not clearly depicting changing patterns of trade specialisation, this table shows that industrialised economies in general exported more than developing countries in all categories of services except travel. In the cases of two major cross-border services – transport and communications – most industrialised economies showed index values not less than -0.2, while developing countries values varied widely from a low of -1.0. The United States is the only country with a comparative advantage – that is positive index numbers – in all categories of services trade.

As Karsenty (1999) noted, travel does not follow the specialisation pattern of cross-border services trade. According to Table 2.11, in both travel and cross-border trade, the share of industrialised countries in trade fell, while there was a marked increase of the share of Asian developing economies in world trade. However, Table 2.12 shows great differences in specialisation patterns between travel and cross-border services. In 1996 most developing countries in Asia were net importers of all cross-border services except travel, where many showed relatively high index values of export specialisation. This is not surprising, since travel exports are demand-oriented activities that reflect the importance of tourism destinations or the quality of certain services such as education or health (Karsenty 1999).

FDI as a mode of service delivery

Services trade data are recorded in a country's balance of payments accounts as services credits (exports) and service debits (imports). These data generally include commercial services that are traded across borders and via the movement of consumers to the location of the service supplier. This definition of services trade is narrower than that used in the General Agreement on Trade in Services, which includes 'commercial presence' as another mode of

Table 2.11 Share in international trade in major activities of services by selected countries and regions, 1990 and 1996 (per cent)

	Transport services 1990 1996		Travel services 1990 1996		Communi- cations, etc.[a] 1990 1996		Insurance, finance 1990 1996		Royalty and licence fees 1990 1996	
Export shares: World = 100										
Asia Pacific industrialised economies										
Aust and NZ[b]	2.1	2.1	1.9	2.6	0.9	0.9	0.5	1.0	0.4	0.4
Japan	7.4[c]	6.7	1.2[c]	0.9	7.4[c]	8.5	-0.3[c]	4.0	7.6[c]	10.2
Canada	1.9	1.8	2.3	2.0	3.1	3.1	n.a.	n.a.	n.a.	n.a.
US	17.4	14.9	17.1	18.2	20.1	21.8	8.8	12.1	46.0	45.6
Asian developing (7)	5.2	6.5	6.5	9.9	5.5	11.8	1.3	2.0	n.a.	n.a.
Korea	1.7	3.1	1.1	1.1	1.4	2.5	0.7	1.0	0.1	0.3
China	1.2	1.0	0.6	2.3	0.4	1.6	0.4	0.1	n.a.	n.a.
ASEAN5[d]	2.3	2.4	4.7	6.4	3.7	7.7	0.2	0.8	0.0	0.0
South America and Africa										
Brazil	0.6	0.0	0.5	0.2	0.3	0.3	0.2	1.2	0.0	0.1
Mexico	0.4	0.4	2.0	1.6	0.5	0.2	0.6	1.0	0.2	0.2
Egypt	0.9	1.0	0.3	0.8	0.7	0.9	0.1	0.1	n.a.	0.1
South Africa	0.5	0.4	0.7	0.5	0.1	0.1	0.6	0.5	0.1	0.1
Western Europe (8)[e]	37.8	35.1	37.1	33.9	50.5	39.9	55.3	46.3	24.3	20.9
France	7.4	6.3	7.2	6.4	10.3	7.3	19.7	9.7	3.6	2.8
Germany	6.8	6.2	4.8	4.0	12.0	9.3	7.9	7.1	5.5	5.0
Italy	4.7	4.7	5.9	6.8	7.3	4.4	4.7	6.1	2.9	0.6
UK	6.5	5.6	5.0	4.5	7.8	7.4	10.7	10.6	7.0	7.2
Import shares: World = 100										
Asia Pacific industrialised economies										
Aust and NZ[b]	2.2	2.4	2.0	1.8	2.1	1.5	0.8	1.7	2.9	2.2
Japan[c]	9.5	9.0	9.1	9.1	10.8	12.2	3.3	7.3	20.1	19.6
Canada	2.1	2.2	4.2	2.7	4.5	3.9	n.a.	n.a.	n.a.	n.a.
US	13.2	11.8	14.6	12.3	15.2	12.0	8.1	11.3	11.0	14.6
Asian developing (7)	7.8	9.6	3.4	6.8	4.6	11.3	3.4	5.4	n.a.	n.a.
Korea	1.7	3.1	1.1	1.8	1.4	2.9	0.6	1.4	0.5	4.8
China	1.2	2.8	0.2	1.1	0.2	1.8	0.2	0.3	n.a.	n.a.
ASEAN5[d]	5.0	3.8	2.2	3.8	3.0	6.7	2.6	3.7	0.7	1.6
South America and Africa										
Brazil	1.1	0.0	0.6	0.9	1.1	0.7	0.3	1.7	0.2	1.1
Mexico	0.9	1.1	2.1	0.8	0.6	0.5	1.1	1.4	1.3	0.7
Egypt	0.5	0.5	0.0	0.4	0.7	0.6	0.2	0.4	n.a.	0.1
South Africa	0.7	0.7	0.4	0.4	0.3	0.2	0.8	0.8	0.5	0.5
Western Europe (8)[e]	32.7	31.6	37.9	36.2	45.2	39.7	50.8	42.3	51.9	38.5
France	6.5	5.5	4.7	4.3	7.6	6.1	21.2	12.2	5.7	5.2
Germany	6.7	6.6	12.8	12.5	10.7	11.6	8.9	4.9	13.4	11.7
Italy	5.3	6.3	4.0	3.9	7.9	5.3	8.9	8.6	6.9	2.0
UK	5.6	5.1	6.9	6.4	6.2	5.2	1.3	1.2	10.5	7.2

Notes:

a World total is calculated from the sum of values reported by 211 individual economies listed in the original data source.

b The figures for royalty and licence fees are for Australia only.

c 1991 figures.

d Includes Singapore, the Philippines, Indonesia, Malaysia and Thailand. Excludes Indonesia for transport services in 1996. Excludes Singapore for transactions of royalty and licence fees.

e The sum of the eight Western European countries listed in Tables 2.9 and 2.10.

n.a. = not available.

Source: World Bank, *World Development Indicators* (compiled from the International Economic Databank, Australian National University, Canberra).

Table 2.12 Trade specialisation in service activities by selected regions and
economies, 1990 and 1996

	Transport services		Travel services		Communications, etc.		Insurance, finance		Royalty and licence fees	
	1990	1996	1990	1996	1990	1996	1990	1996	1990	1996
Asia Pacific industrialised economies										
Aust and NZ	-0.13	-0.13	0.01	0.23	-0.37	-0.23	-0.20	-0.14	-0.67	-0.62
Japan	-0.20	-0.22	-0.75	-0.80	-0.19	-0.16	n.a.	-0.19	-0.36	-0.19
Canada	-0.16	-0.17	-0.26	-0.11	-0.15	-0.09	n.a.	n.a.	n.a.	n.a.
US	0.03	0.04	0.12	0.23	0.17	0.31	0.07	0.15	0.68	0.61
Asia developing										
Korea	-0.10	-0.08	0.07	-0.21	0.04	-0.04	0.10	-0.03	-0.57	-0.86
Singapore	-0.22	-0.10	0.44	0.14	0.39	0.51	-0.80	-0.34	n.a.	n.a.
China	-0.09	-0.54	0.57	0.39	0.37	-0.02	0.41	-0.31	n.a.	n.a.
Philippines	-0.60	-0.76	0.62	0.46	0.61	0.29	-0.62	-0.27	-0.95	-0.96
Indonesia	-0.95	-1.00	0.44	0.43	-0.78	-0.93	n.a.	n.a.	n.a.	n.a.
Malaysia	-0.36	-0.39	0.07	0.26	-0.21	-0.15	n.a.	n.a.	n.a.	n.a.
Thailand	-0.46	-0.50	0.50	0.36	-0.12	-0.11	-0.94	-0.79	-1.00	-0.93
South America and Africa										
Brazil	-0.38	-0.38	-0.04	-0.55	-0.51	-0.34	-0.23	-0.11	-0.64	-0.89
Mexico	-0.48	-0.49	0.00	0.34	-0.11	-0.40	-0.30	-0.08	-0.68	-0.49
Egypt	0.21	0.20	0.77	0.39	0.04	0.23	-0.57	-0.38		0.16
South Africa	-0.27	-0.40	0.24	0.17	-0.52	-0.35	-0.09	-0.10	-0.41	-0.58
Western Europe (8)	-0.03	-0.03	0.03	0.01	0.09	0.02	0.06	0.16	-0.25	-0.17
France	-0.04	-0.01	0.24	0.24	0.19	0.11	-0.01	-0.00	-0.11	-0.17
Germany	-0.09	-0.11	-0.42	-0.49	0.09	-0.09	-0.03	0.29	-0.31	-0.28
Italy	-0.16	-0.22	0.23	0.31	-0.01	-0.06	-0.29	-0.05	-0.31	-0.46
UK	-0.03	-0.03	-0.12	-0.13	0.15	0.19	0.79	0.84	-0.08	0.13

Notes: The specialisation index is calculated as (Export – Import) / (Export + Import); for other notes, see notes in Table 2.11.

Source: World Bank, *World Development Indicators* (compiled from the International Economic Databank, Australian National University, Canberra).

service delivery.[8] The nature of services trade suggests that this is likely to be the dominant mode of delivery for many services. Entertainment, recreation and educational services all require interaction between producers and consumers, and often these services have to be consumed simultaneously with production. As a result, they cannot be transported and therefore are traded across borders. Services such as consulting and tourism services can be delivered through the temporary movement of either producers or consumers, but others require producers to establish a long-term physical presence in the foreign market (Hardin and Holmes 1997).

Foreign direct investment in services is one way of establishing commercial presence for service delivery in the foreign market. Hardin and Holmes (1997) show that FDI in services has increased rapidly over the past two decades, reflecting the growing importance of the services sector in the world economy. They find half the world's FDI stock was in services (around US$1,330 billion) in 1995, the share increasing substantially from 30 per cent in 1970. Services accounted for 60 to 65 per cent of world FDI flows in 1995. There is no

Table 2.13 Services FDI stock as a share of total FDI stock for selected OECD
countries, 1984 and 1994 (per cent)

	Inward FDI services stock		*Outward FDI services stock*	
	1987	*1997*	*1987*	*1997*
Australia	49	52	53	37
Austria[a]	56	65	64	73
Canada	32	27	49	45
France[b]	55	58	50	57
Germany[a]	52	79	31	68
Japan[c]	26	45	48	66
Netherlands[d]	45	55	34	50
United Kingdom[e]	32	50	40	44
United States	47	52	37	49

Notes:
a 1986 and 1996 figures.
b 1989 and 1996 figures.
c 1984 and 1994 figures.
d 1985 and 1995 figures.
e 1987 and 1996 figures.

Source: OECD, *International Direct Investment Yearbook*, various issues.

complete set of country-specific data on FDI in services. Table 2.13 presents
data on selected OECD countries showing that services generally accounted
for about half of all inward foreign investment in 1997. Services also accounted
for the majority of outward FDI stock in most OECD countries. The share of
services in both total inward and outward FDI stock increased for most OECD
countries between 1987 and 1997. Although providing limited information,
Table 2.13 implies that if services traded by foreign affiliates were taken into
account, the share of services in world output would be much higher than
the figures reported in Table 2.5 on exports of commercial services.

CONCLUSION

Despite the limited data and information on services trade, the services sector
is clearly an important and growing part of the world economy accounting
for increasing shares of production, employment and international transactions.

The growth of an economy's services sector is an important part of its
development and is strongly associated with economic growth. The services
sector typically accounts for the largest share of economic activity in
industrialised and newly industrialising economies and a comparable share
of employment. While the proportion of GDP attributable to services is
generally lower in developing countries than developed countries, the services
sector is increasing in importance, even more so if the fact that services are
inputs into all aspects of processing and production is taken into account.

International trade in services has also grown rapidly over the past two decades. The growth of world services trade exceeded that of merchandise trade, and the relative importance of services trade has increased in most countries. Even though world services trade is still dominated by the industrialised countries, their shares of world exports and imports of services are decreasing. In contrast, the relative importance of developing countries, especially in Asia, in world services trade has grown.

Detailed services data are very limited compared with data for merchandise trade. Only a small number of developed countries collect and report services statistics at a relatively disaggregated level. Most countries report data on trade in services in broad categories of transportation, travel, communications, financial services and other services, as reported by this chapter. Among the categories of services, three broadly defined activities – transportation, travel and communications – have accounted for two-thirds of world services exports and imports. The importance of travel and other services gradually increased relative to transport services throughout the 1980s and 1990s.

While the share of the industrialised countries in both travel and cross-border trade showed a common decreasing trend, with a marked increase in the share of developing economies, travel does not follow the specialisation pattern of cross-border services trade. Most developing countries in Asia were net importers of all cross-border services trade but not all were net importers of travel services.

FDI flows and stocks can be used as a proxy for another important mode of service delivery – commercial presence. The increasing importance of FDI in the world economy suggests that the estimation of the share of services in world output would increase substantially if services traded by foreign affiliates or through FDI were taken into account.

Table A2.1 Trade in services as a proportion of trade in goods and services, selected economies and regions, 1980–98 (per cent)

	Export share				Import share			
	1980	1990	1997	1998	1980	1990	1997	1998
World	15.2	18.6	19.4	19.4	16.1	18.7	18.8	18.8
Asia	13.6	14.0	16.0	14.9 [a]	16.4	18.8	19.5	20.3 [a]
Japan	12.6	12.6	13.9	13.5	18.5	26.4	26.5	28.1
China	n.a.	8.5	11.8	11.1	n.a.	7.2	17.4	16.9
NIEs	16.2	14.9	16.3	14.9	11.8	13.9	13.7	15.1
Korea	12.1	12.3	15.7	15.0	12.4	12.6	16.7	19.7
Taiwan	9.1	9.4	12.3	13.1	11.4	20.3	17.5	18.3
Hong Kong	22.1	18.0	16.9	16.4	12.5	11.5	9.8	10.7
Singapore	19.8	19.4	19.6	14.2	10.7	12.3	12.8	15.1
ASEAN4	7.1	15.2	19.6	14.7	12.9	16.4	22.6	22.
Philippines	17.5	26.4	37.6	20.6	13.7	11.7	26.9	23.8
Indonesia	n.a.	8.8	11.3	7.7	n.a.	21.3	28.0	30.3
Malaysia	7.5	11.4	15.9	12.9	20.9	15.6	18.0	16.9
Thailand	17.4	21.4	21.4	19.3	14.9	15.6	21.4	22.6
Other Asia	17.9	18.1	17.1	n.a.	15.3	18.4	18.7	n.a.
India	25.0	20.4	20.2	24.1	16.4	20.1	23.0	24.2
Oceania	13.3	18.5	n.a.	n.a.	19.3	22.1	n.a.	n.a.
Australia	14.3	19.8	22.6	22.1	22.0	24.2	21.8	20.5
New Zealand	14.9	20.3	21.7	n.a.	23.4	25.5	25.2	n.a.
North America	13.3	22.4	22.4	22.6	10.9	16.4	14.6	14.6
Canada	9.5	12.6	11.9	11.8	13.9	18.2	15.2	14.5
United States	14.5	25.1	25.2	25.5	10.1	15.9	14.5	14.6
South America	13.5	16.7	15.3	16.2	18.8	21.4	16.7	16.5
Brazil	7.7	10.6	11.4	13.5	15.1	23.0	21.3	23.7
Mexico	19.5	15.0	9.2	9.2	23.0	20.0	9.5	9.0
Western Europe	20.7	20.3	20.9	21.0	17.0	18.9	19.9	19.9
Austria	33.0	35.5	33.3	33.5	18.9	22.3	30.5	29.6
Benelux	16.9	18.0	18.5	18.3	16.8	18.0	18.4	18.6
France	26.6	23.4	21.7	20.4	18.7	17.7	18.8	17.9
Germany	11.8	10.9	12.7	12.3	17.8	18.2	21.0	20.7
Italy	19.4	22.2	23.1	22.5	13.5	21.5	25.2	24.5
Spain	35.6	33.2	29.5	30.6	13.7	14.8	16.5	17.0
United Kingdom	23.7	22.3	24.6	26.7	17.9	16.7	18.8	19.4
European Union (15)	20.2	19.7	20.3	20.2	16.8	18.5	20.1	19.9
Africa	9.6	15.4	18.0	19.8	22.0	22.1	22.4	22.4
Egypt	43.2	65.1	69.9	n.a.	31.0	26.5	30.6	n.a.
South Africa	10.3	12.8	13.6	13.8	16.1	18.2	15.5	15.4

Note
a Share of Asia and Oceania.
n.a. = not available.

Sources: International Economic Databank, Australian National University; World Trade Organisation, *Annual Report*, 1998.

NOTES

1 For a synthesis on the definition of services, see Castle and Findlay (1988).
2 For further discussion on the framework of services trade data, see Karsenty (1999).
3 'Transport' largely includes freight and passenger transportation by air and sea. 'Travel' is reported as expenditure by non-residents (mostly tourists) while staying in a foreign country. 'Other services' includes items such as brokerage, insurance, communications, leasing and rental of equipment, technical and professional services, property income (royalties), and income generated by the temporary movement of labour.
4 For detailed discussion on services data needs and weakness, see Hoekman (1996).
5 When a country only exports services without any imports, the index number is equal to 1. If the index is –1, the country is only importing services, and not exporting.
6 The data in these tables are mainly from the World Bank, so that the definition of services here is slightly different from 'commercial services' used in Tables 2.5–8, as it excludes construction services but includes government services. It is also important to note that, while goods trade can be disaggregated into hundreds of separate categories based on existing international or national classifications, detailed breakdowns of traded services are very limited for most countries.
7 This grouping is due only to data availability.
8 The GATS includes 'presence of natural persons' as the fourth and final mode of service delivery. This involves an individual, who functions alone or is employed by a service provider and temporarily travels abroad to deliver a service. Services trade via this mode is not explicitly discussed in this chapter.

3 Price-impact measures of impediments to services trade

Malcolm Bosworth, Christopher Findlay, Ray Trewin and Tony Warren

INTRODUCTION

This chapter reviews a seven-step approach to the measurement of impediments to trade and investment in services. It serves as an introduction to a number of aspects of the methodology that is examined in more detail in later chapters.

The focus in this chapter is on the determination of a price impact of impediments to trade in services. We also discuss the assessment of the origin of the price effects. Our approach is to work from the bottom up and allocate impacts to specific measures. This approach is distinct from a top-down approach, for example, where unidentifiable price differences between the services examined and a 'benchmark' service are not attributed to specific impediments.

Seven steps to measuring impediments to trade and investment in services are discussed here. These steps are: defining the industries to be analysed; identifying the specific impediments to trade; making explicit the theoretical link between the impediment and 'prices'; determining the price wedge; identifying the appropriate benchmark market against which to measure the impact of impediments; decomposing the wedge; and incorporating the price-impact data into a general equilibrium model.

After a general discussion of the nature of services trade and investment impediments, we outline each of these steps.

DEFINING IMPEDIMENTS

An impediment to trade or investment in services is any measure that distorts the economy's efficient allocation of resources in the services sector. This definition includes not only measures that restrict trade but also those that may cause an increase in the volume of trade and investment.

It was pointed out in PECC (1995) that all definitions of this type will have limitations. An alternative is to define impediments by example. This could be done by using a list of impediments developed by international institutions such as the United Nations Conference on Trade and Development (UNCTAD) (see UNCTAD and World Bank 1994). The problem is that this method may miss some newer impediments. It would also not provide a conceptual basis for measuring their impact. Whatever approach is used, the coverage of impediments must be comprehensive, not just covering border measures but all modes of supply and incorporating, for example, those investment measures that may impinge on the efficiency of service delivery.

The multilateral General Agreement on Trade in Services (GATS) applied a four-part typology of how international transactions in services can be accessed, namely:

- cross-border flows;
- the movement of a consumer to a supplier's economy;
- the movement of a commercial organisation to the consumer's economy; and
- the movement of an individual supplier to the consumer's economy.

Free trade and investment in services occurs when service providers and consumers are able to interact through whichever mode they decide, free of any regulatory distortions. Any policy that impedes service producers and consumers interacting through any of these modes of supply is an impediment to international service transactions. Following Part III of the GATS, impediments can either violate national treatment or limit market access.

The GATS does not define market access. Article XVI (1) obliges members to grant market access to scheduled industry subsectors, while Article XVI (2):(a)–(f) contains a list of quantitative measures considered to be limitations on market access. Article XVII (1) defines national treatment as treatment no less favourable than that accorded to like domestic services and service providers subject to the limitations and conditions set out in the country's schedule of commitments. An uncomfortable overlap exists between the two commitments, with national treatment being interwoven with market access. Despite this confusion, it appears that the GATS application of market access was applied to broadly cover barriers to both foreign and domestic suppliers, that is competition policy (Mattoo 1996; Snape and Bosworth 1996).

As can be appreciated from the above, our definition of an impediment to trade or investment in services is broader than the GATS approach, covering more than just border measures.

IDENTIFYING AND MEASURING IMPEDIMENTS

In order to maintain some degree of comparability across economies, the UN Central Product Classification (CPC) has been used as the starting point for industry definition, as this was used in the GATS. However, there are various problems associated with using product rather than industry classifications. For example, many government policies apply to industries (e.g. banks) rather than to services (e.g. taking of deposits). Hence, the CPC categories in each of the target industries need to be made to accord with industrial classifications, such as the International Standard Industrial Classification (ISIC), in order to give a more complete picture of the industry parameters (see Table 3.1).

There is a question concerning the level of industry aggregation. Should a broad level be taken, such as insurance in general, or more specific components, such as selected insurances (e.g. car insurance), which could then be aggregated? A more disaggregated approach would be more appropriate in terms of better matching international comparisons but could lead to difficulties in terms of allocating more general industry-level common costs.

Identifying specific impediments

An essential preliminary step to measuring the impact of impediments to trade in services is to identify and establish an inventory of such impediments. This is not easy, given the broad definition of impediments to trade in services, for example encompassing internal regulations under competition policy and their effect on new entrants. Moreover, a key feature of impediments to trade and investment in services is that they tend to be in the form of non-tariff barriers (NTBs), such as licensing requirements, standards, outright prohibitions and so on, which are less transparent and more difficult to measure. There are a large number of such NTBs, as can be appreciated from UNCTAD's database on Measures Affecting Services Trade (MAST) based on the GATS list (see Table 3.2). Even taking GATS' modes of supply approach results in many modes, including commercial presence.

However, the GATS does provide a starting inventory as a result of the requirement that members schedule chosen industries, and the modes of supply within those industries, in which they agree to adhere to the principles of free market access and equivalent treatment of foreign service providers. The GATS schedules present a standstill agreement, rather than a schedule of commitments to future liberalisation. As such, the agreement reflects the extent of market access and national treatment commitment of most members as of 15 April 1994. It provides a registry of service industries that have been liberalised and, by default, those that remained closed or where no commitments had been made. Some industries, such as maritime shipping, were not included in the GATS. Moreover, it is a positive-list approach, in contrast to the negative-list approach by the European Union (EU), North American Free Trade agreement (NAFTA) and the Closer Economic Relations agreement (CER), which require all impediments in the covered sectors to be revealed and do not automatically exclude new sectors from such commitments.

The GATS framework could provide the starting point for defining what is 'trade' in services and what are impediments to services. All four modes of supply should be included in the analysis, ensuring that all impediments affecting trade and investment in services are incorporated. Furthermore, impediments to all potential entrants in the market, including both domestic

Table 3.1 Industry classifications and concordances

Industry	CPC	ISIC
Air transport	73, 74, 88	621, 622, 63, 35
Finance and insurance	81	651
Telecommunications	752	642

and foreign suppliers (market access) and, in particular, national treatment should be examined.

The identification of impediments is aided by the GATS schedules of specific commitments made by various economies. In these schedules, economies list many of their breaches of market access and national treatment, greatly facilitating the identification of relevant impediments. Detailed examination of the relevant legislation and regulation covering air transport, financial services and telecommunications is a necessary first step for this project. Reports by foreign governments and industry associations (e.g. EC 1996; MITI 1996; USTR 1995) have proven helpful in identifying these impediments, as have business practices and other less formal impediments.

One outstanding issue that needs to be taken into account with a sectoral approach is the various cross-sectoral impediments that exist. These include impediments such as general foreign investment constraints and policies on work visas. The effect of these horizontal impediments on each target industry needs to be included into any sectoral analysis.

Making explicit the theoretical link

A more useful inventory than that just discussed would list for each service industry the type of impediment restricting trade, classified in terms of its impact on the market. Once the impediments have been identified, the effect of the policy on actual service outcomes needs to be conceptualised. In some cases, this is a relatively simple task. For example, if the impediment is a quantitative restriction or a restriction on the number of firms in a market, then it is known how this leads to higher prices. The same can be said for poor or no regulation of access to essential facilities. However, there are policies where this linkage is not so clear. One example is the effect on prices of limits on foreign investment in particular firms, as opposed to limits on all new foreign investment. This may impact upon the economics of the market, for example by constraining the introduction of new technologies, but the linkage is less clear.

Determining the relevant price wedge

We use Figure 3.1 to illustrate the effects on prices of various types of impediments. It depicts the various prices (which can also be thought of in

Table 3.2   Categories of measures

Measures affecting market access
a   Limitations on the number of providers
b   Limitations on the total value of service transactions or assets
c   Limitations on the total number of service operations
d   Limitations on the total number of persons that may be employed in a sector
e   Measures which restrict or require specific types of legal entity or joint venture
f   Limitations on the participation of foreign capital
g   Other measures affecting market access

Measures affecting national treatment
a   Discriminatory taxes
b   Discriminatory incentives/subsidies
c   Government procurement policies
d   Local content requirements
e   Nationality, citizenship or residence requirements
f   Other measures affecting national treatment

Measures affecting MFN treatment
a   Integration agreements, as stated in Article V of GATS
b   Reciprocity requirements
c   Bilateral agreements
d   Other measures affecting MFN treatment

Non-discriminatory measures, as stated in Article VI of GATS
a   Licensing procedures
b   Technical standards
c   Recognition of qualifications
d   Other measures related to Article VI of GATS

---

terms of associated costs) that are relevant in determining the effect of an impediment to trade in services. In the figure the quantity axis shows the volumes of some services, such as international telecommunications. The price of the service is shown on the vertical axis. The diagram illustrates the market for this service in one economy. For simplicity, supply curves are horizontal (where marginal cost = average cost).

The lowest price shown in the figure (P_w) is the price at which the service can be delivered by the cheapest supplier(s) on the world market. It is assumed the service is delivered from the home base of that supplier, employing local inputs at home-base prices alongside some internationally traded inputs which it can buy at world prices. It is also assumed the economy of focus is small in world market terms, so that the supply curve at this price is perfectly elastic. If the service is tradable and no impediments to cross-border trade exist, the price expected to be observed in the domestic economy under examination is equal to the world price (P_w).

However, not all services are tradable (in a cross-border sense). Therefore, to deliver its service to local consumers, the world's best-practice firm must

Figure 3.1 The price effects of various impediments to services trade

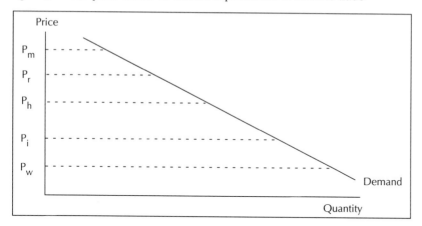

Notes: P~m~ = monopoly price in the home market; P~r~ = regulated price in the home market; P~h~ = competitive price in the home market; P~i~ = the price the best-practice foreign investor can offer in the home market; P~w~ = the world price

invest in the local market. This may involve higher costs (e.g. labour, capital, telecommunications, transport) than the firm faces in its home market. These can be taken into account in the firm's cost function using econometric techniques. Hence, the price it offers is higher than P_w, say at P_i. Therefore, if the service is non-tradable and no impediments to foreign investment exist, the price expected to be observed in a competitive domestic economy is equal to the price the best-practice foreign investor can offer in that market (P_i).

To summarise to this point, the benchmark price n in an economy characterised by no impediments to trade and investment is either P_w or P_i, depending upon whether or not the service is tradable.

If, however, there are impediments to trade and investment, costs and therefore prices are generally expected to be higher. But if the domestic market is relatively competitive, despite being protected from international trade and investment, the price should settle at P_h. P_h is higher than P_i or P_w because international firms operating at world's best-practice are excluded from the market. This assumes that domestic firms cannot obtain the world's best-practice technology.

Suppose now that there is only one domestic supplier (e.g. because of scale economies). If that firm is not regulated and if there is also an impediment to trade in the service, the local supplier can act as a monopolist. It will set its price at P_m (determined as the price at which the profit-maximising quantity of the service – set by the intersection of the marginal revenue curve and its marginal cost line – is demanded). It may instead be the case that the domestic market is regulated and that the local firm is subject to a price cap. In this case, some forms of cost padding can be expected. The reported average cost line is expected to increase to a level of, say, P_r. The regulated price may be at or above this level. For simplicity, the former is assumed.

This model can be used to illustrate the effects of reform:

- If, for example, an economy decides to deregulate its market, but not to liberalise, prices will fall from either P_m or P_r down to P_h.
- If an economy then decides to allow in foreign investors, prices will fall from P_h to P_i.
- Finally, if an economy permits trade from the home base of foreign suppliers, then the price will fall to P_w, assuming it is tradable.

It is the wedge between the various possible prices (or associated costs), in an economy without impediments (P_w or P_i), and the actual price (P_h, P_r or P_m) that is of greatest concern for this project. This wedge will provide the prima facie price impact of the trade barriers.

Identifying the appropriate benchmark market

Once the linkage between impediments and prices has been identified, it is necessary to find a market where such impediments do not exist in order to provide a benchmark against which to measure their impact. The market could be a 'real market', such as the best practice market overseas, or it could be a 'theoretical market', such as a perfectly competitive market. Various benefits and problems are associated with either type of benchmark.

We can illustrate this process by considering a case study. In Australian telecommunications, two real markets and one theoretical market are available to determine the effect on prices of the duopoly on the provision of line links.

The first market that could be used as a benchmark consists of international prices for the provision of a range of telecommunications services. The advantage with this method is the availability of data. The Organisation for Economic Cooperation and Development (OECD) and the International Telecommunications Union (ITU) both produce extensive databases comparing tariffs or charges for various services around the world. The disadvantage with this method is that international prices may not reflect traded services, similar input costs and quality, or liberalised prices. For example, maintenance costs for Singapore Telecom are likely to be significantly less than those faced by Australia's Telstra, given the different geography over which their respective networks operate.

The second market that could be used as a benchmark involves unimpeded domestic prices. The advantage of this method is that cost and quality differentials are no longer an issue (with some minor caveats). The problem is that, aside from a few industries dependent upon essential facilities, access prices are not always available.

The third benchmark market – and the market that will be predominantly used in the Australian research – is the theoretical one of a perfectly competitive market. Equal domestic and international prices do not imply that there are no impediments; for example, similar impediments could apply worldwide (like the international accounting rate system applied in telecommunications). The interest is in a comparison of prices with some measure of long-run marginal cost (LRMC), for example derived from econometric analysis of the cost of supplying the service. The theory underlying the approach is that if the market had no impediments to entry (market access problems) then it would be competitive and prices would be expected to approach LRMC. If there are impediments, however, a cost–price wedge will exist.

The definition of LRMC used is 'the cost of keeping a particular facility alive and well in the long run' (IC 1997). LRMC includes operating costs, normal returns on capital and some payment, say in the form of depreciation on sunk capital, to ensure continued innovation and new investment. While LRMC recovers all costs directly attributable to a particular service, it will not generate revenues necessary to meet unallocatable (common) costs such as administrative costs. The most efficient way to recover these costs is from the service with the most inelastic demand, which is unlikely to be international services.

The major problems with this method are the lack of data and data distorted by cost padding. The problem of cost padding is difficult to overcome because of data issues. However, in some industries, sufficient international data are available to estimate the world's best practice (technically and allocatively efficient) cost function. This cost function, which may not actually apply to any one country, can be estimated using frontier or related techniques such as data envelopment analysis. These functions require a standardised output, for example costs per mainlines in telecommunications, so that analysis can be undertaken across economies. Frontier estimation usually includes estimating bundles of output characteristics. This is like a hedonic price model – an implicit price model which assumes services are composed of a series of (perfectly divisible) attributes (e.g. quality differences) and enables isolation of values which contribute to observed price differences.

Generally, frontier models have not fitted the data well but procedures such as robust estimation techniques can help in this regard (see, for example, Trewin et al. 1995). In other cases, datasets are more limited. Fortunately, the data that are available tend to come from the world's more liberal markets because of the competition policy regimes that affect service industries in these countries.

Decomposing the wedge

Even restricting the focus to price-impact or cost–price wedges, some fundamental issues remain, such as whether these are best decomposed by 'building up' the impact of individual impediments or by 'breaking down' the wedge into components due to impediments and those due to other factors. Our preferred approach is to build up the impact of individual impediments (see IC 1995a). This approach provides conservative estimates by avoiding the unintentioned capture of other factors causing the price differences. It also builds on the earlier stage of listing an inventory of impediments. By enabling the explicit identification of impediments and their price impact, it minimises the danger that international price comparisons may not be made between the same quality service or markets (in equilibrium). The cost function discussed in the previous part provides a basis for a measure of the extent of the wedge. It also provides a base for determining the extent of the costs of individual impediment components, for example, by adjusting factor prices that have been increased by particular impediments.

The further challenge is to design a method by which the impediments can be assessed and incorporated in the analysis of the variation in costs or prices between economies. Ideally, policy impacts would be incorporated directly into models. However, as explained in the introduction to this volume, capturing this extent of detail is often difficult. Instead, policies can be characterised for this purpose using measures based on frequency counts. The issues in the application of frequency measures were also noted in the introduction and applications of the technique are reported in other chapters.

A survey of industry could also be undertaken, designed to elucidate possible reasons for price differentials that are not policy induced, but instead reflect differences in the costs of inputs, the quality of outputs or business practices and other informal impediments. Benchmarking is as much a 'process' as a technique, establishing a framework in which bureaucracy and industry can communicate on the factors that cause differences between domestic and international prices. In an international study of this type, the 'black books' process developed by government and industry of one economy on the impediments they face in other economies could be used (see, for example, EC 1996; MITI 1996; USITC 1995; USTR 1995).

Incorporating the price-impact data into a general equilibrium model

Finally, in order that the impact on the wider economy (e.g. social welfare) of a particular set of impediments to trade in services can be measured, the relatively uninformative price-impact figures and other directly relevant information, such as on quotas, can be analysed in a modified GTAP (Global Trade Analysis Project) model (Hertel 1997) capturing the structure of service industries. This will allow policymakers to quantify the costs of maintaining policies designed to exclude rival domestic and foreign firms from their service markets. Such an approach has been applied with frequency measures (see Brown et al. 1995) and, although a useful first approximation, the approach can be misleading and consequently distort policy advice. A more substantial discussion of the issues of the application of general equilibrium models is reported in Chapter 16.

CONCLUSION

This chapter has described a practical approach for measuring impediments to trade in services. The focus here was on the measurement of the impact of impediments on prices.

One issue that arises in the approach is that of aggregation, undertaken at the subsector level. This should not be so much of an analytical problem. However, it could be a negotiations problem, encouraging sector negotiations such as that on telecommunications, rather than service-wide negotiations, which are likely to offer larger gains, especially for a diverse collection of economies such as in APEC.

The difficulties in working through the steps highlighted a number of areas requiring future research. These include the need for better (e.g. more consistent) price and cost information; a better understanding of the impact of some policies (e.g. in respect of FDI) and other aspects on the market; the econometric estimation of the world's best practice cost functions; and the incorporation of the various forms of information from the earlier steps into economy-wide models measuring the broader impact of impediments to trade in services.

NOTE

The work reported here builds on experience in the preparation of the 1995 Pacific Economic Cooperation Council Survey of Impediments to Trade and Investment in the APEC Region (PECC 1995). The authors acknowledge the research assistance of Gerard Durand and Marpudin Azis, and the general contribution of Greg McGuire. The views expressed in this chapter are those of the authors and should not be attributed to, or taken as representing the views of, the Productivity Commission.

4 Assessing barriers to services sector investment

Leanne Holmes and Alexis Hardin

INTRODUCTION

Foreign direct investment (FDI) plays a key role in services trade. For foreign suppliers of many services, such as communications, financial, retailing and various business and professional services, it is important to establish a commercial presence in a market to allow ongoing direct contact with consumers. Restrictions on FDI can therefore potentially have significant implications for services trade.

Considerable progress has been made in recent years in the analysis of barriers to goods trade and, to a lesser extent, services trade (see Deardorff and Stern 1997; Hoekman and Braga 1997; Hufbauer 1996; OECD 1997a). Estimates of the possible gains from trade liberalisation have helped to provide impetus for the reform process. In contrast, there are still major gaps in the information base and tools for analysis of FDI policies. While there is some evidence of the benefits of investment liberalisation (see APEC 1997a; OECD 1998), more information is needed on the nature and extent of the existing barriers and how they affect services trade and economies generally.

In this chapter, a new method is developed for summarising and quantifying FDI barriers. This method is applied to eleven service sectors in fifteen Asia Pacific Economic Cooperation (APEC) economies.

IDENTIFYING AND CLASSIFYING BARRIERS TO FDI

The first major hurdle in the analysis of FDI barriers is the lack of information on the restrictions imposed in each economy. Some initiatives in recent years have helped to increase transparency, although the new sources of information still have some shortcomings. For example, FDI policies in APEC member economies are now documented and updated in the *Guide to Investment Regimes of Member Economies* (updated in early 1998) and APEC members' Individual Action Plans. However, these information sources are based on material provided by member economies and are often incomplete. World Trade Organisation (WTO) members' listing of some FDI restrictions in the General Agreement on Trade in Services (GATS) has also helped to improve transparency. However, the 'positive list' approach means that many restrictions, particularly those in sensitive sectors, are not included (see Hardin and Holmes 1997).

A further difficulty with establishing an information base on FDI barriers is that a vast range of measures is applied throughout the world, often on a case-by-case basis. For example, the UN Conference on Trade and Development (UNCTAD) has identified a total of 57 different types of FDI restrictions applied throughout the world (UNCTAD 1996). These must be identified, classified and summarised in some way before any analysis can proceed.

Using the three-part classification system suggested by UNCTAD (1996) – restrictions on market entry, ownership and operations of the foreign firm – Hardin and Holmes (1997: Table 4.2) list the major restrictions on inward FDI in service sectors in selected APEC economies. There is a wide range of such restrictions and, while the details vary, some common characteristics seem to be:

- application of some form of screening or registration process, involving various degrees of burden for the foreign investor;
- restrictions on the level or share of foreign ownership, particularly in some service industries, and often in the context of privatisations;
- widespread use of case-by-case assessments, often based on vague national interest criteria;
- widespread use of restrictions on ownership and control (for example, restrictions on board membership), particularly in industries such as telecommunications, broadcasting and banking; and
- relatively limited use of performance requirements or input controls in service industries.

Service sectors tend to be the most heavily restricted sectors in many economies. For example, in Indonesia the activities where foreign investment is completely banned are all in the services sector. Furthermore, six of the eight sectors where foreign investment is banned unless it involves some joint venture with Indonesians are in services (the other two are electricity generation and transmission, and nuclear power generation, which are not classified as service sectors in the GATS). In Japan, foreigners can not hold licences to provide telecommunications services, television or radio broadcasting, air transport or maritime transport services (mining is also restricted). Korea is undergoing an extensive liberalisation process, with foreign ownership restrictions being lifted in 152 industries. However, even at the end of the process in January 2000, 29 industries were still closed to foreign investment. Of these, all but five (in agriculture and fishing) are in the services sector.

Even among the economies with relatively liberal FDI regimes, some foreign ownership restrictions apply in key service sectors. The United States has no screening or authorisation process and no restrictions in most sectors, but it does restrict foreigners from holding broadcasting, common carrier and aeronautical radio licences (as well as licences to operate atomic energy plants). Similarly, Hong Kong has no screening process, but ownership and control restrictions apply in broadcasting (APEC 1998a).

While no sectors are completely closed to foreign investment in Australia, restrictions in addition to those set out in the *Foreign Acquisitions and Takeovers Act 1975* apply for certain sensitive sectors. With the exception of real estate, all of these are in services (banking, civil aviation, shipping, broadcasting, newspapers and telecommunications).

QUANTIFYING BARRIERS TO FDI

In essence, barriers to FDI involve some restriction on the value of foreign investment (say, a limit on the share of foreign ownership in a sector or firm), or some measure that makes the foreign investment more costly (say, by requiring the investor to go through a screening process, or by restricting the inputs used by the foreign firm).

In principle, the impacts of these restrictions on asset prices or prices for the services in the restricted markets would be useful measures of the extent or size of the FDI barriers. These 'tariff equivalents' could provide a basis for comparing FDI regimes across economies and would be a useful starting point for modelling the general equilibrium effects of liberalisation.

However, there are a range of practical and conceptual difficulties in estimating tariff equivalents for FDI barriers. The wide variety of forms of restrictions and their often case-by-case nature complicates the task, even for relatively direct types of restrictions such as limits on the share of foreign ownership. Different limits often apply to different firms in a sector, to different types of foreign investors, and to individual and aggregate foreign investment. As is the case for non-tariff barriers to goods trade, alternatives to simple price or cost wedges often have to be used to summarise the extent of FDI restrictions.

The difficulties with estimating tariff equivalents, or price wedges, are outlined in the following section. Because of these difficulties, we also examine some alternatives to the assessment of impediments to services sector foreign direct investment. These alternatives, based on a frequency measure, are reported in the final section of the chapter.

Tariff equivalents

Restrictions on foreign ownership are applied in selected sectors by all APEC and WTO member economies. In some cases, no foreign investment is allowed in certain sectors, while in others, foreigners may own up to some maximum share of equity in firms within a sector.

These types of restrictions are similar in many ways to quotas on imports of goods. They therefore provide a useful starting point for assessing the extent to which the techniques used in assessing trade barriers to goods can be applied to calculating tariff-equivalent type measures for FDI barriers.

In general, a restriction on the supply of imports (of goods or capital) will lead to some price adjustment to ration the limited supply, and some switching to the next best alternative product or asset – usually a domestically produced good or capital from domestic investors.

Where the FDI is being undertaken to gain access to services markets in a country, the next best alternative may be some other mode of supply, such as delivering financial services via the Internet or sending professional staff temporarily to the country to provide services to clients, without the firm investing directly. In some cases, the next best alternative to the supply of services via foreign investment may be supply using domestic resources (e.g. via licensing arrangements).

The quantity restriction on imports translates into some increase in prices or rates of return. Assuming the next best alternative is a very close substitute for the restricted product or asset, the wedge that is driven between the restricted and unrestricted prices or returns measures the tariff equivalent of the quota. The size of the wedge depends on the nature of supply and demand in the restricted market. In Box 4.1, this is illustrated for the case of a restriction on the supply of foreign capital, where domestic capital is a perfect substitute for the restricted foreign capital. The restriction results in an increase in the rate of return, a reduction in total capital flows and an increase in the share of domestic capital in the total.

If the next best alternative to services delivered via FDI is services delivered by some other mode, the simple partial equilibrium model in Box 4.1 can be reinterpreted in terms of a services market, rather than a capital market. The demand would be for services, while supply would be via FDI or an alternative mode. The restriction would increase the price of services and increase the share of the alternative (and more costly) mode of supply in total service supply.

Moving beyond the simple model to a practical tariff equivalent measure can be difficult. For example, what rates of return or service prices should be compared, and can all the differences be attributed to the effects of the investment restriction? This issue of identifying a benchmark by which performance in a particular sector could be evaluated was also discussed in Chapter 3 of this volume. One issue, also stressed in Chapter 3, is that it is likely that observed price or rate-of-return wedges will reflect factors other than FDI restrictions. For example, differences in rates of return in the telecommunications sector in Australia or New Zealand, where foreign investment is restricted, and the United Kingdom, where it is not restricted, could be due to a range of factors, including different regulatory regimes in telecommunications. Observed differences in rates of return could not be attributed fully to the different foreign investment policies. Removing the FDI barriers may not eliminate the wedge. The wedge may also remain if the domestic and foreign capital are not perfect substitutes, although it would be reduced by removal of the barrier.

Box 4.1 The impact of a limit on the share of foreign ownership

To illustrate the effects of a limit on the supply of foreign capital, assume that the demand for capital in the sector is a declining function of the rate of return (see D_1 in Figure 4.1 below), and that the domestic supply of capital increases with increases in the rate of return. Domestic suppliers of capital to the sector need to be offered higher returns to divert more capital to the sector, to offset any additional risks they may take by reducing their portfolio diversification. Because the domestic economy is small, foreign capital supply is assumed to be perfectly elastic – any amount is available at the world rate of return.

If there were no restrictions on foreign capital, it would meet demand beyond Q_d, up to Q_t. Domestic capital can be supplied at below the world rate of return up to Q_d, but beyond that the foreign capital meets all demand as it is cheaper.

However, now say there is a 25 per cent limit on the share of foreign capital in the market. This effectively places a limit on the amount of foreign capital that can be supplied beyond Q_d. For an increase in foreign capital by one unit, three additional units of domestic capital must be used. Three-quarters of any increase in capital must be met from the domestic market.

The demand curve for domestic capital can therefore be derived (D_2 in Figure 4.1). Domestic demand is three-quarters of total demand, at each price. The domestic demand curve has a slope of 4/3 of the total demand curve. The level of domestic capital supply is set where the domestic demand and supply curves intersect (Q_{dr}), and imports then meet the additional demand (up to Q_{tr}).

With the restriction in place, the rate of return increases, less capital is used, but more of it comes from domestic sources. A measure of the size of the investment barrier is the implicit tariff, which is given by the difference between the actual rate of return in the restricted sector (R_r) and the return on the world market (R_w).

Figure 4.1 The effect of restrictions on foreign capital

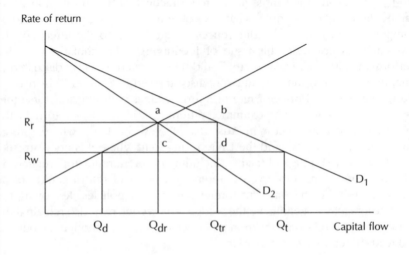

The underlying assumptions about perfect substitutability between imported and locally supplied items are particularly relevant when applying the simple model to the case of FDI. The above analysis is based on a very simple representation of capital (or services) markets. There is demand for capital (or services) in the domestic market, and this can be met from one of two sources. The two sources are perfect substitutes, so that domestic capital (or services supplied via some mode other than FDI) can meet any demand not satisfied by restricted foreign capital.

However, FDI often involves the transfer of firm-specific assets, such as human capital, technology, and international reputation (see Markusen 1995). It is these assets that give the international firm an advantage over domestic firms, making FDI profitable despite the additional costs that must be incurred in managing affiliates in different countries.

In the services sector in particular, FDI may be driven by the desire to establish a commercial presence in a market, where it is the most technically feasible and profitable way to supply a service. Furthermore, service suppliers often compete on non-price terms, with FDI in a range of countries giving them some competitive advantage over purely domestic firms. For example, a global financial enterprise such as American Express may be able to differentiate its products and services from others because of the international facilities it offers, and remain competitive even if it does not offer the lowest prices.

Given these economic factors driving FDI, an observed price or rate of return wedge could not necessarily be interpreted as the result of the restriction on foreign capital. The wedge may reflect the less-than-perfect substitutability between FDI and domestic capital (or FDI and the next best mode of service supply).

The basic concepts illustrated in Box 4.1 are still relevant, as they show that the quantity restriction translates into some equivalent price or rate of return distortion, and the size of the distortion depends on supply and demand in the relevant market. But the difficult parts in assessing FDI barriers are deciding the appropriate market in which to conduct a partial analysis, and deciding how much of any observable price wedge reflects the restriction (as opposed to the less than perfect substitutability), before proceeding to trace the effects through the economy.

The problems in measuring and interpreting price wedges, or tariff equivalents, become even more significant when we move from the simple case of a 25 per cent restriction on the share of foreign capital to more complicated real world regimes. For example, different foreign ownership limits may apply to different firms within a sector – say, Australian telecommunications firms Telstra and Optus. A restriction on foreign share ownership may also be coupled with other operational or establishment restrictions – say, requirements that local labour and other local inputs be used.

In short, while conceptually appealing, tariff equivalents of FDI restrictions are likely to be very difficult to measure and interpret. As is the case in assessments of non-tariff barriers to goods trade, alternatives generally have to be used. Commonly used measures include coverage ratios, such as the proportion of trade covered by barriers, and counts of the frequency with which barriers are observed in each sector (see PECC 1995).

Frequency-based measures

Hoekman (1995) used frequency ratios as a starting point for estimating 'tariff equivalent' measures of the relative degree of restriction of services trade across countries and sectors. The measures were based on information contained in each country's schedule of GATS commitments. Hoekman arbitrarily defined a set of benchmark 'guesstimates' of tariff equivalents for each sector to reflect a country that is highly restricted with respect to market access. A value of 200 per cent was chosen for the most restricted sectors, such as postal and telecommunications services, while values between 20 and 50 per cent were assigned to more open sectors, such as tourism and education services. Each country and sector was then assigned a value related to that benchmark. For example, the benchmark for postal services was set at 200, so for a country with a frequency ratio of 50 per cent for postal services, the tariff equivalent for that sector was 100. For countries that made no commitments for postal services, such as Australia, the frequency ratio was zero and the tariff equivalent for the sector was 200. Different overall country and sector measures can then be calculated, with the values depending on the weights chosen for different sectors and countries.

While these tariff equivalents provide some indication of the relative degree of the restriction of services trade across sectors and countries, their usefulness as a basis for policy development, country comparisons and modelling of the economic effects of FDI barriers is limited, for several reasons.

First, interpreting 'no commitment' in a GATS schedule as meaning that restrictions exist may lead to misleading or biased results. There are many cases where a country does not have restrictions, but has not made commitments for the sector in the GATS. For example, Singapore does not apply restrictions in civil aviation (APEC 1998). However, it does not schedule the subsector in the GATS and is therefore recorded as applying restrictions (with a tariff equivalent of 200) in Hoekman's estimates. Some countries may not schedule some sectors or make commitments simply because they do not have the relevant sectors or activities in their economies. For example, space transport services are scheduled by only three countries. Other services, such as maritime transport and inland waterway transport, are simply not relevant for some countries and therefore no commitments are made. (Australia does not schedule space transport or inland waterway transport.) Furthermore, developing countries make, on average, far fewer commitments than higher income countries, in part reflecting their relatively undeveloped service sectors.

In short, a higher score may not necessarily reflect a less open or liberal policy regime.

Second, all types of restrictions listed in the country schedules are given equal weight in the index. For example, a country that lists a market access restriction in the form of a 49 per cent limit on foreign ownership gets the same score as a country that lists a screening process. No account is taken of the likely differences in economic impact of different types of restrictions. Hoekman does distinguish between measures that are scheduled as unbound and those that are unscheduled, with the former assigned a score of 0.5 in the index and the latter a score of 1. The implicit assumption is that the more substantial restrictions are in the unscheduled sectors. However, as noted above, this may not be reasonable.

Third, the tariff equivalents are simply benchmarks. For example, the 200 per cent for postal services does not mean that prices or returns in the sector are 200 per cent higher than they would be in the absence of restrictions. The restrictions on postal services are simply twice as widespread or frequent as they are in a sector where the tariff equivalent is 100.

Fourth, the tariff equivalents include only market access restrictions, not national treatment. They therefore provide an incomplete indication of the extent of restrictions.

Finally, these GATS-based tariff equivalents combine measures that restrict all modes of service delivery, not only commercial presence and FDI. It is, however, important to distinguish between barriers to FDI and barriers to the other modes of supply, as they are likely to operate through different channels and will need to be modelled in different ways. For example, a particular FDI restriction may be best treated as a tax on foreign investor profits, whereas restrictions on cross-border services trade may be better treated as a wedge between domestic and foreign service prices. Furthermore, the links between cross-border trade restrictions and FDI restrictions cannot be analysed if the two types are lumped together. It is also important to distinguish between FDI and other restrictions for the purposes of policy development. FDI may raise national sovereignty concerns and may therefore need to be addressed separately from cross-border trade.

AN INDEX OF THE DEGREE OF RESTRICTIVENESS OF FDI REGIMES

In a previous paper, we developed alternative indexes of the degree of restrictiveness of FDI (Hardin and Holmes 1997). These measures are extensions of the simple frequency index, addressing several of the shortcomings of Hoekman's approach. For example, instead of being based on the information contained in the positive GATS schedules, and the assumption that unscheduled sectors are restricted, they are based on information on actual restrictions (drawn largely from the APEC Individual Action Plans and the APEC *Guide to Investment Regimes of Member Economies*). Information on the types of barriers and their likely relative economic impacts is incorporated, so that the measures provide a more useful basis for modelling the effects of FDI liberalisation. Furthermore, FDI impediments are identified separately from restrictions on other modes of service delivery, and restrictions on all aspects of FDI, not only market access, are incorporated.

The indexes of the relative degree of restriction (by economy or sector) could be translated into some tariff equivalent or tax equivalent. Here, a completely open FDI regime is assigned an index value of zero, and the corresponding tax rate could be zero, while at the other extreme a complete ban on FDI is assigned an index value of 1, and the corresponding tax rate could be 100 per cent.

There is a range of issues to address in devising sensible and useful indexes, including:

- which impediments to include as separate components of the index;
- the weights to assign to each type of barrier (for example, what should the relative weights be for a screening process involving some vague national interest assessment and a restriction on the ownership or operations of a foreign company?); and
- the weights to assign when aggregating across sectors or countries.

Barriers in the index

The components of the index capture the major types of barriers or impediments, as discussed earlier: restrictions on entry and establishment; restrictions on control and management; and restrictions on operations. These broad categories can be further disaggregated, to take account of the relative restrictiveness of different barriers.

Restrictions on entry and establishment are broken into limits on foreign ownership and requirements for screening and notification. Limits on foreign ownership are further divided into cases where no foreign ownership is allowed, those where it is allowed up to some maximum (say, 49 per cent), and finally those cases where investment in an existing firm is limited, but the same limits do not apply to greenfield investment.

Screening and approval is divided further into: simple requirements that the investor notify the relevant authority and register the investment; approval unless judged contrary to the national interest; and approval only if the investor can demonstrate that the investment will result in a net economic benefit for the country.

There is also substantial variation in the nature and extent of restrictions in the other two broad categories: management and control; and inputs and operations. Separate components of the index could be used to capture these. For example, in terms of ownership and control, a limit on the number of foreign board members may be less onerous than a requirement that the government appoint one board member or that it have the right to veto management decisions. However, making these types of distinctions requires detailed information on FDI regimes in each country and requires a substantial degree of judgment, which complicates the task.

Aggregating across different types of impediments

In assigning weights to different types of barriers, the aim is to ensure that the indexes make economic sense. The weights are set to reflect the relative economic costs of different types of restrictions. For example, a restriction on board membership is likely to be less important in terms of distorting investment patterns and levels than a ban on foreign ownership, and the index does not assign equal weights to these types of measures. Similarly, the index should not have the property that more types of restrictions necessarily result in a higher index value. A single restriction in the form of a complete ban on foreign ownership could involve a higher economic cost than a package of several less onerous restrictions, such as screening requirements and limits on board membership. Fewer restrictions are not necessarily better, and the index reflects this. The suggested set of weights is presented in Table 4.1.

A maximum score of 1 is assigned when there is a complete ban on foreign ownership. A score of 1 is also possible when there is a partial ban on foreign ownership as well as stringent approval, management and operational restrictions. In contrast, a country which applied no restrictions would score 0, while one that used only a simple notification process would score 0.05.

The suggested weights are, of course, arbitrary and may not be particularly relevant to some cases. For example, to deal with situations where foreign ownership limits apply to investment in existing firms but not new ones (or to one existing firm but not another, as with the Australian telecommunications firms Telstra and Optus), the foreign equity weight is halved (Table 4.1). The suggested weights also imply that a limit on foreign ownership could be more restrictive than other impediments, such as input and operational restrictions (0.2) in the form of a local content requirement. In practice, the input restriction may be more distortionary than the equity limit, particularly if the foreign equity limit is not binding. But equally, the local content requirement may not be particularly onerous in some situations. Furthermore, local content and other trade-related investment measures tend not to be applied widely in service sectors.

While there may be some inconsistencies in the results obtained using the suggested categories and weights, they provide a simple and transparent starting point and a useful alternative to measures that treat all types of barriers equally. The sensitivity of the results to the weights chosen is examined in Hardin and Holmes (1997: Appendix A).

Aggregating across sectors and economies

The initial index numbers are calculated for individual GATS subsectors in individual economies. To get an overall FDI restrictiveness index for a country, sector scores would need to be added and, in doing this, the relative importance of sectors must be taken into account. The most obvious way to aggregate would be to weight each sector according to its share in the total

Table 4.1   Components of an index of FDI restrictions

Type of restriction	Weight
Foreign equity limits on all firms	
no foreign equity permitted	1.000
less than 50 per cent foreign equity permitted	0.500
more than 50 per cent and less than 100 per cent foreign equity permitted	0.250
Foreign equity limits on existing firms, none on greenfield	
no foreign equity permitted	0.500
less than 50 per cent foreign equity permitted	0.250
more than 50 per cent and less than 100 per cent foreign equity permitted	0.125
Screening and approval	
investor required to demonstrate net economic benefits	0.100
approval unless contrary to national interest	0.075
notification (pre or post)	0.050
Control and management restrictions	
all firms	0.200
existing firms, none for greenfield	0.100
Input and operational restrictions	
all firms	0.200
existing firms, none for greenfield	0.100

value of services sector output in the country. In practice this is difficult, as disaggregated services output data are not always available. An extension would be to assign higher weights to sectors that supply intermediate inputs (such as transport), to reflect the relatively high economic cost associated with distorting intermediate input markets.[1]

When aggregating across economies, to get an indication of the relative degree of restrictiveness in selected sectors, the most obvious way to weight would be according to the contribution of the economy to the value of world services output (or the value for the relevant group of economies, such as the OECD or APEC). This may also be constrained by data availability.

However, often the aggregation issue will not arise, because subsector measures for each economy will be more useful than aggregated sector or economy measures.

RESULTS FOR SELECTED APEC ECONOMIES

Using the weights for different types of barriers shown in Table 4.1, FDI restrictiveness indexes have been calculated for fifteen APEC economies and eleven of the twelve GATS sectors ('other services' are not included). The sectoral results are simple rather than weighted averages of the results for the GATS subsectors. The index values are summarised in Table 4.2.

Table 4.2 Indexes of FDI restrictiveness for selected APEC economies

	Australia	Canada	China	Hong Kong	Indonesia	Japan	Korea	Malaysia
Business	0.183	0.225	0.360	0.015	0.560	0.062	0.565	0.316
Communications	0.443	0.514	0.819	0.350	0.644	0.350	0.685	0.416
Postal	1.000	1.000	1.000	1.000	1.000	1.000	1.000	1.000
Courier	0.175	0.200	0.275	0.000	0.525	0.050	0.550	0.075
Telecommunications	0.300	0.325	1.000	0.200	0.525	0.100	0.550	0.375
Audiovisual	0.295	0.530	1.000	0.200	0.525	0.250	0.640	0.215
Construction	0.175	0.200	0.400	0.000	0.525	0.050	0.750	0.775
Distribution	0.175	0.200	0.275	0.050	0.525	0.050	0.625	0.075
Education	0.175	0.200	0.525	0.000	0.525	0.200	0.550	0.075
Environmental	0.175	0.200	0.275	0.000	0.525	0.117	0.700	0.075
Financial	0.450	0.375	0.450	0.233	0.550	0.358	0.875	0.608
Insurance and related	0.275	0.425	0.475	0.400	0.575	0.450	0.838	0.600
Banking and other	0.625	0.325	0.425	0.067	0.525	0.267	0.913	0.617
Health	0.175	0.200	0.275	0.000	0.525	0.050	0.550	0.317
Tourism	0.175	0.200	0.283	0.000	0.525	0.050	0.617	0.542
Recreational	0.175	0.200	0.275	0.000	0.525	0.050	0.550	0.175
Transport	0.204	0.235	0.455	0.093	0.525	0.114	0.573	0.122

Table 4.2 (continued)

	Mexico	New Zealand	Papua New Guinea	Philippines	Singapore	Thailand	United States
Business	0.289	0.086	0.300	0.479	0.261	0.775	0.005
Communications	0.739	0.434	0.475	0.758	0.518	0.838	0.345
Postal	1.000	1.000	1.000	1.000	1.000	1.000	1.000
Courier	0.775	0.075	0.300	0.475	0.250	0.775	0.000
Telecommunications	0.705	0.425	0.300	0.975	0.571	0.804	0.200
Audiovisual	0.475	0.235	0.300	0.580	0.250	0.775	0.180
Construction	0.450	0.075	0.300	0.475	0.250	0.775	0.000
Distribution	0.325	0.075	0.300	0.475	0.250	0.775	0.000
Education	0.450	0.075	0.300	0.475	0.250	0.775	0.000
Environmental	0.075	0.075	0.300	0.475	0.250	0.775	0.000
Financial	0.554	0.200	0.300	0.954	0.378	0.875	0.200
Insurance and related	0.575	0.125	0.300	0.975	0.250	0.775	0.000
Banking and other	0.533	0.275	0.300	0.933	0.506	0.975	0.400
Health	0.408	0.075	0.300	0.475	0.250	0.775	0.000
Tourism	0.275	0.075	0.300	0.808	0.317	0.775	0.000
Recreational	0.075	0.075	0.300	0.475	0.250	0.775	0.000
Transport	0.283	0.131	0.300	0.975	0.250	0.780	0.025

Across the sectors, the indexes indicate that communications and financial services tend to be subject to the most stringent FDI controls. Scores are particularly high for the communications sector because many economies impose ownership limits in both telecommunications and broadcasting and also have their postal services closed to foreign entry. The least restricted sectors are business, distribution, environmental and recreational services.

Across the economies examined, Korea, Indonesia, Thailand, China and the Philippines score relatively high, reflecting the foreign ownership bans applied in several sectors, along with restrictions on the management and operation of foreign firms. The United States and Hong Kong tend to have the lowest index values.

The indexes for Thailand and Korea take account of some changes implemented during 1997 and 1998 as a condition of securing financial support from the International Monetary Fund (IMF). For example, in March 1998 Korea eased operational restrictions on foreign banks and brokerage houses, allowing them to establish subsidiaries (Government of South Korea 1998c). Thailand has also announced that foreign banks can now open additional branches. Despite these moves to ease restrictions, the indexes remain relatively high in these economies and in Indonesia, which has also secured IMF funding. However, further liberalisation may occur as reform programs, which have stalled for various reasons, particularly in Indonesia (see Government of Indonesia 1998c), are gradually implemented.

For Australia, the index value is 0.175 for many sectors, reflecting horizontal restrictions (Table 4.2).[2] This index value comprises 0.075 for the approval process (with approval unless the project is contrary to the national interest), plus 0.1 for the management and control restriction that at least two board members of a public company must be Australian. Australia's highest scores are for the communications and financial services sectors.

Figure 4.2 shows index values for communications services (postal, courier, telecommunications and audiovisual services) in selected APEC economies. Australia scores 0.443, reflecting limitations on the foreign ownership of Telstra, a closed postal sector, and foreign ownership and control restrictions on television broadcasting. According to the indexes, China, the Philippines, Thailand and Mexico have the most restricted communications sectors. These economies tend to have tight horizontal restrictions, which result in a high score for all sectors, plus specific restrictions on communications. The United States has the least restricted communications sector, followed by Hong Kong and Japan.

The results for communications services highlight a number of problems with the indexes. First, calculating the index for the whole communications sector as a simple average of the subsector scores means that restrictions (or lack of them) in important subsectors, such as telecommunications, are given insufficient weight. Instead, the index for the sector as a whole is unduly affected by the often relatively tight restrictions in the much smaller postal

Figure 4.2 FDI restrictiveness indexes for communications services in selected
APEC economies

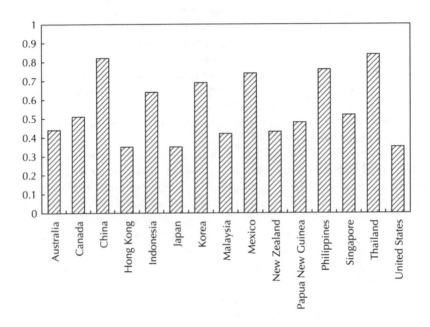

subsector. For example, the telecommunications sector in Hong Kong has a
restrictiveness index of 0.2, but because FDI in postal services is prohibited
and sector scores are derived as the simple average of subsector scores, the
restrictiveness index for Hong Kong's communications sector as a whole
is 0.35.

Thus, in some cases, it may be more useful to examine subsector scores
rather than the broad GATS sector scores (some subsector scores are also
provided in Table 4.2). Figure 4.3 shows FDI restrictiveness indexes for the
telecommunications subsector, which reveal greater variation than those for
the total communications sector. The index for Singapore is relatively high,
reflecting Singapore Telecom's monopoly rights on the provision of wire-
based local and international telecommunications services that ended in 2000.
Japan's index for telecommunications is low because the index for its highly
restricted voice telephony market is offset by its unrestricted value-added
and non-voice telecommunications markets.

Second, countries that do not schedule a sector in the GATS and do not
supply information in the APEC Investment Guide or Individual Action Plans
are assumed to have no restrictions on that sector. This is the case for the
telecommunications sector in Malaysia and Papua New Guinea (for which
only limited information is available), resulting in low index values.

Figure 4.3 FDI restrictiveness indexes for telecommunications services in selected APEC economies

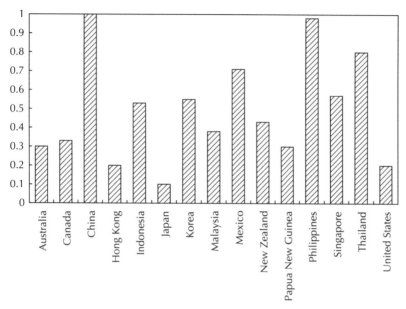

Notes: The higher the score, the more restrictive the economy; the scores range from 0 to 1.
Source: Results estimated as part of this chapter.

Third, to restrict the value of the index to between 0 and 1, multiple restrictions of the same type are counted only once. This may lead to an underestimate of FDI restrictiveness for economies that apply many restrictions of the same type, compared with economies that may impose fewer restrictions of different types. For example, Mexico and New Zealand receive the same score for operational restrictions applying to the motion picture projections subsector, but Mexico imposes four different operational restrictions while New Zealand applies only one.

Finally, the values of the indexes are dependent on the weights that are assumed to apply to different restrictions. As noted, the sensitivity of the restrictiveness indexes to variations in the weights is examined in Hardin and Holmes (1997: Appendix A).

Index values for the financial services sector are presented in Figure 4.4. According to these indexes, the Philippines, Korea and Thailand have the most restricted financial services sectors. The Philippines scores 0.954, reflecting horizontal restrictions (worth 0.475), plus foreign equity restrictions for insurance, banking and other financial services. New Zealand, the United

Figure 4.4 FDI restrictiveness indexes for financial services in selected APEC
economies

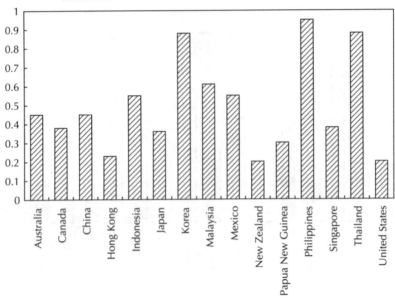

Notes: The higher the score, the more restrictive the economy; the scores range from 0 to 1.
Source: Results estimated as part of this chapter.

States and Hong Kong have the least restricted financial services sectors, all
imposing operational and/or management and control restrictions on some
financial services. Australia scores 0.450 for financial services, reflecting
limitations on foreign ownership of the four major banks (large-scale transfer
of ownership to foreigners is considered contrary to the national interest
(Costello 1997)), and some operational restrictions. China's index for financial
services is relatively low, even though many restrictions are imposed on its
insurance and banking sectors. This is because China applies many restrictions
of the same type, imposing five operational restrictions on FDI in its banking
sector and seven operational restrictions on FDI in insurance and related
services. In each case, only one operational restriction is counted in the
index.

CONCLUSION

This chapter discussed the estimation of tariff equivalents of impediments to
FDI in services. Difficulties in the application of that method were noted and
an alternative approach based on frequency counts of impediments, with
weights applied to different types of impediments in order to calculate an

overall index, was suggested. While there may be some inconsistencies in the results obtained using the suggested categories and weights, they provide a simple and transparent starting point and a useful alternative to measures that treat all types of barriers equally. The method outlined was applied to a number of APEC economies to yield a single index for each of the eleven service sectors in each economy. The indexes summarise the degree of restriction associated with a range of different types of policy instruments.

The work reported here is a first step. For example, when analysing the effects of the FDI restrictions, it may be useful to have more disaggregated measures. One useful distinction may be between those restrictions that impose an additional fixed cost on the foreign investor, such as the cost associated with going through a screening process, and those that add to the marginal costs of the foreign-controlled firm, such as restrictions on the ongoing operations and management of the firm.

For example, instead of being aggregated into a single index, the restrictions in Table 4.1 could be split into two groups: those that affect the fixed costs of entry (equity limits and screening) and those that affect ongoing costs (control and management and input, and operational restrictions). The different effects of these two groups of restrictions could then be examined in a general equilibrium framework, although the scope to do this will depend on having a model where the fixed and marginal costs of foreign-controlled firms are clearly specified and distinct from those of domestic firms. (Modelling issues are discussed in Chapter 16.)

A final issue to consider in constructing the indexes is the appropriate treatment of restrictions that apply across all sectors. As noted above, the horizontal restrictions for each economy are included separately for each sector. An alternative may be to separate out the horizontal restrictions in an economy-wide index, then include only sector-specific restrictions in the sectoral indexes.

NOTES

This chapter is an abridged version of an Industry Commission staff research paper. The Industry Commission has since been amalgamated into the Productivity Commission. The views expressed in this chapter are those of the staff involved and do not necessarily reflect those of the Productivity Commission. The Productivity Commission is the Australian government's principal review and advisory body on microeconomic reform. It conducts public inquiries and research into a broad range of economic and social issues affecting the welfare of Australians. Information on the Productivity Commission, its publications and its current work program can be found on the World Wide Web at <http://www.pc.gov.au>.

1   For Hoekman's tariff equivalents, weights for the GATS sectors were estimated as the share of the sector's output in the total value of services sector output for an 'average' industrialised country. An interesting feature of the estimates is the relatively low weights for some services that are important intermediate inputs.

For example, transport and communications services have lower weights than business services.

2   Horizontal restrictions, as defined in the GATS, are those that apply across all sectors.

5 The identification of impediments to trade and investment in telecommunications services

Tony Warren

INTRODUCTION

The aim of this chapter is to detail a set of frequency indexes of impediments to trade in telecommunications services that moves away from the traditional reliance on the General Agreement on Trade in Services (GATS) or various other trade agreements as the primary source of data. Instead the indexes are generated using recently released data from the International Tele-communications Union (ITU). These are the first indexes of impediments to trade and investment in telecommunications services to be based upon a survey of actual policies, rather than those inferred from commitments made in trade negotiations.

This chapter discusses the nature of impediments to trade and investment in telecommunications services, surveys the existing indexes of impediments to trade in services, and compares them with indexes generated from the ITU database.

IMPEDIMENTS TO TRADE IN TELECOMMUNICATIONS SERVICES[1]

Until the mid-1980s telecommunications services and international trade and investment were viewed as quite separate realms of policy activity. Domestic policy and regulations were developed by governments within the parameters of national telecommunications carriers, monopolistically providing a technologically narrow range of services. International concerns were confined to matters of interconnection, standards and tariffication and were handled cooperatively through the international consultative committees of the ITU or through bilateral agreements among providers of international services (Ergas and Paterson 1991).

However, as telecommunications services have become increasingly internationalised, a host of regulatory impediments to international trade and investment in telecommunications services have come to light. Many of the barriers affecting telecommunications services are similar to those affecting other services, in that laws and regulations impede the ability of producers and consumers to interact across borders through cross-border trade or foreign direct investment (Hill 1977; Sampson and Snape 1985). Other barriers, specific to telecommunications, involve the effective regulation of the dominant carrier.

Impediments to cross-border trade in telecommunications

Impediments to cross-border trade in telecommunications services tend to come in the form of limitations on network access. For example, countries may prevent callback operators or Internet service providers from leasing local network circuits in an attempt to prevent foreign services from being easily available to their citizens.

Technological changes, however, are making many of these restrictions on local circuits less and less effective and it is now almost impossible for governments to prevent their citizens from gaining access to foreign telecommunications services directly through international calls. The rollout of mobile satellite services will make regulation even more difficult (Frieden 1996). Consequently, many restrictions are unenforced or unenforceable, with governments resorting to less direct means. For example, some governments simply impose a ban on callback advertisements as a means of controlling the spread of these services.

Firms seeking to provide cross-border telecommunications services may also encounter limits on so-called rights of non-establishment – the right of a firm to operate and be accessible remotely without being required to have a physical presence in the market. In a bid to obtain foreign technology or to increase domestic employment, local presence may be required by law. While not as onerous as other regulations, such policies can slow the development of international trade in telecommunications services.

Impediments to foreign direct investment in telecommunications

In the industrialised world, impediments limiting commercial presence are the more common barrier to international transactions in telecommunications services (PECC 1995). Many telecommunications service providers have the capability to construct and/or operate alternative telecommunications networks in foreign markets. However, the involvement of foreign capital in the construction and operation of telecommunications infrastructure is often limited by legislation, administrative decree or terms of concession. Limitations range from total exclusion from the entire market to equity caps in 'sensitive' market segments such as basic telephony.

Impediments to commercial presence also impact upon those telecommunications service providers that plan to utilise leased telecommunications networks rather then construct or operate their own. The nature of telecommunications services implies that for many foreign firms, establishment of a physical presence within a market is not technically necessary. However, firms may consider that they need a local presence in order to offer their service on a competitive basis, to provide support services, or because of differences in local business practices or language. Any restriction on a firm's ability to engage in such practices is an impediment to international transactions in telecommunications services.

Regulatory impediments to international telecommunications

One of the most important constraints on new entrants into telecommunications service markets – both foreign and domestic alike – is a lack of effective regulation ensuring fair network interconnection (Hoekman et al. 1996; Noll 1995; Scanlan 1994). Almost all new telecommunications services require some form of access to the existing network. Often this network is controlled by a dominant carrier, which may also be competing with the new entrant in a final product market. The scope for predatory pricing, vertical foreclosure and other anti-competitive practices is potentially extensive. This problem is exacerbated when the dominant carrier is also the industry regulator, a situation still common in countries where a postal and telecommunications ministry is both the regulator and the service provider. In markets where effective competition regulation is not apparent, such behaviour can be an effective impediment to market access.[2]

Another important impediment to all new market entrants is differing technical standards. Standards, and the procedures used in formulating them, have the potential to promote international trade and investment in telecommunications services by facilitating the flow of information between specialised equipment.[3]

Such positive effects depend upon standards being transparent and non-discriminatory. Traditionally, the purpose of most standards was to achieve the technical integrity of discrete national systems. Typically, these standards were developed by monopoly telecommunications operators in conjunction with favoured equipment suppliers with little transparency in either the process or the resulting standard. The aim was to make network and terminal equipment idiosyncratic, such that equipment developed for one national system was incompatible with that developed for another. While such incompatibility was viewed as a means of developing local equipment capabilities, it has resulted in significant barriers to telecommunications trade and investment by forcing service suppliers to adopt incumbent standards in order to connect to the local network.

The GATS framework for listing impediments

A useful mechanism for bringing coherence to these impediments is to use the framework developed for the GATS, which defines impediments as contraventions of either market access or national treatment.

Market access limitations have tended to be defined primarily in terms of quantitative restrictions such as the number of firms allowed in a market. However, the language of Article XVI of the GATS would suggest it covers all limitations on market access and not just limits that target foreign firms (Snape and Bosworth 1996). In this paper, market access limitation will be taken to mean any regulatory impediment to market entry that favours an incumbent over a potential entrant.

The *national treatment* obligation requires members to list all regulatory requirements that differentiate between foreign and domestic service suppliers in terms of benefits given or regulatory obligations that are imposed. These may be limitations on the nationality or residency of directors, foreign ownership restrictions, or preferences given to domestic suppliers in the allotment of frequencies (ITU 1997). Hence, violations of national treatment include all regulatory impediments to market entry that favour residents over foreign service suppliers.

The GATS framework also encompasses all four possible modes of supplying telecommunications services internationally:

Cross-border supply is where a telecommunications service is delivered to the consumer in one territory by a supplier located in another territory. The termination of incoming international calls is the major example of cross-border supply of telecommunications services and continues to be the most significant source of international revenue for most carriers. The most common limitation on this mode of delivery is the prevention of bypass. That is, for example, where a foreign carrier (the consumer) can only utilise a domestic monopolist (the producer) in order to terminate its calls. Callback services may also come within the ambit of this mode of supply.

Consumption abroad is where a consumer receives a service from a fellow national in a foreign territory. Examples in telecommunications of this mode of supply include satellite mobile telephony, calling cards and country direct services. Restrictions on this mode of supply are rare, although some carriers may not provide the necessary interconnection to make calling cards and country direct feasible.

Commercial presence and the *presence of natural persons* are increasingly important modes of supply in telecommunications as foreign companies are more often utilised to develop national networks. However, restrictions on foreign investment are common and range from total exclusion from the entire market to equity caps in 'sensitive' market segments such as basic telephony. All countries limit the movement of personnel, usually through general immigration policy rather than industry-specific restrictions.

FREQUENCY INDEXES AND SERVICES

Non-tariff barriers (NTBs), such as those affecting telecommunications services, are notoriously difficult to identify and measure. As a consequence there are very few studies that systematically identify the barriers that do exist. Frequency-type measures of NTBs affecting services were not produced for many years due to the lack of suitable survey data on impediments. For example, impediments to services are not included in the UNCTAD database on NTBs, often used in studies of impediments affecting manufactures. This lack of data was partially overcome thanks to the requirement of the GATS that countries agreeing to be bound by the GATS disciplines list any barriers they wish to retain in their individual schedules.

Quantification of the GATS schedules commenced with the pioneering work of Hoekman who developed a relatively simple three-category weighting method (Hoekman 1995). There are many limitations with this methodology, most of which are detailed by Hoekman and in the other studies, such as that by PECC (1995), which have adopted this approach. To begin with, the Hoekman methodology does not distinguish between barriers in terms of their impact on the economy, with minor impediments receiving the same weighting as an almost complete refusal of access.

Another major problem with the Hoekman indexes is the coverage of the GATS schedules, which in many cases do not give an accurate picture of the actual barriers that are in place. This is particularly the case for developing economies, many of which continue to struggle with the complexities of the scheduling process. There is also some evidence to suggest that nations with liberal policies are not binding their commitments, so as to maintain a retaliatory capability in future negotiations on market access. Therefore, some industries that are recorded in the Hoekman indexes as impeded may be open, at least to suppliers from some countries. It should be noted that a threat of future retaliation could itself be considered an impediment and as such the data may not be too misleading.

ITU-BASED FREQUENCY INDEXES

This study seeks to address both the data and the weighting problems in relation to telecommunications services. The data used to construct the indexes is sourced from the International Telecommunications Union (ITU). These data have the distinct advantage of being drawn from a survey of actual policies, rather than inferring these policies from commitments made in trade negotiations. In the construction of these indexes, some attempt has been made to weight the data by subjective assessment of the economic importance of various issues.

An attempt has also been made to produce indexes that correspond with the more important distinctions drawn in the GATS context, namely the differences between market access and national treatment and the distinction between trade and investment. It is anticipated that maintaining such a distinction will assist in the use of these indexes in future work modelling the general equilibrium impacts of impediments to trade and investment in telecommunications services.

The data source

The ITU data source used to generate the indexes in this analysis is a report entitled *Telecommunication Reform, 1998*. It was produced in June 1998 by the Development Bureau of the ITU, which intends to publish a similar report annually.

The report is divided into six volumes. Volume I provides an international overview of regulatory reform. Volumes II to VI are organised by region and contain detailed information on the regulatory situation in each ITU member state, including: the regulators and policymakers; legal instruments; governing the sector; institutional profiles; regulatory responsibilities; licensing regimes; private sector participation; market status; and universal service. Usable information was available for 136 countries, some of which are not members of the WTO. Consequently, the country coverage of these measures is significantly greater than would be possible when using GATS schedules to generate indexes.

The key information sets in the ITU report that are used to construct the indexes include:

- *Ownership of the incumbent*: details ownership of the incumbent carrier, including the level of private ownership and the identity of major private investors where applicable.
- *Ownership of other carriers*: details the number and identity of major competitive carriers and their ownership structure. For some countries this is an exhaustive listing, for others with multiple carriers only the major operators are detailed.
- *Degree of foreign ownership allowed*: details, where applicable, the degree of foreign ownership allowed in competitive carriers (i.e. not the incumbent).
- *Degree of market liberalisation*: details the degree of market liberalisation in twelve sectors of the industry, namely local, long distance, international data, telex, leased lines, cellular analogue, cellular digital, paging, cable TV, fixed satellite and mobile satellite. For each sector the ITU notes whether they are characterised by a monopoly, partial competition or competition. *Partial competition* refers to situations where countries retain certain 'non-technical' restrictions which can lead to limits on the number of operators or on geographical coverage. *Competition* refers to the introduction of legislation which allows for unrestricted entry. Unfortunately the ITU has, in the case of mobile cellular services, listed all countries that allow more than one competitor as competitive on the grounds that spectrum availability limits the number of licences that can be issued.
- *Leased line and resale*: details policies towards leased line and resale. Information is provided on whether domestic or international (i) leased lines or private networks, (ii) third party resale or (iii) connections of leased lines and private networks to the PSTN are allowed or are restricted. Where applicable, some details of specific restrictions are provided.
- *Callback*: details whether or not callback services are allowed.

Policy indexes

Using this ITU information, five separate indexes have been constructed. Each corresponds with the more important distinctions drawn in the GATS context, namely the differences between market access and national treatment and the distinction between trade and investment. Data availability means that a distinction is made between mobile and fixed network services only in relation to market access restrictions on foreign investment.

The first policy index is titled MA/Trade. This is an index designed to capture policies that discriminate against all potential entrants (domestic and international) seeking to supply cross-border telecommunications services. It is constructed from the ITU data on individual country policies towards leased lines and resale. There are six observations for each country. A score of 1 was given for each instance where no restrictions were apparent, a score of 0 for any reported restriction or empty cell. Hence an index is created with scores ranging from 0–6.

The second policy index is titled MA/Invest (fixed). This is an index designed to capture policies that discriminate against all potential entrants (domestic and international) seeking to supply fixed network services via investment in the country at issue. The index is a weighted average of the scores from three questions:

- Does competition operate in the market for fixed services? The number of competitors in the fixed market is identified, with the maximum number of competitors constrained at three. This information is drawn from the ITU information on ownership. The maximum number of competitors has been constrained at three to avoid the statistical anomalies created by countries such as the United States and Finland, where the number of carriers is well in excess of one hundred. Three carriers may be sufficient to stimulate competition, although there are no hard and fast rules on the number of competitors in a market and the extent of competition.[4] The scores (1–3) are then multiplied by the weight (3).
- Does policy allow for competition in the market for fixed services? Policy scores for competition in the provision of fixed services are calculated. The ITU data on the degree of market liberalisation were examined in each country in five sectors considered to form the core of fixed network services, namely: local, domestic long distance, international, data, and leased lines. A score of 1 is provided if the ITU found that full competition is allowed, with 0.5 for partial competition and 0 for a monopoly situation and an average score is calculated. The scores (0–5) are then multiplied by the weight (2).
- Is the incumbent privatised? The fraction of the incumbent that is privatised (0.0–1.0) is multiplied by the weight (1).

The weights given to each of these scores reflect a subjective assessment of their relative importance in terms of producing competitive outcomes in the market for telecommunications services. Actual competitors operating in the market are considered more likely to act as a competitive constraint on the incumbent than the threat of competition posed by liberal policies alone. Although contestable markets theory suggests that liberal policies can effect outcomes (Baumol et al. 1982), McAvoy (1995) demonstrated that even with a significant number of competitors, the US long-distance market produced less-than-competitive outcomes during the 1980s.

Privatisation is given the lowest weight, reflecting the theory that in a competitive market, private ownership of the incumbent will result in some additional efficiency gains arising from capital market disciplines. However, in a market that retains monopoly characteristics, privatisation is generally equivalent to a transfer of monopoly rents from the public to the private sector and hence is unlikely to result in significant gains for consumers.[5]

The third policy index is titled MA/Invest (mobile). This is an index designed to capture policies that discriminate against all potential entrants (domestic and international) seeking to supply cellular mobile services via investment in the country at issue. The index is constructed in much the same way as MA/Invest (fixed) – that is it is a weighted average of the scores from three questions:

- Does competition operate in the market for mobile services? In the discussion on ownership of competitive carriers, the ITU also provides information on the number of competitive mobile carriers. A simple count has been made, with the maximum number of carriers again constrained at three. The score (1–3) is then multiplied by the weight (3).
- Does policy allow for competition in the market for mobile services? The ITU data on the degree of market liberalisation in cellular analogue or cellular digital markets was examined in each country. A score of 1 is provided if the ITU found that full competition is allowed in *either* market, a 0.5 for partial competition in *either* market and a 0 if there is a monopoly in both markets. The score (0–1) is then multiplied by the weight (2).
- Is the incumbent privatised? The fraction of incumbent that is privatised (0.0–1.0) is multiplied by the weight (1).

The fourth policy index is titled NT/Trade. This is an index designed to capture policies that discriminate against potential foreign entrants seeking to supply cross-border telecommunications services. It is constructed from the ITU data on individual country policies relating to callback services. The variable is a dummy variable on whether or not callback services are allowed. A 1 indicates callback is allowed, a 0 indicates that it is not.

The fifth policy index, NT/Invest, is designed to capture policies that discriminate against potential foreign entrants seeking to supply fixed or mobile telecommunication services via investment in the country at issue. It

Figure 5.1 Restrictiveness indexes to trade in telecommunications services for the top-20 services trading nations, 1997

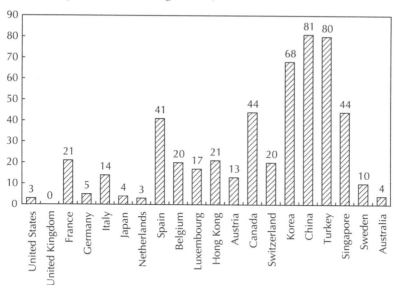

Note: The higher the score, the greater the degree to which an industry is restricted. The maximum score is 100 per cent.

is constructed from the ITU data on individual country policies. The variable represents the percentage of foreign investment allowed in competitive carriers. The ITU does not consistently report limits on foreign investment in the incumbent and hence this was excluded from the index.

Descriptive statistics

The indexes have been calculated for 136 countries. Figure 5.1 provides the unweighted average score across the five indexes for the top twenty services trading nations. A high degree of variation is apparent, reflecting the continuing resistance among many countries to the liberalisation of their telecommunications markets.

The key descriptive statistics for the five indexes are presented in Table 5.1. The significant variation across countries is immediately apparent from the high standard deviations across all indexes. The higher mean for MA/INV (mobile) than for MA/INV (fixed) accords with preconceptions about the relative liberality of mobile markets compared with the more restricted markets for the provision of fixed network services.

The Pearson correlation coefficients between each of the variables are presented in Table 5.2. The notable relationships include the significant correlation between MA/INV (mobile) and NT/FDI (r=0.71). This reflects the

Table 5.1   Descriptive statistics

Variable	Mean	Median	Std Deviation	Minimum	Maxi-mum
MA/Trade	2.35	2.00	2.08	0	6
MA/INV (fixed)	38%	30%	25%	17%	100%
MA/INV (mobile)	56%	67%	30%	0%	100%
NT/Trade	..	0	..	0	1
NT/FDI	48%	49%	44%	0	100%

Table 5.2   Pearson correlation coefficients (and prob > |R|)

	MA/Trade	MA/INV (Fixed)	MA/INV (Mobile)	NT/Trade	NT/FDI
MA/Trade	1				
	(0.0)				
MA/INV (fixed)	0.42	1			
	(0.0001)	(0.0)			
MA/INV (mobile)	0.21	0.64	1		
	(0.0131)	(0.0001)	(0.0)		
NT/Trade	0.57	0.50	0.39	1	
	(0.0001)	(0.0001)	(0.0001)	(0.0)	
NT/FDI	0.34	0.49	0.71	0.38	1
	(0.0001)	(0.0001)	(0.0001)	(0.0001)	(0.0)

reliance of most countries on foreign carriers to provide competition to the incumbent carrier in newly competitive mobile markets. Interestingly, the relationship between MA/INV (fixed) and NT/FDI (r=0.49) is not so pronounced. Countries seem less prepared to use majority-owned foreign carriers as a vehicle for introducing competition into their fixed telecommunications markets. The relationship between MA/INV (mobile) and MA/INV (fixed) (r=0.64) indicates that, while not perfectly correlated (as noted above), countries that liberalise their mobile networks are also likely to liberalise their fixed facilities. Interestingly, the low correlations between MA/Trade and NT/Trade and between MA/Trade and NT/FDI suggest that some countries that fail to liberalise the commercial presence are prepared to allow some competition in the form of private networks (MA/Trade) or callback (NT/Trade). These patterns hold generally for both industrialised and developing economies, although the former are more likely to have liberalised their telecommunications industry.

Table 5.3 Most liberal and illiberal countries in the sample across all indexes

Most liberal countries Country	Average score (5)	Least liberal countries Country	Average score (5)
Finland	5.00	Burkina Faso	0.33
United Kingdom	5.00	Costa Rica	0.33
Netherlands	4.85	Ethiopia	0.33
Denmark	4.83	Malta	0.33
New Zealand	4.83	Syrian Arab Rep	0.33
USA	4.83	Tunisia	0.33
Australia	4.78	Angola	0.40
Japan	4.78	Jordan	0.40
Germany	4.75	Mali	0.40
Chile	4.56	Mozambique	0.40

Table 5.3 lists the top ten most liberal countries and the top ten most illiberal in the sample calculated on the basis of a simple average of the five indexes. There are few surprises in either list, although some explanation may be required for the relative scores among the more liberal economies. The United States fails to receive top billing, despite the popular belief in its openness, because of the reciprocity requirements on access to international leased lines. Australia and Japan come further down the list because of the residual public holdings in Telstra and NTT respectively. New Zealand, which is a very liberal country, fails to achieve the full five points because it has only two operators of mobile phone services. This may highlight a limitation with the indexes. For small economies such as New Zealand, two mobile carriers may be sufficient to achieve highly competitive outcomes, rather than the three carriers required for maximum score in the MA/INV (mobile) index.

Another potential limitation with the indexes, which becomes apparent from examination of the relative scores of various OECD countries, is the lack of any competition policy dimension. As mentioned above, there is often significant scope for incumbent carriers to abuse their residual dominant position, reducing the competitive benefits likely to flow from liberalisation. A simple dummy variable could be constructed to reflect whether particular national telecommunications operators are subject to competition policies.[6] However, such a variable may not reflect differences between competition policies in terms of scope and implementation that can have significant implications for market outcomes. For example, Ergas (1996) highlights how Australia's highly proscriptive competition policy produces inferior outcomes for consumers (as opposed to competitors) compared with the light-handed regime in New Zealand.

Figure 5.2 GATS and ITU-based indexes of restrictiveness to trade in telecommunications services for selected Asia Pacific economies

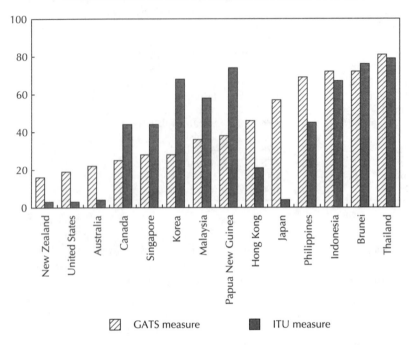

Note: The higher the score, the greater the degree to which an industry is restricted. The
maximum score is 100 per cent.

Source: ITU-based indexes: Warren (forthcoming); GATS-based indexes: Marko (1998b).

COMPARISON WITH GATS-BASED INDEXES

One of the advantages of the indexes calculated in this chapter is that they
are based upon a survey of actual policies, rather than policies inferred from
commitments made in trade negotiations. A comparison of these ITU-based
indexes with the GATS-based indexes is useful partly because the GATS is
still a necessary source of data in other industries and partly because such
comparison will provide some indication of the comprehensiveness of the
GATS schedules.

Figure 5.2 plots the average of the five ITU-based indexes (expressed as a
percentage) against the GATS-based index produced by Marko (1998a) for
selected Asia Pacific nations. The GATS-based index reflects the number of
commitments in telecommunications (without exceptions) that a country has
made in its GATS schedules as a percentage of the total number of
commitments it could have made; the larger the number, the greater the

Table 5.4 Pearson correlation coefficients between ITU-based and GATS-based indexes

	MA/Trade	MA/INV (Fixed)	MA/INV (Mobile)	NT/Trade	NT/ FDI
GATS-based measure	0.61	0.30	0.32	0.49	0.55

implied openness of the country, with 100 per cent implying full liberalisation. The data reported in Figure 5.2 indicate that the GATS schedules provide a useful picture of relative policy, but are far from an accurate reflection – a conclusion consistent with other findings, such as those of McGuire (1998).

The Pearson correlation coefficient between the GATS-based measures and the simple average of the five ITU-based measures ($r=0.64$) confirms this relationship. Interestingly, the correlations between the GATS-based measures and each of the individual ITU-based indexes are highly varied. Table 5.4 reports the Pearson correlation coefficients between each of the variables and the GATS-based index produced by Marko.

The results reported in Table 5.4 indicate a degree of co-relationship between the GATS-based measure and the ITU-based MA/Trade, NT/Trade and NT/FDI indexes, but very little relationship with the MA/INV indexes. It is possible that this reflects the more legalistic nature of the former indexes (i.e. is something allowed or not) verses the more economic nature of the latter indexes (i.e. what are the conditions on the ground in terms of number of carriers). The GATS is more likely to reflect legal rather than economic conditions. The indexes that include aspects of the competitive environment, however, are more likely to be useful for predicting outcomes for consumers in terms of lower prices, higher quality or greater output.

The efficacy of the GATS-based measures can be gauged from Figure 5.1, which compares the rankings (least to most liberal) of the 63 countries on the basis of both measures. The degree of correlation is apparent.

CONCLUSION

This chapter details a frequency index of impediments to trade in telecommunications services that moves away from the traditional reliance on the General Agreement on Trade in Services or various other trade agreements as the primary data source. Five separate indexes are generated using recently released data from the International Telecommunications Union. These data allow for the production, for the first time, of indexes of impediments to trade and investment in telecommunications services that are based upon a survey of actual policies, rather than those inferred from commitments made in trade negotiations.

NOTES

1   This section is drawn from Warren (1995).
2   The exact nature of the most appropriate competition policy is a matter of some debate, see Ergas (1998).
3   For an analysis of the process of standardisation in telecommunications services that also focuses on the use of standards as a mechanism of trade protection, see Mulgan (1991) and Wallenstein (1990).
4   See Landes and Posner (1981) for a detailed critique of the simple assumption that market shares are a useful proxy for market power.
5   However, there is a possibility that privatisation of monopolies could lead to increased output if it reduces the corruption-based incentives for constraining supply. For example, when Bond Corporation took over the incumbent in Chile, output doubled in a short space of time, despite a significant increase in prices.
6   Unfortunately the ITU does not collect data on the application of competition policies.

6 The impact on output of impediments to trade and investment in telecommunications services

Tony Warren

INTRODUCTION

The aim of this chapter is to provide an exploratory foray into the quantification of the impact of impediments to trade and investment in telecommunications services using a quantity-impact approach. Generally, quantity-impact studies have sought to compare actual and benchmark trade volumes. For a variety of reasons this has proved impossible in services, not least because of the lack of bilateral trade data.

In contrast, this chapter develops a method for examining the impact of barriers to entry on the quantities of fixed and mobile telecommunications services actually consumed within a country, rather than the quantity traded. Individual country restrictions on international trade and investment in telecommunications are explicitly modelled using a frequency index of impediments to trade in services generated from International Telecommunications Union (ITU) survey data. The aim is to quantify the comparative impact upon telecommunications consumption of these limits on competition, controlling for other explanatory variables.

The chapter reviews methods for measuring impediments to trade in services, and describes the penetration models used to measure output effects. It estimates the impact on average output in the sample countries if those countries with high barriers were to liberalise and estimates the tariff equivalent of the quantity-impact estimates.

MEASURING IMPEDIMENTS TO INTERNATIONAL SERVICES TRANSACTIONS

A feature of services is that they cannot be produced and then stored for later consumption. Production and consumption are simultaneous, requiring producers and consumers to interact (either directly or via a communications medium) for the service to be rendered. Consequently, many of the barriers to international service transactions come in the form of restrictions on interaction rather than the tariff barriers commonly affecting trade in goods.

In telecommunications, these barriers include impediments to cross-border trade such as limits on network access and restraints on the provision of callback services. Impediments to foreign direct investment are also common in telecommunications, particularly limits on foreign investment in the incumbent carrier (Warren 1995). Telecommunications service providers can also encounter impediments to trade in the form of anti-competitive behaviour by the incumbent carrier, in those countries where the incumbent is unconstrained by effective competition policies or regulatory pressures (Hoekman, Low and Mavroidis 1996).

Non-tariff barriers (NTBs) such as these are notoriously difficult to identify and measure. As a consequence there are very few studies that systematically quantify the impact on economic outcomes of impediments to trade and investment in services. However, the available research on the measurement of NTBs affecting goods trade provides a useful guide on how to proceed. In their extensive review of the literature, Deardorff and Stern (1985) identify two broad methods for quantifying the economic impact of NTBs:

- *price-impact measures* that examine the impact of NTBs on domestic prices by comparing them with world prices; and
- *quantity-impact measures* that compare an estimate of trade volumes in the absence of NTBs with actual trade volumes.

These types of price and quantity-impact measures have been considered impossible to replicate in relation to service industries on grounds of data availability. A world price for many service industries is indeterminate. Similarly, a lack of systematic bilateral services trade data and the highly aggregated nature of the current account data (see Karsenty 1999) limit the potential for traditional quantity-impact models.

As a consequence of these data concerns, it is necessary to identify alternative benchmarks against which to compare actual prices and quantities. Here the market power analysis associated with competition policy or anti-trust regulation is instructive. The aim of such analysis is to compare actual market outcomes with those that would be expected to prevail if the market were competitive (Areeda, Hovenkamp and Solow 1995).

Much research on market power has sought to compare actual prices with marginal costs, taking advantage of the theory that a market free from barriers to entry will result in prices that equate with marginal cost.[1] A similar benchmark can be used to determine where prices would be in the absence of impediments to trade and investment – with marginal cost having to be adjusted to take account of the entry of more efficient foreign firms (Bosworth et al. 1997 and Chapter 5).

An alternative approach is to examine output, since price and output is simultaneously determined in a market. In particular, demand for telecommunications services is likely to be greater the more competitive is its supply. This is because the lower relative prices and higher service quality arising from competition will increase demand, while rivalry in investment will push out supply.

Recently several studies have sought to examine the impact of barriers to entry focusing upon the quantity of mobile telecommunications services consumed within an economy – rather than the quantity traded – and comparing this with international benchmarks (Ralph and Ludwig 1997; Ergas, Ralph and Small 1998). The aim is to quantify the impact upon telecommunications consumption of limits on competition controlling for other explanatory variables. Restrictions on competition are modelled directly by a count of the number of mobile operators in each country at each period.

This chapter develops these earlier studies in two ways. First, the analysis is extended from mobile telephony to include the fixed network services, measured in terms of the number of mainlines per hundred persons. Second, the policy variable is expanded beyond a simple count of the number of operators (fixed and mobile) to include a series of indexes designed to reflect differences in a broad spectrum of telecommunications policies.

PENETRATION MODELS

In this analysis, two separate questions are asked:

1 What impact do impediments to trade and investment in services have on the penetration of the fixed telecommunications network; and
2 What impact do impediments to trade and investment in services have on the penetration of the mobile telecommunications network?

The immediate difficulty with explaining the impact on consumption of impediments to trade and investment is the issue of causality. Does greater liberality in policy cause more extensive network penetration or does a more extensive network allow a country to liberalise its markets? In this paper, causality is explicitly assumed to flow from liberalisation to increased network penetration. In reality, there is likely to be a complex interaction between these variables – an interaction that is difficult to unbundle in the absence of time-series data or appropriate instrumental variables.

A further difficulty with explaining the impact on consumption of impediments to trade and investment is that international differences in consumption are not only a function of differences in policy settings. Rather, the impact of other factors affecting penetration needs to be examined explicitly.

The literature on the determinants of demand for telecommunications – demand both for access to and usage of the telecommunications network – is extensive, although much of the research is unpublished in-house analysis based upon sensitive commercial data and hence is unavailable. Of the published research on this issue, the great majority is based on time-series

US data comparing penetration rates across states.[2] In terms of cross-country differences, recent contributions by the ITU (1994); Bowles and Maddock (1998); Ralph and Ludwig (1997); and Ergas, Ralph and Small (1998) are notable exceptions to an otherwise sparse literature.

The underlying penetration models proposed here are based upon the available cross-country research, with the addition of the policy variables developed by Warren in Chapter 5. The models are specifications of the following forms:

$$Q_i^f = \alpha + \mathbf{x}_i\beta + \varepsilon_i$$

$$Q_i^m = \alpha + \mathbf{x}_i\beta + \varepsilon_i$$

Where Q_i^f relates to the extent of the fixed network and Q_i^m relates to the extent of the mobile network, for $i = 1$ to n countries. The ε_i term is the standard ordinary least squares (OLS) error term.

The $\mathbf{x}_i$ term is a matrix of independent variables that theory and the available literature indicate are important explanatory factors when seeking to determine differences in penetration rates and consumption levels across countries.

Amongst the independent variables analysed in this study, primary emphasis is placed on a series of policy indexes that seek to capture differences between countries in the extent to which they maintain regulatory impediments to trade in services. It is anticipated that countries with fewer impediments will record higher levels of output, other factors being equal. In part the relationship between increased competition (fewer impediments) and increased output is a function of the enhanced allocative efficiencies produced by competition. But as Scherer (1987) has argued, the gains and losses from the reduction of the deadweight loss are usually very small. Instead, the real gains come from the x-efficiency (reduced rent-seeking) and technological efficiencies that flow from competition.

An explanatory factor found to be of primary importance in the literature is income per head. The greater the level of national development, the greater the observed penetration of the telecommunications network. Work by the ITU (1994) in fact finds that 85 per cent of the variation in teledensity (mainlines per unit of population) can be explained by variation in per capita income. An extra US$1,000 of GDP per capita was found to correspond to an average increase of 2.24 lines per 100 people. However, as Bowles and Maddock (1998) note, it is not exactly clear how this result should be interpreted. Income might enter as either a supply-side or a demand-side factor, in that rich countries might be more willing to supply lines just as rich customers may be more willing to pay for them. In reality, it is likely to be a combination of both.

Penetration models also need to account for the differing demographic characteristics of the countries under examination. There are very real differences in the economics of developing a telecommunications network in a densely populated city-state such as Singapore compared with a sparsely populated continent such as Australia. Hence the greater the spread of population, the greater the expected network penetration. Housing density is the most appropriate proxy for this effect in relation to the fixed telecommunications network. Population density is the more appropriate measure for the mobile network.

Quality variables also need to be incorporated into the penetration models. Changes in network quality coupled with changes in technology can radically shift quantities demanded and supplied without policies necessarily changing to allow for increased competition. For example, significant improvements in network technology, coupled with the development of new consumer products such as Web browsers, has resulted in a massive increase in the demand for and supply of data services around the world. Hence, we would expect those countries with higher quality networks to record higher levels of demand, other things being equal. Unfortunately, systematic cross-national measures of network quality are unavailable. Instead, the digitisation of the network is used as a proxy for network quality.

A further independent variable that needs to be accounted for when examining penetration is the presence of waiting lists. The regression models used in this analysis are reduced-form expressions. They contain only those variables that *independently* influence supply and demand for service. Underpinning this specification is the assumption that the markets for fixed and mobile lines are always in equilibrium; that is, at going prices consumers can purchase as many lines as they wish.

The historic existence of substantial waiting lists for fixed line services in many countries casts doubt on the assumption of equilibrium. When demand for fixed line connections greatly exceeds supply it is likely that demand-side factors – in particular income per head – will have a lesser impact on penetration levels than when markets clear. This is because large levels of excess demand imply customers cannot purchase what they want. Thus an increase in income will increase demand, but may have little impact on supply. Rather, excess demand will also rise (Ergas, Ralph and Small 1988).

Some attempt has been made to control for this issue by including an unmet demand variable in the analysis. However, it should be noted that waiting list data can be misleading. Waiting lists are primarily a function of changing conditions rather than a static measure of unmet demand. People do not put themselves on waiting lists unless there is some imminent expectation of demand being met. Thus we would expect to find larger waiting lists in those countries where supply constraints are being removed, rather than in those countries where supply constraints are binding and unlikely to change in the short to medium term.[3]

At the other end of the spectrum, supply may be artificially expanded in many developed countries as a consequence of universal service obligations.

Most countries have in place some form of regulatory requirement for expanding access to the telecommunications network. In some industrialised countries, penetration rates have reached levels whereby almost all households are connected to the fixed network. In these countries, measures of fixed network penetration may be inflated above levels where other explanatory factors would indicate they should be.

Second and third-degree polynomial regression models have been included in this analysis. This is because there is good reason to believe that the take-up of network access is unlikely to follow a linear process as countries develop. Rather, the relationship between network penetration and income may actually take the form of an S-curve. The theory is that as income in poorer countries increases, the number of mainlines or mobile handsets increases more rapidly than GDP as a result of consumption externalities. That is, as income rises, more people can afford to rent a phone line or handset, and when more people are connected, the value of being connected to the network increases. However, at some point, network saturation occurs and demand for new services tapers off. It is likely that this point has been reached in some countries for access to the fixed network but does not yet appear to have been reached for access to the mobile network, where a second-degree polynomial regression model is more appropriate.

DATA DEFINITIONS AND SOURCES

In terms of the full set of variables used, the models can be restated as:

$$Q_i^f = \alpha + Y_i.\beta_1 + Y_i.^2\beta_2 + Y_i.^3\beta_3 + HD_i\ \beta_4 + Qual_i.s_5 + UD_i.\beta_6 + [P_i^f]\ \beta_7 + \varepsilon_i$$

Where $[P_i^f] = (Policy_i, MA/Trade_i, MA/Inv(f)_i, NT/Trade_i.$ or $NT/FDI_i)$

$$Q_i^m = \alpha + Y_i.\beta_1 + PD_i\ \beta_2 + [P_i^m].\beta_3 + \varepsilon_i$$

Where $[P_i^m] = (Policy_i,$ or $MA/Inv(m)_i)$

Details of the dependent variables and their data sources are provided in Table 6.1. Descriptive statistics are presented in Table 6.4.

The most significant independent variables in these models from the point of view of this study, and the most difficult to measure, relate to the extent of impediments to trade in services. This study differs significantly from the mobile penetration research detailed above in that it uses a more targeted measure of impediments to trade in services. Instead of using a simple count of the number of mobile operators in each country to measure competition, a series of policy frequency indexes have been developed for each country in the dataset.

Table 6.1   Dependent variables, definitions and sources

Variable	Description and source
Q_i^f	Mainlines per 100 inhabitants (sourced from ITU, *Yearbook of Statistics: Telecommunications Services Chronological Time Series, 1988–97*, various country tables).
Q_i^m	Cellular mobile subscribers per 100 inhabitants (sourced from ITU, *Yearbook of Statistics: Telecommunications Services Chronological Time Series, 1988–97*, various country tables).

The policy variables used in this study are drawn from an international survey undertaken by the International Telecommunications Union (ITU 1999). This survey provides a systematic description of the telecommunications policy framework in each of the ITU member countries. All data are current for 1997.

Table 6.2 provides a brief summary of the policy variables that can be constructed from this ITU dataset. In Chapter 5 of this volume, Warren provides a more detailed description of these measures. Descriptive statistics are reproduced in Table 6.4. The greater the scores for each of these variables, the more open to services trade and investment the country at issue is considered to be. The significant correlation levels between each of the variables in Table 6.2 (see Table 5.3) means that separate models need to be run to ascertain the impact of each policy measure on network penetration. The combined impact is measured directly by the aggregate policy variable (Policy).

In addition to the policy variables, several other factors affecting penetration rates and consumption levels need to be modelled. Each of the specific variables and their data sources are defined in Table 6.3. Descriptive statistics are provided in Table 6.4.

RESULTS FOR THE FIXED NETWORK PENETRATION MODELS

Table 6.5 presents the results of five third-degree polynomial fixed network penetration regression models. Each model independently assesses the impact on fixed network penetration of each of the policy variables identified in Table 6.2 that pertain to the fixed network (MA/Trade, MA/Inv(f), NT/Trade, NT/FDI and Policy) while controlling for each of the other factors affecting network penetration.

Table 6.2   Policy variables

Variable	Details
MA/Trade: (Score of 1–6)	A variable designed to capture policies that discriminate against all potential entrants (domestic and international) seeking to supply cross-border telecommunications services.
	Constructed from the ITU data on individual country policies towards leased line and resale. The ITU data provides information on whether both domestic or international (i) leased lines or provide networks, (ii) third party resale or (iii) connections of leased lines and private networks to the PSTN are allowed. Hence there are six observations for each country.
	A score of 1 was given for each instance where no restrictions were apparent and a score of 0 for any reported restriction or empty cell.
MA/Inv (f) (percentage)	A variable designed to capture policies that discriminate against all potential entrants (domestic and international) seeking to supply fixed network services via investment in the country at issue.
	Constructed from the ITU data on individual country policies. The variable is a weighted average of the scores from three questions: (i) no. of competitors in fixed market (max 3) multiplied by 3; (ii) average policy scores for competition in the provision of fixed services multiplied by 2; and (iii) percentage of incumbent that is privatised multiplied by 1.
	No. of competitors in fixed market In the discussion on owner ship of competitive carriers, the ITU provides information on the no. of competitive fixed carriers. A simple count has been made. For the purposes of this index, the total no. of carriers has been constrained at 3.
	Average policy scores for competition in the provision of fixed services The ITU provides data on whether a particular country (i) enforces a monopoly, (ii) allows partial competition, or (iii) allows full competition in the following PSTN markets: local service, domestic long distance, international, data, and leased lines. A score of 1 is provided if full competition is allowed, 0.5 for partial competition and 0 for monopoly, and an average score is calculated.
	Percentage of incumbent that is privatised The ITU provides data on the percentage of the incumbent operator that is privatised.

Table 6.2 (continued)

Variable	Details
MA/Inv (m) (percentage)	A variable designed to capture policies that discriminate against all potential entrants (domestic and international) seeking to supply mobile network services via investment in the country at issue.
	Constructed from the ITU data on individual country policies. The variable is a weighted average of the scores from three questions: (i) no. of competitors in mobile market (max 3) multiplied by 3; (ii) policy score for competition in the provision of mobile services multiplied by 2; and (iii) percentage of incumbent that is privatised multiplied by 1.
	No. of competitors in the mobile market In the discussion on ownership of competitive carriers, the ITU provides information on the no. of competitive mobile carriers. A simple count has been made. For the purposes of this index, the total no. of carriers has been constrained at 3.
	Average policy scores for competition in the provision of mobile services The ITU provides data on whether a particular country (i) enforces a monopoly, (ii) allows partial competition, or (iii) allows full competition in either the analogue or digital mobile markets. A score of 1 is provided if full competition is allowed in either analogue or mobile, 0.5 for partial competition and 0 for monopoly.
	Percentage of incumbent that is privatised The ITU provides data on the percentage of the incumbent operator that is privatised.
NT/Trade (1 or 0)	A variable designed to capture policies that discriminate against potential foreign entrants seeking to supply cross-border telecommunications services.
	Constructed from the ITU data on individual country policies. The variable is a dummy variable on whether or not callback services are allowed. A 1 indicates callback is allowed, a 0 indicates that it is not.
NT/FDI (percentage)	A variable designed to capture policies that discriminate against potential foreign entrants seeking to supply fixed or mobile telecommunication services via investment in the country at issue.
	Constructed from the ITU data on individual country policies. The variable represents the percentage of foreign investment allowed in competitive carriers.
Policy (percentage)	An unweighted average of the preceding five policy variables

Table 6.3   Dependent variable definitions and sources

Variable	Description and source
Y	Gross domestic product per capita in US$ (sourced from the IMF's *International Financial Statistics*, International Economic Databank).
Qual	Percentage of mainlines attached to a digital switch (sourced from ITU, *Yearbook of Statistics: Telecommunications Services Chronological Time Series, 1988–97*, various country tables).
UD	International Telecommunications Union estimates of the waiting lists for connection to the public switched network as a percentage of the number of mainlines in operation (sourced from ITU, *Yearbook of Statistics: Telecommunications Services Chronological Time Series, 1988–97*, various country tables).
HD	Household density calculated as the number of households per square kilometre (sourced from ITU, *Yearbook of Statistics: Telecom munications Services Chronological Time Series, 1988–97*, various country tables).
PD	Population density calculated as the number of people per square kilometre (sourced from the World Bank's *World Tables*, International Economic Databank).

Table 6.4   Descriptive statistics

Variable	Mean	Std deviation	Minimum	Maximum
Q_i^f	18.6	20.7	0.11	67.9
Q_i^m	5.4	9.0	0	41.7
MA/Trade	2.4	2.1	0	6
MA/Inv(f)	38%	25%	17%	100%
MA/Inv(m)	56%	30%	0%	100%
NT/Trade	0.2	0.4	0	1
NT/FDI	48%	44%	0%	100%
Policy average	41%	26%	7%	100%
Y	$6,752	$9,740	$86	$41,544
PD	196km²	689km²	2km²	6122km²
HD	52km²	193km²	0.3km²	1807km²
UD	16%	17%	0%	71%
Qual	79%	26%	3%	100%

Table 6.5 Results for the fixed penetration models

Variable	Model 1	Model 2	Model 3	Model 4	Model 5
MA/Trade	-0.46 (0.38)	..	..	..	..
MA/Inv(f)	..	4.73* (2.88)	..	..	..
NT/Trade	..	..	-0.33* (2.01)	..	..
NT/FDI	..	..	..	3.93***.. (1.48)	..
Policy average	..	..	..	..	5.26** (3.11)
Y	0.004*** (0.0003)	0.004*** (0.0003)	0.004*** (0.0003)	0.004*** (0.0003)	0.004*** (0.0003)
Y^2	-6.1E-8*** (0.0)	-6.2E-8*** (0.0)	-6.2E-8*** (0.0)	-6.32E-8*** (0.0)	-6.3E-8*** (0.0001)
Y^3	1.3E-13*** (0.0)	1.3E-13*** (0.0)	1.3E-13*** (0.0)	1.3E-13*** (0.0)	1.3E-13*** (0.0001)
HD	0.001 (0.004)	0.003 (0.003)	0.002 (0.003)	0.003 (0.003)	0.003 (0.0033)
UD	-0.07 (0.05)	-0.08* (0.05)	-0.08* (0.05)	-0.08* (0.05)	-0.08* (0.05)
Qual	-0.13*** (0.03)	-0.14*** (0.03)	-0.14*** (0.03)	-0.13*** (0.03)	-0.13*** (0.03)
Constant	14.47*** (2.49)	12.83*** (2.56)	14.04*** (2.48)	11.75*** (2.56)	12.26*** (2.66)
Adjusted R^2	0.88	0.89	0.88	0.89	0.89

Notes: Reported figures are coefficient estimates; figures in parentheses represent standard errors; * = coefficient estimates are significant at the 90 per cent level; **= coefficient estimates are significant at the 95 per cent level; ***= coefficient estimates are significant at the 99 per cent level.

Each of the models reported in Table 6.5 have a high degree of explanatory power, a finding that is consistent with the other studies that have sought to examine cross-national differences in fixed network penetration. Much of the cross-national variation seems to be explained by differences in average income levels. The use of third-degree polynomials improved the explanatory power of the models, lending support to the hypothesis that the relationship between average income and network penetration is S-curved in shape.

Importantly, for current purposes, both of the policy measures affecting network investment have a significant (at the 90 per cent and 95 per cent confidence levels) and positive relationship with network penetration. Countries that have allowed alternative operators (foreign and/or domestic) to establish and compete against the incumbent operators are countries that have more extensive fixed telecommunications networks than would otherwise be predicted. This is also true for countries that have generally liberal policies, as measured by the aggregate policy variable. These findings are consistent with the hypothesis that liberal policies increase network penetration.

Interestingly, however, the relationship between restrictions on telecommunications trade and the extent of network penetration are not as predicted. The data indicate that there is a weak, but significant, relationship between restrictions on callback (NT/Trade) and network penetration. It is possible that this result reflects the ability of countries that prevent the leakage of revenues from international call services (via preventing callback) to use those revenues to cross-subsidise the further rollout of the fixed network. The relationship between restrictions on leased lines and resale and network penetration is also negative, although this relationship is not significant.

Amongst the other variables included in this analysis, significant unmet demand is, as predicted, negatively related to network penetration. Similarly, household density is positively related to network penetration, but the results are not significant.

The relationship between network quality (as measured by the digitisation of the fixed network) and network penetration is significantly negative. This result is contrary to expectations and may indicate that rather than measuring quality, digitisation simply measures the newness of the network. Countries that have more extensive networks are also likely to have in place a greater number of older analogue switches. A review of the data indicates that many developing countries with very small networks are 100 per cent digitised, while countries such as Australia with extensive network infrastructure retain analogue switches in some remote areas where the network is still to be upgraded.

RESULTS FOR THE MOBILE NETWORK PENETRATION MODELS

Table 6.6 presents the results of two further models. These are second-degree polynomial regression models examining the relationship between a reduced number of independent variables and mobile network penetration. The first model assesses the impact on mobile network penetration, controlling for other factors affecting network penetration, of the mobile specific policy variable identified in Table 6.2 (MA/Inv(m)). The second model assesses the impact of the aggregate policy variable (Policy).

Both of the models detailed in Table 6.6 have a high degree of explanatory power. Much of the cross-national variation seems to be explained by differences in policy and average income levels. In particular, the mobile

Table 6.6 Results for the mobile penetration models

Variable	Model 6	Model 7
MA/Inv(m)	3.02**	..
	(1.32)	
Policy average	..	3.05*
		(1.85)
Y	0.0009***	0.0008***
	(0.00005)	(0.00005)
Y²	-1.9E-9***	-1.9E-9***
	(0.0)	(0.0)
PD	0.001**	0.001**
	(0.0005)	(0.0006)
Constant	-1.92**	-1.3*
	(0.79)	(0.7)
Adjusted R²	0.79	0.78

Notes: Reported figures are coefficient estimates; figures in parentheses represent standard errors; * = coefficient estimates are significant at the 90 per cent level; **= coefficient estimates are significant at the 95 per cent level; ***= coefficient estimates are significant at the 99 per cent level.

specific policy measure (MA/Inv(m)) has a significantly positive relationship with the extent of the mobile network. Countries that have allowed alternative operators (foreign and/or domestic) to establish and compete against the incumbent operators are countries that have more extensive mobile telecommunications networks than would otherwise be predicted. This is also true for countries that have generally liberal policies as measured by the aggregate policy variable. These findings are consistent with the hypothesis that liberal policies increase network penetration.

The use of second-degree polynomials improved the explanatory power of the models, lending support to the hypothesis that the relationship between average income and mobile network penetration is in the earlier stages of the S-curve effect. Mobile penetration rates, unlike the fixed network, are yet to level off, reflecting the early stage of development of mobile networks in most countries. Countries with greater population densities also tend to have greater mobile network penetration.

ESTIMATING QUANTITY IMPACTS AND TARIFF EQUIVALENTS OF POLICY

The results from the regression models detailed above can, where the policy variable is found to have a significant positive relationship with network penetration, be used to estimate the quantity impact of the barriers to trade and investment in telecommunications services in each of the countries under review. Once these quantity-impact measures are estimated, it is a relatively straightforward procedure to calculate a tariff-equivalent of the policies impeding trade and investment.

The quantity impact measure reflects the effect of impediments to trade and investment on network penetration. As detailed above, penetration rates of the fixed and mobile networks in country i are represented by the following equations:

$$Q_i^f = f(Y_{i\cdot}, Y_{i\cdot}^2, Y_{i\cdot}^3, HD_i, Qual_{i\cdot}, UD_{i\cdot}, [P_i^f]) \qquad (1)$$

$$Q_i^m = f(Y_{i\cdot}, Y_{i\cdot}^2, PD_i, [P_i^m]) \qquad (2)$$

Given the functional forms assumed for (1) and (2), it is possible to separate the vector of policy measures out from the other components of the models to derive:

$$Q_i^f = f(Y_{i\cdot}, Y_{i\cdot}^2, Y_{i\cdot}^3, HD_i, Qual_{i\cdot}, UD_i) + b^*[P_i^f] \qquad (3)$$

$$Q_i^m = f(Y_{i\cdot}, Y_{i\cdot}^2, PD_i) + b^*[P_i^m] \qquad (4)$$

where b is the vector of estimated coefficients on the vector of actual policy measures.

Substituting $[P_i^f]^*$ for $[P_i^f]$ and $[P_i^m]^*$ for $[P_i^m]$ in equations (3) and (4) gives:

$$Q_i^{f*} = f(Y_{i\cdot}, Y_{i\cdot}^2, Y_{i\cdot}^3, HD_i, Qual_{i\cdot}, UD_i) + b^*[P_i^f]^* \qquad (5)$$

$$Q_i^{m*} = f(Y_{i\cdot}, Y_{i\cdot}^2, PD_i) + b^*[P_i^m]^* \qquad (6)$$

Where $[P_i^f]^*$ is a vector of maximum policy measures affecting the fixed telecommunications network and $[P_i^m]^*$ is a vector of maximum policy measures affecting the mobile telecommunications network. In this context, maximum policy measures means a fully liberalised policy approach.

Subtracting (3) from (5) and dividing by (3) gives the quantity-impact of liberalising the fixed network in country i (QI_i^f). Subtracting (4) from (6) and dividing by (4) gives the quantity-impact of liberalising the mobile network in country i (QI_i^m).

Given that:

$$(Q_i^{f*} - Q_i^f)/ Q_i^f = QI_i^f = e_i [(P_i^{f*} - P_i^f)/ P_i^f] = e_i PI_i^f \qquad (7)$$

$$(Q_i^{m*} - Q_i^m)/ Q_i^m = QI_i^m = e_i [(P_i^{m*} - P_i^m)/ P_i^m] = e_i PI_i^m \qquad (8)$$

Table 6.7 Quantity impacts (QI) and tariff equivalents (TE) of market access and national treatment restrictions on investment

Country	Model 2		Model 4		Model 6	
	QI %	TE %	QI %	TE %	QI %	TE %
United States	0.0	0.0	0.0	0.0	0.0	0.0
United Kingdom	0.0	0.0	0.0	0.0	0.0	0.0
France	0.9	0.8	5.1	4.5	1.8	1.5
Germany	0.9	0.7	0.0	0.0	1.6	1.4
Italy	3.4	2.9	0.0	0.0	4.4	3.8
Japan	0.7	0.6	0.0	0.0	1.1	1.0
Netherlands	0.6	0.5	0.0	0.0	1.1	0.9
Spain	6.1	5.3	0.0	0.0	7.5	6.6
Belgium	0.6	0.5	3.0	2.6	1.2	1.0
Luxembourg	0.8	0.7	0.0	0.0	2.2	1.9
Austria	3.5	3.0	0.0	0.0	2.2	1.9
Canada	0.3	0.2	3.5	3.0	2.8	2.4
Switzerland	3.3	2.8	0.0	0.0	5.1	4.4
Korea	5.5	4.8	7.0	6.2	9.4	8.5
China	110	1000	267	1000	115	1000
Turkey	29	32	18.9	18.7	63	110
Singapore	4.8	4.2	2.8	2.4	2.9	2.5
Sweden	2.4	2.0	0.0	0.0	2.2	1.9
Australia	0.8	0.7	0.0	0.0	1.8	1.5

where e_i equals the price elasticity of demand; P_i^f equals the estimated price of access to the fixed network in country i; P_i^{f*} equals the price of access to the fixed network if country i were liberalised; P_i^m equals the estimated price of access to the mobile network in country i; and P_i^{m*} equals the price of access to the fixed network if country i were liberalised.

The tariff-equivalent (defined as the percentage addition to the current price arising from the impact of the impediments to trade and investment) can be estimated to equal:

$$(1/(ePI_i^f +1))-1 = TE_i^f \tag{9}$$

$$(1/(ePI_i^m +1))-1 = TE_i^m \tag{10}$$

Table 6.7 details the estimated quantity-impact and tariff equivalents for the world's 20 largest services trading nations resulting from market access restrictions (MA/Inv(f) and MA/Inv(m)) and national treatment restrictions (NT/FDI) on investment. In short, Table 6.7 provides the estimated quantity-impact and tariff-equivalents for models 2, 4, and 6 in Tables 6.5 and 6.6 above.

These models have been chosen because the relationship between policy and penetration is significant and is consistent with theoretical predictions. The price elasticity of demand utilised to calculate the TE for all countries in Table 7 is -1.20 (Albon, Hardin and Dee 1997). This is an unsatisfactory estimate as it relates to the demand for calls rather than network access, but in lieu of better estimates it has been utilised for illustrative purposes. Because of the way the tariff-equivalents are calculated, very large quantity impacts translate into negative tariff-equivalents. Consequently, the maximum tariff-equivalents are constrained at 1,000 per cent. In Table 6.7 this is applicable for China only.

Given the limitations with the elasticity estimates, it is best to focus on the quantity-impact measures in Table 6.7. What these data reveal is a varied picture of the impact on network penetration of barriers to investment, even among the developed economies. Countries such as Australia and Japan, which maintain very minor barriers to investment, are predicted to see only small percentage increases in network penetration as a consequence of complete liberalisation. France, Switzerland and Spain, on the other hand, would achieve more significant gains from liberalisation. The major beneficiaries from reform are primarily the developing economies, where significant increases in penetration are expected if liberalisation of investment rules were to occur.

NOTES

1   The excess of price over marginal cost as a proportion of price is known as the Lerner Index, see Lerner (1934).
2   For an extensive but dated survey, see Taylor (1980). For a more recent example, see Garbacz and Thompson (1997).
3   The author would like to thank Henry Ergas for this point.

7 A price-impact measure of impediments to trade in telecommunications services

Ray Trewin

INTRODUCTION

The aim of this chapter is to identify and decompose the observed wedge between telecommunications prices in a sample of countries compared to a benchmark price. The decomposition of the price wedge relies on the incorporation of additional policy variables and better measures of quality of service into the identification of frontier cost functions.

TELECOMMUNICATIONS REGULATIONS AND QUALITY

The WTO Agreement on Basic Telecommunications Services entered into on 15 February 1997 has been used as a source of information on telecommunications regulations. This agreement is well described by Marko (1998a) who sets out various impediments covered by the agreement using a standard framework of market access and national treatment to examine the four modes of supply (cross border, consumption abroad, commercial presence, presence of natural persons). Examples of impediments relating to cross-border supply include market access being prohibited, prohibitive costs for market access, and underdeveloped or unreliable systems. For consumption abroad an example is callback not allowed; and for commercial presence an example is restrictions on foreign equity participation. In respect of national treatment, price controls are an example of an impediment to cross-border supply. One universal impediment that is not included in the agreement is the application of differential accounting rates. A useful outcome of the Marko analysis in relation to the aims of this chapter is the calculation of a frequency measure of the telecommunication impediments for each country based on commitments (none, partial, full) within the above framework following the approach of Hoekman (1995).

Other measures of telecommunication impediments have been derived by Warren in Chapter 5. The Warren indexes have the advantage over the Marko frequency measure of separately considering specific policies such as callback. This enables the determination of key policies, and the sensitivity of analyses (e.g. measures of inefficiency) to specific policies to be determined by the choice of components making up the measure. Both policy measures will be used in the analysis to follow.

Quality of service is also an important aspect of telecommunications. Generally, better quality services involve higher costs and prices. This aspect should be of little concern so long as consumers have a choice and are aware of the trade-offs involved. In non-competitive situations, however, price often has to be used as a proxy for an unknown quality of service (OECD 1990). This potential market failure in non-competitive situations has sometimes led to regulations being introduced to provide more information on the choice between quality and cost.

On other occasions, however, regulations have restricted trade-offs between quality and price through the designation of a fixed quality of service at a fixed price. These minimum standards tend to become the maximum standards as well. Quality has been considered an 'either/or' attribute that was often decided by engineers within a monopoly telecommunications system rather than the market trading-off the costs and benefits of a particular quality. This 'over regulation' has also been observed where a better service has been introduced that avoids some constraining regulation but which leads to the introduction of even more constraining regulations. Many countries have argued that their telecommunications systems cannot be opened to competition as they need to preserve the quality of the system, as if consumers cannot determine quality and decide what trade-offs they wish to make in a competitive situation. Such an approach to quality can lead to over-servicing and restrict competition and innovation that can open the market up to competition (e.g. satellite technologies in rural services).

Quality is likely to become a more important factor as technological development introduces improved service options. Quality itself can be an impediment, with underdeveloped and unreliable systems constraining the extent of interaction that competitive telecommunication exporters can have with the domestic system.

There are a number of indicators of telecommunications quality. The OECD (1996) used four indicators, namely:

- the number of payphones per 1,000 inhabitants;
- the percentage of clients who could potentially receive itemised billing;
- charges for directory assistance (converted to US$); and
- the number of faults per 100 lines per year.

The first two are positively related to quality and the last two are negatively related. In work reported below, a composite index was formed using equal weights for each of the available indexes. The four indicators were chosen on the basis that information was available on them for all OECD countries. There are other quality indicators (see OECD 1990) such as:

- waiting lists (years);
- number of mainlines or teledensity (number of mainlines per 100 inhabitants);
- repairs (percentage undertaken within 24 hours); and
- callback facility (yes or no).

However, on occasions the differences in country data from such indexes reflect more the different methodologies for collecting the data than real differences in performance (PC 1999). Moreover, the callback quality indicator is incorporated in some of the policy measures, illustrating the difficulty on occasions of separating aspects such as quality from the policy aspects.

In the following sections, reports are presented on how these indicators of policy and of service quality can be used in the analysis of the origins of price differences between countries.

MODELLING TELECOMMUNICATION PRICES, COSTS, REGULATIONS AND QUALITY

The broad outline of the methodology applied in this chapter was reported in Chapter 3 in this volume. In terms of the analysis of price wedges, the ideal price chosen is that which would hold in a theoretical perfectly competitive market. These efficient prices are reflected by long-run marginal costs (LRMC). For this reason, and as the program to be applied in the analysis uses formally specified production or cost functions rather than price functions, the analysis will be in terms of costs not prices. This approach has the added advantage that any rents being earned through higher prices need not be of concern. Cost padding is a concern but it is hoped that the analysis of regulations and other determinants of costs will be able to isolate this. Once a specification of the cost function is determined, this could be used to specify a relationship in prices that could be estimated to test for aspects such as rent seeking. Details of the estimation process are recorded in the appendix to this chapter. In this application, the basic data, obtained from the ITU, consisted of a time series over the period 1982–92 on 37 countries on the total costs of the provision of telecommunications services. Frontier cost functions for the log of total costs were fitted over the full 1982–92 period and for each separate year. Explanators included the standard output and input measures as well as others related to policies and quality.[1]

The base explanators were a constant, the log of output (outgoing calls in million minutes), the log of average annual wages (US$) deflated by purchasing power parity (per cent), the log of bond yield (per cent), the log of mainlines (millions) and teledensity (per 100 inhabitants) as representations of capital and quality, and time (years), perhaps capturing technological change. As outlined in the appendix, FRONTIER 4.1 offers the option of treating time within the error specification as well as an explanatory option and both of these options were chosen. After some preliminary analysis, the dataset was split into two, based on income levels as determined by the ITU (GDP greater or less than US$5,000 before 1982).

The results from the base model in Trewin (1998) are presented in Tables 7.1. In addition to parameter estimates and indications of significance, Table 7.1 and others like it in this chapter include data on three other parameters. Their origin is explained in more detail in the appendix. Briefly, the significance of g is a test of whether any form of stochastic function is required. Whether the mean inefficiency effects are zero or not can be tested via the significance of m. Whether the model is time-variant can be tested via the significance of h.

Table 7.1 presents the final maximum likelihood estimates for the two income sets. These are different in a number of respects such as the sign, values and significance of the estimated parameters. The wages variable has a significant and expected positive sign in the low-income set but is not significant in the high-income set. Although wages are higher in the high-income set, labour costs are smaller relative to capital and other inputs. The capital measure, mainlines, has a significant and expected positive sign in the high-income set but is not significant in the low-income set. This suggests that the low-income systems are labour-intensive and the high-income ones are capital-intensive. In both income sets the purchasing power parity deflator is positive and significant suggesting that telecommunication costs follow the pattern of general costs. The high-income set has a significant positive time parameter. This suggests the high-income systems are more dynamic while the low-income ones are more static.

The quality measure, teledensity, is significant and negative in the low-income set but more significant and positive in the high-income set. The negative sign in the low-income set may be the result of a situation in which a low-quality service in these countries could have high costs in terms of repairs and so on. Higher quality in the high-income set may reflect the availability of additions to a good basic service, such as paging and so on.

Final-year efficiency estimates for the two sets of countries did not fully reflect prior expectations. The major limitation of these results is the lack of a good measure of the quality of the telecommunications system.. This issue and treatment of the policy regimes is the focus of the new analysis discussed in the next section.

Application of the frontier model with policy variables

The first step in the analysis was to add the frequency measure of the telecommunication impediments for each country based on commitments derived by Marko (1998) as a policy variable. As this variable concerns one year, the same values were applied over the whole period of data, implicitly assuming that the policy regimes in each country were the same over the period 1982–92 as reflected in the frequency measure.

Table 7.1   'Base' frontier cost function parameter estimates

Variables	Low income	High income
Constant	0.16	-0.01
Output	0.11	0.03
Wages	0.47*	0.07
Bond yield	-0.06	0.05
Mainlines	0.14	1.15**
Tele-density	-0.46*	0.11**
PPP	0.59**	0.92**
Time	0.02	0.03**
σ^2	0.31*	0.22
γ	0.82**	0.92**
μ	1.01**	-0.31
η	-0.02	0.01

Notes:
* Significant at 5% level;
** Significant at 1% level.

The likelihood estimates in Table 7.2 are different in sign, values and significance, both within the two income sets and with respect to corresponding estimates in Table 7.1. The wages variable is no longer significant but still has an expected positive sign in the low-income set. Again mainlines has a significant and expected positive sign in the high-income set and is not significant in the low-income set. The purchasing power parity deflator is positive and significant again in both income sets, suggesting that telecommunication costs follow the pattern of general costs – the main relationship in the case of the low-income set. The high-income set has a significant positive time parameter, again suggesting more dynamism in this set.[2]

The additional policy variable is positive and significant in the high-income set, suggesting that policies contributed to the cost inefficiencies. The policy variable is not significant in the low-income set. The policy variable has the majority of high-income countries showing a low frequency of impediments but there were a number of outliers such as Singapore, Canada, Japan, Switzerland, Hong Kong and Korea.

The next step in the analysis was to replace the Marko frequency measure of the telecommunication impediments with the indexes derived by Warren in Chapter 5. Difficulties with a composite of such indexes include the choice of components and the weights to assign them. Many experts on the telecommunications sector have strong prior opinions on what countries have open or closed telecommunications policies, just as they do on what countries have high or low-quality systems. If these opinions could be captured via surveys of these experts then they could be used statistically to determine

Table 7.2   Marko 'policy' frontier cost function parameter estimates

Variables	Low income	High income
Constant	0.39	-0.31
Output	0.10	0.04
Wages	0.42	0.01
Bond yield	-0.06	0.08
Mainlines	0.16	1.09**
Tele-density	-0.44	0.15**
PPP	0.60**	0.87**
Policy	-0.02	0.15**
Time	0.02	0.05**
σ^2	0.31**	0.07**
γ	0.82**	0.77**
μ	1.02	0.45**
η	-0.02	0.03*

Notes:
* Significant at 5% level;
** Significant at 1% level.

the significant components amongst the indexes and the weights they should carry in the indexes.

The first approach to determining the weights in the policy variables index was a principal components analysis which is not dependent on such additional information. This approach involves transforming the policy variables to a new set of variables made up of combinations of the policy variables that are pairwise uncorrelated and maximise the explanation of the variance. If the first principal component explains most of the variation then its weights are a good guide to an index that will represent the information contained in the variables. The outcomes of this approach were that the first principal component explained 53 per cent of the variation and had roughly equal weights apart from market access to FDI in the mobile network and national treatment in investment, which both had slightly lower weights.[3]

The second approach to determining the weights in the policy variables index was to use discriminant analysis. This involves constructing a formula from a sample of observations of two or more populations in order to minimise the expected costs of misclassification of new observations to one of the populations (see Figure 7.1). Here a subset of the countries was divided into two groups on the basis of whether they had low or high tariffs on imports of telephone sets, as a proxy for openness. The linear discriminant functions provide a weighted combination of policy variables that maximises the discrimination between the two groups.[4] This suggests that policies concerned with market access for FDI in the mobile network should be given more

Figure 7.1 Discrimination analysis

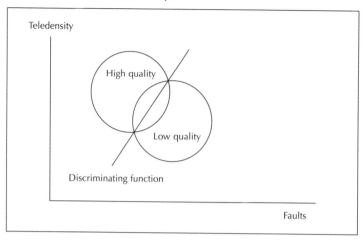

weight than the other policy indexes in an index that would maximise the discrimination between 'open' and 'closed' groups.

The frontier cost functions were first rerun with Warren's five policy indexes entering the functions individually. The results were poor, which could be a result of the strong multicollinearity between the five indexes. When the frontiers were split into high and low-income groups, some of the policy indexes were highly correlated, for example most of the high-income countries allowed callback (the exceptions were Canada, Greece, Korea, Portugal and Spain). These multicollinearity difficulties were addressed by entering a simple average of the five policy indexes as suggested by the principal components analysis. The results of this analysis are presented in Table 7.3.

The likelihood estimates in Table 7.3 are different, both between the two groups and with respect to corresponding estimates in earlier tables. Again mainlines has a significant and expected positive sign in the high-income set. The only explanatory variable that is significant in the low-income set is the purchasing power parity deflator, which is positive and significant in both income sets. Teledensity is again significant and positive in the high-income set.[5]

The additional policy variable is negative and significant in the high-income set, suggesting that as the values of the policies as a group increased, costs fell (e.g. more callback, lower costs).

Undertaking the frontier analysis with market access on FDI (mobiles) as the only policy index, as suggested by the discriminant analysis, resulted in an incorrect sign on the policy variable. To illustrate the benefits of measures such as Warren's indexes in terms of isolating individual policy effects, the

Table 7.3   Warren 'policy' frontier cost function parameter estimates

Variables	Low income	High income
Constant	0.16	0.52
Output	0.13	0.03
Wages	0.51	0.05
Bond yield	-0.04	0.07
Mainlines	0.12	1.19**
Tele-density	-0.44	0.18**
PPP	0.53*	0.91**
Policy	-0.32	-0.47**
Time	0.03	0.0006
σ^2	0.32	0.10**
γ	0.83**	0.85**
μ	0.84	0.60**
η	-0.004	-0.04**

Notes:
* Significant at 5% level;
** Significant at 1% level.

frontier analysis was rerun with the national treatment investment index. The results were sensitive to the choice of individual policy. The results of this analysis are presented in Table 7.4.

The key results in Table 7.4 are that the purchasing power parity deflator plus output and wages are significant in the low-income set. The purchasing power parity deflator is also positive and significant in the high-income set, along with mainlines, teledensity and time. The stochastic frontier parameters are significant. The policy variable is significant and negative in both income sets. This suggests that those countries that allow higher levels of FDI face lower costs.

Application of the frontier model with policy and quality variables

The next step in the new analysis was to add further quality indicators, namely waiting lists (years) and faults per 100 mainlines. Again, as these new variables were only available for the one year, the same values were applied over the whole period of the data, implicitly assuming that the quality regimes in each country were the same over the period 1982–92 as the year in which the quality indicators applied. The results of this analysis are presented in Table 7.5.

The likelihood estimates in Table 7.5 are also different in signs, values and significance of the estimated parameters, both within the table and from corresponding estimates in earlier tables. Output is significant and has an expected positive sign in the low-income set. Mainlines again has a significant and expected positive sign in the high-income set. Again in both income sets the purchasing power parity deflator is positive and significant. In both income

Table 7.4 National treatment FDI 'policy' frontier cost function parameter estimates

Variables	Low income	High income
Constant	0.60	0.52
Output	0.20**	0.004
Wages	0.69*	0.05
Bond yield	-0.01	0.05
Mainlines	0.01	1.17**
Tele-density	-0.43	0.13**
PPP	0.24	0.93**
Policy	-1.74**	-0.33**
Time	0.01	0.03**
σ^2	0.77*	0.51**
γ	0.93**	0.97**
μ	-1.70**	-1.41
η	0.02	0.01

Notes:
* Significant at 5% level;
** Significant at 1% level.

sets the two time parameters are significant and positive. The Marko policy variable is again positive and significant in the high-income set. Of the error component parameters, the m terms in the low-income set are insignificant, suggesting that the stochastic frontier can be represented by a half-Normal distribution.

Of the quality measures, the significant variable in the high-income set is waiting time, which is negative. In the low-income set, significant quality variables are waiting times, with a positive parameter estimate, and faults, with a negative parameter estimate. On the face of it, it would be expected that these additional quality variables would have similar parameter estimates although explanations could be given as to why long waiting times increase costs yet many faults decrease them (e.g. reflect the fixed costs and operating costs in a low, deteriorating capital investment respectively). Another explanation is that the waiting time variable is quite small, being measured in years, and often becomes negative when converted to logs. Most of the higher numbers with positive log values are in the low-income set and this may explain the sign differences on waiting times. The different significant parameter estimates could also be a result of the unrestricted manner in which the quality variables enter the relationships. It is noticeable that some of the quality coefficients are similar, suggesting multicollinearity could be a problem which a fixed combination of quality variables would overcome.

It is worthwhile determining appropriate weights for a quality index to enter the frontier cost function. This index is unlikely to be a simple weighted average as used by the OECD (1996). The weights in the index are likely to

Table 7.5   'Quality' frontier cost function parameter estimates

Variables	Low income	High income
Constant	0.99	-0.59
Output	0.19*	-0.002
Wages	0.53	0.10
Bond yield	-0.03	0.06
Mainlines	0.11	1.06**
Tele-density	-0.33	0.05
PPP	0.39*	0.87**
Policy (Marko)	-.24	0.16**
Waiting times	0.17*	-0.03*
Faults	-0.36*	0.03
Time	0.04*	0.06**
σ^2	0.45	0.05**
γ	0.88**	0.72**
μ	0.60	0.39**
η	0.03*	0.04**

Notes:
* Significant at 5% level;
** Significant at 1% level.

be of separate interest, showing which individual quality measures are more important as well as, as suggested above, overcoming any problems from multicollinearity. They would also incorporate additional information on ranking or grouping the countries, bringing this into the analysis. Again principal components and discriminant analysis were used to determine appropriate weights.

The most appropriate information on which to determine a quality index would be consumer satisfaction with the cost–quality trade-offs offered (BTE 1992). However, data on consumer satisfaction is not collected, only (non-cost) satisfaction with specific services (see ACA 1998). A second-best option may be to classify consumers in competitive countries as satisfied and others not on the basis that competition is more likely to offer the individual cost–quality trade-offs desired. The provision of more specific information on the quality of services offered could be similarly used. Such information relevant to the period of the base analysis is available from the OECD (1990: Figure 5.18) and the BTE (1992: Table 8.1).

The first approach to determining the weights in the quality variables index was a principal components analysis. The outcomes of this approach were that the first principal component explained 60 per cent of the variation and had roughly equal weights for waiting times and faults of just under double the negative of the teledensity weight.[6]

Discriminant analysis was undertaken on the three quality variables of teledensity, waiting times and faults, with the countries split into 'competitive'

Table 7.6 'Quality' frontier cost function parameter estimates

Variables	Low income	High income
Constant	-4.91	-5.13*
Output	0.12	0.01
Wages	0.36	0.05
Bond yield	-0.04	0.06
Mainlines	0.14	1.09**
Tele-density	-0.39	0.11
PPP	0.73**	0.93**
Policy	0.81	1.01**
Waiting times	-0.08	-0.01
Faults	0.37*	0.06
Time	-0.01	0.04**
s^2	0.56*	0.05**
γ	0.91**	0.71**
μ	1.43*	0.39**
η	-0.04**	0.02

Notes:
* Significant at 5% level;
** Significant at 1% level.

and 'non-competitive' groups on the basis of whether they allowed callback or not.[7] This suggests that faults should be given more weight than waiting time and teledensity in a quality index that would maximise the discrimination between 'competitive' and 'non-competitive' groups.

Re-estimating the frontier cost functions with the quality variables entered as a fixed relationship as determined from the first principal component did not lead to superior results. The significance of most of the previous variables are not changed. The new composite quality variable is significant and negative in the high-income set and insignificant and positive in the low-income set.

As mentioned earlier, the calculation of these shocks is more convenient from alternative functional forms. For this reason, the above equation is re-estimated in the double log form with the policy variable entered as (1 + policy) so that the tariff equivalent equals:

$$100[\exp(1 + \text{policy})^{\beta-1}].$$

The results of the re-estimation with this form of policy variable are presented in Table 7.6. The only significant variables in the low-income group are purchasing power parity, faults and the error terms. In the high-income group, mainlines, purchasing power parity, and time are all significant but not the time parameter in the error term.

These parameter estimates were then used to calculate technical efficiency estimates. These are reported in Table 7.7. The nature of these data are

Table 7.7   Technical efficiency, revised Marko policy variable and quality indicators, 1992

Low income	Technical efficiency	High income	Technical efficiency
Chile	3.82	Australia	1.67
China	6.31	Austria	1.31
Hungary	2.61	Belgium	1.55
Iceland	1.16	Canada	1.34
Indonesia	11.96	Denmark	1.43
Ireland	3.22	Finland	1.24
Malaysia	4.31	France	1.74
Mexico	15.41	Germany	1.66
PNG	7.75	Greece	1.11
Philippines	3.06	Hong Kong	1.44
Poland	2.30	Italy	1.71
Thailand	5.25	Japan	1.21
Turkey	4.07	Korea	1.98
		Luxembourg	1.03
		Netherlands	1.43
		New Zealand	1.83
		Norway	1.75
		Portugal	2.08
		Singapore	1.57
		Spain	1.75
		Sweden	1.40
		Switzerland	1.42
		United Kingdom	1.67
		United States	1.48
Mean	5.48	Mean	1.54

discussed in more detail in the appendix to this chapter. Briefly, one of the key features of these results is that the average efficiency of the high-income group is over three times better than the low-income group average. There is also more variation within the low-income country set. In the high-income set, Luxembourg is close to the frontier. Relatively high-cost countries in this set are Portugal and Korea.[8]

If the estimated policy coefficient, β, is close to 1, or full technical efficiency, (as it is in the high-income group) then this gives a one-to-one relationship between the tariff equivalent and the policy variable (e.g. Marko). Thus a 25 per cent change in the Marko frequency measure would translate into an approximate 25 per cent change in the tariff equivalent or prices.[9]

CONCLUSION

There are a number of policy implications that follow from the modelling reported in this chapter. It has been shown via the aggregate frequency measures that telecommunication policy impediments add to the costs of telecommunications in high-income countries. High-income countries appear to be operating under a different economic system to low-income countries – the former more capital-intensive and dynamic than the latter, which appears to be mainly a 'cost-plus', labour-intensive and static system. These last aspects could be reflecting policies in terms of pricing, labour arrangements and competition. Similar but more policy-specific outcomes are evident when separate consideration can be given to specific policies such as national treatment in investment.

Quality was shown to be an important aspect of telecommunication services and one which can be fundamentally affected by regulation. In fact, the addition of the policy and quality variables has explained significant amounts of the previously unexplained inefficiencies. The split into income sets was also important in explaining variation and this aspect interacts with some of the variables, such as quality as measured by waiting times, suggesting care is needed in the use and interpretation of such variables. Some regulation can assist in improving the quality of service by providing necessary information on the quality–cost trade-offs available to consumers. Others can hinder this by imposing fixed standards for set prices which tends to stifle competition and innovation. A competitive market offers consumers a choice of what service they are willing to pay for. This contrasts to a situation where some universal service aspects are built into overheads and no specific charges applied. The long-run benefits of a more competitive, innovative and dynamic system will be difficult to prove without some measures of quality and consumer satisfaction with the service, including cost aspects.

This chapter has advanced the measurement of impediments to international trade in telecommunication services and their impact, in particular in relation to decomposing the price wedge into aspects due to specific policies and quality attributes. Policy and quality indexes have been identified that contribute significantly to telecommunication costs. Individual policies and quality attributes have also been identified. Many of the outcomes make sense and meet prior expectations, for example in terms of their significance and sign, including in relation to outcomes for low and high-income countries. Broad rankings of countries in terms of their policies and the quality of their services also make sense.

The policy and quality indexes have been identified to some extent outside of their impact on measured costs but more could be done in this respect. For example, some information on consumer satisfaction with the quality–cost aspects of the telecommunication services they receive would be invaluable in identifying an appropriate quality index and seeing how much more consumers are willing to pay to receive this quality service. Such information would appear of far greater importance than some of the investigations currently being undertaken on telecommunication services, such as the use of credit by youths in obtaining mobile phone services.

Prior information or surveys might also be useful in determining key policies and their impacts. There is a question of whether some measures of the policies are capturing the required information. For example, do the number of competitors or the degree of FDI allowed fully capture the degree of competition in all cases? Furthermore, many of the policies come as a package and measuring them individually and combining them in some arbitrary fashion may not capture all aspects of such packages.

More recent and comprehensive data on the costs or prices, policy and quality variables would also be invaluable in improving and testing the robustness of the results obtained. For example, more recent cost data would enable the estimated relationships to be tested via their predictive ability.

The analysis is close to a stage where it could provide cost impacts of specific policies as input to modelling the welfare and other broader impacts of such policies – the final step in the approach set out to measuring impediments to trade in services and their economic impact. Using these results to determine the price wedges of countries not in the data analysed here is relatively straightforward if these countries have measures of the policies modelled explicitly. The difficulty arises in determining the stochastic inefficiency measures for these new countries and the impact of a change in policies on such measures. In addition, more than these part-performance measures may be needed to illustrate the full impact of the impediments. For example, it has been shown that such impediments constrain productivity and innovation (Boles de Boer and Evans 1996; Spiller and Cardilli 1997).

APPENDIX: FRONTIER MODELS

In this appendix, the general details on frontier models are illustrated by reference to Figure A7.1, which is similar to a figure presented in Trewin et al. (1995). In analysis of efficiency/inefficiency, it is not the average of observed relationships between inputs and total costs that is of interest but the (often unobserved) minimum possible costs that are expended from a given combination of inputs – the (absolute) frontier cost function C_a. A related concept, but one that will not always correspond to the frontier cost function, involves the envelope encompassing all the input–cost combinations of interest with a '100 per cent-efficient' observation(s) P_b on the envelope. This last concept is also referred to as the best practices frontier (the observed minimum costs obtained) C_b.

The distance an observation lies above its cost frontier measures the degree of technical inefficiency, thus it is a residual measure. The existence of technical inefficiency has been questioned. For example, Mueller (1974) states 'little is known about the role of non-physical inputs, especially information and knowledge, which influence the firm's ability to use its available technology set fully ... Once all inputs are taken into account, measured productivity differences should disappear except for random disturbances'. This seems to be a question of what constitutes an appropriate input. In terms of the policy analysis, it is somewhat irrelevant whether some policy improves the level of 'non-core' inputs such as information, and hence output under Mueller's view, or addresses inefficiencies due to a lack of information under a frontier function approach. There is also the question of whether all inputs can be taken into account, or measured, thus avoiding the need for a residual measure approach.

Technical inefficiency is also represented in Figure A7.1. A production process is technically inefficient if minimum costs are not produced from a given bundle of inputs. The complementary concept of technical efficiency is measured by the ratio of expected costs to minimum costs, for example T_o/T_b in Figure A7.1; that is a comparison of costs at points P_b and P_o, each with the same inputs but with P_b lying on the best practices frontier function C_b while P_o lies on C_o, which is a neutral shift of the frontier C_b that passes through point P_o. The concept could be measured relative to other frontiers, for example the absolute frontier function C_a lying below all the sample points. Here, the ratio will be T_o/T_a or a comparison of costs at points P_a and P_o. The ratio will take values between 1 (efficiency) and infinity in the case of the cost function.

One form of frontier function is the stochastic frontier (Aigner et al. 1977; Meeusen and van den Broeck 1977). Functions, being simplified representations of actual operations, require assumptions regarding the distribution of random errors before they can be used in empirical estimation. The usual assumption made in relation to average functions is a normal distribution, which is symmetric and bell-shaped. The stochastic frontier (a

Figure A7.1 Best practices and absolute frontiers and measures of inefficiency

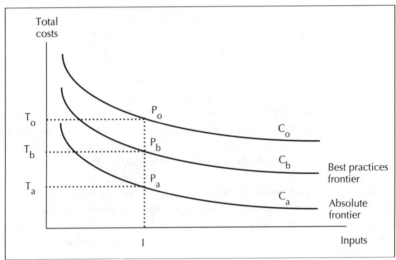

variant of the absolute frontier concept) incorporates two random components: a traditional random error component V_i and a component U_i representing the degree of technical inefficiency. Various one-sided distributional assumptions have been made regarding this additional component. In the deterministic frontier concept (often corresponding to the best practices frontier concept), any variation in country performance is relative to a single frontier and attributed purely to inefficiency. This ignores the possibility of variation due to factors not under the country's control, such as the weather and geography, which are usually incorporated into the random error.

The specific stochastic frontier used in this chapter is set out in Coelli (1996) and can accommodate unbalanced panel data associated with a sample of N countries over T time periods. It incorporates a simple exponential specification of time-varying country effects and is defined by:

$$C_{it} = f(I_{it}; \beta)\exp(V_{it} + U_{it}) \qquad\qquad i = 1,..., N, \qquad t = 1,..., T,$$

and

$$U_{it} = \eta_{it}U_i = \{\exp[-\eta(t - T)]\}U_i \qquad\qquad t \in S(i); \; i = 1,..., N;$$

where C_{it} represents the costs for the ith country in the tth time period; $f(I_{it}; \beta)$ is a suitable function of a vector, I_{it} of factor inputs (and country specific variables), associated with the production of the ith country in the tth time period, and a vector, β, of unknown parameters; the V_{it}s are assumed to be independent and identically distributed $N(0, \sigma_v^2)$ random errors; the Us are assumed to be independent and identically distributed non-negative truncations of the $N(\mu, \sigma_u^2)$ distribution; h is an unknown scalar parameter; and S(i) represents the set of T_i time periods among the T periods involved for which observations for the *i*th country are obtained.

The parameterisation in which σ_v^2 and σ_u^2 are replaced with

$$\sigma_s^2 \circ \sigma_v^2 + \sigma_u^2 \text{ and } \gamma \circ \sigma_u^2/\sigma_s^2$$

is used as γ lies between 0 and 1, which provides a range that can be searched for a good starting point for an iterative maximisation of the likelihood.

In the work reported in this chapter, the program FRONTIER 4.1 (Coelli 1996) was used to obtain maximum likelihood estimates of the frontier cost function parameters and predictors of the efficiencies of individual countries. The dependent variable is the log of costs (in US$m), which is made up of the log of the sum of operating costs, depreciation, net interest paid, taxes on telecommunications income, and other costs. The preferred model can be selected using generalised Likelihood Ratio (LR) tests and these tests suggested a translog function was preferred over a semi-log function. Sargan's LR criterion (Sargan 1964) suggested preference of the semi-log over the levels specification.

Whether any form of stochastic function is required can be tested via the significance of γ. Whether the mean inefficiency effects are zero or not can be tested via the significance of m. Whether the model is time-variant can be tested via the significance of η.

NOTES

This is a redraft of a paper presented at the Impediments to Trade in Services: Measurement and Policy Implications Telecommunications seminar, Canberra, 19 March 1999. A longer version of the paper which contains further discussion of the technical efficiency estimates based on the various models is also available on request to the author. The author would like to acknowledge Marpudin Azis for his research assistance on this chapter and the Australian Research Council for financial support.

1   These latter explanators that, as described below, distinguish frontier from traditional cost functions make the usual interpretation of coefficients in terms of scale and shares difficult. In fact, poor results were obtained when constant returns to scale were imposed by modelling costs per mainline (see Trewin 1998).

2   Of the error component parameters, the m term or mean inefficiency effects are insignificant in the low-income set, suggesting that the stochastic frontier can be represented by a half-Normal distribution.

3   Actual weights were Market Access/Trade = 0.50; Market Access/FDI (fixed) = 0.46; Market Access/FDI (mobile) = 0.39; National Treatment/Trade = 0.49; National Treatment/FDI = 0.39.

4   The first such function was:

-5.6 + 1.1 * log(Market Access/Trade) - 2.5 * log(Market Access/FDI fixed) + 16.3 * log(Market Access/FDI mobile) - 2.0 * log(National Treatment/Trade) -2.9 * log(National Treatment/FDI).

5   Of the error component parameters, only the g term on the requirement for a stochastic frontier in the low-income set is significant. All error component parameters are significant in the high-income group.

6   Actual weights were Teledensity = -0.38; Waiting times = 0.68; and Faults = 0.62.

7   The first discriminating function was -7.6 * 1.5 x log(Teledensity) - 0.2 * log(Waiting time) + 3.5 * log(Faults).

8   Some countries consistently rank well or poorly in terms of the inefficiency estimates whereas others change their rankings depending on the specification. This suggests that the results need to be tested for their robustness or presented in broad terms.

9   This compares to the 20 to 40 per cent figure obtained by the Productivity Commission (1999).

8 Modelling the benefits of increasing competition in international air services

Martin Johnson, Tendai Gregan, Geraldine Gentle and Paul Belin

INTRODUCTION

For over half a century, international civil aviation has been governed by a system of bilateral air service arrangements (ASAs) between countries. There are now some 3,000 ASAs worldwide, 51 involving Australia.

ASAs set out the terms and conditions under which airlines may fly. Typically they specify capacity, frequency, routes, cities, ownership provisions, safety certification, price approval processes and many other details. Tight ASA restrictions on competition and trade have turned the international airline industry into one of the most regulated in the world.

Unlike trade in goods, which is generally free unless specifically restricted, trade in international air services cannot occur unless it is explicitly permitted in ASAs, which include a positive list of activities that an airline is allowed. Various 'freedoms of the air' allow airlines to fly to, from, beyond, and between bilateral partners and other countries. Other positive provisions of ASAs allow airlines to undertake specific activities in foreign bilateral partner countries, such as setting up an office.

Restrictions on trade in goods are generally applied uniformly to all trading partners that are members of the World Trade Organisation (WTO). In contrast, international air services are largely excluded from the WTO's General Agreement on Trade in Services (GATS). Instead, trade in international air services is regulated within an international framework of bilateral agreements, not subject to the most-favoured-nation (MFN) principle.

EFFECTS OF THE CURRENT BILATERAL SYSTEM

The bilateral system restricts airlines' ownership and access to capital, where they fly, the number and frequency of flights, the number of seats they can offer, the types of aircraft they use, and how much they charge. It influences the nature of competition between airlines by controlling market entry and the quantity and variety of rights allocated to particular airlines.

The system also influences airlines' costs – usually increasing costs by restricting airlines' ability to operate efficiently and to develop new markets and more effective networks. Increased costs and restricted competition lead to higher prices.

Regulation of entry, frequency, capacity, routes and prices keeps fares up and impedes the development of new travel products. Liberalisation has already led to greater competition, reduced fares, new routes and destinations, and improved quality of service, but there is considerable scope for further improvements.

Higher international airfares restrict growth in the tourism industry. The Productivity Commission's modelling (see below) suggests that lower fares resulting from Ansett International's entry to seven Asian routes may have increased net passenger movements to Australia by almost 4 per cent in 1997.

Restrictions on city designation and capacity limitations combine to make it costly for foreign airlines to land at secondary gateways, impeding tourism development and the availability of international air freight capacity in regional centres. In Australia a choice has to be made between Sydney and regional gateways, and Sydney is chosen.

The bilateral system has been built on the premise that each country has its own substantially domestically owned and controlled designated national flag carrier(s). The result is an international misallocation of resources as some countries waste precious capital and other resources on inefficient airlines that would not be viable without government support.

The more efficient industries suffer, both from having to compete for capital and other resources and from having to use expensive international air transport. Conversely, those countries with economically efficient airline industries are unable to expand their airlines to their full potential.

The global aviation industry has reached a critical point in its development. The inefficiencies imposed on the world aviation industry by the current bilateral system and the benefits of more efficient, internationally competitive air services are now apparent.

RECENT REFORMS

World trade in most other goods and services is being liberalised in a multilateral framework, producing demonstrable gains in economic welfare. A different system for international air services is increasingly difficult to justify.

Pressures on the bilateral system include:

- strong growth in air services is revealing the inflexibilities and inefficiencies of the system;
- evidence from around the world of the benefits of aviation deregulation;
- the spread of bilateral 'open skies' agreements;
- consumer and business demands for better and seamless air services;
- the use of codeshares, alliances and charters to overcome constraints of the bilateral structure;

- the low profits of most airlines and the growing reluctance of governments to continue subsidising their airlines;
- the pressure of global capital markets on airlines to improve performance;
- privatisation of airlines and airports; and
- the emergence of regional or plurilateral agreements, particularly developments in the European Union.

As evidence mounts of the inefficiencies flowing from anticompetitive regulation of airlines, the bilateral system has been coming under intense pressure. Airlines have attempted to overcome some of the bilateral system's constraints on their operations by entering into various arrangements, such as codeshares and alliances.

Despite liberalisation in many countries, most ASAs, including Australia's, still prevent airlines from operating like other companies. They are restricted in developing efficient networks and innovative travel products.

One reason for the slow progress of reform lies in the ASAs themselves. The positive list of activities that an airline is allowed inhibits airlines from undertaking anything for which there is no specific provision.

Airlines often require their governments to intercede for them before they can develop new or expanded services. In most other areas, international traders are able to do anything that is not constrained by a negative list of specific restrictions. This gives companies much greater freedom to do business and, importantly, to grow and innovate. Moving from a positive list of restrictions in agreements to a negative list, under which all forms of trading would be allowed unless explicitly restricted, would provide a better basis both for liberalisation and for incorporation of air services into the wider multilateral trade negotiating framework.

Many countries, including Australia, have been liberalising their own regulations concerning international aviation. Driven by the United States, bilateral open skies agreements, which remove most traffic and market access constraints on a reciprocal basis, are spreading. Such policies commonly remove constraints on capacity, frequency, city designation, routes, intermediate and beyond rights, and tariff setting. While such bilateral agreements can have some beneficial effects on competition, they are necessarily limited in scope. Furthermore, a series of bilateral agreements among a powerful 'hub' country and a number of 'spoke' countries could exacerbate and entrench the dominant position of the hub.

Multilateral and plurilateral reform

Ultimately, a liberal multilateral agreement under the WTO that covers all or most countries would allow international air services to develop in response to market pressures. Efficient carriers would replace inefficient carriers, and the removal of regulatory barriers to entry would enhance competition.

However, there has been little action so far at the multilateral level. This appears to be an anachronism in today's world trading environment that could be addressed in the next review of the GATS. The Australian Government has recently announced that it will support a review of the treatment of air services in the GATS.

Given the entrenched position of the bilateral system, and the difficulties of negotiating a truly liberal multilateral agreement, plurilateral liberalisation, such as the process followed for the International Telecommunications Agreement, may offer prospects for achieving gains in the short to medium term.

Plurilateral liberalisation could develop from an 'open club' based on a common open skies agreement among participating countries.[1] This would allow all carriers within the group to fly freely among the members, subject to a common set of rules. It should be open to other countries to join on the same conditions. The challenge with a regional or plurilateral agreement is to ensure that it is used as a stepping stone to global liberalisation, not as an exclusive device to favour members. Openness would be an important feature of such agreements.

The open club idea draws on the principles of open regionalism but with an important difference. Under the WTO, signatories are required to treat the products and services of other countries on a non-discriminatory MFN basis – in general they cannot treat the products of one foreign country differently from those of another, except in a free trade area or a customs union. Open regionalism describes the action of a group of countries reducing impediments to trade among themselves, but not creating any new artificial distinctions or discriminating between members and non-members (Elek 1996). For example, APEC commitments to trade reform amount to a coordinated program of unilateral actions by members to reduce trade barriers without discriminating against non-members.

An aviation open club would operate differently. International air transport has been specifically exempted from the GATS. Most countries apparently wish to retain the bilateral system, and that system fundamentally contravenes the non-discriminatory MFN principle. An aviation open club cannot help but discriminate against non-members because it would grow out of the bilateral system. The difference would be that club members would offer one set of rights to all other club members, and other sets of rights (bilaterally) to non-members. Non-members would be free to join, and as membership grew, discrimination between nations would decline. Transparency would be important to ensure that non-members could understand the conditions of membership, and be forewarned about changes to club rules.

The difficulties of establishing such a club should not be underestimated. Not all countries may wish to join a club, or allow certain other countries to do so. Countries with entrenched political or other differences may not wish to cooperate in such a way. Airlines in member countries may have an incentive to resist extending the boundaries of the club if it would mean entry of other more competitive airlines. However, accession would be important because the overall benefits, including benefits to users, would grow as the size of the aviation network grows. Non-members would risk becoming isolated from the increase in air traffic in response to the more liberal conditions available within the club. Countries that may be reluctant to negotiate reciprocal open skies agreements on a bilateral basis may have little choice but to join the club.

To enhance the chances of this plurilateral open club becoming a vehicle for widespread reform, it should:

- not intentionally disadvantage outsiders any more than the bilateral agreements it replaces;
- have transparent rules;
- allow non-members to join on the same terms and conditions; and
- contain provisions relating to competition policy, particularly to constrain significant government subsidies to airlines.

The Australian Government has announced its support for the concept of plurilateral liberalisation.

MODELLING THE WELFARE GAINS FROM REFORM

The Productivity Commission has developed a regional network model to assess the welfare effects of various liberalisation scenarios as part of its inquiry into Australia's international aviation policy. This uses a spatial modelling equilibrium approach whereby airlines use their flight networks to move passengers from their origins to their destinations. Prices and airline networks are estimated in an equilibrium that explicitly accounts for the demand for air travel, the costs and operation of airline networks and the strategic interactions of airlines. A technical paper supporting the modelling is available from the Commission on request and from the Commission's Website (PC 1998a).

Modelling framework

A review of the literature shows that three main approaches have been used to determine the factors that affect prices in air travel markets (PC 1998b). The first approach uses econometric methods to test statistically whether market concentration, demand and cost variables together explain prices better than demand and cost variables alone. The second approach is also econometric. It focuses either on estimating the extent of economies of density or of scale in airline networks, or on estimating productivity differences between airlines. The third approach is based on spatial modelling, and is the approach adopted in this study.

The conceptual framework embodied in the model draws on three articles. The demand specification, drawing on Gillen, Harris and Oum (1997), assumes that airlines' services are imperfect substitutes for each other and that customers care about the price and non-price attributes of travel (e.g. the frequency of service).

The market behaviour of airlines draws on Lederer (1993), who showed the existence of a (unique) non-cooperative equilibrium in an airline model that can be adapted to the purposes of this study. His demand specification differs from that of Gillen, Harris and Oum but also assumes that airlines compete in price and non-price attributes of travel.

The specification of the airlines' networks draws on the work of Hendricks, Piccione and Tan (1995). It internalises network design and disentangles the network passenger flows from passenger demand within an imperfectly competitive framework.

The model is subject to a number of limiting assumptions:

- it captures the industry at a point in time;
- there are no economic conditions for airline entry or exit;
- slot and gate constraints are not taken into account; and
- negotiated capacity exceeds airline demand.

The first two limitations imply that the model is a comparative static, short-run model. No dynamic investment or entry and exit decisions are made. The third limitation exists because the lack of city designation of passengers in the data excludes estimation of any efficiency losses that may result from capacity-constrained airports or from negotiated restrictions on city access. The fourth limitation implies that negotiated flight capacities are not binding constraints on airlines' networks.

Passenger flows and country coverage

This network model concentrates on scheduled passenger services with adjustments to airline costs to account for the absence of other revenue sources, such as freight, in the model. It should be noted that the total gains from liberalisation estimated in the model exclude any collateral gains to freight and mail services.

Passenger movement data is derived from an Avstats survey of responses by travellers for their origin–destination travel by airline (DTRD 1998). Passenger data are for 1995, so that they are consistent in the model with the most recent International Civil Aviation Organisation cost data available at the time (ICAO 1996). However, data for 1997 are used for some simulations.

Two levels of country coverage were used for this study. The broadest coverage aimed to test the robustness of the model for international travel to and from Australia. A narrower coverage was adopted for policy simulations to maintain numerical tractability in the model while allowing for any possible network effects of possible liberalised ASAs.

The broadest coverage includes routes for travel to and from Australia for twelve foreign destinations. Nine correspond to countries or economies – Japan, the Republic of Korea, Hong Kong, Taiwan and China in North Asia, and Indonesia, Malaysia, Singapore and Thailand in Southeast Asia. The other three correspond to regions – North America (the United States and Canada), the United Kingdom/Ireland and the rest of Europe.

Country pairs rather than city pairs were chosen for demand analysis because the Avstats passenger data for individual airlines were only available for country pairs. This is not an issue for many countries, because there is only one major airport (for example, in Hong Kong, Singapore, the Republic of Korea, Taiwan, Thailand and Malaysia). However, the cost data used in this study are city-based. Therefore representative cities must be chosen for the other countries. They are Sydney (Australia), Beijing (China), Tokyo (Japan), Jakarta (Indonesia), Los Angeles (North America), London/Heathrow (United Kingdom/Ireland) and Rome (rest of Europe).

The broadest market coverage captures 78 per cent and 91 per cent of passenger movements between Australia and the relevant country (excluding New Zealand) of Australian residents and foreign visitors, respectively. New Zealand is excluded because travel between Australia and New Zealand is not subject to capacity constraints, although fifth freedom restrictions to third countries apply.

The Japanese, North American and European markets are by far the largest markets (Table 8.1). Inbound foreign visitor flows dominate outbound Australian resident flows in nine of the twelve markets. Japan, the Republic of Korea, Singapore and Taiwan are particularly oriented towards foreign visitors. In contrast, Malaysia, North America, Thailand, United Kingdom/ Ireland and the rest of Europe are only slightly tilted towards foreign visitors. Australian resident movements exceed foreign visitor movements in the remaining four markets (including the rest of the world), although only marginally for China and Hong Kong.

Airline coverage

Because of the bilateral system, travel between two countries is dominated by their national carriers. The remaining market share is distributed to a large number of third-country carriers, some of which are important competitors. The modelling problem is to incorporate the important third-country competition while keeping the problem numerically tractable. This is achieved by omitting from a market those third-country airlines that have a marginal impact on the model solution. The rules used in this study for airline inclusion/ exclusion are found in PC (1998a).

The model's depiction of airlines' shares of the total traffic to and from Australia and the number of markets served by airlines are presented in Table 8.2. Model shares overstate those observed in the Avstats data, while the model's number of markets served understates those observed in Avstats data because of the exclusion of third-country carriers that have marginal influence.

Qantas dominates total flows but each national airline is significant for travel between its own country and Australia. Airlines in the model that

Table 8.1 Passenger movements to and from Australia by market, 1995

Between Australia and:	Australian residents '000	Foreign visitors '000	Total[a] '000
China	108	88	197
Hong Kong	313	284	597
Indonesia	452	282	734
Japan	88	1,573	1,660
Malaysia	183	228	410
North America	721	731	1,452
Korea, Republic of	28	338	366
Singapore	193	414	607
Taiwan	59	308	366
Thailand	153	166	319
United Kingdom/Ireland	599	745	1,344
Rest of Europe[b]	544	784	1,329
Rest of world[c]	955	576	1531
Total	4,396	6,517	10,912

Notes:
a Numbers may not sum to total as a result of rounding error.
b Includes former USSR.
c Excludes New Zealand.
Source: DTRD 1998.

compete with Qantas in most markets are Cathay Pacific Airways, Air New Zealand and Singapore Airlines. Japan Airlines, Malaysia Airlines, Ansett International, British Airways and Thai International compete with Qantas in approximately half the markets. The remainder compete with Qantas in only a few markets.

In total, the model with the broadest coverage has twenty-one airlines serving twelve markets, although most markets are served by only a few airlines. The model captures at least 93 per cent of the passengers travelling on the route for all routes except the United Kingdom/Ireland and the rest of Europe (Table 8.3). Policy simulation results do not depend on these two markets.

Demand for air travel

Aggregate demand for air travel is influenced by many factors including:

- prices by airline and class of ticket;
- passenger type by price sensitivity, time sensitivity and frequency;
- seasonal demand factors;
- frequency of departures/arrivals;
- time flown;
- number of stops;

Table 8.2 Model market share by airline in travel to and from Australia by
market, based on 1995 data

Airline	Total share %	Home market[a] %	Markets served
Qantas	43.1	43.1	12
Singapore Airlines[b]	8.1	37.7	12
Japan Airlines	5.8	26.2	5
Cathay Pacific Airways	5.7	40.2	8
Air New Zealand	5.2	n.a.	9
United Airlines	4.5	28.3	1
British Airways	4.4	16.4	5
Garuda Indonesia	4.1	34.1	4
Malaysia Airlines	4.0	51.2	7
Ansett Australia	3.8	3.8	6
Thai Airways International	1.7	29.5	4
Korean Air	1.7	34.1	2
All Nippon Airways	1.7	8.7	2
Alitalia	1.2	6.9	3
KLM	1.0	4.5	2
Sempati Air	0.9	10.9	1
Olympic Airways	0.8	5.2	3
EVA Airways	0.8	18.0	2
Lufthansa	0.6	4.5	2
Mandarin	0.6	13.2	1
Lauda Air	0.4	2.5	2
Air China	0.3	15.0	1

Notes:
a British Airways' share was calculated using the United Kingdom/Ireland market. Other
European carriers were calculated using the rest of Europe market.
b To illustrate the contents of the table, consider Singapore Airlines. Singapore Airlines carried
8.1 per cent of the total passengers in and out of Australia and 37.7 per cent of the passengers
who cited Singapore as their origin or ultimate destination. Markets comprise Japan, the
Republic of Korea, Taiwan, China, Hong Kong, Malaysia, Singapore, Indonesia, Thailand,
North America, United Kingdom/Ireland and the rest of Europe.
n.a. = not available.

Source: Productivity Commission estimates based on data from DTRD 1998.

- city of origin and destination; and
- nationality of carrier.

Behavioural parameters for these factors are difficult to estimate. One reason
is that the interests of passengers largely coincide with those of the airlines
for some factors. For example, passengers typically want the shortest flight
with the fewest stops. Airlines that minimise costs subject to hub-and-spoke
cost considerations fly more direct routes with shorter flight times and fewer
stops. Estimation is further complicated by the lack of observed differences

Table 8.3   Model share of total passenger movements by route, based on 1995
data

Between Australia and:	Model coverage %	Airlines serving the market
China	96	11
Hong Kong	98	6
Indonesia	94	5
Japan	98	8
Malaysia	93	5
Korea, Republic of	97	6
Singapore	94	5
Taiwan	98	7
Thailand	97	8
North America	93	5
United Kingdom/Ireland	85	14
Rest of Europe	79	14

Source: Productivity Commission estimates.

in air services by airline and in the prices paid for air services by airline.
Only by observing differences in prices and services can the effect of these
demand factors can be estimated.

Demand in the model can be viewed as a two-step process. Travellers
decide whether to travel to a given destination based on an average, quality-
adjusted price of travel to the destination. They then decide which airline to
fly based on the airlines' relative price and frequency of service. The demand
specification relies on four estimated demand parameters: an aggregate price
elasticity, an aggregate frequency elasticity, an airline substitution elasticity,
and a parameter for each airline's distinct qualities. Parameters for the first
three have been estimated and published in the literature (Brueckner and
Spiller (1994); BTCE (1997); Gillen, Harris and Oum (1997), among others).
The last parameter is estimated as a residual during model calibration. See
PC (1998a) for more detail.

Elasticity estimates were taken from studies of non-Australian markets,
augmented by sensitivity analysis, as no estimates of frequency elasticities or
substitution elasticities were available for Australian markets and existing
price elasticity estimates (BTCE 1997) were considered unreliable. Gillen,
Harris and Oum (1997) reported a median value of 0.1 for estimated frequency
elasticities in studies that attempted to measure responsiveness of aggregate
demand to increases in the frequency of flights. They also found that among
econometric studies the median value of the estimated degree of substitutability
between airlines was two.

Network specification

The physical problem the airline faces is designing a network that moves its passengers from their origins to their destinations. In meeting passenger demand for travel, an airline chooses the following:

- frequency of service between cities on the network;
- number and type of aircraft used;
- scheduling of flights in the network; and
- routing/paths of passenger flows across flight sectors.

But its choice among these factors is limited by:

- airport constraints – for example, rights to gates and landing and take-off slots;
- capacity of aircraft by type;
- distances/flight times between cities on the network;
- input lumpiness in aircraft, other physical capital, personnel and periodic maintenance;
- time taken to on-load and off-load passengers and baggage; and
- ASAs.

The airline's economic problem overlays its physical problem and has a number of aspects. One aspect is to minimise the costs of meeting passenger flows in its network while ensuring its chosen quality of service. A second aspect relates to airline pricing across passenger types and ticket classes for which a range of prices is possible. The fixed costs of the network need not be recovered equally across flights and passengers. Yield management systems, for example, seek to fill planes by offering different fares, conditions and times to different types of passengers.

The model simplified the network specification by developing an aggregated annual version of its pricing and network problem which has a solution that is approximately the same as its actual average annual behaviour. Thus, equations in the model ensure that every airline has sufficient aircraft capacity to carry its passengers and that passengers arrive at their destination and return to their origin. Finally, because an aircraft on a given flight sector can have passengers of different origins and destinations, prices in markets will be linked through the costs of flight sectors that markets share.

Network costs in the model have two components. The first is the flight sector component and comprises the costs incurred in moving passengers along the flight sector. The Commission derived its estimates of flight costs from Aerocost2 (BTCE 1997). The second is an overhead component and includes all administrative expenses and the costs of ticketing, sales, commissions and adjustments for overrides.

Flight sector costs

Flight sector costs are divided into three categories:

- flight-specific costs are incurred no matter how many passengers are carried and include costs such as airport landing and take-off charges, fuel needed for an empty aircraft, flight personnel and aircraft maintenance;
- passenger-specific costs are costs that increase incrementally with the number of passengers (and their baggage) on board – essentially increased fuel costs and provisioning; and
- aircraft capital costs are an imputed hourly charge of the leased aircraft multiplied by the block hours of the flight.[2]

Aerocost2 data (BTCE 1997) indicate that passenger-specific costs on a flight are small relative to total flight costs. Industry confirmed this cost structure. For example, passenger-specific costs for a Boeing 747–400 flying with a 75 per cent load factor from Sydney to Tokyo are approximately 15 per cent of total flight sector costs (including the capital cost of the plane).

Overhead costs

The value of overhead costs was computed as being proportional to the total flight sector costs of the network at observed quantities. This proportion was estimated using the International Civil Aviation Organisation's breakdown of costs into various cost categories with adjustments for freight and the above-average flight distances in the region (PC 1998b). The computation estimated an average overhead charge of A$260 per passenger. The industry provided a range of opinions on this estimate and judged it acceptable for working purposes. Its reasonableness depended in part on how cost items, such as maintenance, are allocated to overhead and flight costs categories, and on which sales commissions are included in the net fare.

Little information is available on how network characteristics affect overheads. Discussions with industry suggested that the size of overheads depends on the number of cities served (e.g. airline city offices), the number of passengers carried on the network (e.g. ticketing and sales costs that are included in net fares) and a general network size (e.g. advertising). The modelling adopts a pragmatic approach by assessing the degree to which models need overheads to increase with the passengers carried to replicate observed quantities and prices.[3]

Omitting overhead costs can have economic welfare implications. If overhead costs were excluded from the model, then the returns covering overheads would be wrongly identified as economic rents rather than as the return necessary to recover costs. Prices that do not cover overhead costs represent a transfer from producers to consumers, and cannot be sustained in the long run. The effect of Ansett's entry on Australian economic welfare depends in part on Ansett's overhead cost because overheads are incurred as a cost of entry.

Airline productivity and costs adjustments

The simplification of the model necessitated some adjustments to costs. For example, neglecting the marginal revenue of freight services implicitly imposes too high a marginal cost on passenger services. The share of freight services revenue in scheduled flight revenue is therefore taken to be an estimate of the adjustment to shared flight costs for the marginal revenue from freight service. Aerocost2 flight-specific costs and capital costs are reduced by 15 per cent to account for the exclusion of freight services (PC 1998b). The industry confirmed that these adjustments lead to ballpark estimates of flight costs for Australian carriers.

The Commission constructed model costs for individual airlines over their flight sectors by applying to Aerocost2 data the differences in airline labour costs and productivity as estimated by Oum and Yu (1995).[4] Aerocost2 data were assumed to be representative of flight costs for the Australian airlines and for Air New Zealand.

Oum and Yu's analysis roughly divides most of the airlines competing with Qantas into four categories:

1   Airlines with the lowest wages, lowest input prices and low productivity include Thai International. This combination leads to higher operating costs but significantly lower overheads than those faced by Qantas.
2   Airlines with lower wages, lower input prices and higher productivity include Singapore Airlines, Cathay Pacific Airways and Korean Air. This combination leads to lower operating costs and overheads than those faced by Qantas.
3   Airlines with higher wages, higher input prices and higher productivity include British Airways and United Airlines. This combination leads to similar operating costs but higher overheads than those faced by Qantas.
4   Airlines with the highest wages, highest input prices and low productivity include Japanese carriers and the other European carriers. This combination leads to significantly higher operating costs and overheads than those faced by Qantas.

Oum and Yu (1995) did not report on all the airlines in the model. Omitted or partly covered airlines were allocated to the categories as follows: Air New Zealand and Ansett International are taken as being as productive as Qantas with similar input and labour prices.[5] Malaysia Airlines, Air China, EVA Air, Sempati Air, and Garuda Indonesia are classified in the first group. Finally, Oum and Yu estimated that Lufthansa and KLM were more productive than Qantas with higher input prices (as in the third group). Their labour prices were taken to be those of Alitalia.

The Commission applied Oum and Yu's estimates of airline productivity and cost differences to flight sectors in the following manner. Airline flight sector costs were adjusted for all the productivity differences that Oum and Yu estimated and only for the differences in labour prices according to labour's share in flight costs. Other flight costs were not adjusted because most other costs, such as navigation charges, landing costs, fuel costs and provisioning costs, will be similar for any airline operating over the same flight sector. Overhead costs, although not included in Oum and Yu's analysis, were adjusted by input price differences to reflect different prices for administration, ticketing, office space and the like.

Oum and Yu's estimates were not entirely accepted by industry analysts. For example, analysts pointed out that some airlines include commissions in revenues and costs while others exclude them. Because airline total efficiency depends on a revenue-share weighted average of freight and passenger service output, the use of revenue estimates constructed from differing revenue definitions will lead to biased estimates of relative efficiencies between airlines. Sensitivity analyses were performed to test whether model conclusions depend on the estimated differences in productivity and in input and labour prices (PC 1998a).

Airline behaviour

The model assumes that airlines behave as price-setting oligopolists.[6] Airlines recognise that non-price characteristics lead one carrier's air travel to be an imperfect substitute for another carrier's air travel. Consequently, they have discretion in setting the price of their services. Their price and network choices affect their competitors and the demand for their competitors' products.

Each airline takes into account the network and prices of its competitors (essentially computing the residual demand for its product) and chooses prices and flight frequencies to maximise its profits.[7] An airline equates its marginal cost to the marginal revenues of its residual demand, leading to price discrimination. For example, a return price from Sydney to Tokyo may differ from a return price from Tokyo to Sydney. Prices differ across airlines because their marginal costs and market power differ. A lower cost airline will charge a higher price than that charged by a higher cost airline if its market power can support it.

Model validation

Validation experiments were conducted for the model with broad coverage and for the model with narrow coverage which was developed for the policy simulations. The former is based on a large number of single market formulations without network interactions. The latter is based on a smaller number of markets with network interactions. Computing limits precluded the construction of a network model with the broad coverage while time did not allow for applying all sensitivity experiments to the smaller network model. However, comparisons of similar sensitivity simulations and the cost sensitivity results discussed below indicate that the results for the broad coverage are consistent with those for the narrower coverage.

Validation experiments were performed to assess the range of underlying parameters and airline behaviour assumptions that lead to valid models – models that replicate observed prices and quantities. This was done for a number of reasons.

- The demand, price and cost data are from separate sources. A validation simulation tests whether the data and modelling framework can be treated together as representative of the industry.
- Unlike the demand and price data, the cost data are not observed in the market. They are Aerocost2 estimates that the Commission transformed to its cost classifications. Industry sources suggest Aerocost2 is correct to within a range of 15 per cent. Validation experiments that vary costs by these amounts test whether the initial assessments of the range of demand parameters and behavioural assumptions for valid models are robust to these changes in costs, and whether the costs are representative at all.
- Oum and Yu's estimated differences in airline productivity and input and labour prices are open to question. Therefore, it is important to determine whether conclusions about the validity of demand parameters and Aerocost2 costs depend on their estimates.
- The frequency and substitution elasticity parameters for the model are not based on estimates for Australian markets. Consequently, it is useful to assess whether the range of values for these parameters found in non-Australian markets lead to valid models in Australian markets.[8]
- Inquiry participants were sceptical of the accuracy of the initial price elasticity estimates. Therefore an experiment using price elasticity estimates for non-Australian markets was conducted.
- Validation experiments exclude from future consideration those parameter values that are not capable of reproducing observed quantities and prices within the modelling framework. Thus, they place bounds on parameter values for sensitivity analysis of policy simulations.

A full discussion of the validation sensitivity simulations is found in PC (1998a). The results are summarised here. The valid price-setting models suggest a substitutability between airlines operating on Australian routes that is nearly twice that of the median estimate for non-Australian routes and a frequency elasticity that is approximately the same as the median estimate for non-Australian routes. Simulations that approximately doubled the aggregate demand price elasticity in a valid model did not require significantly different ranges of substitution and frequency elasticities.

Aerocost2 estimates of flight costs are found to provide reasonable cost estimates within the industry's suggested range of plus or minus 15 per cent.

This placed fairly narrow bounds on the range of substitution and frequency elasticity parameters that lead to valid price-setting models. In addition, the demand and cost results are not overturned when airlines' costs are assumed to be identical. This implies that Oum and Yu's estimates would have to understate grossly the degree of input price and productivity differences among airlines to overturn previous results.

Valid price-setting models leave little or no room for overhead costs to be allocated to passengers as a per unit charge. Instead marginal revenue is set equal to marginal flight sector costs to replicate observed prices and quantities. Overhead costs act as barriers to entry and allow airlines to price above flight marginal costs. The profitability of the airline will then depend on whether the wedge it drives between its operating costs and the price of its service covers the overhead costs of its network. Thus, the valid price-setting model depicts an international air travel market in which market power does not guarantee airlines significant economic rents. Airlines can make profits or losses as market conditions dictate. This is because travellers, after accounting for frequency advantages, view flights offered by the various airlines as highly substitutable.

Modelling economic welfare

The model measures the economic welfare benefits of liberalisation by consumer surplus and airline profits for both domestic and foreign markets. Economic welfare changes in an economy are the sum of changes in consumer surplus arising from the availability of air services in the country and the profits of its national carrier(s). Given that prices are net fares, consumer surplus will include not only the consumer surplus of travellers but also any profits and taxes from the net fares further along the marketing chain.

This is a partial equilibrium analysis, so it does not measure the economy-wide benefits of any increase in tourism that may occur as a result of liberalisation. Airport congestion, pollution and impacts on government revenue and price characteristics of air travel are not addressed. Nor is the spillover effect on freight measured. It is presumed that any capacity increases in response to liberalisation will have a neutral effect on freight profitability, although they will result in more freight being carried.

Two partial equilibrium effects do point to likely economy-wide effects, however. Changes in total passenger travel indicate the direction of change in those air services activities that are needed regardless of the nationality of the airline. For example, all air travel to Australia requires baggage handling, boarding-gate staff, air traffic control and terminal infrastructure. Therefore, the export of aviation services is not limited to exports by the Australian carriers. Increased air travel to Australia will lead to a general increase in the demand for all these services. These increases are not included in the calculations of the economic welfare analysis.

Changes in net tourism to Australia are used as an indicator of the direction of change in profits of industries associated with travel (such as tourism).[9] Net passenger movements are better than inbound visitor movements as an indicator of the effect on tourism services because they account for changes in the numbers of Australians that travel abroad (and not at home).

Estimating effects of new entry

One aim of current Australian policy is to encourage new (Australian) entrants in the air services market. Ansett International has entered a number of Asian markets, but the outstanding question is how Ansett's entry has affected prices, travel and economic welfare in Australia and in the other countries it serves.[10] Model results suggest that Ansett's entry:

- reduced airfares;
- increased passenger flows to Australia; and
- increased Australian and foreign net economic welfare.

Simulation specification

Sensitivity simulations, discussed below, were conducted to test the sensitivity of these results to changes in model assumptions. Model results are found to be generally robust.

Two years, 1995 and 1997, are used for simulating the effects of Ansett's entry. As Ansett's market share increased in a number of markets from 1995 to 1997 (Table 8.4), results for 1995 would tend to understate the effects of Ansett's entry. Total demand also increased in this period.

Simulations are conducted by removing Ansett from the model to estimate what the market would have been like if Ansett had not entered it. Other airlines' cost structures are assumed not to change when Ansett is present, though flight sector costs change to reflect altered network choices.

The effects of Ansett's entry on the market can be placed in three categories: cost, competition and demand. The cost effect of Ansett's entry hinges on Ansett's costs relative to the industry. In the network model, Ansett is likely to have lower costs than the industry because Ansett's direct service is less costly than the indirect service offered by third-country carriers.[11] The competitive effect of Ansett's entry is increased competition in price and frequency. Both cost and competitive pressures should reduce prices and increase frequencies of service. The demand effects relate to product differentiation and the frequency of service offered by the larger number of airlines.

One feature of the demand specification and parameter values in the model is that consumers prefer (with total frequency remaining constant) more frequent service on a few airlines to less frequent service on more airlines.[12] That is, although consumers benefit from the lower prices induced

Table 8.4   Ansett's model market share, 1995 and 1997, and growth in total
passengers, 1995–97 (per cent)

| Market | Ansett's market share | | Growth in passengers 1995–97 |
	1995	1997	
China	13	13	43
Hong Kong	17	18	6
Indonesia	10	14	36
Japan	8	9	6
Malaysia	1	10	22
Korea, Republic of	0[a]	10	43
Taiwan	2	18	19
Total	8	12	18

Notes: Results are computed from base data used in the model; only carriers considered in the
model are included;
a Ansett had minimal Korean market share in 1995 and was not included in the model for
   1995.
Source: Productivity Commission estimates based on DTRD 1998.

by increased competition, they face an offsetting effect of reduced flight
quality through the spreading of frequencies over more airlines. In fact,
increased competition can reduce consumer surplus if no significant increase
in aggregate quantity occurs and dominant airlines reduce their frequency of
flights (PC 1998b).

In addition to the frequency effect, Ansett's entry offers the opportunity
for greater product differentiation. Product differentiation increases observed
aggregate demand by better serving existing demand and tapping into latent
demand.[13] For example, if Ansett introduced a new non-stop service between
two cities then, even though the airfare for travel between them may not
change, observed travel between them would increase because people residing
in or near one of the cities obtain better service.[14] Some existing passengers
fly more frequently. Other people who would not fly indirectly now choose
to fly directly. In this example, however, the source of the increased market
diversity reflects both Ansett's decision to provide the service and governments'
decisions to negotiate it. It is not possible to unravel the two. Consequently,
the following results reflect both. The simulation assumes that Ansett
successfully differentiated its service from those of its competitors.

Results

Ansett's entry is estimated to decrease price and increase quantity in every
market it entered in 1995 and 1997 (Table 8.5). The price and quantity effects
tend to be larger for those markets where Ansett obtained higher market
shares. For example, the least affected markets are where Ansett had little
market share in 1995 – Malaysia, the Republic of Korea and Taiwan. By

Table 8.5 Estimated changes in price and quantity by market from Ansett's entry, 1995 and 1997 (per cent)

Between Australia and:	1995	1997
Prices		
China	-4.1	-4.4
Hong Kong	-7.0	-6.8
Indonesia	-7.4	-7.7
Japan	-3.8	-4.3
Korea, Republic of[a]	0.1	-2.4
Malaysia	-0.9	-4.0
Taiwan	-1.1	-4.3
Quantities		
China	2.3	2.6
Hong Kong	5.3	5.3
Indonesia	1.5	3.4
Japan	2.6	3.0
Korea, Republic of[a]	0.1	0.6
Malaysia	0.8	2.7
Taiwan	1.0	2.7

Note:
a Ansett had minimal Korean market share in 1995, and was not included in the Korean demand for 1995.

Source: Productivity Commission estimates.

1997, however, Ansett had increased its market shares. Its estimated effects on prices and quantities are therefore greater in 1997 than in 1995.

Ansett's entry leads to price increases in the Republic of Korea in 1995 through the effects on its competitors' price and frequency choices. Ansett's entry forces third-country airlines to use smaller aircraft to maintain flight frequency as they lose market share. Smaller aircraft are more expensive to operate over the flight sectors in the model. Therefore prices increase.

The increases in quantity imply an increase in some aviation services in Australia regardless of the nationality of airlines.

Ansett's entry is also estimated to have increased Australian and foreign economic welfare in 1995 and 1997 (Table 8.6). In addition to the increase in economic welfare, Ansett's entry is estimated to have redistributed airline profits to consumer surplus through lower prices.[15] In both years, the resulting economic welfare effect, although substantial, is much smaller than the underlying transfer of profit to consumer surplus.

Ansett's entry increases consumer surplus for both Australian and foreign consumers in every country except for the Republic of Korea in 1995 (Table 8.7). The Korean market in 1995 experiences a price increase which reduces Korean consumer surplus. For Australian consumers, the major gains are achieved in Hong Kong and Indonesia in both 1995 and 1997. For foreign

Table 8.6   Estimated changes in Australian and foreign gross profits, consumer surplus and economic welfare from Ansett's entry, 1995 and 1997 (A$m)

	1995	1997
Australian		
Profits (gross)	-41.6	-57.5
Consumer surplus	70.0	89.9
Economic welfare	28.4	32.4
Foreign		
Profits (gross)	-75.9	-121.8
Consumer surplus	88.3	153.5
Economic welfare	12.4	31.7

Source: Productivity Commission estimates.

consumers, the gains are largest in Japan, although Japan's gains are not nearly as big a share of the increase in foreign consumer surplus in 1997 as in 1995.

Projected changes in net passenger movements can be examined to gain a sense of the likely impact of Ansett's entry on the demand for tourism services in Australia (Table 8.8). Ansett's entry leads to larger positive net passenger movements or smaller (in absolute value) negative net passenger movements for four of the countries (Japan, the Republic of Korea, Malaysia and Taiwan) in 1995 and for all countries except China in 1997. The changes in net passenger movements tend to reflect price reductions from Ansett's entry. That is, if net passenger movements are positive (more inbound visitors than outbound residents), then Ansett's entry leads to a bigger positive net passenger movement and consequently a percentage increase in net passenger movements. The negative net passenger movements for China, Hong Kong and Indonesia in 1995 reflect a tilt in Ansett's passengers towards outbound resident movements that is greater than that for the industry. Total net passenger movements are estimated to increase by 2 per cent.

The increase in total net passenger movements is larger in 1997 (3.7 per cent) than in 1995 (2 per cent). This is because the estimated price effects for Malaysia, the Republic of Korea and Taiwan are larger in 1997 than in 1995, leading to a larger increase in net passenger movements in both absolute number and percentage.

Despite their large percentage changes in 1997, changes in net passenger movements for China and Hong Kong make only a small contribution to total net passenger movements. Indonesia and Japan are the most important markets in determining total net passenger flows. The results for China and Hong Kong reflect the balance in the market between the Australian resident and foreign visitor flows, leading to a small base value for net passenger movements. Thus, even though the price reductions from Ansett's entry induce

Table 8.7   Estimated changes in Australian and foreign consumer surplus from Ansett's entry by market, 1995 and 1997 (A$m)

Between Australia and:	1995	1997
Australian consumer surplus		
China	5.5	7.6
Hong Kong	24.2	23.3
Indonesia	36.3	44.6
Japan	3.5	4.6
Korea, Republic of[a]	0.0	1.3
Malaysia	0.5	7.1
Taiwan	0.0	1.4
Total	70.0	89.9
Foreign consumer surplus		
China	3.5	5.4
Hong Kong	16.8	19.5
Indonesia	0.2	10.4
Japan	65.2	79.2
Korea, Republic of[a]	-0.6	11.6
Malaysia	0.9	9.0
Taiwan	2.3	18.4
Total	88.3	153.5

Note:

a Ansett had minimal Korean market share in 1995. It was not included in the Korean demand for 1995.

Source: Productivity Commission estimates.

a small change in net passenger movements and a small contribution to total net passenger movements, the percentage changes in net passenger movements are large.

PLURILATERAL REFORM

The network model has also been used to explore how freeing up airline networks and competition in an open club could affect the economic welfare of club members.

It illustrates the possible benefits and costs of an open club among Australia, China, Hong Kong and Japan. Under the open club scenario, the airlines of these countries are assumed to be able to choose to fly directly between the member countries or set up hub-and-spoke networks anywhere within the club. Consequently, airlines of the open club members would be able to enter any market within the club and construct networks on the basis of market fundamentals with only those restrictions imposed by the capacity and freedom dictates of ASAs with non-member countries.

Because of limitations to the model, data and scenarios, simulation results are illustrations, not predictions, of how the economic forces unleashed by an open club agreement could transform international air travel markets

Table 8.8   Estimated changes in net passenger movements to and from Australia
from Ansett's entry, 1995 and 1997 (per cent)

Between Australia and:	1995	1997
China	-3.1	-47.0
Hong Kong	-7.1	92.8
Indonesia	-2.4	5.2
Japan	2.7	2.9
Korea, Republic of[a]	0.1	0.4
Malaysia	1.4	2.3
Taiwan	1.2	2.7
Total	2.0	3.7

Notes: Net passenger movements are inbound visitor movements minus outbound resident
movements.
a Ansett had minimal Korean market share in 1995. It was not included in Korean demand
for 1995.

Source: Productivity Commission estimates.

inside and outside the open club. The results illustrate that open clubs that
allow airlines to achieve efficiency gains and to construct their most profitable
networks increase the economic welfare of club members. A key to the
model is that all airlines in the open club are assumed to attain a benchmark
level of efficiency as estimated by Oum and Yu (1995).[16] The assumed increase
in efficiency is due to competitive pressures within the club. No incumbent
airline exits any market.

The Commission's modelling examined three scenarios. Under the first,
the airlines of the countries in the open club are freed from restrictions on
their operations and allowed to achieve the benchmark productivity of the
most efficient carrier (for example, Ansett is able to achieve Cathay Pacific's
productivity). In the second scenario, airlines of club members become free
to fly wherever they like within the club, and to enter new markets previously
denied them under the bilateral system (for example, China Air could enter
the Tokyo–Sydney market). Under the third scenario, the two effects are
considered together. In other words, airlines of member countries improve
productivity and are allowed to enter new markets and establish new networks.

Model results for this scenario produce an increase in economic welfare
over the other scenarios because of more efficient and flexible networks,
increased competitive pressure and increased consumer benefits. However,
the non-club economies suffer net reductions in economic welfare.

These model results illustrate the economic forces which could be unleashed
in an open club of countries with a common open skies agreement. The
bigger the club, the bigger the benefits for members and the greater the
disadvantages faced by non-members.

Network effects in open clubs and modelled scenarios

Current ASAs place constraints on airline networks. Open clubs release club members from these constraints inside the club and can tangentially affect markets for travel to non-member countries. Model simulations explicitly consider the two likely network effects of open clubs:

- open club airlines become more efficient; and
- open club airlines can enter all open club markets and fly directly between any two foreign countries in the club.

Less efficient airlines in an open club are forced to lift their game or leave club markets. More efficient airlines will face greater competition as other airlines improve their efficiency. Incentives to improve efficiency will increase because profit opportunities are enhanced for any airline that improves its efficiency or carves out a larger slice of the market. Finally, improvements in network management may spill over from open club markets to all markets in the airline's network.

The *airline efficiency gains* effect is modelled as follows. All airlines in the open club are assumed to attain a benchmark level of efficiency as estimated by Oum and Yu (1995). The assumed increase in efficiency is due to competitive pressures within the club. No incumbent airline exits any market.

Under current ASAs, airlines of open club members must fly through their home country or obtain fifth freedom permission in order to fly passengers from one foreign country to another. Under the open club, they can choose to fly directly between the foreign countries in the club, or set up hub-and-spoke networks with hubs in other member countries to fly passengers between any two spoke countries within the club. Consequently, airlines of open club members will be able to enter any market within the club and construct networks on the basis of market fundamentals with only those restrictions imposed by the capacity and freedom dictates of ASAs with non-member countries.

Market entry with direct flights is modelled as follows. Club airlines can fly direct flights between any two countries in the open club. They can also enter markets for travel between other club members (Japanese carriers can enter the Australia–Hong Kong and Australia–China markets and Chinese carriers can enter the Australia–Japan market). Each entrant is assumed to add 5 per cent to the size of the market.[17] It does this by tapping into latent demand for travel, for example by providing better connections or departure times than incumbents provide. No incumbent airline exits any market.

The effects are used in three scenarios:

- Scenario A applies efficiency gains and market entry with direct flights between foreign countries;

- Scenario B applies efficiency gains only; and
- Scenario C applies market entry with direct flights between foreign countries.

Scenario A reflects that, by freeing airlines to form their most profitable networks, open clubs will unleash many effects. The final two scenarios allow the respective economic effects to be separated.

The choice of club members is illustrative and not based on any expectations by the Commission of the likelihood of any of the countries entering into such a club. The simulations assume the following club, country, market and airline coverage:

- open club members are Australia, China, Hong Kong and Japan;
- country, market and airline coverage is that for the Ansett simulations (markets for travel between Australia and China, Hong Kong, Indonesia, Japan, the Republic of Korea, Malaysia and Taiwan); and
- the club airlines are Ansett, Qantas, China Airlines, China Southern Airlines, China Eastern Airlines, Cathay Pacific, Japan Airlines and All Nippon Airlines.

Club membership was chosen because the distances between China, Hong Kong and Japan allow hub-and-spoke networks to be set up by all club members in any of the countries. In addition, aircraft can fly one long sector from Australia and be turned around to fly a short sector in the northern part of the club within a day, arriving at the final destination at a convenient hour for travellers and within airport curfew times. The latter feature increases aircraft utilisation and the revenue each aircraft can generate in a day. Without the club, aircraft arriving from Australia may have to sit for an extended period at a foreign port to obtain desirable departure and arrival times before returning to Australia.

Limitations of open club scenarios and their implications

Three limitations of the open club scenarios bear specific mention:

- Oum and Yu's efficiency estimates are representative of uniform differences in efficiency between networks;
- assumptions are made in the scenarios regarding airline entry, exit and product differentiation; and
- markets are limited to those involving travel to and from Australia.

The limitations have important consequences for the interpretation of results.

Efficiency estimates

Oum and Yu (1995) formulate their efficiency estimates by constructing indexes of inputs and outputs for each airline. The output index is calculated using a revenue-weighted average of each airline's passenger and freight service output adjusted for average stage length. If these adjustments aggregate outputs correctly, then the estimated efficiency differences are attributable to the relative ability of airline management to produce output with the least amount of inputs.

Three reservations must be stated. First, even if Oum and Yu's methodology and interpretations of efficiency are correct, the estimates are only as good as the data used and the data's comparability across airlines. ICAO data were the primary source of industry information for Oum and Yu. As noted by the industry, airlines use different accounting definitions which may undermine the comparability of ICAO data across airlines. Second, their aggregation of airline output may have deficiencies. For example, other output characteristics, such as the number of cities served or the frequency of service, are omitted (Kirby 1986). The omissions would bias efficiency estimates favourably toward airlines that have lower frequencies of service and serve fewer cities because both characteristics increase network costs for the same number of passengers carried in a network. Third, Oum and Yu did not estimate efficiency and input prices for the Chinese airlines. Chinese airlines' efficiencies and input prices are assumed to be those estimated for Thai Airways.

If Oum and Yu's estimation and interpretation of efficiency differences are reasonably correct and Thai Airways' costs and efficiency are representative of those for Chinese airlines, then Scenario B offers insights into the direction of change that efficiency improvements will push the industry. However, given the above reservations, a more conservative interpretation is that they are a specific formulation of the general effects discussed above and thus illustrate those general effects for a special case.

Entry, exit and product differentiation

The directions of change in airline profits, consumer welfare and, therefore, economic welfare by country depend on the assumption that no airline exits the market.

Under the efficiency gains scenario, the assumption of no exit implies that all airlines improve their efficiency. When all airlines improve to the benchmark, the benchmark airline suffers reductions in profits, because by assumption it is the benchmark. In contrast, the inefficient airlines enjoy increases in profits, because by assumption they improve to the benchmark, competing more vigorously against their erstwhile more efficient competitor.

An alternative and no less plausible assumption is that open club airlines achieve the benchmark efficiency because efficient airlines force inefficient airlines to exit the market. The opposite effect on airline profits would be observed in this case: efficient airlines increase their profits as they dominate markets and inefficient airlines suffer reductions in profits as they lose market share or exit the market.

In the context of direct flights with market entry, the assumptions of no exit and of a modest increase in product diversity imply an unknown a priori net effect on consumer surplus that depends on three factors. First, an assumed entry with no exit of incumbent airlines increases the number of airlines serving a market. Prices can be expected to decrease from the increase in competitors. Second, new entrants on routes are also assumed to add modestly to product diversity, increasing consumer surplus. However, the modest increase also limits their ability to compete effectively in the market. Finally, entry confronts the consumer preference for more frequent service on fewer airlines. The net effect on consumer surplus is only known after the simulation is completed.

In reality, the industry has indicated that a significant market presence is crucial to compete effectively. Obtaining a minimum market presence may not be an optimal strategy. Instead the optimal strategy may be attaining a large market presence. In this case, the product diversity that taps into latent demand may also take customers from incumbents. A long-run outcome may see one or more airlines exit the market.

Travel to and from Australia

Because of data limitations,[18] the model does not explicitly account for markets between non-Australian club members (e.g. the market for travel between Hong Kong and Japan). Consequently, the simulation cannot provide estimates of the total economic welfare effects of the open club. In particular, its estimates omit:

- increases in Australian airline profits and Australian economic welfare from Australian airlines' entry into completely foreign markets;
- decreases in foreign airline profits from Australian airlines' entry into completely foreign markets; and
- increases in foreign consumer surplus in travel between two foreign countries from Australian airlines' entry into those markets.

Implications

Given the limitations of the model and the modelled scenarios as described above, the most reliable estimates of changes in profits, consumer surplus and economic welfare are for open club members in total; they are reported here. Individual country estimates are not reliable and depend strongly on scenario assumptions; they are not reported.

For example, the use of the efficiency estimates and the assumptions of airline entry and exit imply that model results for changes in profits by airline are direct consequences of scenario assumptions and not consequences of any underlying economic behaviour in the model. Therefore, estimated changes in profits by airline in markets for travel to and from Australia have little descriptive worth. They are even less appropriate as estimates of changes in profits by airline for all markets in the open club because, as noted above, the exclusion of completely foreign markets omits likely increases in profits for Australian airlines and likely reductions in profits for foreign airlines. However, the estimated changes in profit for all airlines in club countries are more reliable and relevant because they do not imply specific winners and losers. They estimate the total effect on profits across all airlines, reflecting the net change in profits among airlines.

Results for Australian markets

The net economic welfare gains in all three scenarios show a large gain for club members and a small loss for non-club countries (Table 8.9). The principal reasons for the results can be traced to the modelled effects of open clubs:

- As club airlines' productivity improves, their costs fall and they compete more vigorously against other airlines by cutting their prices or increasing the frequency of their services.
- Freed from the constraints of current ASAs, all club airlines redesign their networks to serve better their markets to and from Australia. In doing so they can offer both direct flights and indirect flights in a hub-and-spoke system. Direct flights keep costs down, while the hub-and-spoke system increases frequency of service.
- Market entry by club airlines on routes increases competition because it is assumed that no incumbent airlines leave. The competitive pressures of entrants increase with their size because large entrants compete more strongly against incumbents in frequency and ticket prices.

Scenario A combines all these effects. Scenario B isolates the first effect. Scenario C isolates the second and third effects. But there are some important interactions between the three effects, so that the results of Scenario A are not simply the sum of results for Scenarios B and C. The separate impacts of Scenarios B and C are discussed first before their combined impact in Scenario A is analysed.

Scenario B results

Scenario B shows that the man beneficiaries of efficiency improvements are consumers (Table 8.9). The consumer surplus gains in club countries are nearly ten times the size of the increased club airline profits. In non-club countries, consumer surplus increases while the profits of non-club airlines fall. In addition, the fall in profits for all airlines (club and non-club combined) suggests that efficiency gains are passed on to consumers, while airlines that improve their efficiency take profits from their rivals.

Efficiency gains are passed on to consumers through lower prices and increased flight frequencies. Consumer surplus increases in both club and non-club countries as a result. Prices in non-club markets fall because club airlines become more efficient in all their markets, and they lower prices to passengers flying to non-club destinations. Examples of this could be more efficient uses of aircraft in club and non-club countries. In addition, the competitive lessons learned in open club competition can be applied in non-club markets too. These lessons could be in the areas of network design, fleet usage and marketing, among others.

Airlines that become relatively more efficient (all club airlines except the benchmark) gain at the expense of those that become relatively less efficient (non-club airlines and the benchmark). Consequently club airlines' profits increase in total, while non-club airlines' profits fall. Competitive forces compel club airlines to pass on some of these cost savings to consumers through lower prices. This would create pressures for non-club airlines to either join the club, improve their efficiency or scale back their presence in markets served by club airlines.

Scenario C results

In Scenario C, the assumed increases in the number of airlines competing on routes between club members lead to price reductions in most club markets, profit declines for club and non-club airlines, and consumer surplus and economic welfare gains in club countries.

The price falls in Scenario C are driven by increased competition in the markets that club airlines enter and by their ability to cut costs by flying passengers directly to their final destinations. Club airline profits fall in Scenario C mainly as a result of the price falls. Non-club airline profits fall because they are unable to modify their networks to reduce costs while club airlines enter markets and restructure their networks.

Consumer surplus increases in open club countries because prices fall, frequency increases and the number of airlines connecting some club countries to Australia rises. Consumer gains in club countries are more than twice as large as profit losses. Economic welfare increases as a result.

Non-club consumer surplus declines marginally. This result is not surprising since non-club flights remain constrained and cannot benefit from the open club's improved network design or greater competition. In fact, the increase in direct flights by some club airlines out of Australia reduces the number of flights in some airlines' hub-and-spoke networks. This reduces their frequency of service to non-club destinations and adversely affects the consumer surplus of those non-club countries.

Scenario A results

The results of Scenario A are best explained as the efficiency gains of Scenario B compounding the competitive and network effects of Scenario C – improving productivity enhances the competition of freer networks. In particular, Scenario A shows:

- greater profit declines in moving from Scenario C to Scenario A come mostly at the expense of airlines in non-club countries (an A$8 million

Table 8.9 Estimates of changes in net economic welfare from various open club scenarios (A$m)

	Scenario A *Efficiency gains plus direct flights and market entry by club airlines on routes to and from Australia* *1997*	Scenario B *Efficiency gains* *1997*	Scenario C *Direct flights and market entry by club airlines on routes to and from Australia* *1997*
Club members[a]			
Profit (gross)	-38.4	15.6	-30.4
Consumer surplus	291.6	152.1	73.2
Economic welfare	253.2	167.6	42.8
Non–club members			
Profit (gross)	-29.7	-24.7	-4.3
Consumer surplus	23.4	24.3	-0.3
Economic welfare	-6.3	-0.4	-4.6

Notes: Estimates exclude economic welfare effects in markets between non-Australian countries in the club. These could not be estimated due to the lack of data on prices and passenger flows (by origin–destination and airline) between non-Australian countries in the club. Markets covered are between Australia and: China, Japan, Hong Kong, Malaysia, Republic of Korea, Taiwan and Indonesia.

a Club countries are Australia, China, Hong Kong and Japan. Club airlines are Ansett, Qantas, China Airlines, China Southern Airlines, China Eastern Airlines, Cathay Pacific, Japan Airlines and All Nippon Airlines.

Source: Productivity Commission estimates.

reduction in club profits compared to a A$25 million reduction in non-club profits); and

- more vigorous competition increases consumer welfare by approximately 20 per cent more than the sum of Scenarios B and C would suggest.

In addition, the combined effects of efficiency gains and direct flights with market entry lead to considerable gains in club member consumer surplus and economic welfare with, by comparison, small changes in club airline profits. For non-members there is a net economic welfare loss, despite the spillover efficiency benefits from open club airlines, because non-club airlines lose competitiveness to club airlines.

The gains in club members' consumer surplus are because the three open club effects have increased the vigour of competition, resulting in prices being pushed down.

The combined effects of productivity improvements, network design changes and market entry have a compound, rather than additive, effect on the degree of competition within the club. Within the club, new entrants compete with incumbents on price, frequency and cost, raising the level of competition above that in Scenarios B and C. Unlike in Scenario B, incumbents cannot afford to retain some of the benefits of the productivity improvement, because new entrants can undercut them by charging prices that are closer to reduced costs faced by club airlines. These price effects are reflected in the consumer surplus and profit results across the three scenarios.

The deep price cuts within the club in Scenario A result in open club consumer surplus rising substantially. For club countries the increase in consumer surplus is greater than the sum of consumer surplus gains in Scenarios B and C.

Non-club consumer surplus increases as club airlines' productivity gains and frequency increases spill over into their non-club operations. Because there is no entry to these markets, the effects of Scenario A are approximately the sum of those for Scenarios B and C.

In Scenario A, club airlines sustain a net fall in the profits on their operations to and from Australia, which is a result of these price falls. Consumers benefit from lower prices, increased frequency and greater choice. This result indicates that most of the benefits from the efficiency gains and improved network designs are passed on to passengers. The change in the net economic welfare of club countries is strongly positive because the gains in consumer surplus more than offset the combined profit declines of the eight club airlines.

Non-club countries suffer a small loss in their economic welfare as a result of the open club. This is because the profit decreases suffered by their airlines are greater than the gains in consumer surplus by non-club residents. Both effects are driven by the price falls to non-club destinations.

Network design changes as a result of the open club

Simulations A and C show that club airlines create new networks which utilise direct flights and hub-and-spoke systems. These new network designs permit airlines to fly lower cost direct flights from a club member, while increasing frequency of service via a hub-and-spoke system. These changes are illustrated for Ansett, Cathay Pacific and Qantas (Table 8.10). Scenario B reflects the old network constraints which prevent Ansett and Qantas using Hong Kong as a hub and Cathay from flying its passengers directly to Japan from Australia.

Table 8.10 shows the network changes in both Scenarios A and C are:

- Cathay Pacific chooses to fly most of its Australia–Japan passengers directly, rather than flying all of them through its Hong Kong hub. It continues to fly the remainder of these passengers via Hong Kong.
- Ansett switches to using Hong Kong as hub for all its China-bound passengers, who are flown to Hong Kong then transferred on to smaller aircraft for the flight to China.
- Qantas continues to fly the vast majority of its open club passengers directly to their destinations from Australia. However, it too finds Hong

Table 8.10 Shares of passengers flying from Australia to selected open club destinations using direct and indirect routes, selected club airlines (per cent)

Passengers by airline and origin–destination	Scenario A		Scenario B		Scenario C	
	Direct route	Indirect route	Direct route	Indirect route	Direct route	Indirect route
Cathay Pacific						
Australia to Japan	58	42	0	100	63	37
Australia to China	0	100	0	100	0	100
Ansett						
Australia to Japan	100	0	100	0	100	0
Australia to China	0	100	100	0	0	100
Qantas						
Australia to Japan	100	0	100	0	100	0
Australia to China	94	6	100	0	94	6

Source: Productivity Commission estimates.

Kong a useful hub for marginally increasing the frequency of its services to China, thereby giving it a competitive advantage.

The unconstrained networks of the open club allow airlines to construct networks that provide better services in both price and quality terms. As the sectors that club airlines are allowed to fly increase, the airlines are able to increase flight frequency by establishing hub-and-spoke networks to service passengers flying between club countries. The model results show that Hong Kong is preferred as a hub over Beijing and Tokyo. Club airlines weigh up the cost savings from lower cost direct flights against the competitive benefits of greater frequency to many of their destinations by using Hong Kong as a hub. Airlines choosing to set up hub-and-spoke systems also incur marginally higher costs as they trade off higher costs from operating smaller aircraft on some flight sectors serving a hub against the competitive advantages of increased frequency.

CONCLUSION

This model was constructed to provide some measure of the economic welfare effects of anticompetitive restrictions in international air services arrangements. It showed clearly that the interests of the community and those of airlines do not necessarily coincide, as consumer benefits from lower prices can also reduce airline profits. Yet the stance of much international aviation policy has been directed to supporting national airlines rather consumers and user industries such as tourism.

Analysis such as that provided through this model helps to illustrate the costs and benefits of alternative policy arrangements. This model was developed quickly to provide analysis for an inquiry into Australian international aviation policy. Data were limited to Australian routes and passengers. Despite these limitations, the approach appears to be a useful one for analysing policy change by a single country or many.

Extending the model to include other countries' routes and passenger data, and refining airline cost, revenue and productivity information, could provide a useful tool for future international aviation policy analysis.

NOTES

This article is based on work conducted by the authors at the Australian Government's Productivity Commission as part of an inquiry into international air services policy. Much of the text is drawn from that report or from an associated technical paper. The authors' views do not necessarily represent the views of the Australian Government. The inquiry report is available from the Australian Government Publishing Service or on the Commission's Web site at <http://www.pc.gov.au/inquiry/aviation/index.html>.

1   See PC 1998a, pp. 234–9 for a thorough discussion of the concept of an open club.
2   The block hours of a flight denote the time elapsed from the aircraft leaving the departure gate to arrival at the arrival gate. Aerocost2 employs annual block hour use data in computing the hourly charge of the lease. Annual block hour use is representative of observed usage for each aircraft type operating in Australia. It is a consequence of network design and may be affected by changes in ASAs. Such changes would be incorporated in model simulations as a change in airline productivity rather than as a reduction in the hourly charge.
3   For example, one industry source suggested an imputation of a share of overhead as a charge per revenue passenger kilometre. Unfortunately, time did not permit constructing a model and performing the relevant simulations with this overhead assumption.
4   The study by Oum and Yu (1995) is the most comprehensive and up-to-date study available on different airline networks' productivity levels, input prices and competitiveness.
5   One industry analyst suggested that Air New Zealand had significantly lower labour costs.
6   Other behavioural assumptions were tested and rejected (PC 1998b).
7   Equilibrium is the point at which the choices airlines assume for their competitors are consistent with the choices their competitors make (PC 1998b).
8   Qantas also warned that using elasticities for countries other than Australia could produce misleading results.
9   Net passenger movements are inbound visitor movements minus outbound resident movements. A positive projected change means that inbound visitor passenger movements grew by more than outbound resident passenger movements. When net passenger movements are negative (more Australian outbound traffic than foreign inbound traffic), a positive projected change means the difference grew smaller. When net passenger movements are positive, a positive projected change means the difference grew larger.

10 This study does not account for recent changes to Ansett's network as a result of the Asian economic crisis.

11 Results reported in Productivity Commission (1998b) did not have a large cost effect, because the model was based on the single market models described above. Results reported here rely on the network model and therefore differ from those in the draft report.

12 For example, passengers who miss flights can board the next flight offered by the same airline without undue delay. Similarly, time-conscious business travellers can travel on the same airline at times that allow them to coordinate with appointments at their destination and return to their origin without undue delays.

13 Latent demand is demand that would otherwise not be served. Incumbents' airlines have incentives to create product diversity but only if it increases current profits. In contrast, entrants have enhanced incentives to create product diversity precisely because it takes profits away from incumbents.

14 Lederer (1993) represents this as a reduction in the total cost of travel which includes, for example, the passenger's valuation of time in travel, possible delays and the convenience of a non-stop flight.

15 These results are presented in an aggregated manner to protect detailed confidential data provided by airlines.

16 Oum and Yu (1995) estimated that Cathay Pacific is the most efficient airline among the open club airlines.

17 Five per cent was chosen for illustrative purposes. It is less than one half that observed for Ansett in its smallest market. Thus it represents a minimum market penetration that entrants would aim to achieve. Nevertheless, the Commission stresses that this is an assumption only and the results flowing from it are illustrative, not forecasts. A greater or lesser level of additional traffic could be assumed, thereby affecting the magnitude but not the direction of the results.

18 For example, for non-Australian routes there were no price data or passenger origin–destination data as found in Avstats.

9 Regulatory reform in the maritime industry

Jong-Soon Kang and Christopher Findlay

INTRODUCTION

Shipping is the major mode of supply for world exports and imports. Efficient and competitive international maritime transport services (MTS) are therefore vital for a productive world economy. Policies or practices restricting competition and inflating the costs of international MTS or reducing the quality of services can therefore have a significant impact on the world economy and could seriously undermine the economy-wide gains from broader microeconomic reform and trade liberalisation.[1]

Restrictions on MTS are also important in the context of international commitments to liberalise trade in services. The negotiating group on maritime transport services (NGMTS) within the World Trade Organisation (WTO) aims to establish a multilateral framework of principles and rules for trade in services, with a view to expansion of such trade under conditions of transparency and progressive liberalisation. Since the outset of the Uruguay Round negotiations on MTS in September 1986, there have been continuous efforts to deliver a consensus about the global maritime order and shipping policies between the major maritime nations and among global economic organisations like the WTO, the United Nations Conference on Trade and Development (UNCTAD) and the Organisation for Economic Cooperation and Development (OECD). Regardless of increasing pressure for liberalisation, these efforts failed to devise a more liberal trading system or even to gain an acceptance of the relevance of the General Agreement on Trade in Services (GATS) principles. The most recent talks were the negotiations on MTS within the WTO (WTO/NGMTS) in July 1996. However, this set of multilateral negotiations was again suspended after some progress, but there was a failure in delivering a schedule on specific commitments. These negotiations started again in 2000.

Some reasons for the difficulties in reaching consensus include: private interests affected by the new system; national perceptions of carrier interests and the extent to which gains are more likely under bilateralism; constraints imposed by accepting the roles of existing institutional structures; and an unwillingness to permit foreign establishments or firms in domestic markets or routes (Choi et al. 1997).

This chapter discusses aspects of the regulatory scheme in MTS and the future prospects for liberalisation in the international MTS industry, focusing on liner shipping services.

MARITIME TRADE AND THE CURRENT REGULATORY SCHEME

World maritime trade volumes grew at an average annual rate of 3.6 per cent, from 2.6 billion to 3.7 billion tonnes, for the 1970–80 period (Table 9.1). In the 1980s, however, the figure slowed to an average rate of 0.8 per cent a year. Momentum was regained in the 1990s, attaining an average annual growth rate of 3.1 per cent between 1990 and 1997. In 1997 total cargo reached 4.95 billion tonnes, recording its twelfth consecutive annual increase. Total cargo shipment grew slightly in 1998 and is estimated to have reached only just above 5 billion tonnes, due mainly to sluggish trade in tanker cargoes (UNCTAD 1998b).

The international cargo shipping operation can be split into two types: liner and non-liner shipping. The liner fleet includes container, conventional, roll-on/off and multi-purpose vessels, among which container vessels are the main type. Non-liner vessels are predominantly specialised bulk carriers, including tankers and most dry (and/or liquid) bulk carriers. While liner shipping provides scheduled services to set timetables, non-liner shipping tends to supply specialised services under contract.

Non-liner carriers dominate in terms of trade volumes, as major commodities carried under contract include grains and minerals such as coal, iron ore and steel. Table 9.1 shows that tanker cargo, such as crude oil and petroleum products, currently represents above 40 per cent of the world's total volume of shipments, though its share is continuing to decline from the more than 50 per cent level in the 1970s and early 1980s. In the case of dry cargo, its share continued to grow, from about 45 per cent in the 1970s to 57 per cent in the 1990s. While the 'main bulk' share of dry cargo has dropped since the mid-1980s, accounting now for around 23.5 per cent, that of other dry cargo has gradually increased since the 1970s. This growing importance of dry cargo in maritime transportation could be mainly attributable to the significant expansion of general/utilised cargo trade, which moved mainly on liner trade routes (UNCTAD 1998).

While non-liner tankers and bulk carriers dominate in terms of trade volumes, liners are far more significant in value terms because they tend to carry relatively high-value and low-volume cargoes. World liner shipments of containerised cargoes have continued to expand. Total liner shipments were estimated to have increased by 7.7 per cent in 1997 over the previous year and to have expanded further, by 3–4 per cent, in 1998 (UNCTAD 1998b).

Table 9.1 International maritime trade volumes, selected years
(million tonnes loaded; per cent in parentheses)

| | Tanker cargo | Dry cargo | | Total |
		Main bulk[a]	Other cargo	
1970	1,440 (55.3)	448 (17.2)	717 (27.5)	2,605
1975	1,644 (53.5)	635 (20.7)	790 (25.7)	3,072
1980	1,871 (50.5)	796 (21.5)	1,037 (28.0)	3,704
1985	1,495 (44.2)	857 (25.3)	1,066 (31.5)	3,382
1990	1,755 (43.8)	968 (24.2)	1,285 (32.1)	4,008
1995	2,049 (44.1)	1,082 (23.3)	1,520 (32.7)	4,651
1997	2,172 (43.9)	1,157 (23.4)	1,624 (32.8)	4,953
1998[b]	2,181 (43.1)	1,200 (23.7)	1,684 (33.3)	5,064

Notes:
a Grain, iron ore, coal, bauxite/alumina and phosphate.
b Estimates only.

Source: UNCTAD 1998b.

Regardless of the rapid development in liner shipping services, however, international competition in these services has been regulated for over a century through international cartels, which are known as 'conferences', even though there are also non-conference liners, including individual operators and consortia.[2] This form of cartel is protected from competition laws in most economies which would otherwise make it illegal.[3] While conference arrangements provide members with an opportunity to reduce costs and shippers also benefit from such arrangements, this has been the main regulatory scheme in the world liner shipping industry.

In addition to conferences, a number of other instruments of a regulatory or promotional nature at the international or national level have shaped the function of liner shipping. Even though promotional policies are of considerable importance and tend to distort competition, regulatory policies even more directly affect market mechanisms and structures. The basic reasons for regulating shipping services are to restrain the concentration of power in shipping conferences or other forms of alliance, on the one hand, and to protect national interests from international competition, on the other. Policies or practices which have had a significant impact on competition in international shipping services include the UN Liner Code, bilateral agreements on access to cargo, and national policies of financial support and non-financial measures for domestic industries.

Shipping conferences

Shipping conferences represent one of the oldest forms of cartel in the world and have been a feature of international liner shipping for well over a century, with the first operating on the route between the United Kingdom and Calcutta in 1875 (Frank and Bunel 1991). There are currently approximately 300 conferences operating worldwide, each of which tends to limit its activities to one leg of a particular route or trade between two or more countries. Most conferences have fewer than 10 members, although there are some with as many as 50. Shipping companies are often members of several conferences (Yong 1996).

Conferences differ from other cooperative arrangements, such as alliances, in that their agreements take a variety of forms but commonly involve collusion to set prices and limit competition among members. The conference members jointly set a schedule of freight rates, which then applies to all members. They also set the maximum frequency of sailings by each company along what was usually a multiport route (Dick 1996). There are basically two types of conferences: closed and open.

Closed conferences are traditional forms of shipping cartels, not only setting freight rates but also allocating cargo quotas and restricting membership (Frank and Bunel 1991).[4] New entry to any line was also vigorously blockaded or opposed under this scheme. Occasionally there was an attempt by a shipping organisation to run as a non-conference line, which also was usually stoutly resisted in order to deter other such initiatives (Dick 1996). By controlling total capacity and allocating it among members, closed conferences may avoid the problem of excessive service competition and excess capacity. Even if able to find the lowest average cost for a supply arrangement, they may not necessarily provide the incentives for members to meet consumer demand in the most efficient way. Closed conferences are banned in the United States but allowed in most other economies. A prime example of this type includes the Far Eastern Freight Conference, in which the UK and European liners are major players.

Open conferences set the freight rates on a route but do not allocate cargo shares among members. There are no entry and exit barriers in this type of conference. As members are operating under common carriage rules, rates are the same for a given service type to all shippers (Butz 1993). The conference normally sets prices above costs. Given the inflexibility of freight rates to allocate market shares, members generally compete in terms of service quality, which may in turn result in excessive service competition.[5]

Conferences have been the subject of many reviews throughout the world since the beginning of the 1900s, and there are many different views on their economic effects and public interests. In the first major review, the British Royal Commission on Shipping Rings, commissioned in 1906, did not reach a consensus and majority and minority reports were released (PSA 1993).

The pro-conference argument is that, by coordinating capacity, setting stable prices and limiting competition between members, conferences can offer at the lowest average cost the types of services that shippers demand.[6] Shipping conferences may have ensured the stable supply of MTS by preventing unexpected fluctuations in freight rates due to changes in consumer demand. It is also clear that conferences generate benefits for members in terms of higher profits, compared with independent operations. In terms of cost savings, there are clearly scale economies associated with any given ship, from sharing capacity rather than providing a given service with separate vessels.

However, there is no conclusive evidence that cost savings have been generated through coordination and passed on to consumers. On the contrary, there is some overseas evidence that conference price setting has inflated shipping rates (ECLAC 1998). Moreover, conferences established market power for their members, restricting the entry of newcomers, especially from developing countries, and delaying improvement in the quality of shipping services. They tried to sustain their market power through tactics such as bilateral agreements and cargo reservations, even though in some cases the cartel members appeared to argue for more open shipping markets (Ghang et al. 1998). Even if cost savings are generated, part of these savings is not necessarily transferred to shippers and hence probably not passed on to the consumers and producers of shipped commodities or even to the wider economy.[7]

This regulatory system of conferences was gradually undermined by containerisation throughout the 1960s and 1970s. There was also increased competitive pressure from new entrants operating independently, even though world maritime trade was still controlled largely by the shipping cartels of the traditional maritime states of Europe, the United States and Japan. To achieve the necessary economies of scale with containerisation, lines merged their conference rights into consortia. This trend was further developed into forming global alliances.[8] In consortia, liner operators not only share transport capacity but also harmonise their schedules and ports of call. Alliances generally do not involve price setting and they are gradually being used more widely in international shipping, partly because they do not attract the attention of regulators (Gardner 1997). Such mergers were also a way of mobilising the huge amounts of capital needed to containerise an entire trade, not only to build the ships but also to supply the necessary facilities to handle them in each port. The consequence was a gradual shrinkage in the number of principals, but this did not strengthen the conferences because of new entry (Dick 1996).

In the late 1970s, there also emerged non-conference lines offering independent semi or full container services at a frequency varying between weekly and fortnightly. These are mostly based in the newly industrialising economies of East Asia. They include Evergreen (Taiwan), Yang Ming (Taiwan), Cosco (China), Hanjin (Korea), Hyundai (Korea) and Norasia (Swiss). In the 1980s they vigorously undercut conference rates, leading to a complete realignment of the conference consortia. These new entrants not only replicated existing schedules but also had privileged access to a national cargo base and an existing network. By 1995 it was estimated that the share of these non-conference lines in the world liner shipping market was about 40 per cent (Dick 1996).

UN Liner Code

It had been difficult for developing countries to join the shipping conferences. Even when allowed to join, they were treated unequally in many cases. One approach to solving this problem was adoption of the United Nations Convention on a Code of Conduct for Liner Conferences (UN Liner Code) in 1974.

The UN Liner Code stipulated that contracting parties have equal rights of cargo sharing and agreed a cargo reservation formula of 40:40:20 (exporter: importer: the third flag), which came into effect in October 1983. The core of the code was to support the entry of shipping firms from developing countries into international liner services by eroding the monopoly power of existing shipping conferences. However, it is also true that the UN Liner Code allows a new type of shipping conference by dividing the international shipping market into segmented regional or south–north activities, hence restricting competition. Industrialised countries have argued that this code is another justification of protectionism in developing countries.

Bilateral agreements on access to cargo

Through bilateral agreements, many countries have been applying most-favoured-nation (MFN) and national treatment (NT) principles to cargo allocation and the use of port facilities. In a bilateral cargo allocation agreement, two countries agree on terms of cargo-sharing practices (e.g. half each).[9] To avoid the accusation that they have completely eliminated cross traders, the partners of such bilateral agreements leave a part of their trade to the third flag. The cargo shipping formula of 40:40:20 specified in the UN Liner Code is a multilateral agreement on cargo reservation to avoid such conflicts. However, the United States and some industrial countries have not yet ratified the code, arguing that this again restricts free shipping.

National policies

Since the British Navigation Acts of Cromwell in the seventeenth century, government involvement and the adoption of a regulatory approach have been the rule rather than exception in the international MTS industry. The objectives of protectionism are to expand a country's own merchant fleet to the size and structure desired and determined by the needs of the national economy and/or to maintain the established position of the country's merchant fleet. In general, the national regulatory scheme takes two forms: financial support and non-financial regulations, such as control of market access and cargo reservation.

Financial support

This measure usually takes the form of subsidies and financial support such as tax incentives or assistance for shipbuilding or operation costs, aiming at the development of shipping activities or sometimes at the maintenance of the already established position of the national merchant fleet. While most developing countries subsidise their MTS industries in various ways, many industrial countries also do so directly or indirectly through their financial systems.[10]

Non-financial regulations

In an effort to reserve the largest possible share of the country's seaborne trade, foreign firms are restricted from entering, or operating in, the domestic market. This restriction is one of the strongest forms of shipping protectionism since it decisively eliminates competition from foreign carriers.

To control market access by foreign firms, many countries control foreign ownership of domestic fleets and/or restrict foreign direct investment in maritime-related projects such as the construction or management of national ports. The employment of foreign workers in national ports or ships is also often restricted or controlled.

In many cases, foreign operations on domestic routes are also restricted in the form of cargo reservation. Most developing countries adopt this measure to protect domestic shipping firms. In many industrial countries, cargo reservation is not expressly stipulated in the text but is, in fact, exercised indirectly through administrative and other guidelines. For instance, the US government adopts an extremely wide range of protectionist measures, such as cargo reservations and intervention by the Federal Maritime Commission in the internal matters of shipping conferences operating to and from US ports, in an effort to protect US firms whose competitiveness may be weakened by higher operating costs.

Cargo preferences are also used sometimes to create better conditions for domestic carriers in the country's trade. At least formally, foreign competition is not completely eliminated by reservation systems.

FORCES FOR CHANGE

Countries with strong and competitive fleets are more likely to take the position of shipping liberalism, while those with weak fleets and a vulnerable market position intend to protect what they see as their interests against competition from more efficient foreign carriers. It is a conflict not only between traditional maritime powers and developing countries but also among industrial countries. There are increasing pressures on governments to achieve freer international trade in maritime services. These stem not only from market forces but also from international negotiations through the WTO regime and from technological developments in various parts of the industry.

All of these forces have, in turn, offered not only enhanced services and overall efficiency in operation but also reductions in operating costs and freight rates, promoting the liberalisation process in pursuit of all the benefits that are expected to flow from the operation of freer markets. Liberalisation is expected to permit firms to pursue economies of scale, to promote international division of labour and specialisation, to enhance effective management and to improve service menu and quality. Shippers will be the immediate beneficiaries, but the reduction in natural protection through reduced transport costs will also facilitate trade in other sectors.

Market pressure

As discussed above, international shipping has witnessed the demise of the traditional system of liner conferences and the formation of multinational consortia, partly in response to containerisation. Another force for change stems from the rapid growth of East Asian economies since around 1970. Developing countries in Asia doubled their share of world ship registration from 7.8 per cent in 1980 to 16.8 per cent in 1997, while the figure for industrial countries dropped from more than 50 per cent to 27.4 per cent in the same period (Table 9.2). In the case of open-registry countries, UNCTAD (1998b) analysed that developing countries' share has also increased since 1980 when such open-registered tonnage was negligible, reaching one-quarter in 1997. On the other hand, the overall share of industrial countries has been on a downward trend, representing two-thirds of the total tonnage registered in 1997 (UNCTAD 1998b). In the 1990s competitive pressure from new developing country entrants and the growing demand for global logistics brought about the disintegration of the consortia and the advent of huge global alliances that united the Asia–Europe, transpacific and transatlantic trades (Dick 1996).

Intensifying competition has firstly brought about a new combination of shipping services, as new entrants mostly from developing countries not only replicated existing schedules but also reconfigured networks. For example, newly entered Asian independent challengers, which were more heavily involved in the transpacific trade than most of the established European operators, introduced worldwide services using the same ships to link trades between Europe, East Asia and North America, and transatlantic trades. Cargo to or from the east coast of the United States was loaded at Pacific coast ports onto container trains instead of being carried by sea and through the Panama Canal (Dick and Rimmer 1993).

Since the 1980s intensifying competition has forced all operators to establish combined and integrated transport systems and to focus on port-to-port transit times. The drawback of using huge container ships on multiport transport is extended transit time. In this situation, lines offering direct service from Korea, China or Taiwan to specific ports are therefore attracting cargo from other lines offering service only by roundabout routings or transshipment. The

Table 9.2 Distribution of tonnage registration by groups of countries, 1980 and 1997 (gross registered tonnes based; per cent of world total)

	1980	1997
World total[a]	414.5	523.7
Industrial countries	51.7	27.4
East and Central Europe (incl. former USSR)	7.7	4.4
Developing countries	12.5	22.6
Asia	7.8	16.8
Other developing countries	4.8	5.7
Major open-registry countries	27.6	44.1
Rest of the world	0.5	1.6

Notes: Excluding the US Reserve Fleet and the US and Canadian Great Lakes fleets, which in 1996 amounted respectively to 3.0, 1.0 and 1.2 million grt (gross registered tonnes); Mid-year figures for 1980 and end-of-year figures for 1997.
a Figures in million tonnes.

Source: UNCTAD 1998b.

established operators with larger ships have responded by increasing frequency but altering the sequence of ports for alternate sailings (Dick 1996). The development of combined transport systems has also stimulated new procedures and policies relating to risk bearing or insurance, bringing about reduction in freight rates as well as simplification of the freight system.

Increasing competition has also enhanced the quality of services. The most important part has been the innovation of fixed-day, weekly sailings which allow regular shippers to program production runs and delivery of cargo almost to the hour. The leading operators have also put a great deal of effort into improving the speed and convenience of booking cargo door-to-door and handling paperwork. P&O and Nedlloyd, in particular, have diversified heavily into land transport in order to be able to offer an in-house door-to-door service. Competition has forced all operators to compete in terms of door-to-door service – they cannot just dump cargo on the wharf and leave it to the shippers' agents to sort it out (Dick 1996).

In the 25 years since the introduction of containerisation, the level of freight rates has fallen dramatically. The decline was triggered in the early 1980s by the entry of the new independent lines, which undercut conference rates by 25–30 per cent (Dick and Kentwell 1991).[11] Rates have remained flat in the 1990s, as lines have battled for market share by a huge expansion of capacity. With capacity growing much faster than demand at least until 1998, however, there is likely to be continuing downward pressure on real rates.

The need to respond to the global transport requirements of large container shippers has also brought about moves by major carriers to enter into global alliances. Table 9.3 lists the current major global alliances and their container shipping capacities. By the end of 1997, global alliances made up nearly 50

Table 9.3 Estimated capacity of major global alliances in container shipping, 1997

	Vessels	*Capacity*[a]
Grand Alliance		
Hapag-Lloyd, MISC, NYK, OOCL, P&O Nedlloyd	242	547,197
New World Alliance		
Hyundai, MOL, NOL/APL	172	294,403
Maersk/Sea-Land Group	201	447,371
Evergreen	108	228,248
Hanjin Group (United Alliance)		
Hanjin/DSR-Senator/Cho Yang/UASC	122	270,408
K-Line/COSCO Group		
COSCO/K-Line/Yangming	226	381,936

Notes:
a Total capacity in TEUs (20-foot equivalent units).
Source: UNCTAD 1998b.

per cent of the world fleet, bringing about a completely new dimension to competition and a concentration process in international shipping services (UNCTAD 1998b). The degree of concentration by these carriers is even larger on the major trade routes, where more than 75 per cent of capacity is provided by major lines either individually or in the context of global or trade-related alliances. The present process of competitive positioning by companies will lead to further concentration, as is shown by the merger of P&O and Nedlloyd to create a company with a carrying capacity of 221,000 TEUs (20-foot equivalent units), making it the third-largest container carrier in the world (UNCTAD 1998b).

World liner shipping markets are still undergoing important structural changes that will have a lasting impact on the way the industry operates. In addition to the emergence of new entrants into international MTS markets, the globalisation of maritime transportation companies is an important part of increasing market pressure for liberalisation. Following global operation by multinational firms or global alliances especially in liner shipping areas, transnational or stateless systems are being established through the internationalisation of business operations.[12] As global management is becoming more common, its adoption is being accelerated. In that context, most liners have been promoting strategic alliances with other operators. This will promote the emergence of large-scale transnational liner groups through global alliance, or mega operators through international mergers and acquisitions. The process of globalisation of overall trade and industrial production also has affected demand for transport and related services and has forced all transportation companies to better adapt services to the requirements of the trading community.

Technological developments

Since the advent of the first giant containerships in 1971–73, there has been no further significant technological innovation but a series of improvements. The most dramatic improvement has been the increased size of ships (see Table 9.4). The first series of containerships in the 1970s were about 2,000 TEUs at the maximum, with a length of around 210 metres. By the mid-1980s, sizes were above 4,000 TEUs and 270–300 metres. Intense competition in the 1990s has seen the size of new orders grow to 6,000 TEUs and more than 300 metres since 1996.[13] Shipyards have already drawn up plans for the construction of even larger ships. Other changes have been the switch from steam turbine to slow-speed diesel as the means of propulsion, increased automation and smaller crew sizes, open-hatch design, and less frequent docking cycles (Dick 1996).

There have been continuous improvements in sailing speed as well. In the 1960s the average speed of 1,000 TEU containerships was about 16 knots, which increased to current rates of about 25 knots for 6,000 TEU ships. Efforts to realise technological breakthroughs in the speed of ships continue to be made, especially in passenger ships and short-distance liners. Under development include new ships like the 1,000 TEU TSL (Techno Super Liner), with a speed of 50 knots per hour. The technology is also expected to be applied to medium-sized cargo liners in approximately 2005 and to large liners in around 2015 (KMI 1998).

There has also been technological improvement in cargo loading and unloading in an effort to enhance overall efficiency in the transport system. In particular, productivity gains based on the use of advanced technologies, such as electronic data interchange, have been remarkable. The developments in this area also include shipboard automation, acceleration and increased size of the port facility. In the case of container stevedoring, the multiple hoist system is gradually replacing the single hoist method.

Policy framework

All of these changes in the provision of shipping services, in market structures and in technologies have contributed to reduction of unit costs for high-volume operations, which was a necessary response to low freight rates and smaller profit margins. These changes further raised the issue of policy reform programs at the global as well as national levels. In general, national-level programs consist of the privatisation of state-owned shipping companies and other maritime infrastructure and the reduction of discriminatory regulations to service suppliers in both shipping and auxiliary service sectors. All these issues have been growing concerns of the international community.

There have been, in fact, both protectionist and liberal shipping policies coexisting in the international MTS arena. The core of shipping liberalism is that shippers have to have the right to a free choice of carrier. That is, the merchant marines should operate on the freight market without any

Table 9.4   Technological improvement in containerships

	1960s	1970s	1980s	1984+	1992+	1996+	2000+
Length (m)	190	210	210–90	270–300	290–320	305–10	355–60
Width (m)	27	27	32	37–41	38–47	38–40	38–40
Draught (m)	9	10	11.5	13–14	13–14	13.5–14	15
Knots	16	23	23	24–24.8	25	25	?
TEU	1,000	2,000	3,000	4,000+	4,900+	6,000	6,000

Source: KMI 1998.

intervention from governments and their agencies. A general spirit of liberalism has been represented by the OECD Maritime Transport Committee. The committee has been the sole intergovernmental body that meets regularly to deal with problems of international shipping policies. The essence of its task is to discourage state interventions and to prevent the further spread of discriminatory practices.

The work of the committee basically involves securing agreement to broad principles for the application of competition policy to international liner shipping. The Code of Liberalization of Shipping, adopted in 1961, lays down certain principles. Even though it was written about 40 years ago, it continues to influence the international maritime order. The sections in the code dealing with shipping can be summarised as follows:

- Governments should apply no pressure on shippers as to the choice of ship to carry their cargoes. This choice should be a matter of a normal commercial consideration.
- Governments should refrain from discriminating against those of their importers/exporters who wish to use foreign ships by imposing export/import licences, refusing to grant them foreign exchange or forcing them to employ home-flag vessels.
- Government-controlled organisations should also conduct their business on the basis of normal commercial principles.

However, there are no countries practising these principles to the full extent. For some governments, shipping policy raises national sovereignty concerns and there is a high degree of government involvement in their shipping industries, so governments are reluctant to commit to multilateral rules. Many believe that the concept of shipping liberalism as shown in the OECD Code is more a slogan than a reality (Ghang et al. 1998).

Not only within OECD but also in the rest of the world, the United States and the European Union are the most influential economies in international maritime policy and law. The US government has been discussing the revision of the Shipping Act of 1984 since the early 1990s and has reached the final stages of passing the Shipping Reform Act. This new Act will have considerable influence on the world shipping community. In contrast, the European Union has been maintaining the position and legal principles which were established during the 1980s. Although the United States and the European Union are trying to remove the gaps in policy between them, concerning competition policy in particular, there are some unsettled issues which may cause conflict because of the different scope of, and criteria applied to, their respective legal regimes (Ghang et al. 1998).

Nevertheless, the OECD Maritime Transport Committee has played an important role as a forum for multilateral action on international maritime transport services. Now all issues of liberalisation in the international shipping industry are on the agenda of the most recent global reform programs of the GATS.

WTO/GATS AND NEW INTERNATIONAL SHIPPING REGIME

The General Agreement on Trade in Services is the most recent example of an instrument aimed at opening markets and creating a fair trading environment for all maritime service providers. That is, the international service sector, including MTS, is governed by the GATS under the WTO regime, which is now the greatest institutional force pushing the international MTS sector towards freer trade. The GATS general principles, including MFN treatment, are to be adopted unconditionally by all member countries, but principles of market access and national treatment can be applied according to the result of negotiations on commitments. The following describes the multilateral negotiation process in the WTO.

Uruguay Round negotiations

The objective of the Uruguay Round negotiations on MTS is to provide multilateral regulations that will ensure the liberalisation of trading in this sector. Major agenda items of the MTS during the negotiations were sectoral tests which examine the major principles and regulations to be stipulated in the GATS, the formulation of sectoral annex of the MTS, and bilateral negotiations for commitments. Although the negotiations failed to reach an agreement, the round was fruitful since the application of the framework provisions of the GATS to MTS was agreed upon and the liberalisation of trading in MTS was promoted through bilateral negotiations (Choi et al. 1997).

WTO negotiations

In compliance with the Decision on the Negotiation on Maritime Transport Services, adopted in April 1994, the NGMTS was established. The mandate of the NGMTS was to hold comprehensive negotiations to secure commitments in international shipping, auxiliary services, and access to and use of port facilities, leading to the elimination of trade restrictions within a fixed timescale.

The WTO/NGMTS has held sixteen meetings since its inception in April 1994. At the time of suspension of the negotiations, 42 governments (counting the EU and its member states as one) had elected to participate fully in the negotiations. Another fifteen governments were observers.

In October 1994, the NGMTS surveyed the participating countries' MTS market structures and regulatory issues. In all, 35 of the full participants and observer governments responded to the questionnaire survey. The NGMTS also examined outstanding technical and conceptual issues. There were technical matters relating to the scheduling of commitments on international shipping, auxiliary services, access to and the use of port facilities and multimodal transport services. Modifications of the draft schedule, including alternative approaches which would enable participants to reschedule commitments, were also considered.

At the end of June 1995, participants began submitting draft commitments on MTS to serve as the basis for bilateral request/offer negotiations. At the time of suspension of negotiations, 24 countries had submitted conditional offers. During the negotiations, participants made it clear that their offers were conditional upon the quality and extent of the commitments made by others. Frequent rounds of bilateral negotiations were also held among participants.

WTO/NGMTS member governments agreed to suspend negotiations on 28 June 1996 and to resume on the basis of existing or improved offers at the time of the further round of comprehensive negotiations, which was scheduled to begin this year.

During the Uruguay Round negotiations on the MTS, 32 countries submitted their final commitments to be included in the schedule of specific commitments as an integral part of the GATS. The next round of negotiations started in 2000, and further rounds will be held periodically thereafter, with a view to achieving a progressively higher level of liberalisation in MTS. Such negotiations are to be directed to the reduction or elimination of the adverse effects on trade in MTS, with the aim of promoting the interests of all participants on a mutually advantageous basis and to secure a balance of rights and obligations.

If negotiations this year proceed successfully, a new paradigm for MTS could be created. The implications are summarised in Table 9.5. Under this regime, the principle of MFN treatment will be more widely applied and the GATS schedule will be universally adopted in the settlement of trade frictions. Allowing time for negotiation to proceed, and for an implementation period, one scenario is that international shipping could then be completely liberalised by 2010. Before this time, domestic routes would also be targets for liberalisation.

APEC AGENDA

Choi, Kim and Findlay (1997) have observed that about 22 per cent of the world merchant fleet are national-flag ships of APEC member economies. They also noted that these economies made a great contribution to the MTS

Table 9.5   New shipping regime under GATS general principles

	GATS general principles	Relevance to shipping regime
MFN/Non-discrimination	Unconditional application	Removal of cargo reservation and other discriminatory measures
Transparency	Prompt (at least by the time of enforcement) announcement of all relevant measures pertaining to/affecting the operation of the GATS	Transparency in government practices in cargo preference, private agreement/measures between operators, any measures for cargo reservation and subsidies, technical standards, and so on
Increasing participation of developing countries	Promotion of service industries in developing countries	Removal of cargo allocation in developed countries; promotion of technology transfer and application; support for staff training; investment in ships
General exceptions	When related to national security or culture	For example, transportation of military items

negotiations. Among the 42 full participants of the WTO/NGMTS, 15 were APEC members and, of the 24 countries that submitted conditional offers at the end of WTO/NGMTS, 8 were from the APEC region. However, they also noted that there was no concerted effort towards a single or harmonised voice of APEC members throughout the negotiations. Moreover, APEC member economies showed deep reservations over suggestions made by the United States, including the recognition of multimodal transport in the MTS negotiations, legislation on the transport of Alaska North Slope Oil, and technical matters relating to the scheduling of commitments. Box 9.1 provides summary profiles of the activity of APEC member economies during the Uruguay Round and WTO negotiations on MTS.

The services sector is a challenge for the liberalisation process because of the constraints which have made it more difficult to achieve a 'big bang outcome'. There is, however, an opportunity for groups of like-minded countries to promote services sector liberalisation. Bora, Findlay and Warren (1997) argue this point in the context of existing formal trading arrangements, such as the ASEAN Free Trade Agreement (AFTA) and the Closer Economic Relations (CER) Agreement. APEC, a higher level organisation which operates in a less formal fashion, has complementary contributions to make to both subregional initiatives and to global negotiations. One of APEC's contributions could be to provide a framework in which subgroup activities take place. To do so, its members could:

- reassert the relevance of the GATS principles to maritime transport;
- make clear the impediments to international trade in MTS amongst its members (going beyond the GATS by detailing impediments rather than just commitments to liberalise);[14]
- monitor the terms of any agreements amongst its members on transport services;
- comment on competition policy principles, or the compatibility of existing rules, which might be applied;[15] and
- assert the relevance of its investment principles to this sector.

APEC can therefore help define the relevant end-points for regional approaches to services trade liberalisation and act as a monitor of the milestones which the participants set themselves. APEC members would be expected to record any commitments they make unilaterally or to regional arrangements.

The review of the efforts among APEC economies demonstrates, particularly in the western Pacific, a strong interest in a more liberal MTS regime. There is, therefore, widespread, although not universal, explicit support among APEC members for change. Members may be interested in a discussion of targets and strategies for the MTS negotiations in the WTO before they resume, the outcome of which would be a further contribution of APEC.

For example, the bundling and sequencing of services sector negotiations in the WTO is not yet well defined. The isolation of individual service sectors in negotiating processes is one explanation of why some failed to reach a conclusion. One suggestion is therefore to bundle MTS negotiations with other service sectors, and liberalisation of the cargo sector as a whole has been suggested before by the Pacific Economic Cooperation Council (PECC) (see Pangestu et al. 1996) as one way of making progress.

Attempts at the liberalisation of maritime services have so far failed in the global trade negotiations and air transport has been completely excluded, as Choi et al. (1997) explain. On the other hand, land transport has been dealt with in the multilateral round, and multimodal services have also been discussed. The main remaining issues in these areas appear to be those related to investment. All these services could be brought together under the one banner so as to pursue 'free freight'.

It has been suggested that putting all these modes on the table at the same time would help mobilise support for reform in economies where otherwise there is resistance to change when dealing with one sector at a time – for example, resistance to maritime reform might be offset by strong support among air cargo companies. The scope for grouping these sectors may be an important element in raising the degree of interest in this process in the North American economies.

Given that the WTO negotiations have begun again, APEC itself is not the appropriate place to set out to negotiate new arrangements for MTS, or MTS bundled with other services. APEC members could discuss some principles

Box 9.1 APEC member activities in MTS negotiations

Australia made commitments on MTS in its final schedules in the UR negotiation and reinstated it in the WTO negotiations. The offer covers the binding of the following issues with GATS: international MTS and auxiliary services; international rental of vessels with crew; storage and warehousing services; maritime forwarding services; customs clearance services; and preshipment inspection. Australia presented a discussion paper on 'Scheduling Options for Multimodal Transport' (WTO Doc. S/NGMTS/9, 8 March 1996, p.1), to deal with outstanding scheduling issues, particularly the issue of multimodal transport services.

Canada made UR commitments, major contents of which are international MTS, maritime agent services and maritime freight forwarding services (WTO Doc. S/NGMTS/W/8, 18 July 1995). Canada requested MFN exemption for the reciprocal tax exemption for the non-Canadian resident international cargo carriers.

Chile submitted a WTO conditional offer, which included international MTS (passenger and freight), towing and tug services, container station and depot services, loading and unloading services, and storage and warehousing services (WTO Doc. S/NGMTS/W/8, 16 February 1996). Chile filed a MFN exemption for the bilateral cargo-sharing agreement with Brazil signed in 1974.

The People's Republic of China made UR commitments which included international MTS and auxiliary services. MFN exemption was requested for cargo-sharing agreements and joint ventures.

Hong Kong made UR commitments for international MTS (excluding passengers) and auxiliary services.

Indonesia made UR commitments and submitted a WTO improved-offer which included international MTS (passengers and freight).

Japan reinstated its UR offer, including international MTS and maritime auxiliary services (maritime cargo handling, container station and depot, maritime agency) and port services (WTO Doc. S/NGMTS/W/8, 18 July 1995, pp. 35–44).

The Republic of Korea made UR commitments and a WTO improved offer, including international MTS and maritime auxiliary services such as shipping agent, maritime freight forwarding, ship brokering, maintenance and repair of ships, international rental of ships, customs clearance, warehousing and cargo handling services.

Malaysia made UR commitments, including international MTS, shipping agent services, salvage services.

New Zealand reinstated UR commitments, including international MTS, storage and warehousing services and maritime freight forwarding services. New Zealand requested the MFN exemption to recruit the officers aboard its flag carriers from Ireland, Hong Kong, United Kingdom, Canada, Malaysia and Singapore.

Papua New Guinea made UR commitments.

The Republic of the Philippines made UR commitments, including international MTS, international rental of vessels without crew, ship maintenance and repair services. The Philippines requested MFN exemption for the cargo allocation, applying the formula of UN Liner Code.

Singapore made UR commitments, including international MTS (excluding passengers), shipping agent services and ship brokering services. Singapore sought MFN exemption for the bilateral agreements with Korea, China and Vietnam.

Chinese Taipei participated as an observer in WTO/NGMTS.

Thailand made UR commitments, including international MTS, freight forwarding services and port services for the freight suppliers of maritime auxiliary services, the applied equity ratio was 60/40 and for all other forms of commercial presence and minority equity participation not exceeding 49 per cent. Thailand sought MFN exemption for measures based on bilateral agreements with China and Vietnam but confirmed that these agreements had never been implemented and should be repealed or amended on a non-discriminatory basis (WTO Doc. S/NGMTS/6, 3 August 1995, p. 2).

The United States withdrew its UR offer and has not resubmitted it.

Source: Reproduced from Choi et al. 1997.

under which these sorts of negotiations could proceed, for example by documenting impediments (or verifying existing datasets), refining end-points (such as free trade in MTS by 2010), or by discussing modes of negotiation (such as the scope of the negotiating bundle).

APEC could also develop complementary programs in economic and technical cooperation. Liberalisation of foreign investment regimes will lead to the transfer of shipping technology, including management methods. Other programs in which governments might take a direct interest include cooperation to transfer the experience in constructing policymaking institutions, in establishing industry training schemes, in privatising ports or financing their development, and so on. These programs might overlap with measures associated with the facilitation of trade in shipping services, for example, anticipating the extent of technological change and the challenges that will arise for current standards or common practices in shipping or in cargo handling.[16] Care is required not to duplicate existing effort.[17]

CONCLUSION

In this paper we reviewed issues concerning the regulation of international maritime transport services. We noted the pressures on the current arrangements from events in the market, from technological change and from multilateral negotiations through GATS/WTO. We stressed the lack of progress so far in the latter but highlighted the continuing pressure for change. The next step is the new round of WTO negotiations. In the beginning of this new century, similar progress to what was made via specific agreement for basic telecommunications and financial services could be achieved for maritime transport, with a specific agreement moving beyond the standard GATS framework to deal with issues such as the treatment of liner shipping in competition laws. Such progress will certainly require that the signatories to the agreement jointly recognise the potential benefits of opening the market to the forces of competition.

We also discussed a series of contributions that the APEC process could make to those negotiations, alongside effort already in progress in other institutions, including the OECD. APEC could contribute to achieving a greater degree of transparency in the impediments to trade in this service. Of particular relevance is the contribution that preliminary discussions in APEC processes might make to the choice of a mode for the negotiations and to the definition of a goal for the WTO process. We suggested that a proposal to bundle negotiations on the cargo transport services sectors is worth further consideration. The scope to develop complementary economic and technical cooperation programs, or trade facilitation programs, in APEC was also noted. These could include, for example, a process for discussing standards, dealing with issues in the application of competition policy, and developing policy regimes to promote infrastructure development.

NOTES

1   For example, if the shipping market is restricted or uncompetitive, the benefits of cost reductions from reform and/or trade liberalisation in the related sectors, such as waterfront and inland transportation, may be limited or largely captured by some shipping operators rather than spread throughout the economy.

2   A shipping conference can be defined as an unincorporated association of two or more ocean carriers carrying on two or more businesses, each of which includes providing liner cargo shipping services.

3   Shipping conferences are in general exempt from antitrust laws in many countries, including the United States and Canada. For example, the US Shipping Act of 1984 eliminated the public interest standard of antitrust law.

4   They also commonly undertake the pooling of earnings, either gross or net of costs. This type is called a pool account conference.

5   In order to secure a market share at given freight rate, members increase the service offered, which increases the cost of their services.

6   For example, if the ship designated to sail on a particular journey has mechanical problems, the conference can arrange to have a backup and so minimise the cost to customers. If there is excess demand for capacity on a scheduled trip, the conference can arrange to allocate additional capacity to the task. With a large number of vessels in its combined fleet, a conference may also be able to offer more frequent services, as it does not have to wait for vessels to return from a particular journey.

7   Conferences would only result in benefits for shippers if they produce cost savings that are, at least in part, passed on to shippers and/or increases in the quality of service supplied at given freight rates. The extent to which shippers benefit from the cost savings that conference members make depends on the bargaining position of the shippers. If they have the option of switching to an alternative transport provider, they should be able to negotiate a share of the savings in the form of lower freight rates. If shippers demand more frequent and reliable services, and are prepared to pay for those quality characteristics, they may benefit from conferences even if freight rates are not lower. If they also value stable prices, they may benefit from having access to the fixed, published freight rates of conferences, rather than market-determined rates.

8   Alliances are global, rather than route-specific, agreements to cooperate in setting timetables, sharing capacity, purchasing port services, and providing some associated services.

9   Cargo reservation may also take a unilateral form: that is, where a country unilaterally decides to reserve a part or all of its seaborne trade for domestic carriers.

10   See USDT (1993) for the status of international maritime subsidies.

11   Another structural change has been a reversal in the flow of cargo. Until the 1970s the main tonnage and revenue-paying cargoes were from Europe to Asia. The industrialisation of East Asia has meant that the main flow is now in the other direction, so that export cargo from Europe now enjoys heavily discounted back-haul rates that can be less than US$1,000 per box. See Dick (1996) for further details.

12   See Dick (1996) for further discussion on the formation of global alliances in the 1990s.

13   However, not all operators were equipped with large container ships over 2,000 TEUs. In 1985, only around 15 per cent of the world container capacity was provided by vessels of more than 2,000 TEUs. This share went up to 60 per cent of existing cellular fleet and 72 per cent of the slots on order in 1997 (UNCTAD 1998).

14   The 1997 report of the OECD's Maritime Transport Committee says that, in 'respect of maritime trade in services negotiations … the Committee prepared a stocktaking of existing impediments to maritime and multimodal transport in non-OECD countries. This stocktaking will assist MTC members in ranking the various impediments, such as access to cargoes and obstacles to maritime investments, and will facilitate the development of possible negotiating strategies' (from <http://www.oecd.org//dsti/sti/ transpor/sea/prod/ar97.htm> Matters Related to the World Trade Organisation (WTO), accessed 24 October 1998). This stocktake could be reviewed and updated within the APEC process. It was also reported that, 'during 1997 the Committee completed a comprehensive Inventory on Support Measures and Arrangements provided to International Shipping. The information collated in this inventory, together with similar information from selected non-Member economies, was used in preparing a report which is the first stage of a wider study on support measures. This wider study will aim to establish full transparency on all types of support arrangements granted to alleviate employment costs, support measures provided to the shipping companies and those granted to owned and controlled vessels.'

15   The OECD's MTC has also examined competition policy issues in the maritime transport sector. It concluded that incompatibilities in competition policy were a problem (see DSTI/SI/MTC(98)1).

16   Further work is required on the scope of these issues, and their implications for policy reform and other forms of international cooperation. The PECC has begun planning a 'futures' project for the transport sector, one aim of which is to identify the business and policy challenges in transport over the next couple of decades.

17   The OECD's MTC, for example, has a work program on 'substandard shipping'. See <http://www.oecd.org//dsti/sti/transpor/sea/news/roundtab.htm> (accessed 24 October 1998).

10 Restrictiveness of international trade in maritime services

Greg McGuire, Michael Schuele and Tina Smith

INTRODUCTION

Efficient and competitive delivery of international maritime transport services is vital for trade-oriented economies. Along with air services, shipping is one of the main modes of international transport. Imposing restrictions on maritime services can adversely affect the price, reliability and quality of these services. But a necessary first step in assessing such impacts is identifying and quantifying the restrictions. This chapter presents a comprehensive list of restrictions on maritime services, compiled from a number of sources. A restrictiveness index then summarises and quantifies the nature and extent of these restrictions for 35 economies.

DEFINING RESTRICTIONS

Restrictions on trade in maritime services are barriers that limit maritime service suppliers from entering or operating in a market. Such restrictions are typically imposed by governments through legislation and regulation. Regulation of maritime services can be discriminatory or non-discriminatory against foreign service suppliers. Discriminatory regulations treat foreign maritime service suppliers less favourably than domestic maritime service suppliers and often aim to restrict trade. For example, foreign suppliers may be prohibited from providing services around the coast of a country. Non-discriminatory regulations treat domestic and foreign maritime service suppliers equally, but can still restrict activity, for example, by requiring mandatory use of a designated supply of port services by domestic and foreign suppliers. Such restrictions may be more burdensome than necessary to achieve a competitive and safe maritime industry.

Multilateral trading forums aim to reduce restrictions while recognising the freedom of members to maintain regulation to ensure the safety of their maritime industry. Governments are generally permitted to set their own maritime regulation objectives – for example, being internationally competitive and meeting acceptable safety standards.

All government regulation or restrictions on maritime services are covered by the restrictiveness index developed and reported in this chapter. In general, trade restrictions, by reducing competition in maritime services will reduce efficiency in that market. But sometimes regulation that limits competition is necessary to deal with 'market failure' and to meet particular social objectives. For example, some regulation of maritime services is considered necessary to ensure the safe and efficient delivery of these services.[1] However, it is difficult to make an assessment on the merits of regulation for different economies with different preferences on the scope and level of regulation.

RESTRICTIONS ON TRADE IN MARITIME SERVICES

A list of government regulations or restrictions on the entry and operations of maritime services has been compiled from a number of sources. The primary source of information is a 1994 questionnaire distributed by the WTO's Negotiating Group on Maritime Transport Services (NGMTS 1994). The questionnaire, designed to facilitate the exchange of information in a common format, covered the structure of maritime services markets and the regulations applying to maritime services. Supplementary information has been taken from:

- the GATS schedules for each WTO member assessed in this chapter, covering information on restrictions applying to maritime transport, port and auxiliary services (WTO 1994);
- WTO Trade Policy Reviews, which describe regulation applying to maritime services, trade restrictions and trade policies for WTO members (WTO 1996, 1997a, 1998a);
- the National Trade Estimate Report on Foreign Trade Barriers, from the Office of the US Trade Representative, which covers information on restrictions on maritime services for most economies (USTR 1998);
- an OECD paper covering restrictions on maritime and multimodal trade in selected non-OECD countries, which records restrictions in the provision of maritime and related services (OECD 1997c);
- APEC Individual Action Plans, which list restrictions and liberalising commitments in reports covering services, investment, competition and deregulation (APEC 1997b, 1998b); and
- the TradePort Web site, which covers information on restrictions for most economies (TradePort 1998).

A consolidated listing and description of restrictions on maritime services has been compiled from the above sources of information for 35 economies. The maritime services covered are bulk, liner and inland waterways shipping services, and port facilities. The information on restrictions dates from 1994 to the end of 1998 and, as far as possible, reflects the existing restrictions applying to maritime services. While a comprehensive list can be drawn from these sources of information, some recent developments may not necessarily be included.

Restrictions specific to maritime services and major 'horizontal' restrictions on all services are included in the list of restrictions. The horizontal restrictions on all services, including shipping, are those on the movement of people, on direct investment, and on the composition of the board of directors. The approach taken here is to quantify all restrictions on maritime services regardless of whether the restrictions are specific to maritime or not. Table 10.1 outlines some common restrictions on maritime services.

RESTRICTIVENESS INDEX METHODOLOGY

An index methodology has been used to quantify the nature and extent of restrictions on international trade in services. An index uses available information on regulations to quantify the extent to which comparable economies have more or less restrictive trading regimes for services. Table 10.2 outlines the restrictiveness index used for maritime services.

The index has been developed by first grouping the restrictions identified from the sources of information listed earlier. The restrictions are divided into two groups – those affecting commercial presence, and other restrictions. The reason for distinguishing between commercial presence restrictions and others is so that the former can ideally be modelled as restrictions on the movement of capital, while the latter can be modelled as restrictions on trade in maritime services.

Restrictions on commercial presence affect the ability to become established in an economy and provide maritime services. The commercial presence restriction grouping covers restrictions on maritime service suppliers flying the national flag, the form that commercial presence can take, direct investment in shipping service suppliers, direct investment in onshore maritime service suppliers, and the permanent movement of people. The other restrictions grouping covers cabotage, the transportation of non-commercial cargoes, port services, the discretionary imposition of restrictions including for retaliatory purposes, membership of the United Nations Liner Code, governments permitting the operation of conferences, bilateral maritime agreements on cargo sharing, the composition of the board of directors and the temporary movement of people.

Within these common restriction categories, the degree of restrictiveness varies. An index has been developed by assessing the differing degrees of restriction – from most restrictive to least restrictive – for most categories. The greater the restriction on maritime services, the higher or more restrictive the score. Scores range from 0 (least restrictive) to 1 (most restrictive). A score is assigned for each restriction category that best reflects the type of restriction imposed by an economy.

Table 10.1 Examples of restrictions on maritime services

Restriction	Description of restriction
Right to fly the national flag	Requires ships to be registered or licensed to provide maritime services on domestic and international routes. The conditions on registration may include having a commercial presence in the domestic economy, the ship being built and owned domestically, and meeting seaworthiness and safety requirements.
Cabotage	Restricts shipping services on domestic or coastal routes to licensed vessels that meet certain conditions. Shipping services between domestic ports may be required to be carried out by domestically owned, operated, built and crewed ships.
Cargo sharing Bilateral agreements	Stipulates the allocation of cargo on particular routes between parties to bilateral and multilateral agreements. Agreements between two economies that primarily restrict the supply of shipping services and the allocation of cargo. Some bilateral agreements also restrict the use of port facilities.
UN Convention on a Code of Conduct for Liner Conferences (UN Liner Code)	Stipulates that conference trade between two economies can allocate cargo according to the 40:40:20 principle. Forty per cent of tonnage is reserved for the national flag lines of each economy and the remaining 20 per cent is to be allocated to liner ships from a third economy. The Code also entitles any national flag shipping line to be a member of a conference and to fix freight rates.
Conferences	Restricts the free and open participation of maritime service suppliers. Conference members set freight rates and schedules. Conferences may be open or closed. Open conferences have unrestricted entry and exit, and freight rates are set on a route. Closed conferences set freight rates, allocate cargo and restrict membership. Governments usually permit the existence of conferences though exemptions from price setting and collusion provisions of domestic competition legislation.
Port services	Requires ships to use a designated supply of port services. These services include pilotage, towing, tug assistance, navigation aids, berthing, waste disposal, anchorage and casting off.

Sources: Kang et al. 1998; White 1988; WTO 1998a.

The calculation of scores for the 'right to fly the national flag' and 'port services' restriction categories is different. These categories cover a number of restrictions that are mutually exclusive. Restrictions in these categories are the addition of separate restrictions. For example, a score of 0.55 is assigned

Table 10.2 Restrictiveness index for maritime services

Category weightings[a]			Score	Restriction category
R[b]	MFN[c]	Total[d]		
				Restrictions on Commercial Presence
0.143	0.008	0.15		*Conditions on the right to fly the national flag*
			0.40	Commercial presence is required in the domestic economy.
			0.30	50 per cent or more of equity participation must be domestic.
			0.20	50 per cent or more of the crew are required to be domestic.
			0.10	Ship must be registered.
0.095	0.005	0.10		*Form of commercial presence*
			1.00	Measures which restrict or require a specific type of legal entity or joint venture arrangement.
			0.50	Shipping service suppliers must be represented by an agent.
			0.00	No restrictions on establishment.
0.095	0.005	0.10		*Direct investment in shipping service suppliers* The score is inversely proportional to the maximum equity participation permitted in an existing shipping service supplier. For example, equity participation to a maximum of 75 per cent of an existing shipping service supplier would receive a score of 0.25.
0.095	0.005	0.10		*Direct investment in onshore maritime service suppliers* The score is inversely proportional to the maximum equity participation permitted in an existing onshore maritime service supplier. For example, equity participation to a maximum of 75 per cent of an existing onshore service supplier receives a score of 0.25.
0.019	0.001	0.02		*Permanent movement of people*
			1.00	No entry of executives, senior managers and/or specialists.
			0.80	Executives, specialists and/or senior managers can stay a period of up to 1 year.
			0.60	Executives, specialists and/or senior managers can stay a period of up to 2 years.
			0.40	Executives, specialists and/or senior managers can stay a period of up to 3 years.
			0.20	Executives, specialists and/or senior managers can stay a period of up to 4 years.
			0.00	Executives, specialists and/or senior managers can stay a period of 5 years or more.

Table 10.2 (continued)

Category weightings[a]			Score	Restriction category
R[b]	MFN[c]	Total[d]		
0.095	0.005	0.10		*Other Restrictions*
				Cabotage
			1.00	Foreigners generally cannot provide domestic maritime services.
			0.75	Foreigners that fly the national flag can provide domestic maritime services.
			0.50	Restrictions on type and length of time cargoes can be carried.
			0.00	No cabotage restrictions.
0.095	0.005	0.10		*Transportation of non-commercial cargoes*
			1.00	Private shipping service suppliers cannot carry non-commercial cargoes.
			0.50	National flag shipping service suppliers can carry non-commercial cargoes.
			0.00	No restrictions on access to non-commercial cargoes.
0.095	0.005	0.10		*Port services*
			0.30	Some restrictions on access to ports.
			0.20	Mandatory use of pilotage.
			0.15	Mandatory use of towing.
			0.10	Mandatory use of tug assistance.
			0.05	Mandatory use of navigation aids.
			0.05	Mandatory use of berthing services.
			0.05	Mandatory use of waste disposal.
			0.05	Mandatory use of anchorage.
			0.05	Mandatory use of casting off.
0.048	0.003	0.05		*Discretionary imposition of restrictions, including for retaliatory purposes*
			1.00	Governments are able to impose selective restrictions.
			0.00	Governments are unable to impose selective restrictions.
0.048	0.003	0.05		*United Nations Liner Code*
			1.00	Economy is party to the code and applies Article 2 of the code.
			0.75	Economy is party to the code but does not apply Article 2 of the code.
			0.00	Economy is not party to code.
0.048	0.003	0.05		*Government permits conferences*
			1.00	Government permits the operation of conferences.
			0.00	Conferences are subject to effective competition.
0.050	n.a.	0.05		*Bilateral maritime services agreements on cargo sharing*
				The score for an economy is taken from the 35 by 35 matrix of bilateral agreements on cargo sharing.

Table 10.2 (continued)

Category weightings[a]			Score	Restriction category
R[b]	MFN[c]	Total[b]		
0.019	0.001	0.02		*Composition of the board of directors*
				The score is inversely proportionately to the percentage of the board that can comprise foreigners. For example, a score of 0.80 is allocated where 20 per cent of the board of directors of a maritime service supplier can comprise foreigners.
0.010	0.001	0.01		*Temporary movement of people*
			1.00	No temporary entry of executives, senior managers and/or specialists.
			0.75	Temporary entry of executives, senior managers and/or specialists up to 30 days.
			0.50	Temporary entry of executives, senior managers and/or specialists up to 60 days.
			0.25	Temporary entry of executives, senior managers and/or specialists up to 90 days.
			0.00	Temporary entry of executives, senior managers and/or specialists over 90 days.
0.952	0.048	1.00		*Total*

Notes:
n.a. = not applicable.
a Totals may not add due to rounding.
b R is the restriction category weighting.
c MFN is the most-favoured-nation category weighting.
d Total of restriction category and most-favoured-nation category weightings.

where there are some restrictions on access to some ports and there is mandatory use of pilotage and berthing services.

We assigned weights to restriction categories by making an a priori assessment of the cost of restrictions to economic efficiency. Hardin and Holmes (in Chapter 4), Warren (in Chapter 6), OECD (1997b) and Claessens and Glaessner (1998) provide examples of weightings to apply to restriction categories. From these papers and the research conducted for this chapter, we made a judgement about the cost to economic efficiency of different restrictions. Restrictions that we considered to impose a greater cost on economic efficiency are given a greater weighting. For example, restrictions on direct investment in shipping service suppliers are generally considered to be more restrictive and a greater cost to economic efficiency than those restrictions on the movement of people (see Table 10.2).

We calculated an index score separately for domestic and foreign maritime service suppliers, to quantify the extent to which regulation restricts domestic and international competition. The foreign index covers restrictions relevant to foreign maritime service suppliers and the domestic index covers restrictions relevant to all maritime service suppliers. Non-discriminatory restrictions on the right to fly the national flag receive the same score under the domestic and foreign index. A higher score is assigned under the foreign index than under the domestic index where the conditions on foreigners are more onerous than on domestic suppliers. The difference between the foreign and domestic index score is a measure of discrimination against foreigners.

A key question is how to deal with most-favoured-nation (MFN) exemptions. These typically allow economies reciprocal or preferential treatment with a particular set of partner economies. If the details of such treatment were known, this information could be built directly into the computation of the index as so far described, but on a bilateral basis. If an economy granted preferential treatment on the movement of people to a partner economy, for example, and the extent of this preferential treatment were known, its index score for this restriction category could be computed separately for that partner economy and would be lower than against other economies. Unfortunately, the information sources typically do not spell out the nature or extent of reciprocal or preferential treatment. Thus, a different, admittedly less satisfactory, approach has had to be taken.

In this chapter, the foreign index covers MFN exemptions for maritime services and the movement of people, and bilateral agreements on cargo sharing. The type of exemption or bilateral arrangement is scored, rather than adjusting each restriction category for any reciprocal or preferential arrangement between two economies. The scoring still recognises that an economy that applies an MFN exemption or bilateral arrangement to one or a number of economies has lower restrictions overall than an economy without such an arrangement. Thus, economies with MFN exemptions or bilateral arrangements receive a lower score than economies without these arrangements.

MFN exemptions for maritime services and the movement of people are scored under a separate index. As noted, an MFN exemption permits an economy to discriminate between economies. The MFN exemptions scheduled under the GATS are used as a source of information. They specify the sectoral coverage, the economies to which they apply and the intended duration. These exemptions can apply to selected or all WTO members. Table 10.3 outlines the scores for the two types of MFN exemptions: preferential treatment and reciprocity.

MFN exemptions are assigned scores in a matrix to measure how the 35 economies treat one another. For example, suppose economy A has a preferential treatment MFN exemption with economies B, C and D on cabotage and port services. For this purpose, the European Union is treated as a single economy, since it rather than its member states applies the exemptions. So there are 20 economies and the matrix is 20 by 20. In the matrix, economies B, C and D receive a score of 0 and the sixteen remaining economies receive a score of 1. The score of 0 shows that economy A has lower or no restrictions with economies B, C and D. The score of 1 shows that A has more restrictions

Table 10.3 Scores for MFN exemptions – maritime services and movement of people

Score	Type of MFN exemption
1.00	No MFN exemption
0.50	MFN exemption with reciprocity with selected or all economies
0.00	MFN exemption with preferential treatment with selected or all economies

with the remaining sixteen economies. The total score of 16 is divided by 19 to obtain a pro rata score for the number of economies to which the MFN exemption is not applied. The denominator of 19 reflects the number of economies that economy A can potentially trade with, since it cannot have an exemption with itself. Thus, the score for economy A for cabotage and port services is 0.84.

This score is multiplied by the respective MFN weighting for cabotage and port services (see Table 10.2). MFN exemptions make up 5 per cent of each restriction category and approximately 5 per cent of the overall foreign index weight. The 'bilateral maritime agreements on cargo sharing' category receives no exemption weighting. (This is discussed later.) The exemption score for each EU economy is the same. MFN exemptions do not apply to the domestic index.

The foreign index also covers a 35 by 35 matrix for bilateral agreements. The European Union is split to reflect the bilateral agreements of individual member states. Economies with bilateral agreements on cargo sharing are considered to be more liberal than those economies without such agreements. The methodology for calculating a score for bilateral agreements is similar to that for MFN exemptions. However, the average score for an economy is included in a separate restriction category: bilateral maritime agreements on cargo sharing. This reflects that the agreements mainly cover cargo sharing. Little or no information is available on other restrictions in bilateral agreements that would allow the construction of a more comprehensive index. MFN exemptions covering bilateral agreements are included in the bilateral matrix and not in the MFN exemption matrix. Table 10.4 outlines the scores applied to bilateral agreements. This restriction category is given a weighting of 5 per cent.

Fewer restriction categories are relevant for the domestic index than for the foreign index. The domestic index excludes restriction categories covering cabotage, the discretionary imposition of restrictions including for retaliatory purposes, the United Nations Liner Code, bilateral maritime agreements on cargo sharing and the movement of people. Scores from the MFN exemptions

Table 10.4 Scores for bilateral maritime services agreements on cargo sharing

Score	Type of bilateral agreement
1.00	Two economies do not have any bilateral maritime agreement involving cargo sharing
0.00	Two economies have a bilateral maritime agreement which involves cargo sharing

and bilateral agreements on cargo sharing matrixes are also excluded. Governments do not generally apply these restrictions to domestic maritime service suppliers. For example, governments do not typically restrict the movement of their nationals within domestic borders. These restriction categories effectively receive a score of 0 in the domestic index. Thus, the foreign index score for an economy will always be greater than the domestic index score. The maximum possible foreign index score is 1. The maximum possible domestic index score is 0.665 (Table 10.5).

The index methodology has been applied to actual restrictions rather than to stated limits. Some statutory restrictions may not necessarily amount to actual restrictions. For example, an economy may restrict foreign equity participation in an existing shipping service supplier to 15 per cent, but government approval may usually be granted to invest above this limit. The index methodology has been applied to the actual restrictiveness, after taking into account approvals above stated limits. Thus, a restriction that is applied as prescribed receives a higher score than a restriction where government approval is usually forthcoming.

RESULTS FOR 35 ECONOMIES

The restrictiveness index has been calculated for economies where comprehensive information about restrictions on maritime services could be gathered from the sources outlined earlier in the chapter. Information was gathered for 35 economies, covering the major regions of the world – Asia, Europe, North America and South America.

Restrictions on maritime services vary significantly among economies. Some economies have few restrictions, while others have a broad range of restrictions. Most economies require ships to be registered and to meet safety requirements. Several economies apply these general entry requirements together with more stringent measures which restrict trade in maritime services.

Canada, EU members, New Zealand and Singapore are relatively open to trade in maritime services, while India, the Philippines, Thailand and the United States are relatively closed economies (Figures 10.1, 10.2 and 10.3).

Table 10.5 Relevance of restriction categories for foreign and domestic indexes

Restriction category	Relevant for foreign index	Total weight[a]	Relevant for domestic index	Total weight[a]
Restrictions on commercial presence				
Conditions on the right to fly the national flag	Yes	0.150	Yes	0.143
Form of commercial presence	Yes	0.100	Yes	0.095
Direct investment in shipping service suppliers	Yes	0.100	Yes	0.095
Direct investment in onshore services	Yes	0.100	Yes	0.095
Permanent movement of people	Yes	0.020	No	n.a.
Other restrictions				
Cabotage	Yes	0.100	No	n.a.
Transportation of non-commercial cargoes	Yes	0.100	Yes	0.095
Port services	Yes	0.100	Yes	0.095
Discretionary imposition of restrictions, including				
for retaliatory purposes	Yes	0.050	No	n.a.
United Nations Liner Code	Yes	0.050	No	n.a.
Government permits conferences	Yes	0.050	Yes	0.048
Bilateral maritime agreements on cargo sharing	Yes	0.050	No	n.a.
Composition of the board of directors	Yes	0.020	No	n.a.
Temporary movement of people	Yes	0.010	No	n.a.
Total weighting or highest possible score		1.000		0.665

Notes:
n.a. = not applicable.
a Totals may not add due to rounding.

Asia Pacific economies

Foreign index

India, Korea, the Philippines and Thailand are the most restricted markets for maritime services in this region (Figure 10.1). These economies all have several significant restrictions. India does not permit foreign involvement in the supply of coastal freight services, does permit liner conferences to form and set freight rates, and has several mandatory port services which may only be supplied by Indian service suppliers. Korea allows for the formation of liner conferences and has several mandatory port services that are reserved

Figure 10.1 Restrictiveness indexes for selected Asia Pacific economies and Turkey

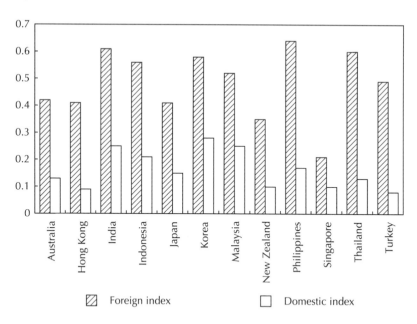

Notes: The higher the score, the more restrictive the economy; scores range from 0 to 1.
Source: Results estimated as part of this chapter.

for Korean service suppliers. Korea reserves the right to impose counter-measures where Korean operators are subject to unfair or discriminatory practices. The Philippines and Thailand impose minority foreign equity limits on the ownership of both shipping service suppliers and associated onshore services. They also require government cargoes to be carried by their respective flagships.

Indonesia, Malaysia and Turkey also obtained relatively high foreign index scores. Indonesia and Malaysia require a commercial presence in the form of a joint venture to provide maritime services. Indonesia also stipulates that all non-commercial cargo be carried by a government-owned shipping line. Malaysia and Turkey limit foreign equity participation in domestic shipping lines to a minority and restrict the activity of foreign vessels in their coastal trade. Malaysia also requires that all non-commercial cargo be carried by government-approved Malaysian vessels.

Australia, Hong Kong, Japan and New Zealand have relatively open markets. All of these economies limit the activity of foreign vessels in coastal trade and permit liner conferences. Australia and New Zealand exempt liner conferences from competition policy legislation. The most open market in this region is Singapore, which has only minor requirements relating to the mandatory use of pilotage and tug services.

Domestic index

India, Korea, Malaysia and Singapore impose several restrictions on their domestic and foreign maritime service suppliers. Korea extends the same treatment regarding mandatory port services to all service suppliers operating in the domestic market. Singapore affords the most equal treatment to foreign and domestic maritime service suppliers, with the difference reflecting only restrictions on the movement of people. The Philippines, Thailand and Turkey treat foreign maritime service suppliers significantly less favourably than domestic firms.

American economies

Foreign index

Brazil, Chile and the United States are the most restricted markets in this region (Figure 10.2). Brazil and Chile restrict foreign equity participation in domestic shipping service suppliers to a minority. Brazil also requires that two-thirds of crew members be Brazilian nationals, and foreign vessels are not permitted to participate in coastal trade unless they are party to a bilateral agreement with Brazil. Brazil has bilateral agreements on cargo sharing with Argentina, Chile, Germany and Portugal. The United States has a highly restricted market for maritime services. The *Merchant Marine Act 1920* (the Jones Act) requires that all goods transported by water between US ports be carried in US owned, operated, built and crewed ships. The United States reserves the right to impose retaliatory measures on routes served by US ships as well as routes served by foreign ships but carrying US cargo.

Colombia and Mexico achieved moderate foreign index scores. These economies restrict foreign equity participation in shipping service suppliers and onshore services to a minority, and require that the majority of crews on flag vessels be nationals.

The most open markets in the region are Argentina and Canada, which both have relatively liberal access regimes. Argentina has some restrictions on foreign vessels participating in coastal trade and reserves the right to impose counter-measures in response to unfair practices in maritime services. Canada also imposes limits on foreign participation in coastal trade and permits liner conferences.

Domestic index

Chile and the United States treat foreign maritime service suppliers significantly less favourably than domestic firms. The remaining economies in this region moderately discriminate against foreign maritime service suppliers. Chile limits the participation of foreign vessels in its coastal trade, and the United States imposes several entry restrictions to its ports against selected economies and prohibits all entry by Korean vessels.

Figure 10.2 Restrictiveness indexes for selected American economies

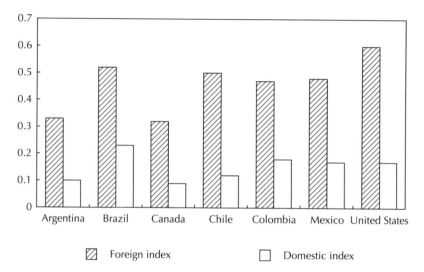

European economies

Foreign index

Germany, Italy, Spain and Sweden are the most restricted markets in this region for trade in maritime services (Figure 10.3). All of these economies reserve the right through relevant shipping legislation to impose retaliatory measures against unfair practices. These economies also require that foreign maritime service suppliers wishing to fly the national flag be owned by a national or EU-registered service supplier. In addition, Germany deems that a number of port services are mandatory and that domestic operators be government approved. Spain requires that maritime service suppliers have a domestic representative agent, and Sweden limits foreign equity participation in domestic shipping and onshore service suppliers.

Austria, Belgium, Finland, France, Ireland, the Netherlands and Switzerland achieved moderate scores. Austria, Belgium, France, Ireland and the Netherlands require that maritime services be supplied through a domestic commercial presence. Finland requires mandatory pilotage, to be provided by an approved Finnish service supplier. Switzerland excludes foreign equity participation in domestic shipping service suppliers.

Figure 10.3 Restrictiveness indexes for European economies

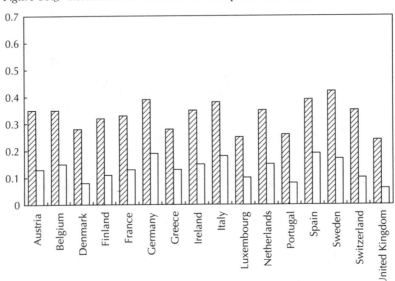

Notes: The higher the score, the more restrictive the economy; the scores range from 0 to 1; as noted earlier, inland waterways are covered by this study.

Source: Results estimated as part of this chapter.

Denmark, Greece, Luxembourg, Portugal and the United Kingdom are the most open markets in the region. Denmark and Portugal require the mandatory use of pilotage, while Greece also requires the mandatory use of towing and tug assistance for larger ships. In Luxembourg, foreign maritime service suppliers wishing to register maritime service suppliers in the Luxembourg Shipping Register must be more than 50 per cent owned by EU nationals or must be an EU company with an office in a member state. The United Kingdom is a party to the United Nations Liner Code.

Domestic index

All economies in this region impose several restrictions on their domestic maritime service suppliers, which are also imposed on foreign suppliers. Most economies apply the same conditions to foreign and domestic maritime service suppliers wishing to fly the national flag and require all ships, whether foreign or domestic, to use mandatory port services such as pilotage.

Some qualifications on measurement

The reliability of the index for different economies is dependent on the quality and depth of information. The available list of restrictions for 35 economies that is used here has been compiled from the best known sources of information. However, given the number of economies covered, some restrictions may not have been captured or may have been scored differently from the way in which they are applied in practice. A more stringent index could be developed if a greater depth of information on restrictions were available.

The index does not take into account the different natural endowments of economies. Some have no or few restrictions on maritime services because they are landlocked and have no or few inland waterways. For example, Luxembourg's location contributes to a low score because several restriction categories, including cabotage and port services, are effectively not applicable. Some economies may require high restrictions on maritime services to safeguard against accidents. For example, the United States requires mandatory pilotage for the entry of ships into some ports. This may be entirely appropriate if foreign pilots lack the experience to berth a ship safely in technically difficult and hazardous ports.

Some restrictions may not necessarily fit within a restriction category. Certain restrictions may only apply in one economy and are not covered by a restriction category in the index. These restrictions are not directly assigned a score but are used as background information in assigning appropriate scores in some restriction categories.

The results provide no indication of the safety of the maritime industry. There is usually a trade-off between competition and safety. The removal of some restrictions on entry and operations may reduce the costs of maritime services but sacrifice the safety of such services. For example, removing the requirements for ships to be registered and seaworthy may reduce entry costs to a market but may also jeopardise safety in the industry.

CONCLUSION

An index methodology has been developed and applied to quantify the restrictiveness of maritime service markets in 35 economies, based on information on restrictions ranging from 1994 to the end of 1998. There is a large range between the most restrictive and the least restrictive economies. Brazil, Chile, India, Indonesia, Korea, Malaysia, the Philippines, Thailand and the United States have the most restricted markets against foreigners. These markets are characterised by strict conditions on the right to fly the national flag and restrictions on the carriage of certain cargoes. Governments in these economies also permit liner conferences to form and operate, and they reserve the right to impose discretionary retaliatory measures. Brazil, Chile, the Philippines and Thailand restrict foreign equity participation in domestic maritime service suppliers to a minority.

Brazil, India, Indonesia, Korea and Malaysia apply a number of restrictions equally to domestic and foreign maritime service suppliers. These markets are characterised by the equal application to both domestic and foreign suppliers of restrictions on the form of commercial presence and conditions to fly the national flag, as well as the mandatory use of port services such as pilotage. Singapore affords the most equal treatment to foreign and domestic maritime service suppliers, with the difference accounted for entirely by restrictions on the movement of people.

Chile, the Philippines, Thailand, Turkey and the United States are the most discriminatory. These economies treat foreign maritime service suppliers significantly less favourably than domestic suppliers – the difference between the foreign and domestic index scores. These economies are also some of the most restricted economies.

NOTES

The authors are employed by the Australian Productivity Commission. Ms Tina Smith contributed the bulk of this chapter while on vacation employment with the Commission. The views expressed in this chapter are those of the staff involved and do not necessarily reflect those of the Productivity Commission. The Productivity Commission is the Australian government's principal review and advisory body on microeconomic reform. It conducts public inquiries and research into a broad range of economic and social issues affecting the welfare of Australians. Information on the Productivity Commission, its publications and its current work program can be found on the World Wide Web at <http://www.pc.gov.au>.

1   The GATS recognises the right of domestic regulators to impose minimum standards and conditions, which include qualification requirements and procedures, technical standards, licensing and authorisation (OECD 1994).

11 Price impact of restrictions on maritime transport services

Jong-Soon Kang

INTRODUCTION

Maritime transport is the main way of delivering cargo in international trade. In Australia, for instance, approximately 99 per cent of import volumes and 96 per cent of export volumes were transported by sea in the 1995–96 period (PC 1998c). Although the growth rate of air cargo transport is much faster, maritime transport is also expanding, with annual cargo shipped increasing for the thirteenth consecutive year to reach 5.06 billion tonnes in 1998 (Table 9.1). World economic growth relies heavily on international trade; therefore efficient and competitive shipping services are vital for a productive world economy. As discussed in Chapters 9 and 10 of this book, the maritime transport industry is subject to various forms of restrictive policies or practices that constitute significant impediments to trade. Such impediments to trade hinder competition and inflate the costs of shipping services and can therefore have a significant impact on the world economy.

This chapter investigates the impact of restrictions on maritime services trade on shipping prices or costs. A simple partial-equilibrium econometric model, incorporating cross-country and bilateral trade data, is used to test the proposition that impediments to trade in shipping services will increase transport costs and hence the shipping margins of traded products.

BASIC PRICE-IMPACT MODEL

The method and theoretical framework applied in this chapter was outlined in Chapter 3. As a first step in establishing an empirical model for estimating the price impact of restrictions on shipping services, shipping expenses (or margins) in bilateral trades are used as a proxy for price. Shipping margins (M_{ij}) for products shipped from country i (exporter) to country j (importer) are derived from comparisons of the FOB values at the point of export and the CIF values at the point of import. Letting EX_{ij} represent the observed FOB export value reported by the ith country as exported to the jth country and IM_{ji} represent the observed CIF value reported by importing country j for products imported from country i, shipping margins can be expressed as:

$$M_{ij} \equiv \frac{IM_{ji}}{EX_{ij}} = 1 + \delta = \mu \qquad (1)$$

Variable δ represents transport costs, and the term μ ($= M_{ij}$) > 0 is the CIF/FOB ratio for the commodity shipped from i to j. The CIF/FOB ratio is not affected by a rise of commodity prices because it is expressed in relative terms. However, any factors affecting transportation costs of shipping from i to j should change this ratio.

The model aims to estimate the impact on shipping margins (M_{ij}) of bilateral restrictions on trade in maritime services trade (R_{ij}). It will then allow for the impact of other variables such as the distance between trade partners (D_{ij}), and the scale of bilateral trade (SC_{ij}).

$$M_{ij} = f(R_{ij}, D_{ij}, SC_{ij}) \qquad (2)$$

where i and j (i $\neq$ j) = 1, 2, ..., n. If the Cobb-Douglas functional form of equation (2) is chosen, the relationship between M_{ij} and its arguments can be represented as:

$$M_{ij} = c \ (R_{ij})^{\alpha} \ (D_{ij})^{\beta} \ (SC_{ij})^{\gamma} \qquad (3)$$

where c is a constant term and α, β and γ are coefficients of R_{ij}, D_{ij} and SC_{ij} respectively. The coefficients are estimated in natural logarithmic forms, yielding:

$$\ln (M_{ij}) = C + \alpha \ln (R_{ij}) + \beta \ln (D_{ij}) + \gamma \ln (SC_{ij}) \qquad (4)$$

where $C = \ln c$ and the coefficients represent elasticities – that is, percentage changes in the margins in response to a unit percentage change in the corresponding variable.

In this model the coefficient of R_{ij} is expected to have positive sign ($\alpha > 0$), since higher restrictions on shipping services in either country will increase transport costs and hence the CIF/FOB ratio. This could be the result of the protection of inefficient operators and therefore higher costs. It could also occur as a result of the reduction in competition in markets for shipping services (Francois and Wooton 1999). As distance increases between trading partners, shipping margins should also increase ($\beta > 0$). The scale effect should be negative ($\gamma < 0$), since the margin is expected to be a decreasing function of the size of bilateral trade along a given route (Gehlhar et al. 1997).

DEFINITION OF VARIABLES AND CHARACTERISTICS OF DATA

McGuire et al. (in Chapter 10) provide an index to restrictions on shipping trade for 35 countries. Basic trade data used in the construction of M_{ij} and SC_{ij}

are from the Global Trade Analysis Project (GTAP) 4 Data Base, where the data are benchmarked to 1995 (McDougall et al. 1998). These two sources provide information on 23 countries: Australia; New Zealand; nine Asian countries (Korea, Japan, Hong Kong, the Philippines, Malaysia, Indonesia, Singapore, Thailand and India); five EU members (Denmark, Germany, Finland, Sweden and the United Kingdom); three North American countries (the United States, Canada and Mexico); and four South American economies (Argentina, Brazil, Chile and Colombia). A bilateral, cross-sectional dataset is established, which generates 506 observations for each variable.

Bilateral shipping margins (M_{ij})

The margin M_{ij} is calculated from the CIF/FOB ratio for the products shipped from country i to country j, with import and export data from the GTAP 4 database. Trade data upon which GTAP 4 is built originate from United Nations COMTRADE statistics (Gehlhar et al. 1997). As the UN COMTRADE database is one of the most complete and exhaustive databases in terms of commodity and country coverage, it is not surprising that there are problems of data availability, consistency and reliability.[1] There is a problem of inconsistency between reported export data and reported import data in COMTRADE, with export values reported on an FOB basis often exceeding the corresponding import values reported on a CIF basis. An effort was made in the GTAP project to reconcile these discrepancies by adjusting trade data with estimates of country-specific and commodity-specific biases in reporting exports and imports.[2] CIF/FOB ratios calculated with the GTAP 4 database should provide a more reliable set of bilateral trade margins compared with those in COMTRADE, although Gehlhar (1998) stresses that there are still problems in using CIF/FOB ratios as accurate trade margins.

The GTAP 4 database produces trade margins based on all modes of transportation, but to calculate shipping margins only the share of maritime transportation in total trade is required. These data, however, are incomplete and since maritime transportation is the main method of trade, this chapter uses trade margins as a proxy for shipping margins.

International trade margins vary widely across traded commodities (Gehlhar et al. 1997). Trade margins tend to be higher for lower value products: agricultural goods generally have low values per tonne compared with non-agricultural or manufactured goods, and therefore higher trade margins. Table 11.1 shows trade margins in broad categories of commodities in the 23 countries listed above. The countries are categorised as either developing or industrialised. In the table, M_{wi} refers to the margins for the products shipped from the world to country i and M_{iw} represents those shipped from country i to the world. In most of the listed countries, except Australia, Indonesia, Mexico, Colombia, Brazil and Chile, the trade margins on imports (M_{wi}) of manufactures are smaller than on agrifood products. In the case of the margins on exports (M_{iw}), only Colombia shows a value for manufactures greater than that for agrifood products. The table shows also that values for M_{iw} and M_{wi}

on agrifood products vary more widely across countries than those on manufactures. Another interesting point revealed in Table 11.1 is that, with only a few exceptions, export margins for products shipped from the world to developing economies are generally greater than those for exports to industrialised countries. In most economies in the table, the trade margins for their exports to the world are greater than those for their imports from the world ($M_{iw} \geq M_{wi}$).

While figures in Table 11.1 represent one-sided trade margins where either partner is the rest of the world, the M_{ij} variable used in the model in this chapter represents bilateral trade margins for all 23 countries. In estimating the margins function, bilateral margins data and other relevant data aggregated at the level of the manufacturing average are used. The agriculture and food sectors are excluded, since agrifood products are in general considered subject to a quite different set of policy measures and are much bulkier and more expensive to transport than manufactures. Inclusion of agrifood data could bias the estimation results by creating an underestimation or overestimation of the impacts of dependent variables on trade margins in equation (4).[3]

Bilateral restrictions on trade in maritime services (R_{ij})

McGuire et al. (in Chapter 10) quantified restrictions in shipping trade and constructed index numbers using various information sources in 35 countries from 1994 to the end of 1998. A foreign index quantifies the extent of all restrictions applying on foreign maritime services suppliers seeking to enter and/or operate in the domestic market, while a domestic index represents the extent to which both domestic and foreign suppliers are subject to the same restrictions. The difference between the foreign and domestic index scores is the extent to which foreigners are treated less favourably than domestic service suppliers. The foreign index is always higher than the domestic index, and therefore is used here as the basis of the variable R_{ij}.

Table 11.2 shows foreign and domestic restrictiveness indexes for the 23 countries examined in this chapter. The higher the value, the more restrictions there are on trade in maritime services. The table shows that, as with trade margins, industrialised countries generally have less-restricted markets for maritime services than developing economies. The foreign index registers values between 0.20 and 0.42 for all industrialised economies except the United States, which has the fourth-highest level of restrictions (at 0.60) among the 23 countries. Among the developing economies, Argentina has a relatively low foreign restrictiveness figure at 0.33. The other developing countries have much higher values ranging from 0.47 up to 0.64. The domestic index varies far less for both industrialised and developing groups, and across countries. The values range between 0.06 and 0.19 for the industrialised economies and between 0.09 and 0.28 for the developing economies.

The R_{ij} that is needed for estimating equation (4) is an index of the bilateral relationship – that is, restrictions on shipping services for bilateral trade

Table 11.1 Trade margins across broad categories of commodities by country, 1995

	Total commodities		Agrifood products		Manufactures	
	M_{wi}	M_{iw}	M_{wi}	M_{iw}	M_{wi}	M_{iw}
Industrialised countries						
Sweden	1.05	1.07	1.10	1.17	1.04	1.06
Hong Kong	1.05	1.23	1.07	1.52	1.05	1.22
Singapore	1.06	1.14	1.28	1.45	1.05	1.13
Denmark	1.06	1.11	1.09	1.18	1.06	1.08
Canada	1.07	1.07	1.11	1.22	1.06	1.06
Finland	1.07	1.07	1.11	1.14	1.07	1.07
Germany	1.07	1.08	1.11	1.14	1.07	1.08
US	1.08	1.15	1.15	1.53	1.07	1.10
UK	1.08	1.09	1.20	1.17	1.06	1.08
New Zealand	1.09	1.30	1.10	1.53	1.09	1.11
Australia [+]	1.14	1.24	1.11	1.56	1.14	1.14
Japan	1.18	1.14	1.71	1.28	1.08	1.14
Developing countries						
Mexico [+*]	1.08	1.07	1.06	1.13	1.08	1.06
Indonesia [+*]	1.14	1.13	1.14	1.17	1.14	1.13
Colombia [+]	1.14	1.15	1.10	1.14	1.15	1.15
Malaysia [*]	1.15	1.11	1.56	1.31	1.13	1.09
Chile [*]	1.15	1.12	1.12	1.22	1.16	1.09
Korea	1.16	1.16	1.54	1.21	1.12	1.16
Argentina	1.17	1.22	1.18	1.27	1.16	1.17
Brazil [+*]	1.21	1.16	1.12	1.21	1.22	1.13
Thailand [*]	1.22	1.16	1.53	1.26	1.20	1.13
Philippines [*]	1.30	1.11	1.53	1.22	1.27	1.09
India [*]	1.46	1.15	1.59	1.21	1.45	1.14
World Total	1.12	1.12	1.25	1.25	1.10	1.10
	(5,183)	(4,639)	(580)	(464)	(4,603)	(4,175)

Notes: $M_{wi} = (IM_{iw} / EX_{wi})$ and $M_{iw} = (IM_{wi} / EX_{iw})$, where i = 1, 2, ..., 23, and w = world; IM_{ww} and EX_{ww} for each commodity categories in parentheses (in billion US dollars); countries in each group are listed in ascending order of M_{iw} for total commodities; + M_{wi} for manufactures) ≥ (M_{wi} for agrifood products); * $M_{wi} ≥ M_{iw}$ for manufactures.

Source: GTAP 4 Data Base.

between two countries, i and j. However, the index in Table 11.2 is one-sided and applies to all partners. It is not R_{ij}, but can be denoted as R_{iw} or simply R_i, representing the restrictions on shipping services for country i's trade with any part of the world. Therefore, considering that bilateral trade is affected by restrictions in both exporter and importer countries, the restrictiveness indexes in both trading countries (that is, R_i and R_j) are used for proxy variables for the bilateral index of restrictiveness and replace R_{ij} in equations (3) and (4). Accordingly, equation (4) becomes:

Table 11.2   Index of restrictiveness of international trade in maritime services

	Foreign	Domestic		Foreign	Domestic
Industrialised economies			*Developing economies*		
Singapore	0.207	0.105	Argentina	0.331	0.095
United Kingdom	0.239	0.062	Colombia	0.469	0.181
Denmark	0.284	0.081	Mexico	0.478	0.171
Finland	0.315	0.114	Chile	0.503	0.124
Canada	0.320	0.090	Malaysia	0.520	0.252
New Zealand	0.352	0.105	Brazil	0.521	0.228
Germany	0.390	0.190	Indonesia	0.558	0.209
Hong Kong	0.403	0.090	Korea	0.582	0.280
Japan	0.408	0.147	Thailand	0.601	0.133
Sweden	0.415	0.166	India	0.605	0.252
Australia	0.416	0.128	Philippines	0.644	0.171
United States	0.600	0.171			

Note: Countries in each group are listed in ascending order of the foreign restrictiveness index.

Source: McGuire et al. (Chapter 10).

$$\ln (M_{ij}) = C + \alpha_1 \ln (R_i) + \alpha_2 \ln (R_j) + \beta \ln (D_{ij}) + \gamma \ln (SC_{ij}) \qquad (5)$$

Equation (5) is further extended to implement different characteristics of components of the restrictiveness index. McGuire et al. (Chapter 10) note that restrictions for different economies are broadly divided into two groups–those affecting commercial presence (denoted as R_i^c or R_j^c) and other restrictions such as those on cabotage and port services (denoted as R_i^0 or R_j^0). They argue that the reason for distinguishing R_i^c from R_i^0 (or R_j^c from R_j^0) is so that the former can be modelled as restrictions on the movement of capital while the latter represents restrictions on trade in maritime services. In exporting country i, products will be exported by a domestic maritime service supplier, by a foreign supplier who set up a commercial presence in the domestic market, or by a foreign supplier operating from its home base. Either R_i or its two components R_i^0 and R_i^c would represent the exporter's restrictiveness variable in equation (5). With respect to restrictions in importing country j, R_j^0 will have a direct impact on shipping margins of imported products. However, restrictions on commercial presence in country j, (R_j^c) may not have a direct or significant impact on the margins of the products imported to the country. That is, R_j^c may have, if any, a minimal or very indirect impact on international competition in the supply of shipping services in exporting country i and hence on shipping margins M_{ij}. This implies that $R_j (= R_j^0 + R_j^c)$ should not enter into equation (5) as an aggregate but separately as R_j^0 and

R_i^c to allow different degrees of impact. Alternatively, only R_i^0 alone should be included if there is expected to be no significant impact of R_i^c.

Table 11.3 shows the restrictive index for commercial presence (R_i^c) and that for other restrictions R_i^0, which sum to the foreign index numbers in Table 11.2. It shows that countries with a higher R_i^0 also have a high R_i^c and vice versa: there is some kind of linear relationship between these two components of R_i. The relationship between R_i^0 and R_i^c is plotted in Figure 11.1, showing that the correlation between the two variables is close to 0.5. This figure implies that there may be some multicollinearity problem when both components of the restrictiveness index for either importer i or exporter j enter together into equation (5).

To address these problems, equation (5) can be rewritten as:

$$\ln (M_{ij}) = C + \alpha_{11} \ln (R_i^0) + \alpha_2 \ln (R_j)$$

$$+ \beta \ln (D_{ij}) + \gamma \ln (SC_{ij}) \tag{6}$$

or as its fully extended form:

$$\ln (M_{ij}) = C + \alpha_{11} \ln (R_i^0) + \alpha_{12} \ln (R_i^c) + \alpha_{21} \ln (R_j^0) + \alpha_{22} \ln (R_j^c)$$

$$+ \beta \ln (D_{ij}) + \gamma \ln (SC_{ij}) \tag{6'}$$

In equations (6) and (6)', the α coefficients are all expected to have positive signs. While α_{22} may not be significantly different from zero, α_{11} and α_{12} are expected to have positive signs but are likely to be affected by the multicollinearity between R_i^0 and R_i^c

Distance (D_{ij})

The ideal distance data would be mileage for water routes from port to port, but instead data from the *Times Atlas of the World* of average geographical mileage (in thousand kilometres) between capital cities are used as a proxy.

Scale of bilateral trade (SC_{ij})

The sum of the value of manufacturing exports from i to j and those from j to i is used to represent the scale of bilateral trade between i and j. That is,

$$SC_{ij} = EX_{ij} + EX_{ji} \tag{7}$$

The volume of trade between countries would be a better measure, but this is not available in the same measurement for all manufactures. Instead FOB value data from the GTAP 4 Data Base, deflated by billion US dollars, is used for a proxy for trade volume.

Table 11.3 Foreign index of restrictions on maritime services trade

	R_i^c	R_i^o		R_i^c	R_i^o
Industrialised economies			*Developing economies*		
Singapore	0.037	0.170	Argentina	0.045	0.285
United Kingdom	0.045	0.194	Colombia	0.239	0.285
Denmark	0.045	0.238	Mexico	0.260	0.218
Finland	0.074	0.242	Chile	0.203	0.300
Canada	0.038	0.282	Malaysia	0.261	0.259
New Zealand	0.088	0.264	Brazil	0.152	0.369
Hong Kong	0.131	0.259	Indonesia	0.235	0.323
Germany	0.145	0.258	Korea	0.226	0.356
Japan	0.131	0.277	Thailand	0.239	0.362
Sweden	0.178	0.237	India	0.261	0.344
Australia	0.185	0.231	Philippines	0.273	0.371
United States	0.199	0.401			

Note: Countries in each group are listed in ascending order of the foreign restrictiveness index.

Figure 11.1 Correlation between restrictions on commercial presence and other restrictions on maritime services trade

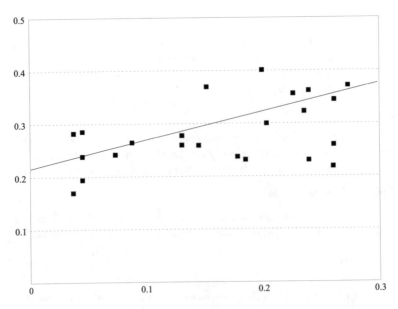

Note: y axis is R_i^o, x axis is R_i^c, with $COR(R_i^o, R_i^c) = 0.480$; $R_i^o = 0.22 + 0.36 R_i^c$ (F = 6.28; t = 2.507).

ESTIMATION RESULTS AND POLICY IMPLICATIONS

In an effort to let different bilateral relationships enter the model, dummy variables are constructed as follows:

d_{11} = 1 when both exporter i and importer j are industrialised economies, and 0 otherwise;

d_{10} = 1 when i is a industrialised economy and j is a developing economy;

d_{01} = 1 when i is a developing economy and j is a industrialised economy; and

d_{00} = 1 when both i and j are developing economies.

The first three constant dummies entered into equations (5) and (6), and extended forms of (6), and the constant term of the equation represents d_{00}. The regression results differ for exporters depending on whether countries are industrialised or developing, but this is not the case for importers. That is, coefficients of d_{11} and d_{10} or of d_{01} and d_{00} are not statistically different from each other in all regressions of (5), (6) and extended forms of (6). The data are then regrouped to identify exporters as either industrialised or developing economies regardless of the type of importing country as follows:

d_1 = 1 when exporter i is an industrialised economy for any importer j, and 0 otherwise; and

d_0 = 1 when exporter i is a developing economy for any importer j.

Table 11.4 shows the results of ordinary least squares estimations of equations (5), (6), the extended forms of (6), with a constant dummy d_1, and multiplicative or slope dummies for all components of restrictiveness variables.[4]

The models in Table 11.4 share many common features and the estimation results are very close in terms of the sizes of the coefficients and test statistics. Of the models presented in Table 11.4, nevertheless, model (6) has slightly better statistical results and is chosen as the representative model. Allowing some structural differences between the d_1 group and the d_0 group, model (6) can then be written as:

$$\ln (M_{ij}) = 0.3388 + 0.1416 \ln (R_i) + 0.0443 \ln (R_i^\circ) + 0.0011 \ln (D_{ij})$$
$$- 0.0049 \ln (SC_{ij}), \text{ for all } i = \text{developing economies } (d_0); \text{ and}$$

$$\ln (M_{ij}) = 0.1414 + 0.0225 \ln (R_i) + (0.0443 \sim 0.0128) \ln (R_i^\circ) + 0.0011 \ln$$
$$(D_{ij}) - 0.0049 \ln (SC_{ij}), \text{ for all } i = \text{industrialised economies } (d_1).$$

The important outcomes of these estimations and the policy implications of the estimation results in Table 11.4 can be summarised as follows:

Table 11.4 Impact of maritime services restrictions on trade margins

	(5)	(6)	(6-1)	(6-2)	(6-3)	(6-4)	(6-5)	(6-6)
R_i	0.1400	0.1416	0.1407	n.a.	n.a.	0.1414	n.a.	n.a.
$d_1 \cdot R_i$	-0.1180	-0.1191	-0.1180	n.a.	n.a.	-0.1186	n.a.	n.a.
R_i^o	n.a.	n.a.	n.a.	0.1054	0.1051	n.a.	0.1056	0.1046
$d_1 \cdot R_i^o$	n.a.	n.a.	n.a.	-0.0816	-0.0812	n.a.	-0.0811	-0.0797
R_i^c	n.a.	n.a.	n.a.	0.0262	0.0264	n.a.	0.0262	0.0262
$d_1 \cdot R_i^c$	n.a.	n.a.	n.a.	-0.0240	-0.0244	n.a.	-0.0243	-0.0243
R_j	0.0270	n.a.	n.a.	n.a.	n.a.	n.a.	n.a.	n.a.
$d_1 \cdot R_j$	-0.0083	n.a.	n.a.	n.a.	n.a.	n.a.	n.a.	n.a.
R_j^o	n.a.	0.0443	0.0278	0.0452	0.3982	0.0429	0.0457	0.0285
$d_1 \cdot R_j^o$	n.a.	-0.0315	n.a.	-0.0421	-0.0322	-0.0401	-0.0326	n.a.
R_j^c	n.a.	n.a.	n.a.	0.0003	0.0043	0.0011	n.a.	n.a.
$d_1 \cdot R_j^c$	n.a.	n.a.	n.a.	0.0077	n.a.	0.0071	n.a.	n.a.
D_{ij}	0.0017	0.0011	0.0011	0.0006	0.0008	0.0011	0.0006	0.0006
SC_{ij}	-0.0044	-0.0049	-0.0048	-0.0051	-0.0050	-0.0049	-0.0051	-0.0050
C	0.2964	0.3388	0.3165	0.4200	0.4193	0.3386	0.4203	0.3965
d_1	-0.1574	-0.1904	-0.1495	-0.2484	-0.2517	-0.1869	-0.2519	-0.2086
F	35.3	35.6	41.2	22.8	25.0	27.8	27.7	30.9
$\bar{R}^2$	0.3221	0.3238	0.3231	0.3215	0.3221	0.3229	0.3225	0.3216

Notes: All variables except d_1 are in natural log forms; F refers to F-statistic of the model; $\bar{R}^2$ refers to the adjusted R^2; –: variable not used in estimation. Coefficients with t-statistic which can reject H_0 at a 80% confidence level but not at a 90% level are italicised. Coefficients with t-statistic which cannot reject H_0 at a 80% confidence level are underlined.
n.a. = not available.

- The restrictions on commercial presence of maritime services in importing countries (R_i^c) have no significant impact on the shipping margins of exported products (see models (6-2), (6-3) and (6-4). The exclusion of this variable and its slope dummy slightly improves the model.
- Other restrictions on services trade (except those on commercial presence) appear to differently affect the shipping margins of importing countries. Differences are observed between the d_1 and d_0 groups, even though the statistical probability of accepting these differences is less than 90 per cent but higher than 80 per cent. This implies that, for industrialised countries, the impact on shipping margins of percentage changes in maritime services restrictions in exporting or importing countries, or both, will be close to, or probably in many cases less than, the impact observed in the developing economy group.

   While trade margins are generally higher for products shipped to developing economies (Table 11.1), changes in maritime services restrictions in any trading partner will have a greater effect on the margins of their exports. This is partly because restrictions are generally higher in developing countries than in industrialised economies. This implies that there is a greater scope for maritime services liberalisation in developing economies, and that the impact of these reductions on shipping charges will be higher.

- When R_i is separated into R_i^o and R_i^c in the estimations, the coefficients of these components are significantly different from each other and also vary between the cases of the d_1 and d_0 groups (see (6-2), (6-3), (6-5) and (6-6)). However, the possibility of multicollinearity biasing the estimation results cannot be excluded. Nevertheless, it is noted that the coefficients of R_i (and also of $d_1 \cdot R_i$) in other models (as in (6), (6-1) and (6-4)) are very close to the sum of coefficients of R_i^o and R_i^c (and also of $d_1 \cdot R_i^o$ and $d_1 \cdot R_i^c$). These statistical results may imply that the impact of R_i can be decomposed into those of R_i^o and R_i^c [5]

- Geographical distance to destinations seems not to have a significant impact on shipping margins, despite the variable having correct (positive) signs in the estimations.[6] The variable may have been significant if sea-route distance between major ports had been used.

- The scale of the bilateral trade has some positive impact on trade margins. This effect does not differ for the different types of bilateral trade relationships (that is, between the d_1 and d_0 groups) and the size of the impact is similar across the models. Although the estimation results show smaller unit shipping margins for larger trading partners, the absolute size of the elasticity of the margins with respect to the scale of bilateral trade is relatively small compared to the margins with respect to trade liberalisation of maritime services.

- The maritime services restrictions imposed by exporting countries (R_j) appear to have in general a much greater impact on margins than those imposed by importing countries (R_j or R_i^o). However, the possibility of the reverse result – that is, the coefficient of R_i^o being greater than that of R_i – cannot be totally excluded when the exporters are industrialised economies (see, for example, (6) in Table 11.4).

- While the restrictions on commercial presence imposed by importing countries R_i^c do not assert a significant impact on shipping margins of imported products, those in exporting countries (R_j^c) certainly raise the costs of shipping their exports. In exporting countries, lowering restrictions on maritime services such as cabotage and port services has a greater effect on margins than reducing restrictions on the commercial presence of foreign suppliers.

- Coefficients of the dummy variable d_1 are statistically significant, implying structural differences of the model when exporters are industrialised countries or developing economies. The signs of the coefficients for d_1 indicate that, at a given level of restriction, margins are lower when the exporter is an industrialised economy, other things being equal.

CONCLUSION

This chapter has developed a model to measure the impact of shipping restrictions on transport margins. The results demonstrate that it is possible to allow for differences in bilateral trade relationships and in policy choices when explaining variations in margins between economies.

The chapter highlighted a number of policy implications for liberalising the international shipping industry. The most important one is that a low degree of restrictions in any trading partner is necessary in order to have low shipping charges. The benefits of eliminating restrictions on shipping services appear to be higher in low-income countries. The benefits will come not only from the reduction in costs but from increased competition, which will lead to improved service quality, an increase in the number of suppliers, and lower mark ups over costs.

The simple model constructed in this chapter could be advanced in various ways. Better data for all variables, particularly appropriate bilateral data, is the first step to improve the model. Searching for new explanatory variables such as bilateral freight rates and the quality of the port, which are thought to affect transport costs but not to be correlated strongly with the other factors, is equally important. Since many variables enter into the single equation reduced form with a high possibility of endogeneity of some explanatory variables, it may be useful to adopt the approach of simultaneous equations. Modelling can also be developed to simultaneously derive other impacts such as welfare effects and, possibly, quantity impacts.

Furthermore, the increased sophistication of the techniques for measuring the restrictiveness of policies will provide a more powerful model to make explicit the mechanisms by which policy choices affect market outcomes. As the extent of modelling work expands and data increases, the restrictiveness variable itself may be determined endogenously.

NOTES

1   For further details of problems in UN COMTRADE and numerous efforts to tackle these, see Gehlhar et al. (1997: pp. 76–7).
2   See Gehlhar et al. (1997) for detailed reconciliation process in GTAP 4 database.
3   It would be ideal to use a more dissaggregated sectoral margins function, where similar levels of unit transport costs can be observed, allowing trade margins to be more accurately compared across bilateral transactions. This more disagreggated approach is left for further studies.
4   Estimates do not include slope dummies for the distance and scale variables, since no differences in the coefficient on these variables are evident in any models. The estimation results of the models with slope and constant dummies showed slightly higher $\overline{R}^2 s$ than those only with a constant dummy.
5   That is, using the notations in the equations (6) and (6)' it can be expressed as: $(\alpha1 \cong \alpha11 + \alpha12)$, and $(\alpha11 > \alpha12)$.
6   However, exclusion of this variable did not improve the estimation results.

12 Restrictiveness of international trade in banking services

Greg McGuire and Michael Schuele

INTRODUCTION

Banking services are important intermediate inputs to other sectors of an economy. Such services facilitate transactions, pool and allocate financial resources, and provide services to manage risk. They need to be supplied in a competitive, efficient and stable environment.

Governments impose restrictions on trade in banking services to achieve various objectives. Some restrictions may aim to restrict trade deliberately, while others may be imposed for prudential reasons. Prudential requirements or restrictions are usually necessary to ensure the efficiency and stability of a banking system.

This chapter first of all discusses the nature of the restrictions on trade in banking services. It then provides a comprehensive list of such restrictions, compiled from a number of information sources. An index methodology, similar to that in Chapter 10, is then used to summarise and quantify the nature and extent of these restrictions in 38 economies, covering the Asia Pacific region, the Americas and Europe.

PRUDENTIAL AND NON-PRUDENTIAL REGULATION

Prudential regulation is aimed at ensuring the stability of a banking system by preserving solvency, limiting risks and protecting bank deposits. Capital and liquidity requirements are common forms of prudential regulation. Banks are required to hold minimum levels of capital to reduce the risk of loss to depositors, creditors and other stakeholders and to assist regulators in pursuing the overall stability of the industry (BIS 1997). Banks are required to hold liquid assets to ensure that they can cope with increases in demand for loans or withdrawal of deposits (RBA 1996). This regulation is clearly aimed at limiting the risk and preserving the solvency of banks.

Prudential regulation restricts a bank's business but adds to its stability. Wallis et al. (1997) argue that, while regulation imposes costs both directly on the financial system and on the wider economy, it adds to the stability of a financial system provided there is an appropriate balance between prudential and efficiency considerations. Prudential requirements are not aimed at restricting trade.

Prudential requirements are generally similar across economies. They are often based on the Core Principles for Effective Banking Supervision of the Basle Committee on Banking Supervision. These principles have been endorsed by authorities from about 120 countries and are used by the International Monetary Fund (IMF) and the World Bank for evaluating supervisory regimes around the world (BIS 1998).

The Core Principles are minimum requirements and they may be supplemented by other measures designed to address particular conditions or risks in the financial systems of individual economies (BIS 1997). The importance of economies being able to vary and have overall control of prudential requirements is recognised in multilateral trading agreements. Under the General Agreement on Trade in Services (GATS), the scheduling of prudential regulation is optional, where prudential measures are those aiming to ensure the integrity and stability of a financial system (IC 1997).

This chapter summarises and quantifies the extent of non-prudential regulation that may restrict trade inappropriately. In Chapter 13, a model is used to estimate separately the influence of prudential and non-prudential regulation on the net interest margins of banks.

Non-prudential regulations frequently affect a bank's ability to operate efficiently in a market. For example, banks may be restricted from extending their distribution networks through branches and automatic teller machines. This clearly limits their ability to penetrate and compete effectively in a banking services market.

It is sometimes difficult to classify financial regulation as purely prudential or non-prudential. The licensing of banks has both competition and prudential aspects. Factors affecting competition may include limitations on the number of licences, as well as conditions on a licence, such as being directed to lend to specific sectors (e.g. housing, small business). Such limitations have been treated as a restriction on competition. But the various initial capital and liquidity requirements needed to obtain a banking licence have been treated as prudential.

As outlined in Chapter 10, restrictions on trade in services are barriers that can limit service suppliers from entering or operating in a market and they can be discriminatory or non-discriminatory.

RESTRICTIONS ON TRADE IN BANKING SERVICES

A list of government non-prudential regulations on entry and operations for banking services has been compiled from a number of sources. The GATS schedules for financial services are the starting point for compiling a list of restrictions for each economy (WTO 1998b, 1998c). The information in the schedules is limited, however, by the positive-listing approach, the optional nature of scheduling prudential measures and the absence of specific criteria for distinguishing between prudential and non-prudential measures. The schedules are supplemented by other sources of information in order to capture financial sector developments in some economies:

- WTO (World Trade Organisation) Trade Policy Reviews, which describe financial regulatory structures, trade restrictions and trade policies for WTO members (WTO 1995, 1996, 1997a, 1998d);
- the National Trade Estimate Report on Foreign Trade Barriers from the Office of the US Trade Representative, which covers information on restrictions for most economies (USTR 1998);
- APEC (Asia Pacific Economic Cooperation) Individual Action Plans, which list restrictions and liberalising commitments in reports covering services, investment, competition and deregulation (APEC 1997b, 1997c);
- a Common List of Barriers to Financial Services Trade report prepared by the WTO Financial Leaders Group, which gives a list of restrictions on trade in financial services for Asian and South American economies (FLG 1997);
- information provided by Indonesia, Korea and Thailand to the IMF as a requirement for receiving standby credit facilities, which outlines the structure of and developments in financial services sectors (Government of Indonesia 1998a, 1998b, 1998c; Government of South Korea 1997a, 1997b, 1997c, 1998a, 1998b, 1998c; Government of Thailand 1997, 1998a, 1998b, 1998c); and
- the TradePort Web site, which covers information on restrictions for most economies (TradePort 1998).

A consolidated listing and description of non-prudential restrictions on banking services has been compiled from the above sources of information for 38 economies, as at 31 December 1997. The sources of information are, as far as possible, matched to this date. The resulting index of restrictions to trade in banking services is later incorporated into the model of Chapter 13 to estimate the effect of trade restrictions on the interest margins of banks. The econometric model uses interest margins data of banks for the closest financial year ending prior to 31 December 1997.[1]

Restrictions specific to banking services and major 'horizontal' restrictions on all services are included in the list. The horizontal restrictions on all services, including banking services, are those on the movement of people, on direct investment and on the composition of the board of directors. The approach taken here is to quantify all restrictions on banking services, regardless of whether the restrictions are specific to banking or not.

Some of these sources provide little or no information on restrictions for some economies. While a fairly comprehensive list of restrictions can be drawn from these sources, some financial sector developments may not be covered.

Table 12.1 Restrictiveness index for banking services

Category weightings[a]			Score	Restriction category
R^b	MFN^c	$Total^d$		
				Restrictions on Commercial Presence
0.190	0.010	0.20		*Licensing of banks*
			1.00	Issues no new banking licences.
			0.75	Issues up to 3 new banking licences with only prudential requirements.
			0.50	Issues up to 6 new banking licences with only prudential requirements.
			0.25	Issues up to 10 new banking licences with only prudential requirements.
			0.00	Issues new banking licences with only prudential requirements.
0.190	0.010	0.20		*Direct investment*
				The score is inversely proportional to the maximum equity participation permitted in an existing domestic bank. For example, equity participation to a maximum of 75 per cent of a bank would receive a score of 0.25.
0.095	0.005	0.10		*Joint venture arrangements*
			1.00	Issues no new banking licences and no entry is allowed through a joint venture with a domestic bank.
			0.50	Bank entry is only through a joint venture with a domestic bank.
			0.00	No requirement for a bank to enter through a joint venture with a domestic bank.
0.019	0.001	0.02		*Permanent movement of people*
			1.00	No entry of executives, senior managers and/or specialists.
			0.80	Executives, specialists and/or senior managers can stay up to 1 year.
			0.60	Executives, specialists and/or senior managers can stay up to 2 years.
			0.40	Executives, specialists and/or senior managers can stay up to 3 years.
			0.20	Executives, specialists and/or senior managers can stay up to 4 years.
			0.00	Executives, specialists and/or senior managers can stay a period of 5 years or more.
				Other Restrictions
0.143	0.007	0.15		*Raising funds by banks*
			1.00	Banks are not permitted to raise funds in the domestic market.
			0.75	Banks are restricted from raising funds from domestic capital markets.
			0.50	Banks are restricted in accepting deposits from the public.
			0.00	Banks can raise funds from any source with only prudential requirements.

Table 12.1 (continued)

Category weightings[a]			Score	Restriction category
R[b]	MFN[c]	Total[d]		
0.143	0.007	0.15		*Lending funds by banks*
			1.00	Banks are not permitted to lend to domestic clients.
			0.75	Banks are restricted to a specified lending size or lending to government projects.
			0.50	Banks are restricted in providing certain services such as credit cards, leasing and consumer finance.
			0.25	Banks are directed to lend to housing and small business.
			0.00	Banks can lend to any source with only prudential restrictions.
0.095	0.005	0.10		*Other business of banks – insurance and securities services*
			1.00	Banks can only provide banking services.
			0.50	Banks can provide banking services plus one other line of business – insurance or securities services.
			0.00	Banks have no restrictions on conducting other lines of business.
0.048	0.003	0.05		*Expanding the number of banking outlets*
			1.00	One banking outlet with no new banking outlets permitted.
			0.75	Number of banking outlets is limited in number and location.
			0.25	Expansion of banking outlets is subject to non-prudential regulatory approval.
			0.00	No restrictions on banks expanding operations.
0.019	0.001	0.02		*Composition of the board of directors* The score is inversely proportionately to the percentage of the board that can comprise foreigners. For example, a score of 0.80 is allocated where 20 per cent of the board of directors of a bank can comprise foreigners.
0.010	0.001	0.01		*Temporary movement of people*
			1.00	No temporary entry of executives, senior managers and/or specialists.
			0.75	Temporary entry of executives, senior managers and/or specialists up to 30 days.
			0.50	Temporary entry of executives, senior managers and/or specialists up to 60 days.
			0.25	Temporary entry of executives, senior managers and/or specialists up to 90 days.
			0.00	Temporary entry of executives, senior managers and/or specialists over 90 days.
0.950	0.050	1.00		*Total*

Notes:
a Totals may not add due to rounding.
b R is the restriction category weighting.
c MFN is the most-favoured-nation category weighting.
d Total of the restriction category and most-favoured-nation category weightings.

RESTRICTIVENESS INDEX METHODOLOGY

An index methodology has been used to quantify the nature and extent of restrictions on international trade in services. An index uses available information on regulations to quantify the extent to which comparable economies have more or less restrictive trading regimes for banking services. Table 12.1 outlines the restrictiveness index used for banking services.

An index has been developed by first grouping the restrictions identified from the sources of information listed earlier into common restriction categories. Restrictions for different economies are divided into two groupings: those affecting commercial presence and other restrictions. As noted in Chapter 10, the reason for distinguishing restrictions on commercial presence from other restrictions is so that the former can ideally be modelled as restrictions on the movement of capital, while the latter can be modelled as restrictions on trade in banking services.

Restrictions on commercial presence affect the ability to become established in an economy and provide banking services. The commercial presence restriction grouping covers restrictions on licensing, direct investment, joint venture arrangements and the permanent movement of people. The 'other restrictions' grouping covers restrictions on raising funds, lending funds, providing other lines of business (insurance and securities services), expanding banking outlets, the composition of the board of directors and the temporary movement of people.

The index applies only to restrictions on domestic banks and the subsidiaries of foreign banks. This is the main form of delivery of banking services. Restrictions on foreign bank branches are excluded from the index. This is because the results from this chapter are used in Chapter 13 to estimate the effect of restrictions on the net interest margins of banks, and data are insufficient to estimate the net interest margins and capital of foreign bank branches.

Within these common restriction categories, the degree of restrictiveness varies. An index has been developed by assessing the differing degrees of restriction, from most restrictive to least restrictive, for most categories. The greater the restriction on banking services, the higher or more restrictive the score. Scores range from 0 (least restrictive) to 1 (most restrictive). For each category, a score is given that best reflects the type of restriction imposed by an economy.

As in Chapter 10, we assigned weights to restriction categories by making an a priori assessment of the cost of restrictions to economic efficiency. Hardin and Holmes (in Chapter 4), Warren (in Chapter 6), OECD (1997a) and Claessens and Glaessner (1998) provide examples of weightings to apply to restriction categories. From these papers and the research conducted for this chapter, we made a judgement about the cost to economic efficiency of different restrictions. Restrictions that we considered to impose a greater cost on economic efficiency are given a greater weighting. For example, restrictions

Table 12.2 Scores for MFN exemptions: banking services and movement of people

Score	Type of MFN exemption
1.00	No MFN exemption
0.50	MFN exemption with reciprocity with selected or all economies
0.00	MFN exemption with preferential treatment with selected or all economies

covering the licensing of banks are generally considered to be more restrictive and a greater cost to economic efficiency than those restrictions on the movement of people (see Table 10.2).

We calculated an index score for domestic and foreign banks to separately quantify the extent to which regulation restricts domestic and international competition. The foreign index covers restrictions relevant to foreign banks, and the domestic index covers those applying to all banks. Non-discriminatory restrictions limiting the number of new banking licences receive the same score under the domestic and the foreign indexes. A higher score is assigned under the foreign index than the domestic index where no foreign bank licences are issued. The difference between the foreign and domestic index score is a measure of discrimination against foreigners.

A key question is how to deal with most-favoured-nation (MFN) exemptions. The treatment is the same as in Chapter 10. Briefly, MFN exemptions for banking services and the movement of people are scored under a separate index. As noted, such an exemption permits an economy to discriminate between economies. The MFN exemptions scheduled under the GATS are used as a source of information. They specify the sectoral coverage, the economies to which they apply and the intended duration. These exemptions can apply to selected or all WTO members. Table 12.2 outlines the scores for the two types of MFN exemptions: preferential treatment and reciprocity. The development of an MFN exemption matrix and the calculation of an exemption score is the same as in Chapter 10. The MFN exemption matrix for banking services is 23 by 23.

Fewer restriction categories are relevant for the domestic index than the foreign index. The domestic index excludes the categories covering bank entry through joint venture arrangements and the movement of people. Scores from the MFN exemption matrixes are also excluded. Governments do not generally apply these restrictions to domestic banks. Thus, the foreign index score for an economy will always be greater than the domestic index score. The maximum possible foreign index score is 1. The maximum possible domestic index score is 0.808 (Table 12.3).

As in Chapter 10, the index methodology has been applied to actual restrictions rather than to stated limits. Some statutory restrictions may not

Table 12.3 Relevance of restriction categories for foreign and domestic indexes

Restriction category	Relevant for foreign index	Total weight	Relevant for domestic index	Total weight
Restrictions on commercial presence				
Licensing of banks	Yes	0.200	Yes	0.190
Direct investment	Yes	0.200	Yes	0.190
Joint venture arrangements	Yes	0.100	No	n.a.
Permanent movement of people	Yes	0.020	No	n.a.
Other restrictions				
Raising funds by banks	Yes	0.100	Yes	0.143
Lending funds by banks	Yes	0.100	Yes	0.143
Other business of banks – insurance and securities services	Yes	0.200	Yes	0.095
Expanding the number of banking outlets	Yes	0.050	Yes	0.048
Composition of the board of directors	Yes	0.020	No	n.a.
Temporary movement of people	Yes	0.010	No	n.a.
Total weighting or highest possible score		1.000		0.808

Notes:
a Totals may not add due to rounding.
n.a. = not applicable.

necessarily amount to actual restrictions. For example, an economy may restrict foreign equity participation in a bank to 15 per cent, but government approval may usually be granted to invest above this limit. The index methodology has been applied to the actual restrictiveness, after taking into account approvals above stated limits. Thus, a restriction that is applied as prescribed receives a higher score than a restriction where government approval is usually forthcoming.

RESULTS FOR 38 ECONOMIES

The restrictiveness index has been calculated for economies where comprehensive information about restrictions on banking services could be gathered from the sources outlined earlier in the chapter. Information was gathered for 38 economies, covering the major regions of the world – Asia, Europe, North America and South America.

Restrictions on banking services vary significantly among economies. Common restrictions are limitations on the number of bank licences available, restricting foreign entry to only joint ventures with new domestic banks, limiting foreign equity participation in domestic banks, and restricting operations. More restricted economies apply to all or a combination of these restrictions. The less restricted economies have few restrictions on entry and operations.

Argentina, Canada, New Zealand and the United States are relatively open to trade in banking services, while India, Indonesia, Malaysia and the Philippines are relatively closed economies (Figures 12.1, 12.2 and 12.3). The scores for some economies with relatively open banking services markets may reflect only restrictions on the movement of people.

Asia Pacific economies

Foreign index

India, Indonesia, Malaysia and the Philippines are the most restricted banking services markets in this region (Figure 12.1). These economies are all characterised by very tight entry controls and restrictions on business operations. India denies access for foreign banks. Indonesia does not permit new foreign bank entry and prohibits existing foreign banks from attracting deposits from public enterprises. Malaysia has a multitude of restrictions on commercial presence, ownership and operation and, consequently, has the most restricted foreign index score among the 38 economies. The Philippines limits foreign equity participation to a minority and applies a non-discriminatory economic means test on applications to establish a commercial presence or to expand existing operations.

Korea, Singapore, Thailand and Turkey all obtained moderate foreign index scores. These economies have at least one significant restriction that limits foreign access to their markets for banking services. Korea has restrictions on the level of foreign equity, and rules directing foreign banks to lend to certain sectors. Singapore's banking sector is restricted through minority foreign equity controls and operational controls – foreign banks may not open new sub-branches or establish off-premise automatic teller machines (ATMs). Thailand has minority foreign equity limits and issues a limited number of new foreign bank licences.[2] Foreign banks in Turkey may only provide banking services and are restricted from providing insurance and securities services.

The most open market in this region is New Zealand. New Zealand has few entry and operational requirements. Australia, Hong Kong, Japan and South Africa also have relatively open markets. Australia's restrictions on acquiring any of the four major banks contributes to a higher score. In assessing an application for a foreign bank to acquire a major bank, the government applies the principle that any large-scale transfer of Australian ownership of the financial system to foreigners would be contrary to the national interest (Costello 1997). Hong Kong has some restrictions on the expansion of operations of foreign banks. Japan does not allow banks to provide insurance services and imposes strict rules on those offering securities services. South Africa has strict rules on foreign banks accessing deposits from the parent company and the lines of business that they may undertake.

Figure 12.1   Restrictiveness indexes for selected Asia Pacific economies, South Africa and Turkey

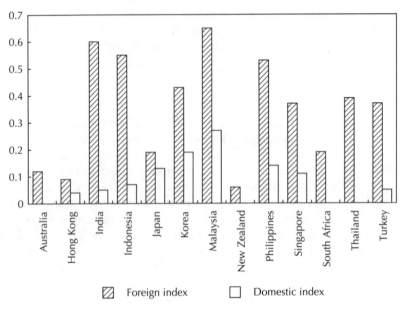

Note: The higher the score, the more restrictive an economy; scores range from 0 to 1.
Source: Results estimated as part of this paper.

Domestic index

Japan, Korea, Malaysia and the Philippines impose several restrictions on their domestic banks that are also imposed on foreign banks. Malaysia has the most restrictions on all banks of the 38 economies. Korea, Malaysia and the Philippines place numerous restrictions on bank lending. Korea limits all banks from raising funds through issuing certain types of securities. Japan limits banks to mainly providing banking services. India, Indonesia, Korea, Malaysia, the Philippines, Singapore, Thailand and Turkey are the most discriminatory against foreign banks, treating them significantly less favourably than domestic banks.

American economies

Foreign index

Brazil, Chile and Uruguay are the most restricted banking services markets in this group (Figure 12.2). Brazil denies access to new foreign banks, limits

Figure 12.2 Restrictiveness indexes for selected American economies

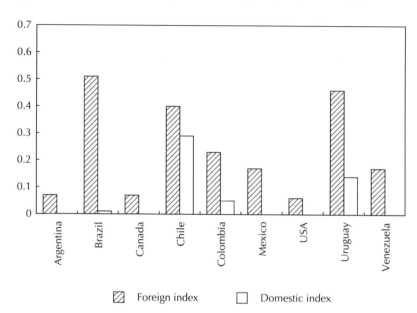

Foreign index ▨   Domestic index ☐

Note: The higher the score the more restrictive an economy; scores range from 0 to 1.
Source: Results estimated as part of this paper.

foreign equity participation in domestic banks to a minority, and entry is only permitted through joint ventures with new domestic banks. Chile limits the total number of banking licences and the only form of entry is via a joint venture unless a licence becomes available as a result of a bank merger. Uruguay's score largely reflects the limited number of new banking licences that are available, as well as strict operational rules applying to foreign banks.

Colombia, Mexico and Venezuela all obtained fairly low foreign index scores. Colombia applies an economic needs test to new financial services and limits the ability of foreign banks to raise funds from the domestic market. Mexico limits foreign equity participation in banking services to a minority. Venezuela also applies an economic needs test to new financial services and prohibits foreign banks from undertaking deposit business in the domestic market.

Argentina, Canada and the United States are the most open markets in the region. These economies have few entry and operational requirements other than those on the movement of people.

Domestic index

In this region, Chile has the most restrictions on all banks. It is characterised by a limited number of licences and the prohibition on banks conducting insurance and securities business. Uruguay's score reflects the fact that the number of licences for new banks may not exceed 10 per cent of the number in the previous year. Argentina, Canada, Mexico, the United States and Venezuela all achieved domestic index scores of zero. Brazil, Colombia and Uruguay are the most discriminatory against foreign banks.

European economies

Foreign and domestic index

The European Union economies and Switzerland have few restrictions and all registered low foreign index scores of 0.07 (for all 15 EU economies) and 0.08, respectively. For the domestic index, these economies scored zero – there are no identified restrictions that are applied equally to domestic and foreign banks.

European economies restrict the movement of people and also have an MFN exemption giving preferential treatment to nationals of the European Union and the European Free Trade Association. Switzerland's foreign index score is slightly higher because it requires foreign banks to obtain approval to expand branch and agency networks.

Comparison of indexes and GNP per capita

A comparison of foreign index results with gross national product (GNP) suggests that economies with less restricted banking services sectors tend to have higher GNP per capita. The foreign index results are compared for 23 economies and the European Union (Figure 12.3).

Other studies find a similar relationship between the openness of trade and income. Levine (1996) found that economies with financial systems that are better at performing key financial services functions tend to be economically developed, have higher income per capita and grow at a faster pace than those with less developed financial systems. PECC (1995) found a positive relationship between wealth and openness, in that APEC member economies with a higher number of GATS commitments also tend to have higher GDP per capita.

Some qualifications on measurement

As in Chapter 10, the reliability of the index for different countries is dependent on the quality and depth of information. The complete list of restrictions has been compiled from the best known sources of information. However, given the number of economies covered, some restrictions may not have been captured or may have been scored differently from the way they are applied in practice. A more stringent index could be developed if a greater depth of information were available.

Figure 12.3 Foreign restrictiveness indexes and GNP per capita at PPP prices (1996)

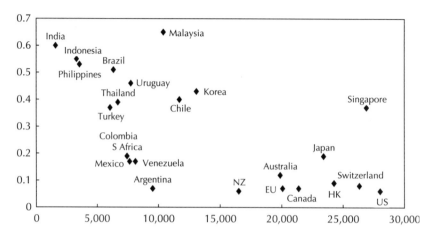

GNP per capita at PPP prices (US$)

Notes: Purchasing power parity (PPP) prices based on World Bank surveys undertaken since 1993. GNP per capita at PPP prices is used; GNP per capita using official exchange rates tends to undervalue low and middle-income economies with relatively low prices (World Bank 1998).

Sources: World Bank (1998) and results calculated as part of this paper.

Some restrictions may not necessarily fit within a restriction category. Certain restrictions may apply only in one economy and are not covered by a restriction category in the index. In such cases, it was necessary to interpret the information so as to obtain a score for the relevant category. In addition, some restrictions are not directly assigned a score but are used as background information in assigning appropriate scores in some categories.

CONCLUSION

An index methodology has been developed and applied to quantify the restrictiveness of banking services markets in 38 economies. The index captures regulatory regimes as at 31 December 1997 and excludes prudential regulation. There is a large range between the most restrictive and the least restrictive economies. Brazil, Chile, India, Indonesia, Korea, Malaysia, the Philippines and Uruguay are most restricted for international trade in banking services. These economies prohibit or restrict foreign bank entry. Brazil, Indonesia, Korea, Malaysia and the Philippines limit foreign equity participation in domestic banks to a minority. These economies also have varying restrictions on banks raising and lending funds, and expanding the number of banking outlets.

Chile, Japan, Korea, Malaysia, the Philippines and Uruguay apply a number of restrictions equally to domestic and foreign banks. Chile, Malaysia, the Philippines and Uruguay have similar or the same restrictions on the number of licences available for all banks. These economies are also characterised by restrictions on all banks providing other services such as insurance and securities, restrictions on expanding the number of banking outlets, and restrictions on lending.

Brazil, India, Indonesia, Malaysia, the Philippines and Thailand are the most discriminatory. These economies treat foreign banks significantly less favourably than domestic banks – the difference between the foreign and domestic index scores. These economies are also some of the most restricted economies for banking services.

NOTES

The authors are employed by the Australian Productivity Commission. The views expressed in this chapter are those of the staff involved and do not necessarily reflect those of the Productivity Commission. The Productivity Commission is the Australian Government's principal review and advisory body on microeconomic reform. It conducts public inquiries and research into a broad range of economic and social issues affecting the welfare of Australians. Information on the Productivity Commission, its publications and its current work program can be found on the World Wide Web at <http://www.pc.gov.au>.

1   McGuire and Schuele (1999) apply an index methodology to restrictions on financial services for Asia Pacific economies for the year ended 1998.
2   Thailand has recently eased ownership limits in its banking sector to satisfy certain conditions for the IMF standby credit facilities. As outlined earlier, the inventory of restrictions is as at 31 December 1997.

13 The price impact of restrictions on banking services

Kaleeswaran Kalirajan, Greg McGuire, Duc Nguyen-Hong and Michael Schuele

INTRODUCTION

Restrictions on international trade in banking services affect the quality and price of banking services. Restrictions are imposed for differing reasons. Prudential controls are usually justified on the grounds of preserving the efficiency and stability of the banking system. Other restrictions are sometimes imposed deliberately to restrict trade in banking services. But both prudential and non-prudential restrictions can protect domestic banks from international competition and may increase the price of banking services.

Banks provide a wide range of financial services including deposit-taking, lending, insurance and securities. Although modern banks are diversified entities, their core business remains the matching of depositors and lenders, or intermediation (NBER 1998). The price of providing intermediation services can be measured by a bank's interest margin – generally, the difference between the interest rate banks charge on their loans and the rate that they pay on their deposits. Restrictions on trade in banking services can increase the interest margin or the price of banking services. Here a model is developed and applied to 694 banks in 27 economies to assess the impact of non-prudential, or trade, restrictions on the interest margins of banks.

RESTRICTIONS AND THE INTEREST MARGINS OF BANKS

High bank profitability can reflect a lack of competition arising from restrictions on bank operations (see Sorsa 1997). Both prudential and non-prudential restrictions impose costs on banks that may be passed through into prices. Prudential standards increase the costs of banks by requiring them to allocate resources to limit risk to an acceptable level. Non-prudential restrictions can protect domestic banks from domestic and international competition. This may allow domestic banks to charge higher prices for their services.

The interest margin of banks can be used to measure the price of banking services. As noted, the interest margin is generally the difference between a bank's lending rate and its deposit rate or cost of funds. Restrictions on banking services can increase the interest margins of banks. There is evidence that economies that permit foreign bank entry have lower gross interest margins and are more efficient than economies with more restrictive policies (see Terrell 1986).

Ho and Saunders (1981) note that if banks are risk averse, they will want to use a positive interest margin to handle timing differences between the supply of deposits and the demand for loans. The interest margin of banks will be affected by factors that affect the likelihood and cost (to the banks) of such timing differences, including interest rate volatility and the concentration of banks in the market (as discussed below).

This chapter estimates the price impact of non-prudential restrictions on the interest margins of banks. In order to obtain such a measure, it is necessary to identify all of the factors affecting bank interest margins before isolating the impact of non-prudential restrictions on interest margins.

MODELLING THE EFFECT OF RESTRICTIONS ON BANK INTEREST MARGINS

Ho and Saunders (1981) integrated the hedging and expected utility approaches of bank behaviour into a model to analyse the determinants of bank margins.[1] They showed that bank interest margins include a pure interest spread, covering the opportunity cost of holding required reserves and default premiums on loans. The pure spread is affected by four factors – managerial risk aversion, the size of transactions undertaken by a bank, the market structure of the banking sector and interest rate volatility. The integrated model was applied to a sample of US commercial banks. The results demonstrated that the pure spread can be identified empirically and that interest rate volatility is a significant determinant of the pure spread.

Saunders and Schumacher (1997a and 1997b) enhanced the model developed by Ho and Saunders to find that greater regulation of banks could increase bank interest margins and the cost of banking services to consumers above the pure spread. They also found that an increase in firm concentration in the banking market and in interest rate volatility would contribute to higher bank interest margins through an increase in the pure spread.

Saunders and Schumacher (1997a) estimated the effect of regulation on the net interest margin (NIM) of banks. NIM, an accounting measure, is the sum of total net interest income divided by total interest-earning assets. Saunders and Schumacher identified the following determinants of the NIM:

- the pure spread, the determinants of which (market structure, interest rate volatility) are constant across all banks in an economy in any given year;
- prudential regulations, as measured by reserve (liquidity) and capital requirements; and
- any shortfall of other revenue over costs, as measured by non-interest expense minus other operating income and divided by total average assets.

Saunders and Schumacher performed a two-stage estimation to distinguish the determinants of the NIMs of banks. In the first stage, they regressed net non-interest expenses, capital and liquidity requirements on the NIMs for each bank in an economy, thereby separating the influence of bank-specific variables from the pure spread. In the second stage, they performed a cross-country estimation to find the effect of market structure and interest rate volatility on the pure spread.

The two-stage estimation separates the influence of bank-specific and economy-wide variables on the NIMs of banks. This approach overcomes an important statistical problem. It avoids the use of a single equation containing both bank-specific and economy-wide variables. Moulton (1986) argues that such a combination of variables in a single equation could lead to bias in the model estimates as a result of group effects – banks within an economy, and hence the estimation errors, may be correlated. This is because banks within an economy operate in the same banking sector, distinct from banking sectors in other economies. Thus, a single-stage estimation could produce a biased estimate.

Saunders and Schumacher (1997a) applied their model to six selected European economies and the United States from 1988 to 1995. In the first stage of the estimation, they found that prudential regulations – reserve and capital requirements – and net non-interest expenses have a significant and positive impact on the NIMs of banks. In the second stage, at the economy level, they found that market structure and interest rate volatility were significant determinants of the pure spread in most economies, and therefore of the NIMs of banks in these economies.

Saunders and Schumacher (1997b) found a similar result in the application of the model to Mexican banks. They found that capital requirements have a significant and positive impact on the NIMs of banks in Mexico. They found no relationship between reserve requirements and the NIMs of banks, and attributed this result to Mexico having eliminated all reserve requirements in 1991. In the second stage, they found that interest rate volatility is a significant determinant of the pure spread and therefore of the NIMs of banks in Mexico.

Estimating the impact of restrictions on trade in banking services on the net interest margins of banks

This study extends the two-stage Saunders and Schumacher model to estimate the impact that non-prudential restrictions on international trade in banking services have on the NIMs of banks. Non-prudential restrictions may limit competition in the market for banking services in an economy and therefore increase the potential for existing banks to charge more for their intermediary services. This estimate is then used to derive the price impact of non-prudential restrictions on trade in banking services in different economies.

A measure of non-prudential restrictions has been calculated in Chapter 12 – a trade restrictiveness index for trade in banking services for 38 economies.

The trade restrictiveness index quantifies the extent to which banks are protected from international competition by restrictions on trade in banking services.

In the first stage, NIMs are regressed on bank-specific measures of prudential regulation – capital requirements (K_{ij}) and reserve or liquidity requirements (L_{ij}) – and net non-interest operating expenses (NIE_{ij}) across all banks j in all economies i. Economy-specific constants from this regression measure that component of a NIM that depends on economy-wide variables – the pure spread, plus economy-wide non-prudential regulations. This component is called the interest spread.

The interest spread becomes the dependent variable (S_i) in the second stage. The interest spread is regressed on economy-wide determinants of the pure spread, plus any premium for non-prudential trade restrictions. The second stage and the first stage are not estimated simultaneously, thus bank-specific and economy-wide stages remain separate.

First-stage estimation

In the first stage, the NIM of banks in an economy is represented by the following function:

$$\text{In } (NIM_{ij}) = \alpha_0 + \alpha_1 \text{ In } (K_{ij}) + \alpha_2 \text{ In } (L_{ij}) + \alpha_3 \text{ In } (NIE_{ij}) + \sum_{i-1}^{27} D_i \qquad (1)$$

where

a_o	constant;
K_{ij}	capital of bank j in economy i;
L_{ij}	liquidity of bank j in economy i;
NIE_{ij}	net non-interest operating expenses of bank j in economy i;
D_i	economy-specific dummy variables for economies i = 1 to 26; so that
$a_o + D_i$	interest spread (S_i) in the second stage.

As outlined in Chapter 12, bank regulators require banks to hold sufficient amounts of capital and liquidity to limit risk and preserve the solvency of banks. Generally, the more capital a regulator requires a bank to hold, the higher the opportunity cost to the bank. A bank's capital could be used for purposes other than maintaining stability and covering the possibility of defaulting loans. A bank may opt to hold capital above the minimum requirements imposed by bank regulators if the required amount of capital is perceived to be insufficient to cover the level of credit risk exposure (see Chapter 12). Banks can recoup the opportunity cost of holding capital by including the cost in their NIM.[2]

Banks are required to hold liquidity to ensure that they can cope with increases in demand for loans or withdrawal of deposits. Banks are required to hold reserve cash and short-term securities for emergencies. Bank regulators typically pay no interest, or less than the market interest rate on these funds. The cost imposed on banks depends on the amount of funds required to be held for liquidity purposes and the difference between the market rate and the interest rate, if any, paid by banking regulators. Banks can also recoup the cost of holding required reserves by raising their NIMs.

Capital and liquidity are the main prudential requirements on banks. Other prudential requirements include licensing requirements, initial capital requirements and limits on the extent of credit and market risk exposures.

Net non-interest operating expenses are costs incurred by a bank that contribute to the cost of operation. They are costs other than interest expenses and have been measured net of the account-keeping fees that are earned by banks. The expenses include essential infrastructure costs for a bank such as wages, property, office equipment and depreciation. An increase in net non-interest operating expenses may also be passed onto consumers through an increase in the NIMs of banks.

A double log functional form has been used in the first stage to take account of unidentified non-linearity in the regressors – capital (K_{ij}), liquidity (L_{ij}) and net non-interest operating expenses (NIE_{ij}). Economy-specific dummy variables are used to capture the economy-specific influences on the NIMs of banks.

Second-stage estimation

The interest spreads (S_i) of banks in each economy are estimated to be a function of interest rate volatility (IV_i), market structure (MS_i) and non-prudential restrictions, as measured by the trade restrictiveness index (TRI_i). The second stage of the estimation is performed across all economies.

The interest spread of an economy is represented by the following function:

$$S_i = b_0 + b_1 IV_i + b_2 MS_i + b_3 TRI_i \qquad (2)$$

where

S_i the interest spread for economy i – first stage constant (a_0) plus economy-specific dummy variable (D_i);
IV_i interest rate volatility in economy i;
MS_i the market structure of the banking sector in economy i; and
TRI_i the trade restrictiveness index score in economy i.

A specification without a logarithmic transformation was found to provide the best fit at the second stage.

Interest rate volatility measures fluctuations in short-term money market interest rates for an economy. Banks manage the timing mismatch between deposits and loans through the short-term money market. Banks borrow from the short-term money market when the amount required for loans is greater than the amount of deposits available. A rise in short-term money market interest rate increases the cost of funds – a refinancing risk. Banks invest in the short-term money market when deposit availability is greater than the demand for loans. Banks earn interest on otherwise idle funds. A fall in the short-term money market interest rate reduces revenue earned – a reinvestment risk. Therefore, greater interest rate volatility increases interest rate risk for a bank and reduces bank profits. Banks may offset lower profits by increasing their interest spread.

NIMs might also be expected to vary with the overall level of interest rates. But there tends to be a strong correlation between the level of interest rates and interest rate volatility so that the inclusion of the interest rate volatility variable can help control for this effect.

The market structure variable reflects the concentration of banks in an economy. The fewer the banks, the lower is the perceived elasticity of demand for, and supply of, funds and the higher will be the prices, or interest spreads, charged for intermediatory services.

Foreign and domestic trade restrictiveness indexes identify the extent to which international and domestic competition may be restricted (see Chapter 12). The foreign index quantifies the extent to which foreign banks seeking to enter and/or operate in the domestic market are treated less favourably than domestic banks. The domestic index estimates the extent to which restrictions apply to domestic and foreign banks equally. The above model is estimated twice to separate out the effects of the foreign and domestic index. This avoids problems associated with correlation between the two indexes, which could lead to inaccurate estimates of the coefficients on the foreign and domestic trade restrictiveness indexes.

Data sources and issues

The data used in this paper are both bank-specific and economy-wide variables. The first stage of the estimation is with bank-specific variables – net interest margins (NIM_{ij}), the capital ratio (K_{ij}), the liquidity ratio (L_{ij}) and the non-interest expense (NIE_{ij}) of bank j in economy i. The second stage of the estimation is with economy-wide variables – interest rate volatility (IV_i), market structure (MS_i), the foreign restrictiveness index (TRI_i foreign) and the domestic restrictiveness index (TRI_i domestic).

The principal source of data on banks in this study is Disclosure's Worldscope database (Disclosure 1999). Saunders and Schumacher (1997a) used this database to estimate the determinants of bank NIMs for seven economies. Other data sources are the International Monetary Fund's International Financial Statistics (IMF 1995, 1996 and 1997) and Chapter 12 for the trade restrictiveness index.

The Worldscope database provides standardised accounting data on publicly listed companies across economies. The econometric exercise covers 694 national and state commercial banks in 27 economies, as identified by the United States' Standard Industrial Classification (SIC). The data on net interest income and net non-interest operating expenses is from the Worldscope database for the nearest financial year of banks ending before 31 December 1997. Data on all other variables from the database is for the nearest financial year ending before 31 December 1996. This study covers commercial banks that primarily provide financial intermediation services, that is banks that engage in deposit-taking and lending. Banks that primarily engage in insurance, securities and other services are excluded from the dataset. Only banks with positive NIMs and those where data on all variables are available are included in the dataset.

The NIMs are expressed as the ratio of net interest income and account service fees to interest-earning assets for selected banks in each economy. This definition of banks' NIMs takes into account the increasing importance of fee payment for banking services, which can result in lower interest spreads. There is usually a trade-off between NIMs and fees (RBA 1994). Interest-earning assets comprise bank lending and investments by banks in securities.

Capital and liquidity ratios are used to represent the prudential variables capital (K_{ij}) and liquidity (L_{ij}). The capital ratio is Tier 1 capital divided by the total assets of selected banks in each economy. This is a proxy for the capital requirements imposed by banking regulators. Tier 1 capital is the permanent capital that would allow banks to absorb losses without being obliged to cease trading and is defined to be the sum of common stock, preferred stock and retained earnings.

Table 13.1 provides a summary and explanation of the data used for each economy. Bank-specific variables are the arithmetic mean for each economy. The economy-specific variables are presented in the form that they are used in the estimation.

Most economies have followed the Bank for International Settlements (BIS) risk-weighted standard of capital adequacy since 1988. The BIS Accord recommends a minimum ratio of 8 per cent capital to risk-weighted assets in addressing credit risk where the capital base comprises Tier 1 and Tier 2 capital. Tier 1 capital is required to comprise at least half of the total capital requirement. Bank credit exposures are taken into account by weighting the assets according to their risk categories and converting off-balance sheet contracts into their credit equivalents.

An ideal way to measure the impact of capital requirements is to derive the BIS risk-weighted standard as it is applied to banks by regulators in various economies. The lack of data on various capital components, asset items and off-balance sheet activities for all banks in the Worldscope database renders this impossible. There are also wide differences in the definition of capital as applied between economies, especially in relation to Tier 2 capital (Barth et al. 1995; IMF 1998).

The net non-interest operating expenses variable is calculated as the ratio of non-interest operating expenses (less other operating income) to interest-earning assets. As noted, net non-interest operating expenses includes staff

Table 13.1 Summary data for 27 economies

Economy	Number of banks	NIM_{ij}^a	K_{ij}^b	L_{ij}^c	NIE_{ij}^d	IV_i^e	MS_i^f	Foreign TRI_i^g	Dom-estic TRI_i^g
Argentina	2	7.62	6.61	4.92	3.32	8.24	0.46	0.07	0.00
Australia	9	4.99	3.24	3.59	2.46	0.70	0.91	0.12	0.00
Austria	7	2.95	1.56	3.85	1.80	0.11	0.78	0.07	0.00
Belgium	5	2.24	0.67	0.30	1.61	0.53	1.00	0.07	0.00
Canada	7	3.59	4.86	0.82	2.13	3.09	0.80	0.07	0.00
Chile	5	7.43	5.23	12.49	4.26	6.08	0.87	0.40	0.29
Colombia	8	13.63	4.11	6.88	7.70	17.42	0.73	0.23	0.05
Denmark	38	7.14	10.30	8.49	4.21	0.35	0.82	0.07	0.00
France	29	3.70	2.20	1.30	2.50	0.24	0.73	0.07	0.00
Germany	21	1.74	1.81	1.06	1.18	0.33	0.45	0.07	0.00
Greece	12	8.17	3.64	13.95	4.70	6.70	0.87	0.07	0.00
Hong Kong	13	4.68	2.34	2.74	1.52	0.79	0.91	0.09	0.04
Indonesia	14	5.75	7.01	2.84	2.23	8.42	0.61	0.55	0.07
Italy	39	6.00	2.55	3.79	3.42	0.82	0.43	0.07	0.00
Japan	109	2.16	2.96	4.94	1.64	0.19	0.28	0.19	0.13
Malaysia	13	5.20	3.04	10.05	1.56	0.82	0.56	0.65	0.27
Netherlands	5	3.28	0.83	0.19	1.75	0.33	1.00	0.07	0.00
Philippines	15	8.33	9.33	11.41	3.80	1.93	0.34	0.53	0.14
Portugal	6	4.19	4.63	4.21	6.69	2.87	0.79	0.07	0.00
Singapore	5	3.69	2.70	16.36	1.09	0.01	0.90	0.37	0.11
South Korea	19	4.43	3.08	8.60	3.40	1.70	0.43	0.43	0.19
Spain	19	5.23	2.73	1.40	3.35	2.81	0.76	0.07	0.00
Sweden	5	2.90	1.62	0.71	1.51	2.51	0.98	0.07	0.00
Switzerland	21	3.91	2.85	1.08	2.52	0.50	0.88	0.08	0.00
Thailand	14	3.71	3.05	2.62	1.80	0.94	0.63	0.39	0.00
UK	10	12.38	9.05	1.35	7.54	0.37	0.82	0.07	0.00
US	244	6.15	6.53	4.57	3.16	0.07	0.33	0.06	0.00
Average	25.70	5.38	4.02	4.98	3.07	2.55	0.84	0.19	0.05

Notes:

a NIM_{ij} is the average NIM or the sum of total net interest income plus total fee income divided by total interest-earning assets for selected banks in each economy.

b K_{ij} is Tier 1 capital divided by total bank assets for selected banks in each economy.

c L_{ij} is total cash divided by total bank assets for selected banks in each economy.

d NIE_{ij} is non-interest expenses minus operating income divided by interest-earning assets for selected banks in each economy.

e IV_i is the variance of annualised quarterly deposit interest rates in each economy.

f MS_i is the lending market share of the four largest banks as a percentage of the total bank lending market in each economy, estimated from Worldscope. TradePort data were used to compute this ratio for Argentina.

g TRI_i is a measure of the trade restrictiveness of each economy.

h NIM_{ij}, NIE_i, MS_i and IV_i are for the financial year of banks ending before 31 December 1997. K_{ij} and L_{ij} are for the nearest financial year ending before 31 December 1996. TRI_i, is taken from Chapter 12 of this volume.

Sources: Disclosure 1999; TradePort 1998; and Chapter 12.

costs, equipment, depreciation, taxes and other operating costs. This proxy can reflect variations in bank operating costs across all banking services, for example variations in labour costs or costs associated with bank branches.

The measure of interest rate volatility is computed as the variance of annualised quarterly deposit interest rates from 1994 to 1996 (IMF 1995, 1996 and 1997).

The market structure variable is the total bank lending assets of the four largest banks in each economy as a percentage of the total bank lending market. The market structure variable ranges from 0 to 1. A market structure value of close to 1 indicates a market where a small number of banks have a large share of the market.

The available bank-specific data have some limitations. The reporting of company information on a consolidated basis means that bank-specific variables, such as NIMs, are affected by both domestic and foreign banking services. Ideally, only domestic banking services should be covered to capture the impact of restrictions applying to each respective economy. In addition, the database may not be comprehensive in the coverage of the banking services market for a particular economy.

Data on the trade restrictiveness indexes for economies are drawn from the results in Chapter 12. Restrictions are grouped into common categories and a score is calculated based on the restrictiveness of banking services in an economy. Scores range from 0 to 1. The higher the score, the more restrictive an economy's banking sector. The foreign and domestic trade restrictiveness scores for 38 economies are based on the best available information as at 31 December 1997.

RESULTS

First-stage results

The capital ratio is a significant determinant of the NIMs of banks (Table 13.2). The estimated coefficient indicates that a 1 per cent increase in the capital ratio will lead to an estimated 0.06 per cent increase in NIMs of banks, holding the other variables constant.[3] Thus, the opportunity cost of holding capital is reflected in higher NIMs.

Net non-interest operating expenses are a significant determinant of NIMs (Table 13.2). The coefficient estimate is 0.67 and is statistically significant – a 1 per cent increase in net non-interest operating expenses will lead to an estimated 0.67 per cent increase in NIMs of banks, holding the other variables constant. Thus, higher net non-interest operating expenses are passed on to consumers through higher NIMs.

The relationship between the NIM of banks and the liquidity ratio is positive but not statistically significant (Table 13.2). Other studies of bank NIMs have also found this relationship to be weak (Angbazo 1997; Saunders and Schumacher 1997b). It is difficult to determine the reason for the lack of

Table 13.2 Coefficient estimates from the first-stage estimation

Explanatory variable	Coefficient estimate
Capital ratio	0.060*
	(0.020)
Liquidity ratio	0.001
	(0.029)
Net non-interest operating expenses	0.674*
	(0.056)
Adjusted R^2	0.783

Notes: Figures in parentheses represent standard errors; the estimates have been corrected for heteroscedasticity; * coefficient estimates significant at the 5 per cent level.

Source: Results estimated as part of this chapter.

significance of the liquidity ratio variable, but it may reflect cash being too narrow a definition of liquidity. Some banks may substitute their cash reserves for other less liquid short-term assets, such as short-term government securities, that are not captured by a measure of cash (Goldstein and Turner 1996).

The estimated equation is statistically robust. The adjusted R^2 is 0.78, that is the model explains 78 per cent of the variation in NIMs.

The interest spreads for 27 economies estimated in the first stage vary from 0.22 for Portugal to 1.32 for Malaysia. Argentina, Colombia, Hong Kong, Indonesia, Malaysia, Netherlands, the Philippines and Singapore have spreads greater than 1. Australia, Chile, Denmark, Greece, the United Kingdom and the United States have spread values between 0.8 and 1. Austria, Belgium, Canada, France, Germany, Italy, Portugal, Spain, Sweden and Switzerland have values less than 0.8 (Figure 13.1).

The interest spreads for 27 economies estimated in the first stage vary from 0.22 for Portugal to 1.32 for Malaysia. Argentina, Colombia, Hong Kong, Indonesia, Malaysia, Netherlands, the Philippines and Singapore have spreads greater than 1. Australia, Chile, Denmark, Greece, the United Kingdom and the United States have spread values between 0.8 and 1. Austria, Belgium, Canada, France, Germany, Italy, Portugal, Spain, Sweden and Switzerland have values less than 0.8 (Figure 13.1).

Second-stage results

The second stage estimates the impact of market structure, interest rate volatility and trade restrictions in a banking services market on the interest spreads of banks operating in an economy. The model is estimated using the foreign and domestic trade restrictiveness indexes separately.

Figure 13.1 Interest spreads for 27 economies

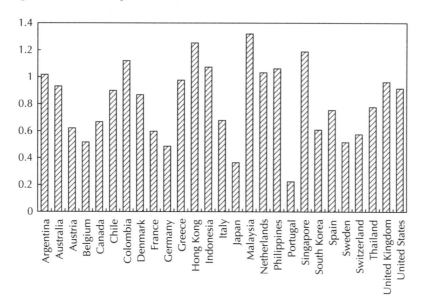

Note: Because of the functional form of equation (1), the units of measurement are the log of the interest rate.

Source: Results estimated as part of this chapter.

Results using the foreign trade restrictiveness index

The foreign trade restrictiveness index is a significant determinant of the interest spreads of banks operating in an economy (Table 13.3). The estimated coefficient indicates that a maximum value of 1 in the foreign trade restrictiveness index will lead to an increase of 0.73 of a percentage point in the interest spread of banks operating in an economy, holding all other variables constant. Foreign trade restrictions protect domestic banks from foreign competition. The lack of competition enables domestic banks to charge higher prices for their services, as reflected in higher interest spreads and increased profits (see Sorsa 1997).

Interest rate volatility is a significant determinant of the interest spreads of banks operating in an economy. The estimated coefficient indicates that a unit increase in interest rate volatility will lead to an increase of 0.015 of a percentage point in the interest spreads of banks operating in an economy, holding all other variables constant. An increase in interest rate volatility increases the risk to a bank of undertaking intermediatory services. The subsequent increase in costs from refinancing and reinvestment risk increases interest spreads.

There is a weak relationship between market structure and interests spread of banks operating in an economy. The coefficient estimate for market structure is 0.18, and it is not statistically significant. One reason for this result is that, for several economies, data were only available for a small number of banks, leading to possible bias in the calculation of the market concentration ratios (see Table 13.1).

The estimation is statistically robust. The adjusted R^2 is 0.19 ($R^2 = 0.29$), which is acceptable for a cross-sectional estimation. Greene (1990) states that in terms of R^2 values normally encountered in application using cross-sectional data, values of 0.50 are relatively high.

Results using the domestic trade restrictiveness index

The estimation using the domestic trade restrictiveness index generated no meaningful results. The estimation had low explanatory power, as reflected by the very low adjusted R^2. The low explanatory power of the model is mainly attributable to only 9 of the 27 economies receiving a domestic index score other than 0 (Table 13.1). Because of this lack of sample variation, it is not possible to draw any useful conclusions from the results of this estimation about the impact of domestic non-prudential restrictions on the interest spreads of banks.

PRICE IMPACT OF NON-PRUDENTIAL RESTRICTIONS

The results from the two-stage estimation are used to calculate a price-impact measure for non-prudential restrictions on trade in banking services for each economy. The measure reflects the effect that non-prudential restrictions on international trade in banking services can have on the NIMs of banks for the 27 economies.

Calculating a price-impact measure for non-prudential restrictions on trade in banking services

The price-impact measure reflects the effect of non-prudential or trade restrictions on bank NIMs. The NIM of bank j in economy i is represented by the following function:

$$\text{In NIM}_{ij} = f \ (\text{in } K_{ij}, \text{ In } L_{ij}, \text{ In NIE}_{ij}, S_i) \tag{3}$$

where S_i is an economy-specific variable represented by:

$$S_i = g(MS_i, IV_i, TRI_i) \tag{4}$$

Given the functional forms assumed for (3) and (4), it is possible to separate the trade restrictiveness index from the other components of the NIM to derive:

$$\text{In NIM}_{ij} = f \ (\text{In } K_{ij}, \text{ In } L_{ij}, \text{ In NIE}_{ij}, MS_i, IV_i) + b^*TRI_i \tag{5}$$

Table 13.3 Coefficient estimates from stage two using foreign index

Explanatory variable	Coefficient estimate
Interest rate volatility	0.015*
	(0.008)
Market structure	0.184
	(0.144)
Foreign trade restrictiveness index	0.732*
	(0.242)
Constant	0.437*
	(0.195)
Adjusted R^2	0.193

Notes: Figures in parentheses represent standard errors; the estimates have been corrected for heteroscedasticity; * coefficient estimates are significant at the 5 per cent level.

Source: Results estimated as part of this chapter.

where b is the estimated coefficient on TRI_i in the second-stage estimation. Taking the antilog of both sides gives:

$$NIM_{ij} = NIM_{ij0} * e^{0.73 * TRIi} \tag{6}$$

where NIM_{ij0} includes all influences other than TRI_i. Since $e^0 = 1$, NIM_{ij0} also measures what the NIM would be in the absence of any non-prudential trade restrictions. Thus,

$$NIM_{ij} / NIM_{ij0} = e^{0.73 * TRIi} \tag{7}$$

and

$$100* (NIM_{ij} - NIM_{ij0}) / NIM_{ij0} = 100* (NIM_{ij} / NIM_{ijo} -1)$$

$$= 100* (e^{0.73 * TRIi} -1) \tag{8}$$

This gives the price impact of trade restrictions for any particular value of the trade restrictiveness index TRI_i.

The price effect for the 27 economies

The price impact varies for each economy, depending on the value of the foreign and domestic trade restrictiveness index for each economy. The price impacts for each of the 27 economies are presented in Table 13.4. As noted, a meaningful coefficient could not be estimated for the domestic index, so the values in Table 13.4 assume that it is the same as the coefficient on the foreign index.

Price impacts using the foreign trade restrictiveness index

The price impacts from restrictions on foreign banks range from 5 to 60 per cent (Table 13.4). That is, the price of banking services or the NIMs of banks are 5 to 60 per cent higher than they would be in the absence of non-prudential or trade restrictions.

The price-impact measures for Indonesia, Malaysia and the Philippines are the highest of the 27 economies – at more than 45 per cent. These economies are characterised by very tight entry controls and restrictions on business operations. They limit foreign equity in domestic banks and prohibit new foreign bank licences.

Chile, Singapore, South Korea and Thailand have a price impact of between 30 and 40 per cent. These economies all have at least one major restriction on the entry and operation of foreign banks.

Colombia and Japan have moderate price impacts of 18 and 15 per cent, respectively. Both of these economies are relatively open but apply some restrictions – Colombia restricts deposit-taking by foreign banks and Japan restricts banks from providing insurance and securities services.

Argentina, Australia, Canada, the EU economies, Hong Kong, Switzerland and the United States have price impacts of less than 10 per cent. These economies have relatively few non-prudential restrictions on foreign banks. EU member states only impose restrictions on the movement of people and also an MFN exemption giving preferential treatment to EU economies and Switzerland. Australia has some restrictions on foreign ownership of banking assets.

Price impacts using the domestic trade restrictiveness index

These price-impact measures are an indication of the effect of regulation applying equally to domestic and foreign banks, and range from 0 to 23 per cent (Table 13.4). That is, the price of banking services or the NIMs of banks are up to 23 per cent higher than they would be in the absence of non-prudential restrictions on all banks.

Chile and Malaysia have a price-impact measure that results in a moderate increase in price of at least 20 per cent. Chile limits the number of new banking licences and prohibits banks from conducting insurance and securities services. Malaysia allows no new banking licences and requires that banks undertake compulsory lending to certain parts of the Malaysian community.

South Korea and the Philippines are the only other economies that have a price-impact measure larger than 10 per cent. Both of these economies impose restrictions on the type and scale of lending that may be undertaken by banks.

Table 13.4 The effect on net interest margins or price for 27 economies
(per cent)

Economy	Price effect using the foreign TRI$_i$	Price effect using the domestic TRI$_i^a$
Argentina	5.34	0.00
Australia	9.30	0.00
Canada	5.34	0.00
Chile	34.00	23.67
Colombia	18.35	3.73
European Union[b]	5.32	0.00
Hong Kong	6.91	2.97
Indonesia	49.32	5.26
Japan	15.26	9.99
Malaysia	60.61	21.86
Philippines	47.36	10.79
Singapore	31.45	8.39
South Korea	36.72	14.93
Switzerland	5.95	0.00
Thailand	33.06	0.00

Notes:
a Uses the coefficient estimate for the foreign trade restrictiveness index as a proxy.
b The European Union grouping excludes Finland, Ireland and Luxembourg; refer to Table 13.1 for restrictiveness index scores for the 12 EU Member States.

Source: Results estimated as part of this chapter.

Japan, Singapore, Indonesia, Colombia and Hong Kong have a price-impact measure of less than 10 per cent. The remaining economies all have a price-impact measure of zero. Chapter 12 provides greater detail on restrictions on trade in banking services for the 27 economies.

CONCLUSION

A model has been developed to estimate the effect of non-prudential restrictions on trade in banking services on the NIMs of banks for 27 economies. A two-stage estimation procedure is used to produce the best linear unbiased estimator. The first stage estimates the effect of capital and liquidity ratios and net non-interest operating expenses on NIMs of banks. The capital ratio and net non-interest operating expenses variables are significant determinants of NIMs.

The second stage estimates the effects of interest volatility, market structure and a trade restrictiveness index on the interest spread of an economy. Interest volatility and the trade restrictiveness index are significant determinants of the interest spread. Non-prudential or trade restrictions on foreign banks contribute to higher NIMs than would be expected in the absence of such restrictions.

Non-prudential or trade restrictions on foreign banks in 27 economies raise the prices or NIMs by 5 to 60 per cent. Removing such restrictions in protected banking markets such as Chile, Indonesia, Malaysia, the Philippines, Singapore, South Korea and Thailand could be expected to produce significant reductions in the price of banking services or bank NIMs.

NOTES

The authors are employed by the Australian Productivity Commission. The views expressed in this chapter are those of the staff involved and do not necessarily reflect those of the Productivity Commission. The Productivity Commission is the Australian Government's principal review and advisory body on microeconomic reform. It conducts public inquiries and research into a broad range of economic and social issues affecting the welfare of Australians. Information on the Productivity Commission, its publications and its current work program can be found on the World Wide Web at <http://www.pc.gov.au>.

1   The hedging behaviour model assumes that banks are risk averse and aim to minimise the risk arising from the different maturities of assets and liabilities. This leads banks to have an interest spread to cover the costs arising from the uncertainty of different maturities of assets and liabilities. The expected utility model assumes that banks attempt to maximise profit or the expected utility of profit.
2   Angbazo (1997) used an augmented dealership model of interest spreads to find that default risk is a significant determinant of net interest margins of large banks.
3   The double log functional form allows the coefficient estimates to be inter-preted as elasticities.

14 Trade in education services and the impacts of barriers to trade

Steven Kemp

INTRODUCTION

Education is a vital ingredient in economic growth and development, as it plays an important role in overcoming income inequality and increasing the skills of the workforce. The growth of education services has paralleled the total growth of the services sector. Public expenditure on education as a proportion of GNP has remained fairly constant since 1980 – at around 5 per cent for developed countries and 4 per cent for developing countries (Table 14.1). Public expenditure on education per inhabitant, however, doubled over the same period, with the rate of increase more significant for developed countries.

The significant increase in public spending per capita on education reflects the value governments place on education. Knowledge-based industries, including education, professional services and information technology services, have for a long time been seen as driving economic development. International transactions in services have become more relevant given the growth of the knowledge-based sectors and the increasing mobility of labour. Advances in information and communications technologies have enabled the rapid growth in services trade, as documented in Chapter 2.

This chapter examines the pattern of trade in education services and reviews the types of restrictions to trade within different modes of supply. The listings of restrictions by World Trade Organisation members in the General Agreement on Trade in Services (GATS) schedules are used to construct comparative indexes.

FOREIGN STUDENT MOBILITY

Since World War II there has been a rapid growth in the number of foreign students in higher education, and international education has become increasingly important in world services trade. Over two-thirds of trade is between the industrialised countries, as host nations, and the developing countries, who are the principal demanders of foreign education. North America, Europe and Oceania are net exporters of educational services, while

Table 14.1 Public expenditure on education

	Public expenditure on education as % of GNP				Public expenditure on education per inhabitant ($)			
	1980	*1985*	*1990*	*1994*	*1980*	*1985*	*1990*	*1994*
World total	4.8	4.8	4.8	4.9	126	124	202	252
Africa	5.3	5.7	5.6	5.9	48	40	41	41
America	4.9	4.9	5.2	5.3	307	375	521	623
Asia	4.0	3.9	3.7	3.6	37	39	66	93
Europe	5.1	5.1	5.1	5.4	418	340	741	982
Oceania	5.6	5.6	5.6	6.0	467	439	715	878
Developing countries	3.8	4.0	4.0	3.9	31	28	40	48
Industrialised countries	5.1	5.0	5.0	5.1	487	520	914	1,211

Source: UNESCO Statistical Yearbook 1997.

Asia, South America and Africa are net importers. Table 14.2 shows that North America and Europe received 84 per cent of the world's foreign students in 1996, with three-quarters of the students coming from Asia and Europe. From 1990 to 1995 the number of foreign students worldwide increased by some 280,000, with most of this growth stemming from Europe and Asia. While nearly 80 per cent of European foreign students studied in Europe, nearly half of all Asian foreign students travelled to North America (Davis 1998).

Trade in tertiary educational services is not a new phenomenon. UNESCO has been recording the movement of foreign tertiary students since the 1950s. In 1996 over 1.6 million students, or about 95 per cent of the known world total, undertook higher education abroad in the top 50 host countries (UNESCO 1998). There is no international data available for other education sectors, but higher education is certainly the most important sector in terms of foreign student flows. In 1950 there were just over 100,000 foreign tertiary students and the number doubled in each of the decades between 1950 and 1980. The growth slowed after 1980, but this appears to reflect the general slowdown in higher education enrolments, as the number of foreign tertiary students as a proportion of the global total has remained fairly constant at around 2 per cent.

The rapid growth in foreign student numbers led several countries to question the cost of subsidising students from abroad, and government policy in a number of countries (the United Kingdom, Canada and Australia) shifted from providing aid to encouraging trade. Each introduced differential fees for foreign students to more fully reflect the cost of supply. Education has become a target for export and education fairs have become popular among foreign governments and education institutions as a means of recruiting Asian students.

Table 14.2 Higher education students abroad, 1996

Host region				Sending region			
	Total	North America	South America	Europe	Oceania	Asia	Africa
North America	493,481	53,604	23,580	73,156	4,561	308,108	29,929
South America	12,678	0	9,505	552	0	0	0
Europe	862,098	36,220	22,387	385,265	3,033	231,398	137,925
Oceania	47,971	1,343	113	1,659	7,625	34,671	924
Asia	165,493	4,858	946	8,290	953	124,961	9,386
Africa	28,379	349	146	3,742	164	6,850	15,200
Total	1,610,100	97,219	56,659	477,463	15,883	714,500	192,624

Note: 55,752 students not specified by sending region.
Source: UNESCO 1998.

Cross-border exports of education services include the tuition and living expenses of foreign students studying in a particular country, while cross-border imports consist of the tuition and living expenses of a country's residents who study abroad. The UNESCO data covers trade in education services at the tertiary level, but not services provided by primary and secondary institutions, or by institutions offering adult and other education services, such as English language instruction. A conservative estimate of the value of the global market for higher education, based on foreign students spending US$18,000 a year on fees and living expenses, is around US$30 billion. If secondary and vocational education sectors were included, the global market for educational services would exceed US$50 billion.

The United States is the leading exporter of higher education services, accounting for over 30 per cent of world exports (Table 14.3). In 1997–98 the value of overseas students in higher education in the United States was estimated at US$8 billion (Davis 1998). If other education sectors are included, the value rises to approximately US$10 billion. Education is now the United States' fifth largest services export. The five leading exporters of higher education services (the United States, the United Kingdom, France, Germany and Australia) receive over two-thirds of the world's foreign students.

In just over a decade, education has become a major export industry in Australia. In 1997–98 education was Australia's third largest services export, accounting for 12.4 per cent of services exports. The value of education exports to the Australian economy is estimated at A$3.2 billion, comprising A$1.6 billion in fees and A$1.6 billion in expenditure on goods and services by overseas students. Australia's exports of education services have grown at an annual average rate of 26 per cent over the past decade, more than double the rate of overall services exports. Australia dramatically increased

Table 14.3 Leading exporters of higher education services

Country	Year	Foreign students	Total enrolment	% foreign
United States	1997–98	481,280	14,350,000	3.4
United Kingdom	1997	198,064	1,978,089	10.0
France	1993–94	170,574	2,083,232	8.2
Germany	1995–96	159,894	2,144,169	7.5
Australia	1998	72,183	671,853	10.7
Japan	1994–95	53,511	3,917,709	1.4
Canada	1995–96	31,435	849,595	3.7

Sources: AIEF 1998; Davis 1998; HESA 1998; UNESCO 1998.

its share of the global market in higher education from less than 1 per cent in 1980 to over 5 per cent by 1998 (AIEF 1998; UNESCO 1998).

Nearly half of all foreign students come from Asia. Table 14.4 lists the main importing countries in Asia and the number of students going to the host countries of the United States, the United Kingdom and Australia. These three countries accounted for 46 per cent of all foreign students and over half of Asia's foreign students in 1997.

MODES OF SUPPLY

The GATS identifies four modes or channels for supplying services to foreign consumers all of which apply to education services.

Mode 1: Cross-border supply – this is the supply of a service across boundaries when neither the consumer nor the supplier move. Examples for education include distance education or education courses conducted through the Internet. While relatively insignificant, this mode of supply is expected to become more prominent over time.

Mode 2: Consumption abroad – the consumer travels to the supplier's country to consume the service, for example foreign students travelling overseas to study. Currently the bulk of trade in education occurs via this mode.

Mode 3: Commercial presence – the supplier establishes a physical presence in the overseas country, usually through foreign direct investment. An education provider may establish a new campus or form a joint venture with an existing institution in the foreign country. This mode of supply has grown in importance in Southeast Asia, with Australian, British and American educational institutions establishing 'twinning' arrangements with institutions in Singapore, Malaysia and Hong Kong.

Mode 4: Presence of natural persons – the supplier temporarily moves to the consumer to supply the service, for example, academics travelling abroad to conduct courses.

Table 14.4 Leading Asian importers of higher education services (1997)

| Sending country | Host countries – Number of foreign students | | |
	Australia	United Kingdom	United States
China	1,875	2,660	46,958
Hong Kong	9,674	7,767	9,665
India	2,367	2,302	33,818
Indonesia	6,051	894	13,282
Japan	1,449	4,665	47,073
Korea	1,470	1,872	42,890
Malaysia	12,810	18,015	14,597
Singapore	12,107	5,646	3,843
Taiwan	1,676	2,903	3,855
Thailand	2,302	2,087	15,090
Subtotal	51,781	48,811	231,070
All foreign students	64,188	198,064	481,280

Sources: AIEF 1998; Davis 1998; HESA 1998.

A country's balance of payments statistics record trade in services occurring through cross-border supply, consumption abroad and the presence of natural persons. Transactions involving commercial presence are reported separately as investment income in the balance of payments. Cross-border trade (Modes 1, 2, and 4) accounts for most of the trade in education services, with consumption abroad being the most dominant mode of supply. For the United States, it is estimated that this form of trade accounts for 90 per cent of education services trade (WTO 1998e). For Australia, the consumption abroad mode of supply accounts for around 85 per cent of education services trade (AIEF 1998). Commercial presence is the next most important mode of supply. Each of the main exporting nations, the United States, Australia and the United Kingdom, have been establishing branch campuses in foreign countries offering pre-university foundation courses, undergraduate and postgraduate programs, and English Language Intensive Courses for Overseas Students (ELICOS). For Australia, the commercial presence mode of supply is becoming quite significant. Most of the recent growth in foreign students in higher education is due to offshore enrolments in Singapore, Hong Kong and Malaysia. Several Southeast Asian countries are actively encouraging foreign education institutions to establish campuses to help meet the increasing demand for higher education and reduce the outflow of students and foreign exchange. There are also a number of partner or twinning arrangements between domestic and foreign institutions, giving local students the ability to undertake a foreign degree. Local tutors are employed to teach the overseas curriculum over two to three years, with students able to study overseas in their final year.

RESTRICTIONS TO TRADE IN EDUCATION SERVICES

There are relatively few data sources for identifying and measuring the extent of trade and investment restrictions with respect to education services. The GATS schedules are a starting point for examining members' limitations with respect to market access and national treatment in education services. Prior to the GATS, there was no systematic means of identifying impediments to trade in services industries on a multilateral basis. A major problem in identifying the extent of trade restrictions in education is that it is one of the least committed service sectors, with only a quarter of GATS members scheduling commitments. This low level of commitment may be due to the substantial role of the government in the provision of education services. The most committed sectors in terms of the proportion of member countries scheduling commitments include tourism (93 per cent), financial services (75 per cent), business services (73 per cent) and communication services (70 per cent). Table 14.5 lists those countries with commitments to education categorised by five subsectors: primary, secondary, higher, adult and other. Only five countries list commitments in all five categories (the Czech Republic, Lesotho, Norway, Sierra Leone and the Slovak Republic).

The GATS schedules list each member's limitations concerning market access and national treatment for each of the four modes of supply. Market access covers any measure that restricts or limits access of foreign suppliers to the domestic market. National treatment covers limitations which treat a foreign supplier less favourably than a domestic supplier. Within each subsector of education and for each mode of supply, countries can offer either a full commitment or a partial commitment with respect to market access and national treatment. A full commitment indicates that no restrictions or limitations exist, in other words trade and investment is unrestricted for that sector. A partial commitment requires a country to specify the nature of the restriction in place. Both full and partial commitments are said to be binding in that no further restrictions can be introduced. By scheduling either full or partial commitments, benchmarks are established which enhance regulatory transparency. Where a country makes no commitment, the mode of supply is labelled unbound. This implies that restrictions on market access and national treatment may be maintained and/or additional restrictions may be imposed in the future. Countries undertaking no commitment make no contribution to regulatory transparency.

Table 14.6 summarises market access commitments for education services for the first three modes of supply. Commitments for Mode 4 (presence of natural persons) were similar for other service sectors, guaranteeing entry to certain categories of people, subject to their qualifications. For trade in education to flourish it is crucial that the consumption-abroad mode is relatively unimpeded as restrictions on students' ability to travel to an overseas destination would have the greatest potential effect on trade. Such restrictions would include emigration requirements, visa restrictions, foreign exchange

Table 14.5 Summary of specific commitments – education services

Countries	Primary	Secondary	Higher	Adult	Other
Australia		X	X		X
Bulgaria	X	X		X	
Congo RP			X		
Costa Rica	X	X	X		
Czech Republic	X	X	X	X	X
European Union	X	X	X	X	
Gambia	X			X	X
Ghana		X			X
Haiti				X	
Hungary	X	X	X	X	
Jamaica	X	X	X		
Japan	X	X	X	X	
Lesotho	X	X	X	X	X
Liechtenstein	X	X	X	X	
Mali				X	
Mexico	X	X	X		X
New Zealand	X	X	X		
Norway	X	X	X	X	X
Panama	X	X	X		
Poland	X	X	X	X	
Rwanda				X	
Sierra Leone	X	X	X	X	X
Slovak Republic	X	X	X	X	X
Slovenia		X	X	X	
Switzerland	X	X	X	X	
Thailand	X	X		X	
Trinidad and Tobago			X		X
Turkey	X	X	X		X
United States				X	X
Total number of schedules	20	22	21	19	12

Source: WTO 1998.

requirements and non-recognition of qualifications. Most countries have made full commitments with respect to consumption abroad within each category of education. Mode 1 (cross-border supply) was also relatively unimpeded, with 80 per cent or more of countries listing full commitment in higher, adult and other education services. The few partial limitations for Mode 1 refer to restrictions such as the granting of financial assistance for studies abroad, restricting the supply of the service only to foreign students, and nationality requirements.

Commercial presence is becoming more important in education trade and it is this mode of supply that is the most restricted. In primary, secondary and higher education services, most countries list some restrictions, with only a third listing full commitment.

Table 14.6 Overview of market access commitments for education services

Sector	Members with full commitment for Modes 1-3[a]	Cross-border supply (Mode 1)			Consumption abroad (Mode 2)			Commercial presence (Mode 3)		
		Full[a]	Partial[b]	No[c]	Full[a]	Partial[b]	No[c]	Full[a]	Partial[b]	No[c]
Primary	3[1]	10	4	6	16	1	3	7	11	2
Secondary	5[2]	12	4	6	18	1	3	8	12	2
Higher	6[3]	16	3	2	18	1	2	7	12	2
Adult	10[4]	16	2	1	18	1	–	12	6	1
Other	6[5]	11	1	–	12	–	–	6	4	2

Notes:

a Full commitments: no limitations listed, without considering horizontal limitations.

b Partial commitments: limitations listed.

c No commitment: unbound.

1 Gambia, Lesotho, New Zealand.

2 Australia, Ghana, Lesotho, New Zealand, Slovenia.

3 Australia, Congo RP, Lesotho, New Zealand, Slovenia, Switzerland.

4 Bulgaria, European Union, Gambia, Haiti (only rural centres), Japan (only foreign language instruction), Lesotho, Mali, Rwanda, Slovenia, Switzerland.

5 Australia (English language instruction), Gambia, Ghana (specialist only), Lesotho, Norway (education not leading to state recognised degrees), United States.

Source: WTO 1998e.

In several principal host nations, notably Australia and the United Kingdom, capacity constraints may limit the growth of foreign students studying abroad. Both these countries have a foreign-to-domestic student enrolment ratios in excess of 10 per cent. Growth in education exports via commercial presence is therefore likely to become more significant for both these countries.

Table 14.7 lists the specific types of restrictive measures applying to market access. Most of the restrictions listed occur within Mode 3 – commercial presence. These include restrictions on the number of suppliers, the type of legal entity, the participation of foreign capital, and other measures limiting access. Most of these restrictions occur within the primary, secondary and higher education sectors. Very few restrictions are recorded in the consumption-abroad mode.

A similar pattern is depicted in Table 14.8, which lists the restrictive measures applying to national treatment. Again the consumption-abroad mode is relatively unimpeded with no restrictions for primary, secondary or higher education. Three types of measures account for most of the restrictions regarding national treatment: nationality requirements (23), authorisation requirements (22) and measures concerning licensing, standards and qualifications (17). Most of these measures involve Modes 3 and 4. Restrictions on the temporary movement of people will have an adverse effect on the ability of foreign suppliers to establish a commercial presence in the foreign market. Most educational institutions establishing new or twinning campuses require staff to frequently travel to the offshore campus to undertake administration and teaching. Students enrolled at these institutions normally expect to have some contact with overseas educators during their program. Foreign academics are an important part of the marketing of these programs and any restriction limiting the movement of overseas teachers is likely to reduce the success of these offshore campuses and therefore constitute a serious trade impediment.

FREQUENCY MEASURES OF TRADE RESTRICTIONS IN EDUCATION

Applying the approach discussed in earlier chapters in this volume, restrictiveness indexes can be constructed for education services based on a count of the types of commitments made by each country with respect to each of the five subsectors. With four modes of supply and two categories of limitations (market access and national treatment), there are 40 possible commitments. A full commitment in a particular supply mode is assigned a score of 0, a partial commitment is assigned a value of 0.5 and an unbound commitment receives a score of 1 (i.e. the higher the value, the more restrictive the country). Education sectors that are not scheduled are treated as unbound and given a score of 8 (four modes with two types of limitations). Countries that made no commitments with respect to any of the five subsectors receive the maximum score of 40, while countries that made full commitments are assigned a score of 0. The frequency scores for each country are expressed

Table 14.7 Types of restrictive measures – market access (by number of schedules)

	Mode	a	c	d	e	f	g	h	Total
Educational	1	–	–	–	3	–	8	3	14
services	2	–	–	–	–	–	4	–	4
	3	3	1	–	18	7	19	11	59
	4	–	–	3	–	–	–	16	19
Primary education	1	–	–	–	1	–	2	1	4
	2	–	–	–	–	–	1	–	1
	3	–	–	–	5	2	5	2	14
	4	–	–	1	–	–	–	4	5
Secondary education	1	–	–	–	1	–	2	1	4
	2	–	–	–	–	–	1	–	1
	3	–	–	–	5	2	5	2	14
	4	–	–	1	–	–	–	4	5
Higher education	1	–	–	–	–	–	2	1	3
	2	–	–	–	–	–	1	–	1
	3	2	–	–	5	1	6	3	17
	4	–	–	1	–	–	–	4	5
Adult education	1	–	–	–	–	–	2	–	2
	2	–	–	–	–	–	1	–	1
	3	1	1	–	2	1	2	2	9
	4	–	–	–	–	–	–	1	1
Other education	1	–	–	–	1	–	–	–	1
	2	–	–	–	–	–	–	–	–
	3	–	–	–	1	1	1	2	5
	4	–	–	–	–	–	–	3	3

Notes: The b grouping of restrictive measures was not relevant for education services and was therefore not included in this table.

a　Number of suppliers.
b　Value of transactions or assets.
c　Number of operations.
d　Number of natural persons.

e　Types of legal entity.
f　Participation of foreign capital.
g　Other market access measure.
h　National treatment limitation.

Source: WTO 1998e.

as a fraction and the index for each subsector is adjusted to reflect the importance of that subsector in trade. Higher education is the most traded sector and receives a higher weighting of 0.4, while each of the remaining four sectors are allocated a weighting of 0.15. It is possible to attach separate weights to each of the four modes of supply but this was not done.

Figure 14.1 reports index values between 0 and 1 for the 29 countries listing commitments to education. It appears that education services are highly restricted, as most countries record values greater than 0.5. The countries with the highest values (such as Ghana, Haiti, Mali, Rwanda and the United States) had scheduled commitments for only one or two of the five sectors. Other countries receiving a relatively high score were Costa Rica, Japan and Thailand. These countries, while listing most of their sectors, had left a large

Table 14.8 Types of restrictive measures – national treatment (by number of schedules)

	Mode	a	b	d	e	f	g	h	m	n	Total
Total educational services	1	–	2	3	–	–	–	3	–	–	8
	2	–	2	–	–	–	–	–	–	–	2
	3	–	2	15	–	5	–	11	–	3	36
	4	1	2	5	3	12	1	8	2	1	35
Primary education	1	–	–	1	–	–	–	1	1	–	2
	3	–	–	3	–	1	–	2	–	1	7
	4	–	–	2	1	3	–	3	1	–	10
Secondary education	1	–	–	1	–	–	–	1	–	–	2
	3	–	–	4	–	1	–	2	–	1	8
	4	–	–	2	1	3	–	3	1	–	10
Higher education	1	–	–	1	–	1	–	1	–	–	2
	3	–	–	4	–	1	–	3	–	–	8
	4	1	–	1	1	3	1	–	–	1	8
Adult education	1	–	1	–	–	–	–	–	–	–	1
	2	–	1	–	–	–	–	–	–	–	1
	3	–	1	2	–	1	–	2	–	1	7
	4	–	1	–	–	2	–	–	–	–	3
Other education	1	–	1	–	–	–	–	–	–	–	1
	2	–	1	–	–	–	–	–	–	–	1
	3	–	1	2	–	1	–	2	–	–	6
	4	–	1	–	–	1	–	2	–	–	4

Notes: The following categories of restrictive measures were not relevant for education services: c, i, j, k and l.

a Tax measures.
b Subsidies and grants.
c Other financial measures.
d Nationality requirements.
e Residency requirements.
f Licensing, standards, qualifications.
g Registration requirements.
h Authorisation requirements.
i Performance requirements.
j Technology transfer requirements.
k Local content, training requirements.
l Ownership of property/land.
m Other national treatment measure.
n Market access limitation.

Source: WTO 1998e.

Figure 14.1 Education services – restrictiveness index 1

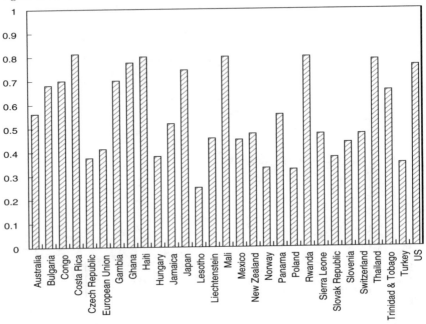

proportion of their commitments as unbound. The group of countries with the lowest values (such as the Czech Republic, the European Union, Hungary, Lesotho, Norway, Poland, the Slovak Republic and Turkey) had commitments in at least four of the five sectors and had given a full commitment to most delivery modes.

This first index assumes that unscheduled or unbound sectors are totally restricted, but this may not be the case. The United States, for example, has not scheduled its higher education sector, yet it is the world's leading exporter of higher education services. If unscheduled sectors are treated as being unrestricted, that is, given a score of 0 rather than 1, then a different degree of restrictiveness emerges, as shown in Figure 14.2. In the first index, more than half of the countries receive a score greater than 0.5, while only one country scores less than 0.3. In the second index, only one country receives a score greater than 0.5 (Japan), while 21 countries score less than 0.3. The conclusion from this second index is that education services are relatively unrestricted, which is consistent with the rapid growth in education trade over the past decade.

CONCLUSION

Barriers to trade in services encompass regulations that restrict or deny foreign service suppliers access to domestic markets or place foreign suppliers at a competitive disadvantage to domestic suppliers. The GATS schedules are one of the few data sources for identifying and measuring the extent of trade

Figure 14.2 Education services – restrictiveness index 2

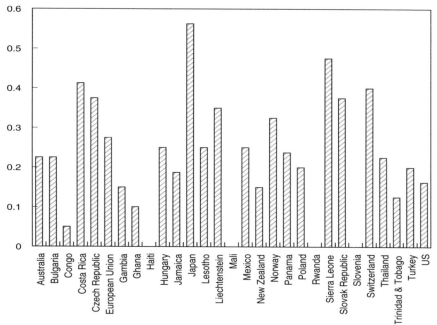

and investment restrictions with respect to education services. A major problem in using these schedules is that education is one of the least committed service sectors, with only a quarter of member countries scheduling commitments. However the data available indicates that consumption abroad is the least restricted mode of supply, while most countries list some form of restriction for commercial presence. Efforts at liberalising trade in education therefore would be more valuable if directed at removing restrictions on foreign investment.

Restrictiveness indexes constructed in this chapter for education services are based on frequency counts of the commitments made by member countries in each of the five education subsectors. While these measures suffer from a number of weaknesses they do provide a useful benchmark for comparing the extent to which countries are committed to setting policy goals toward reducing impediments to services trade.

Some of the weaknesses in these indicators of restrictiveness include the following:

- many countries have not made commitments to some or all of the education sectors;
- the GATS schedules do not provide information on all impediments to trade and investment within each sector; and
- there is little attempt to quantify the importance of different restrictions or different modes of supply.

Many of the world's leading exporters or importers of education services, such as Canada, China, Korea, Hong Kong, Malaysia and Singapore, do not appear in the index because they have not scheduled education in their GATS commitments. There are high returns in further work to collect more information on the policy regime in these economies and to consider more carefully the relative importance of various restrictions on the different modes of supply.

15 Measuring barriers to market access for services: a pilot study on accountancy services

Alessandra Colecchia

INTRODUCTION

This chapter attempts to develop a conceptual framework within which measures affecting market access in professional services can be looked at in an integrated way.[1] Rather than limiting the analysis to commitments scheduled by Organisation for Economic Cooperation and Development (OECD) countries under the World Trade Organisation's General Agreement on Trade in Services (GATS), the chapter looks at a broader range of governmental measures affecting conditions of entry, access and presence in markets for professional services. These are drawn from the list of measures reported in a database compiled in the context of ongoing OECD work on professional services, together with information compiled by the WTO secretariat from a questionnaire on the regulation of accounting services in Member Countries. A methodology is developed that translates qualitative regulatory information into a quantitative indicator of 'restrictiveness' of barriers affecting trade and investment in professional services. While specifically targeted to professional services in the first instance, this methodology may be flexible enough to apply generically to the analysis of impediments to market access for other categories of services.

Measures affecting the international delivery of professional services are looked at comprehensively with the aid of a flowchart. This helps in giving a single snapshot overview of what restrictions are in place in any particular market. Although the information available is qualitative in nature, owing to the regulatory dimension of barriers to trade and investment in professional services, numerical values are assigned to the various measures with a view to delivering a synthetic quantitative indicator of the relative restrictiveness of relevant regulatory practices. Because such practices differ considerably in nature, scope, frequency and importance (e.g. those affecting the temporary entry of service suppliers versus those affecting conditions of commercial presence), they are not strictly comparable and cannot be ranked easily. For this reason, the paper proposes to convert the qualitative information on the presence of a restriction to a simple 0 or 1 indicator. The value of 0 is assigned in instances where no restrictions apply, while 1 denotes the presence of a fully market-access inhibiting measure. Where restrictions or various regulatory requirements do apply, the paper attempts to rank their degree of restrictiveness. The ranking is therefore performed *within* each category of restrictions in order to reduce – indeed largely avoid – intractable problems of comparability *across* restrictions.

To normalise the various measures of restrictiveness and ensure some level of comparability across restrictions, benchmark weights are constructed for each category of restrictions. The benchmark score represents the maximum degree of trade and investment liberalisation compatible with the attainment of legitimate regulatory concerns. The construction of a synthetic indicator of protection, obtained by aggregating the various restrictiveness indexes found in the flowchart, can be viewed as performing a signalling function. That is, by looking at the flowchart of a country characterised by a higher index of restrictiveness, one can hopefully diagnose more easily the most important impediments to market contestability. In turn, this could help identify those measures towards which scarce negotiating resources could be directed.

The methodology is applied to the regulatory regimes governing the accountancy profession in four OECD member countries (Australia, France, the United Kingdom and the United States) in 1997, and this is reported in an appendix.

EXPLAINING THE METHODOLOGY

The flowchart asks a hypothetical service provider a sequence of questions in the right order about supply of services into a market. These questions start with 'can the service be provided at all' and, if so, by progressing to questions about the conditions attached thereto, it is possible to identify which measures affect the provision of the service, which of those impair market access, and to what degree. In constructing the index of trade restrictiveness, the focus is on regulatory measures which affect the service provider's access to a market. Examples of access-impairing measures include nationality requirements, residency requirements and licensing requirements.

As evident in work reported in other chapters in this volume, such an approach requires reliable and fairly comprehensive information. Thus an initial methodological challenge is to ensure that the framework can be applied to sufficient and accurate data. While the OECD's professional services database does not contain all the regulatory measures applicable to professional services, it still features those practices which experts (drawn from governmental circles, licensing bodies and practising professionals) regard as being the most relevant ones affecting the provision of professional services by foreign suppliers. Because professional services, such as legal and accountancy services, are generally provided by individuals or firms, this chapter focuses on regulations that act as barriers to the movement of natural persons and to the establishment of a commercial presence in supplying such services. Therefore, restrictions on the temporary movement of people and the establishment of commercial presence, as well as the broad area of recognition of qualifications and facilitating practices, need to be examined in an integrated way, based on their effects on market access.

A second methodological challenge is to create an index that synthesises different measures (e.g. those affecting the movement of natural persons and those affecting commercial presence, or those which restrict and/or facilitate the provision of a service). Obviously, such measures are not strictly comparable. To deal with this, the qualitative information on the presence of a restriction is converted into a simple 0 to 1 indicator. The ranking describes the extent of the restrictiveness of the measure within the scale of 0 to 1, with a value of 0 applied when there is no restriction in place, while 1 means that a restriction prohibiting market access is in place. This ranking is performed internally to each sectoral restriction.

This index of restrictiveness allows for comparisons across markets and can be used to identify equivalent levels of restrictiveness in the international liberalisation process. An example of the index's utility in respect of qualifications requirements arises with accountancy services, where there seems to be general consensus on the desirability of eliminating restrictions based on nationality and residency requirements. To date, most attention has been devoted to the promotion of the international harmonisation of qualification requirements.[2] With the index approach, as the indicator would reflect the implicit cost of obtaining the necessary qualifications, it might be possible to target a reduction in those costs as an objective to be achieved through liberalisation.

However, this applies only to cross-country comparisons at a given sectoral level (i.e. it would be misleading to compare indexes of restrictiveness that are constructed in isolation at the sectoral level). It would also be desirable for the methodology to utilise quantitative indexes which are broadly comparable *across* sectors, so that, for example, a given restrictiveness rating in one sector may be considered as equivalent to that obtained in another sector.

A special contribution of the work reported in this chapter is the manner in which benchmarking is introduced. The interpretation of the position of particular economies relative to benchmarks has been discussed elsewhere in this volume. Here, the benchmark adopted is the maximum level of openness to international trade liberalisation compatible with the attainment of a minimum level of essential/legitimate regulatory objectives. The benchmark may differ across sectors, but each measure within a sector will be weighted against its sectoral benchmark. Thus the relative market-access impeding effect of a measure in one particular sector may be compared with the effect of an identical or similar measure in another sector. The benchmarking approach also permits sectoral aggregation into an overall index of trade restrictiveness.

THE METHODOLOGY

Constructing the flowchart: asking the right questions

Figure 15.1 summarises the series of questions to a hypothetical services supplier which are the key to the methodology applied in this work. The first question to be asked is whether foreign provision of the service is permitted (this applies regardless of whether the foreign service provider is a firm or an individual). If this is permitted, it will typically be regulated, with the pertinent regulations being those licensing requirements which need to be met in order to practice the regulated activity.

Licensing requirements may apply to both individuals and firms and include, as prime examples, registration requirements, membership of a recognised professional body, professional indemnity insurance, honesty and minimum-age requirements. Together with associated administrative procedures for securing the licence, such requirements belong to the realm of domestic regulation. In WTO terms (GATS Article VI: 4), licensing requirements are permitted so long as they do not constitute unnecessary barriers to trade in services. At this stage, this means only that they should be based on objective and transparent criteria that are not more burdensome than is necessary to ensure the quality of the service, and that the procedures for administering them should not, in themselves, form a restriction on the supply of the relevant service. Regarding discrimination, foreign service providers should be treated the same (most-favoured-nation treatment), unless an exemption for that sector has been scheduled by the regulating country; and national treatment (i.e. the same treatment to foreign service providers as to domestic ones) is required only if a commitment to this effect has been scheduled by the regulating country.

Even if market access is restricted for a foreign provider, the second question to ask is whether a profession can be practised at least to some degree. The question of restricted practice (including temporary licensing regimes) versus full practice involves a finer analysis of qualification requirements and procedures. These comprise one element of licensing requirements and can give rise to discrimination and trade and investment-distorting barriers. Differences exist across countries in the level of qualification required to provide a given licensed service as well as in the functions that are assigned by law to various professions. The central issue from a market-access perspective is whether or not regulations are more burdensome than necessary. The access-inhibiting effects of restricting the delivery of a service through a particular mode of supply depends on the characteristics of the service involved. Legal services are mainly provided by individuals, while accountancy services are essentially provided (in the global marketplace) by a limited number of large firms (the 'Big Six'). Nevertheless, recent OECD work on professional services has made clear that the issue of freedom of choice between individual provision and provision through establishment is important

Figure 15.1 Asking the right questions

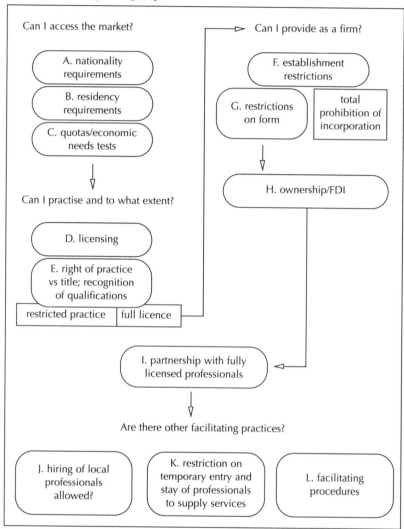

in the eyes of practitioners. Even if a service can be provided by individuals, discriminatory restrictions on incorporation may, by limiting the choice of mode of supply, exert significant access-impairing effects.

Foreign professionals are generally able to practice licensed activities only by becoming part of the local profession, although they may be able to practice on the basis of their domestic credentials in a restricted manner (e.g. a foreign legal consultant who can only practice international and home law but not the law of the host country).

There may also be alternative ways of providing services to a market. The following questions may thus assume some relevance: (i) whether partnerships with fully licensed professionals are permitted; (ii) whether local professionals can be hired; and (iii) whether there are measures to facilitate the temporary entry and stay of foreign professionals. For the purpose of the following analysis, the third subset of measures are viewed as facilitation practices. Responses to a recent WTO questionnaire on accountancy services revealed that 86 per cent of member countries did not maintain special requirements for the hiring of local professionals. In the remaining countries, local hiring is either restricted in some measure or simply forbidden (5 per cent of the cases). Over 40 per cent of the countries in the sample do not maintain facilitation procedures governing the temporary entry and stay of foreign professionals. In countries where such procedures exist, they seemingly do not appear to differ from procedures used for admitting foreign professionals on a more permanent basis (e.g. via residency requirements, economic needs tests/quotas, labour-market tests) (WTO 1997c).

Assessing relative restrictiveness

Figure 15.1 shows twelve categories of measures, but not all are restrictions – some are designed to facilitate trade. Within each category of measures, this chapter ranks relative degrees of restrictiveness. A restriction such as a nationality or permanent residency requirement can be applied fully or, under conditions of reciprocity, only to a subset of countries. The recognition of foreign qualifications can, for its part, be assessed in terms of 'automaticity'. A qualification can be recognised automatically or may require a provider to incur certain costs, such as examination or local training costs. Each restriction or facilitating practice can be associated with a range of weights depending on their importance for securing effective access in a market. This allows potentially important gains in flexibility: the range within which rankings may be attempted can and indeed will be likely to differ across various service categories (and not only within the area of professional services).

Attributing the weights

The weights can be positive (i.e. add to the degree of restrictiveness), as in the case of restrictive measures, or negative, as in the case of facilitating practices. It should be noted that the overall assessment will depend importantly on the type of qualitative information available on any given country/profession appearing in the OECD database (this information is not always exhaustive or coherent). To the extent that such information is less than fully comprehensive or accurate, the conclusions may be biased and much less robust.[3] A discussion of the weighting system and some examples related to accountancy services are presented below.

Separate rankings can be obtained also by taking into account just the restrictions and not the facilitating practices. A separate ranking for restrictive qualification requirements could similarly be useful in charting an area that the WTO Working Party on Professional Services deems as its top investigative priority (WTO 1997c). It could also serve a useful purpose in the context of encouraging greater recourse by professional licensing bodies to mutual recognition agreements (MRAs).

The weights should be refined in order to be consistent with each other. For example, the weight attributed to having automatic recognition of qualifications must always be greater than the sum of weights attributed to having the ability to obtain restricted practice plus the weight associated with the possibility of full partnership with fully titled professionals. Differing ways of achieving the same substantive degree of market openness in professional services should ideally be attributed the same score.

Benchmarking

A major objective is to design a framework that can be applied, in principle at least, to all services despite the existence of 'natural' differences in predominant modes of supply, in relevant barriers to their provision or in key regulatory objectives and concerns. While accountancy services are predominantly supplied internationally by six large firms, the provision of legal services is still very fragmented, with services being provided largely by national firms and by a small (but growing) number of firms with offices outside of their national base. The flowchart takes into account barriers affecting both the movement of natural persons and conditions of commercial presence. Although barriers to commercial presence can constrain the cross-border provision of legal services, they might not always be binding given that the movement of natural persons remains the most prominent mode of supply for such services.

Different benchmarks for accountancy and legal services are used and country indexes of restrictiveness are constructed as deviations from such benchmarks. Hence, a particular barrier that is considered to be restrictive in the case of accountancy can be regarded as less restrictive in the case of legal services. The key is thus to define a level of protection/openness considered to be the 'norm', that is, the level that is normally applied by all countries given certain regulatory objectives (e.g. consumer protection, confidentiality and accountability). As a benchmark one could take into consideration: (i) the flowchart of the most liberal country in that particular service sector (e.g. the United Kingdom, in the case of accountancy); or (ii) a hypothetical flowchart in which the best practice for every measure is assessed by taking into consideration *de minimis* regulatory objectives.

The weighting system

A measure of overall restrictiveness is obtained by summing up the individual 'within measures' scores contained in the flowchart. This involves summing the scores attributed to: (i) nationality requirements; (ii) licensing requirements;

(iii) the possibility of establishing a commercial presence and the forms such a presence can take; (iv) the issues of firm ownership and restrictions on partnership; as well as (v) a cluster of facilitation practices, ranging from conditions governing the hiring of local professionals to the temporary entry and stay of professionals.

This section discusses the ranking of the restrictions within each measure and their score, corrects the 'within restriction' scores through weightings that more accurately reflect the market-access impairing effect of the restriction or requirement and discusses consistency constraints.

Weighting within measures

Two types of weights can be used for purposes of delineating the relative importance or market-access inhibiting effects of various regulatory practices. Horizontal weights involve the use of a range set between 0 and 1. The attributed weight (w) is equal to 1 if a requirement or restriction applies, to 0 if it does not, and set at values between 0 and 1 in instances where measures apply only occasionally (i.e. 1>w>0).

Vertical weights are selected on the basis of a qualitative/rule-of-thumb ranking of regulatory practices, ranging from most to least restrictive (and average restrictiveness in between). Figure 15.2, which depicts market-access restrictions affecting the provision of various services (boxes A to C in Figure 15.1), highlights the operation of the weighting system described above:

- *nationality and residency requirements* are measures to which horizontal weights can be applied;
- *residency requirements* can be ranked using vertical weights, and range from most (permanent residency) to least restrictive (requirement of having just a domicile in the host country); and
- *quotas/economic needs tests* are measures to which 'least restrictive' can be assigned in instances when they are required in principle but not enforced in practice due to various agreements among professional associations and/or licensing bodies.

A second broad category of measures to focus on concerns qualification requirements and the implicit cost of obtaining such qualifications (see area D in Figure 15.3). Measuring restrictiveness in this area involves both positive and negative weightings, the outcome of the *licensing requirements + recognition of qualifications* routine being the net result of adding up positive (where licensing requirements apply) and negative values (costs incurred in having foreign qualifications recognised).

Measures governing the *recognition of qualifications* are ranked on a 'cost' basis. The cost to a foreign professional of having his/her qualifications recognised in order to be granted a full licence will vary from mere red tape costs, to having to undergo a period of local training, or to the more

Figure 15.2 Market access for individual providers

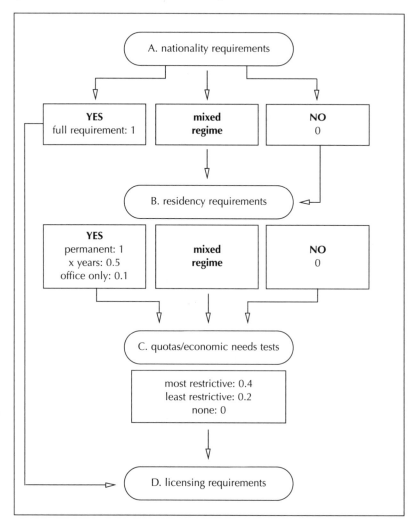

burdensome requirement of having to submit to a more comprehensive set of local examinations. In cases where more than one requirement applies, the total score would equal -1 times the absolute value of the product of the scores of each requirement. For example, if both exams (-0.6) and local training (-0.8) were required, the score attributed would equal -0.48.

In cases where such requirements apply only to some categories (e.g. public auditing) or where procedures differ across various service categories, the score would be obtained as follows:

Figure 15.3 Licensing and recognition of qualifications

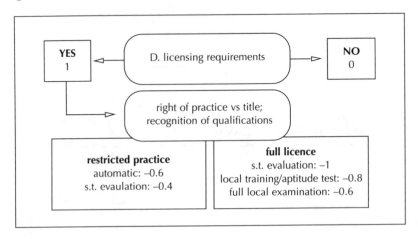

$\sum_{j}\sum_{i}(1+w_{ij})p_j$ where w_{ij} is the (negative) weight given to requirement i and applied to professional category j, and p_j is the percentage share of category j in the overall profession.

A third area in the flowchart (area E to G) concerns the broad array of measures affecting conditions of establishment (see Figure 15.4). Such measures include:

Discriminatory *restrictions on incorporation*[4] A total prohibition on incorporation is a clear-cut restriction to market access. While often non-discriminatory in nature, such measures nonetheless restrict the choice of the mode of delivery for both domestic and foreign suppliers, and penalise those foreign firms in whose home countries services are most commonly delivered through a corporate presence. The score assigned to such measures is 0.8 (smaller than a full nationality requirement owing to the latter measure's discriminatory character).

The main regulatory issue relating to 'allowed forms' of incorporation concerns questions of limited versus unlimited liability. The box 'restrictions on form' refers to cases in which limited liability corporations are allowed (e.g. limited liability partnerships). Forms of limited liability are ranked using a dual benchmark. *Norm* characterises forms of limited liability corporations which are typically subject to 'minimum' regulatory concerns (e.g. France). *Above norm* applies to countries whose regimes tend towards a greater degree of restrictiveness.

Restrictions on FDI, control and ownership[5] While restrictions on control and ownership of professional firms are not generally expressed in a discriminatory manner, their burden tends to weigh more heavily on the ability of foreign firms to contest a national market. Such restrictions are,

Figure 15.4 Restrictions on establishment

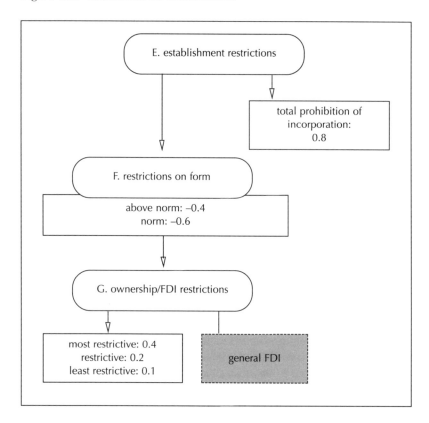

accordingly, often viewed as a form of *de facto* discrimination. In the accountancy sector, these restrictions are not viewed as a serious impediment to entry as all but one (i.e. Arthur Andersen) of the Big Six firms operate through a network of international affiliations with local firms rather than on a parent/subsidiary basis (Piggot 1996: 103). Recourse to local partnerships, which might not always be the optimal means of delivering some professional services, may well have developed in reaction to existing restrictions on ownership. These restrictions are attributed the following scores: (i) most restrictive – ownership and control requiring residency or citizenship; (ii) restrictive – ownership and control requiring a majority of locally licensed professionals; and (iii) least restrictive – ownership and control requiring a minority of locally licensed professionals. Restrictions typically relate to the obligation of being a member of an approved local accountancy body. Such requirements are taken into account where relevant.

Correcting the scores

Each requirement or restriction will be attributed the score indicated in each subroutine. In principle each requirement can apply generally or be limited in scope. Accordingly, the scores are corrected by weights as indicated below. In the flowcharts, boxes indicating 'mixed regime' are subroutines in which corrections are applied.

Professional categories Some regulatory requirements apply only to some categories within the profession. (This is typically the case of auditors within the accountancy profession. In Australia, for example, residency requirements apply only to auditors and liquidators.) In this case the total score resulting from a subroutine will be multiplied by a weight of one (w=1) if the requirement applies generally, and by w<1 if the requirement applies partially. The weight should ideally reflect the importance of the category in question.

Reciprocity Some countries impose regulatory requirements on the basis of reciprocity considerations (as is often the case in Mexico). In this case the score attributed to a subroutine is the average of all the scores attributed to other countries for the same subroutine.

Regional agreements The granting of regional preferences within regional trade arrangements means that some regulatory requirements apply only to a certain geographical area (e.g. nationality requirements applied only to non-European Economic Area or non-European Union nationals). Depending on the sample of countries under consideration one might want to correct for this factor. In the case of a database such as that developed by the CIME, and which is mainly composed of European countries, one might want to consider a requirement applied only to non-EU countries as relatively less restrictive than a requirement applied to every country in the sample. Scores can be corrected by multiplying them by weights varying with the size of the geographical area: for example w=0.4 for the EU and w=0.6 for the EEA.

Consistency constraints

The values assigned to the different restrictions are not important *per se*. More important is the ability to address barriers to the provision of professional services by looking comprehensively across countries at all possible impediments to market access. Here are some examples:

- restricted practice + full automatic partnership (i.e. at no cost) should always be smaller than full practice at no cost: -0.6 + (-0.3) = -0.9 < -1;
- allowing limited liability forms of incorporation should be considered as a more liberal practice than allowing only unlimited liability partnerships (limited liability forms (-0.6 or -0.4) > unlimited liability partnership (-0.3)); and
- unfettered provision by an individual supplier implies a score equal to 0.

Equivalent (i.e. in terms of restrictiveness/openness) ways of providing a service can be determined by the parties themselves. If negotiating parties agreed on the qualitative equivalence between granting a full licence at some cost and allowing restricted practice plus free partnerships, such 'packages' could be exchanged at the negotiating table. It is important to note the interdependence between establishment restrictions and licensing requirements. Firms can often only be established or controlled by locally licensed professionals. Similarly, two countries applying the same types of restrictions on establishment might still have differing levels of overall protection due to differences in the implied cost of acquiring a licence.

CONCLUSION

This chapter has proposed a methodology that could help in evaluating countries' relative level of protection in service sectors. The key elements of this framework are: (1) the use of all available information on the relevant measures affecting trade in professional services (as defined by experts) and these measures are summarised in an integrated fashion with the aid of a flowchart; (2) the construction of restrictiveness indexes to rank barriers affecting trade in professional services; (3) the imposition of 'consistency' constraints on the weights assigned to each measure; (4) the definition of a benchmark score within each restriction to normalise the measures and allow restrictions to be compared and aggregated into an index, with the benchmark score representing the maximum level of trade liberalisation that could be deemed compatible with the satisfaction of legitimate regulatory objectives; and (5) the construction of a synthetic indicator of protection, obtained by aggregating the restrictiveness indexes along the flowchart, which functions as a signal. By looking at the flowchart of a country characterised by a higher index of restrictiveness, it is possible to see where the problem lies and where liberalisation efforts should be targeted.

Both the assessment of the relative restrictiveness of measures and the construction of the benchmark flowchart are flexible and could likely be adapted to other types of services. An obvious shortcoming of the methodology proposed in this chapter is that its various assessments involve a fair degree of subjectivity. This is unavoidable given both the regulatory, hence qualitative, nature of impediments to trade in services and the inherent shortcomings in the availability and completeness of regulatory information/data. Still, the chapter has attempted to impose some constraints on the weights attributed to each measure so as to ensure a more consistent evaluation across measures. As well, the use of survey information and expert opinion in constructing benchmarks aims to reduce the level of subjectivity. The point is that both the consistency constraints and the benchmarks to be used can be agreed upon (i.e. negotiated) by countries. Countries can hopefully converge around some notion of an optimal level of regulation in a particular area indicated in the flowchart; agree to achieve the recognition of qualifications through various means (e.g. mutual recognition agreements); and reach agreement on equivalent ways of delivering a service. They can similarly be encouraged to adopt greater facilitating practices (e.g. allowing the temporary movement of foreign providers) when they are not ready to remove restrictions in other areas (e.g. on forms of establishment).

One final dimension emphasised by the chapter's analysis is the desirability for countries to look at the entire range of measures affecting conditions of entry, access and presence in markets when negotiating and setting their liberalisation priorities in services discussions. While this chapter has emphasised a range of access-impeding governmental measures, there are other practices, public or private, that may potentially reduce the international contestability of services markets. Indeed, for some professions, the ability to compete for government procurement contracts (including at the sub-national level) may be key to securing effective access to a market (e.g. consulting engineering). Similarly, there may well be professions where private anti-competitive conduct and differences in the coverage and/or enforcement of national competition laws might feature prominently in the market-access equation (Sauvé 1995a). In developing the methodology further, and possibly applying it to other service categories (including beyond professional services), it may be desirable to attempt to measure the degree to which other types of measures, public and private, can restrict trade, investment and the competitive process more generally. This in turn would require strengthened efforts at data collection, regulatory cooperation and government–industry dialogue.

APPENDIX: AN APPLICATION OF THE METHODOLOGY TO ACCOUNTANCY SERVICES

This section applies the methodology described earlier to four OECD countries (the UK, France, Australia and the United States), using information on regulatory regimes in place in 1997. Reading the country-specific flowcharts (see Figures A15.1–4) from the top left part, the weights assigned are those corresponding to the shaded boxes. The footnote at the bottom of each flowchart shows the calculations of each country's overall protection index (P). In the chapter, three 'within-measure' indexes are identified: (i) the market-access restrictiveness index; (ii) the cost-of-qualification index; and (iii) the facilitating-practices index. The third index is less reliable since the availability of information in the database varies considerably across countries. That is why a restrictiveness index (R), which excludes facilitating practices, has also been calculated.

To construct benchmark weights in the accountancy sector for the different areas of the flowchart, information contained in the published proceedings of the last two OECD workshops on professional services is used. Particularly useful is the result of an enquiry into the policy rationale of measures such as restrictions on establishment, nationality and local presence requirements. To gain a better sense of what experts consider to be the optimal level of liberalisation in accountancy services, one can turn to the specific policy recommendations made at the Third OECD Workshop on Professional Services (20–21 February 1996).

Based on the information described above, it would appear that nationality and prior residency requirements are on the retreat in OECD countries and do not really have much of a pertinent policy rationale in the case of accountancy services. Residency requirements come in many variations, ranging from permanent residency requirements to temporary residency requirements or the adoption of a domicile. Of the four countries examined here, the United Kingdom is completely liberal in this respect while France applies a *de minimis* requirement (only a professional address is required). In Australia, there is no stipulated residency requirement but in practice the Australian Securities Commission may refuse to register auditors and liquidators who are not residents in Australia. Moreover, the country's corporation law stipulates that at least one member of an auditing company must be a registered company auditor who is ordinarily resident. In the US, except in few jurisdictions, citizenship is not required for licensing accountants while many states require residency and/or an in-state office (i.e. a local presence).

Measures that restrict the form of establishment are important in the accountancy sector. The main motivations behind them are to preserve the non-commercial character of the practice of accountancy or the personal responsibility of professionals. Many of these restrictions have been removed and in the OECD database sample limitations on forms of incorporation are not maintained in the accountancy sectors in Finland, Greece, Iceland, Mexico, Norway, Switzerland and the United Kingdom. We take the 'norm' to be that

Table A15.1 Protection indexes for the four countries

	Index	Ranking
1	Market-access restrictiveness index (A+B+C+E+F+G)	UK = 0.2 France = 0.6 Australia = 1.15 US = 1.55
2	cost of qualification index (D)	France = 0.1 Australia = 0.1 UK = 0.3 US = 0.4
3	facilitating practices index (H+I+J+K)	UK = -0.5 France = -0.4 Australia = -0.3 US = -0.3
4	overall index (P)	UK = 0 France = 0.3 Australia = 0.85 US = 1.25
(4-3)	restrictiveness index (R) (i.e. without the facilitating practices index)	UK = 0.5 France = 0.7 Australia = 1.15 US = 1.55

for which all the forms of establishment are allowed except some forms of limited partnership. This is the case of France where some forms of companies[6] are not allowed for statutory auditors and chartered accountants on the grounds of protecting the non-commercial character of those professions.

Restrictions on investment and ownership are based on the nationality of the owner or on the origin of the licence they hold. In both cases such restrictions are taken into account in the area of the flowchart concerning licensing requirements. Those are the binding restrictions since it is usually the case that shareholding in professional firms is restricted to individuals, which hampers attempts to develop parent–subsidiary relationships even if the firms involved were all to be locally licensed. The benchmark chosen is that of ownership and control requiring a minority of locally licensed professionals. The overall benchmark score is constructed in such a way so that the total index (restrictions plus facilitating practices) is equal to zero.

To construct the final index the deviations of each 'within measure' score from the benchmark are aggregated and the corrected overall index (P bar) and restrictiveness index (R bar) are obtained.[7] It bears noting that the ranking of the sample of countries is not affected in this specific case, though it could be in other instances.

Table A15.2 Benchmark weights

Box	Measure	Bench-mark weight	Benchmark rationale
A	nationality requirements	0	restrictions on nationality should be abolished
B	prior residency and local presence requirements	0.1	prior residency requirements should be abolished, minimum local presence requirements to assure regulatory and enforcement processes (e.g. local office)
C	quotas/economic needs tests	0	
D	qualification requirements	0.2	aptitude tests
E, F	restrictions on form	0.3	only limited partnerships should be restricted
G	ownership restrictions	0.1	ownership and control requiring a minority of locally licensed professionals
H	partnership with fully licensed professionals	-0.3	
I	hiring of local professionals	-0.2	
J–K	restrictions on temporary entry and stay of professionals to supply services	-0.2	

Table A15.3 The corrected protection and restrictiveness indexes

	P	P bar	R	R bar
UK	0	-0.2	0.5	-0.2
France	0.3	-0.1	0.7	0
Australia	0.85	0.55	1.15	0.45
US	1.25	0.95	1.55	0.85

Figure A15.1 Barriers to the provision of accountancy services, Australia

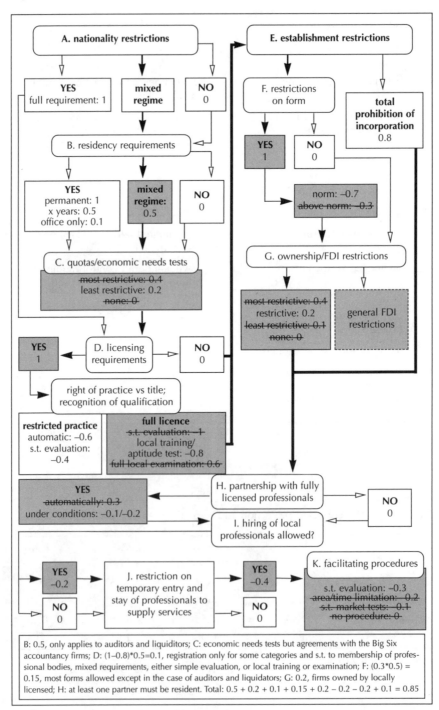

Figure A15.2 Barriers to the provision of accountancy services, France

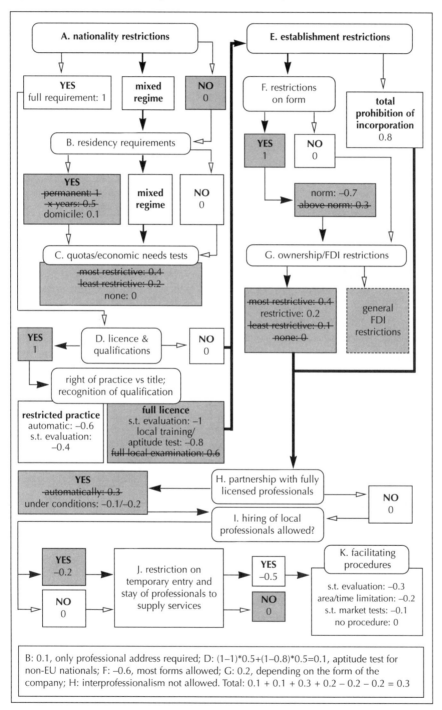

B: 0.1, only professional address required; D: (1–1)*0.5+(1–0.8)*0.5=0.1, aptitude test for non-EU nationals; F: –0.6, most forms allowed; G: 0.2, depending on the form of the company; H: interprofessionalism not allowed. Total: 0.1 + 0.1 + 0.3 + 0.2 – 0.2 – 0.2 = 0.3

Figure A15.3 Barriers to the provision of accountancy services, United Kingdom

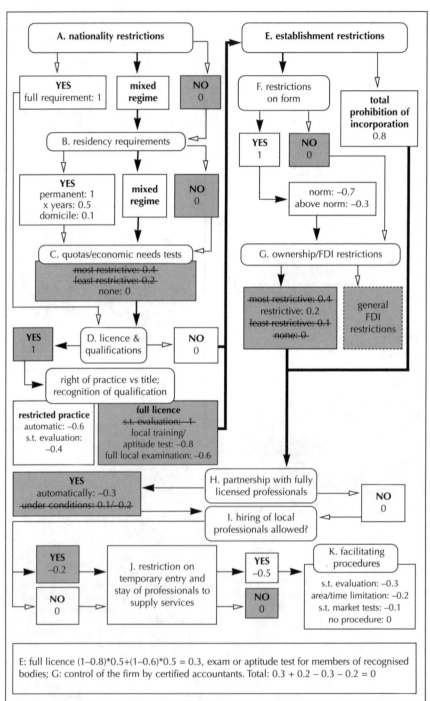

E: full licence (1–0.8)*0.5+(1–0.6)*0.5 = 0.3, exam or aptitude test for members of recognised bodies; G: control of the firm by certified accountants. Total: 0.3 + 0.2 – 0.3 – 0.2 = 0

Figure A15.4 Barriers to the provision of accountancy services, United States

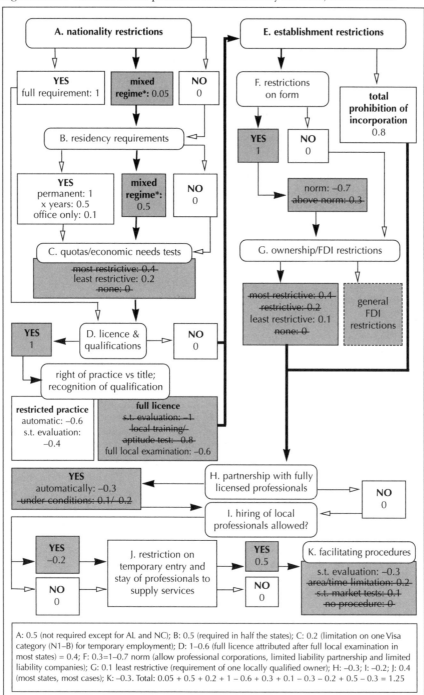

A: 0.5 (not required except for AL and NC); B: 0.5 (required in half the states); C: 0.2 (limitation on one Visa category (N1–B) for temporary employment); D: 1–0.6 (full licence attributed after full local examination in most states) = 0.4; F: 0.3=1–0.7 norm (allow professional corporations, limited liability partnership and limited liability companies); G: 0.1 least restrictive (requirement of one locally qualified owner); H: –0.3; I: –0.2; J: 0.4 (most states, most cases); K: –0.3. Total: 0.05 + 0.5 + 0.2 + 1 – 0.6 + 0.3 + 0.1 – 0.3 – 0.2 + 0.5 – 0.3 = 1.25

NOTES

The views expressed in this chapter are the author's and should not be attributed to the Organisation for Economic Cooperation and Development or its member countries. The chapter was written when the author was working in the OECD Trade Directorate and has greatly benefited from interactions with colleagues. The author is especially grateful to Crawford Falconer, Bernard Hoekman, Patrick Low, Aaditya Mattoo and Raed Safadi for helpful comments and discussion. A special thanks goes to Pierre Sauvé and Rachel Thompson for all the encouragement and valuable drafting suggestions. Rachel Thompson, also of the OECD Secretariat, presented highlights from this chapter at the Measuring Impediments to Trade in Services workshop hosted by the Productivity Commission (of Australia), 30 April–1 May 1998, in Canberra.

1   This methodological proposal was prepared for the OECD Trade Committee Working Party in September 1997. The working party did not choose to pursue this methodology. Instead, subsequent work has focused on advancing the construction of sectoral and cross-sectoral inventories of barriers to trade in services, which are being ranked in three broad categories of restrictiveness.

2   The efforts of the WTO Working Party on Professional Services have been directed towards the production of guidelines for mutual recognition agreements/arrangements in the accountancy sector.

3   Fortunately, this is a matter for which the OECD traditions of peer review and constant exchanges of regulatory information can be put to good use with a view to enhancing the overall quality of information contained in the database.

4   GATS Article XVI on market access requires member states to include in their commitments provisions against 'measures which restrict or require specific types of legal entities through which a service supplier may supply a service'.

5   General FDI restrictions should be taken into consideration in assessing countries' relative openness to service provision, as these are deemed barriers to access in the sense of GATS Article XVI (market access). Since such data is still unavailable (although the negative lists of non-conforming measures by signatories to the Multilateral Agreement on Investment might produce useful information in this regard), such restrictions are not taken into consideration in measurement terms but still mentioned in the flowchart as a reminder of their potential significance.

6   *Societé en nom collectif* and *societé en commandite*.

7   The following computations are obtained:

P_{UK} = (0-0)+(0-**0.1**)+(0-0)+(0.3-**0.2**)+(0-**0.3**)+(0.2-**0.1**)+(-0.3+**0.3**)+(-0.2+**0.2**)+ (0-**0.2**) = **-0.2**

P_{FR} = (0-0)+(0.1-**0.1**)+(0-0)+(0.1-**0.2**)+(0.3-**0.3**)+(0.2-**0.1**)+(-0.2+**0.3**)+ (-0.2+**0.2**)+(0-**0.2**) = **-0.1**

P_{AUST} = (0-0)+(0.5-**0.1**)+(0.2-0)+(0.1-**0.2**)+(0.15-**0.3**)+(0.2-**0.1**)+(-0.2+**0.3**)+ (-0.2+**0.2**)+(0.2-**0.2**) = **0.55**

P_{US} = (0.05-0)+(0.5-**0.1**)+(0.2-0)+(0.4-**0.2**)+(0.3-**0.3**)+(0.1-**0.1**)+(-0.3+**0.3**)+ (-0.2+**0.2**)+(0.2-**0.2**) = **0.95**

R_{UK} = (0-**0**)+(0-**0.1**)+(0-**0**)+(0.3-**0.2**)+(0-**0.3**)+(0.2-**0.1**) = **-0.2**

R_{FR} = (0-0)+(0.1-**0.1**)+(0-0)+(0.1-**0.2**)+(0.3-**0.3**)+(0.2-**0.1**)= **0**

R_{AUST} = (0-**0**)+(0.5-**0.1**)+(0.2-0)+(0.1-**0.2**)+(0.15-**0.3**)+(0.2-**0.1**)= **0.45**

R_{US} = (0.05-0)+(0.5-0.1)+(0.2-0)+(0.4-0.2)+(0.3-0.3)+(0.1-0.1) = **0.85**

16 Issues in the application of CGE models to services trade liberalisation

Philippa Dee, Alexis Hardin and Leanne Holmes

INTRODUCTION

One of the distinguishing features of the General Agreement on Trade in Services (GATS), the key forum for multilateral liberalisation of services trade, is the inclusion of commercial presence as a mode of service delivery. The other modes – cross-border supply, consumption abroad and temporary movement of people – all result in trade transactions that are captured, albeit very imperfectly, in balance of payments accounts, on which the services trade structures of existing computable general equilibrium (CGE) trade models are based. Commercial presence does not. It represents a mode of delivery that would need to be added explicitly to most existing model structures. This is the first challenge in the application of CGE models to services trade liberalisation.

The second challenge, highlighted in Chapter 4, is how to characterise the non-discriminatory restrictions on market access and the discriminatory restrictions on national treatment that apply to services trade. What are the appropriate tax or tariff equivalents of these restrictions, on what production or trade flows should they apply, and who gets the rents? Only once these issues have been decided can CGE models be used to analyse the impact of services trade liberalisation, via the reduction or elimination of these tax or tariff equivalents.

PAST MODELLING OF SERVICES TRADE AND FOREIGN DIRECT INVESTMENT

Model frameworks

Only a few attempts have been made to model the impacts of liberalising investment in a general equilibrium framework. The approaches adopted in these studies can be divided broadly into three groups. The first group does not model foreign direct investment (FDI) explicitly but, when examining the impact of services trade liberalisation, it implicitly includes the reduction of FDI barriers. The second group of studies does not explicitly model FDI or the reduction of investment barriers; it simulates the effects of investment liberalisation by making assumptions about the variables which increased capital mobility may affect. The third group explicitly models FDI and captures many of the important economic characteristics of FDI which are not included in the other studies. While the approaches in the third group have some shortcomings, they provide a sound basis for examining the implications of investment liberalisation for Australia.

The first group of studies includes those that use Hoekman's (1995) estimates of tariff equivalents to examine the impacts of services trade liberalisation (see, for example, Brown et al. 1995; Brown et al. 1996; Dee et al.). These estimates include barriers to services traded cross-border, via the temporary movement of people and via FDI. Therefore, estimating the impacts of reducing these tariff equivalents necessarily includes the reduction of barriers to FDI. There are a number of problems with this approach, the most important being that the models do not capture the important economic characteristics of FDI. For example, foreign-owned firms typically benefit from their parents' firm-specific assets. Hence, the demand and production characteristics of foreign affiliates need to be modelled as distinct activities from other production activities in both the host and home economies.

A good example is Brown et al. (1996) who model trade liberalisation in services under various assumptions using a general equilibrium framework. The authors argue that the movement of factors from the exporting country to the importing country, as in FDI, to provide a service does not pose a problem within their model. Such factors are still part of their home country's factor markets, and the fact that they happen to be located abroad should not matter for the determination of the various market equilibria.

This approach to modelling FDI liberalisation has some appeal as it does not require a restructuring of most general equilibrium models. Barriers to FDI are combined with barriers to services traded cross-border and removing them results in cheaper services and increased services trade for the liberalising economy.

However, the possible benefits of FDI and its role in services trade are not modelled, so important effects such as the scope for foreign varieties of non-tradable services to be consumed in the host economy via FDI are not captured. Furthermore, this approach requires that services traded via FDI are included in the initial database as exports and imports of services for each region. This is not usually the case in general equilibrium models. Brown et al. (1996) use balance of payments data to assemble their services database. As noted, these data do not capture the value of services traded through FDI. This means that, although the barriers to FDI are being removed as part of services trade liberalisation, the original levels of services traded failed to include services traded through FDI.

The authors note that they do not take account of changes in FDI that might occur as a result of changes in the rate of return on capital. Therefore, removing impediments to FDI does not result in higher levels of FDI in the liberalising country as would be expected. An additional problem raised by Brown et al. (1996) is their assumption that all factors of production are regarded as participating in the factor markets of their country of origin. Often services traded via FDI require factors to be employed from the importing country's factor markets. For example, most foreign subsidiaries are staffed, at least to some extent, with local labour. This will matter for the effects of trade on the economies involved.

In the second group of studies, FDI is not modelled explicitly and barriers to FDI are not incorporated explicitly. Investment liberalisation is assumed to affect certain variables, such as the extent of capital mobility, and the effects of this are then simulated. For example, Bora and Guisinger (1997) use a general equilibrium model which incorporates international capital mobility. No distinction is made between portfolio investment and FDI. Investment liberalisation is modelled by increasing capital inflows to liberalising economies by varying degrees.

Donovan and Mai (1996) use the MEGABARE model to estimate the effects of trade liberalisation under standard and high degrees of capital mobility. They assume that removing investment barriers will result in increased capital mobility. No distinction is made between portfolio investment and FDI. Investment in the model is a function of the differential between national and global rates of return. The parameter that determines the responsiveness of investment to changes in rates of return is initially set to achieve a plausible pattern of international capital flows. To represent a more liberal investment regime, the degree of capital mobility in the model is increased fourfold over the standard value.

McKibbin and Wilcoxen (1996) also allow international capital mobility in their general equilibrium model: G-Cubed. However, they do not attempt to model the impact of investment liberalisation directly. Instead, they examine the impact of a rise in total factor productivity in the services sector, which they consider a plausible side effect of trade liberalisation in services in the context of the GATS. While FDI is not included explicitly in the model, the economy-wide data presumably cover the activities of both domestic and foreign firms. Therefore, the productivity of both domestic and foreign firms operating in the domestic economy is assumed to increase as a result of services trade liberalisation. The improved performance of services results in resources being channelled into that sector. These resources come from other sectors in the economy as well as from overseas. The increase in return to capital in the services sector leads to an inflow of foreign financial capital into physical investment in the liberalising economy.

The third group of studies overcomes many of the problems discussed above by incorporating FDI into a general equilibrium model in a way consistent with theoretical work. The main feature of these models is that they recognise the links between parents and foreign affiliates, and they differentiate between foreign and domestic firms within a given region.

The first of these studies, Markusen et al. (1995), compares the impact of trade liberalisation with and without multinational firms in an industry with increasing returns to scale and imperfect competition. The models are applied to the North American (Canada, Mexico and the United States) auto market, with the rest of the world supply explicitly modelled and endogenous. While the scope of this study is narrow and does not include investment liberalisation, their methodology and results are useful when considering how to model the role of FDI and the effects of reducing barriers to it.

The principal difference between the model with multinational firms and that with only national firms is the response of a firm's market share to trade liberalisation. In the multinational model, a firm's US market share includes imports from its branch plants in Canada and Mexico. Thus, additional cars imported from Mexico to the United States constitute an increase in the combined market share of US firms because the Mexican exporter is US owned. Other general equilibrium models ignore multinationality (or FDI) and impose an assumption that a firm's domestic production equals its market share. In the national model, a car imported into the United States from Mexico constitutes an erosion of the US firm's market share.

Therefore, holding rest-of-world imports constant, an import from Mexico in the multinational model lowers the North American firm's perceived elasticity of demand and raises its markup. The same import in the national firm model raises the North American firm's perceived elasticity of demand and lowers its markup. Markusen et al. (1995) therefore hypothesise that the presence of multinational firms, or FDI, reduces the benefits of trade liberalisation.

It is important to note that the results of this study are dependent on the assumption that multinational firms coordinate price and quantity decisions across markets to maximise global rather than regional profits. It is not clear whether this is generally the case in services markets or if some foreign affiliates make their own price and output decisions. Obviously, the extent of international coordination by multinationals will determine the relevance of the anti-competitive effects identified by Markusen and others and, therefore, the extent to which FDI affects trade liberalisation.

The second study is more general in terms of incorporating FDI into a general equilibrium framework. Petri's (1997) model of FDI distinguishes between the activities of domestic and foreign-owned firms at the microeconomic level. Petri provides for production linkages between parents and subsidiaries. This is accomplished by identifying three types of requirements in the input structure: value-added inputs; inputs sourced from parents; and other intermediate inputs. Therefore, it overcomes the problem identified in Brown et al. (1996) of assuming that all factors of production are from the country of origin.

The demand side of the model differs from the conventional approach. The Armington assumption that product varieties are differentiated by place of production is replaced with the assumption that they are differentiated by both country of ownership and place of production.[1] The resulting demand system means that foreign varieties are available not just as imports, but also as local purchases from the subsidiaries of foreign firms. Petri notes that an important economic implication is that FDI does not merely promote increased production of a commodity in the host economy; it also changes how the products of that economy enter world demand. The FDI mechanism has important implications for modelling services trade liberalisation because it allows foreign varieties to be consumed in non-tradable sectors through the presence of foreign firms. This is an important characteristic of FDI that is not included in the first group of studies, which require all foreign products to be imported.

The allocation of capital across regions is modelled in an optimising framework which allocates capital to the highest return activities, but also takes into account investor preferences for a particular mix of investment instruments. The capital allocation function therefore relies not only on the investment's expected rate of return, but also on the investor's utility function, which minimises risk. This is analogous to consumer choice among goods subject to a budget constraint and yields similar functions for relating investment allocations to prices of assets. Thus, the allocation of capital between sectors and between domestic and foreign investments is not based on arbitrage conditions assuming perfect substitution, but on a constant elasticity of substitution (CES) formulation with less than perfect substitutability.

Treatment of services trade barriers

Petri models barriers to FDI as a tax on FDI profits. Therefore, such barriers affect the rate of return on FDI stocks and hence discourage FDI flows into the region imposing the barriers. Reducing or removing FDI barriers increases the returns to FDI stocks, which results in more foreign investment being allocated to the liberalising country or region. As noted in Hardin and Holmes (1997), not all FDI restrictions are best treated as a tax on the returns to FDI. Nor does the search for high returns necessarily explain all of the motivations for undertaking FDI. Nevertheless, this approach to modelling barriers to FDI seems to be a reasonable place to start.

Many past studies (Brown et al. 1995; Brown et al. 1996; Dee et al. 1996; Petri 1997) which attempt to estimate the impacts of services trade and/or investment liberalisation have used tariff equivalents estimated by Hoekman (1995). These tariff equivalents were calculated on the basis of scheduled commitments under the GATS. Therefore, they include barriers that are applied on all four modes of supply identified by the GATS, including FDI. The limitations of these estimates are identified by Hoekman (1995) and are discussed in Chapter 4.

The implications of applying the estimated tariff equivalents to just services trade (as in Brown et al. 1996), or just FDI (as in Petri 1997), may not be important because the limitations of Hoekman's estimates mean that the results of the studies that use them provide only an indication of the impacts of services and/or investment liberalisation. Hoekman (1995) notes that care must be taken in allowing for a wide range of 'benchmark' tariff equivalents when the GATS-based tariff equivalents are used to model the impacts of liberalising services trade. However, if modelling results are to provide insights into the role of FDI and the linkages between trade and investment liberalisation, then FDI and barriers to it need to be modelled explicitly.

Studies that do not use Hoekman's tariff equivalent estimates have tended to use even more arbitrary measures of investment restrictions. For example, Bora and Guisinger (1997) model the impact of investment liberalisation by varying the ratio of FDI flows to gross investment. Three cases are examined: high, medium and low. The high case involves doubling the 1995 ratio, the low case increases it by 30 per cent, while the middle case is between these two estimates. The authors do not distinguish between FDI and portfolio investment and do not allow for foreign firms in the domestic economy. Their results, therefore, reflect only the impact of a capital inflow on domestic firms. Donovan and Mai (1996) use a fourfold increase in the capital mobility parameter as a proxy for investment liberalisation, because of the difficulties with quantifying investment barriers.

Data

Bilateral investment flows and stocks data at a disaggregated industry level are available only for a few countries. Even data for services traded cross-border are weak compared with those on merchandise trade (see Box 16.1). The only study which attempts to incorporate FDI flows and stocks into a general equilibrium framework is Petri (1997). Other studies assume that services traded via FDI are incorporated in balance of payments data, or make use of more aggregated capital flow and stock data within the models.

A WAY FORWARD

The general equilibrium modelling framework developed by Petri (1997) captures some of the features of FDI identified in the theoretical literature that are important when examining the impacts of liberalisation. Petri's framework recognises that foreign-owned firms benefit from their parents' assets by modelling them as distinct from domestic-owned firms, both in terms of demand and production characteristics. Petri also allows foreign affiliates to be linked to parents through intermediate input flows. His model distinguishes between varieties produced by the foreign affiliate and those produced by domestic firms of the host economy or by subsidiaries of other parents.

As noted, reducing FDI barriers in Petri's model is equivalent to reducing taxes on the profits earned by foreign affiliates. As profits increase, foreign affiliates can offer lower prices to domestic consumers. Increased profits also

Box 16.1 Services data

The main source of data on trade in services is the balance of payments (BOP), which has many weaknesses. BOP statistics are often inconsistent between countries. For example, a user of BOP statistics cannot be certain that what is reported for exports of port services by country A consists of the same items reported as exports of port services by country B. Coverage of BOP statistics is also often incomplete. At virtually any level of aggregation, some nations may not report information on a certain item. This results in biased figures when data are added across countries to arrive at regional totals, and discrepancies when comparing world imports and exports for a category.

Information on trade by origin and destination is not available on a comparable and detailed basis. In general, the amount of detail or disaggregation for data on trade in services is very limited. Trade data on a volume basis are not available. This makes it very difficult to determine what proportion of growth in a category in a given year is due to inflation as opposed to improvements in quality.

Comparability of BOP statistics over time is difficult because methodologies and definitions employed by countries may vary between years. It is also difficult, if not impossible, to relate services trade statistics to domestic production and employment data. To some extent, this is because different countries include different items in various components of the current account. More important is that trade data are simply too aggregated, so that concordances have little meaning.

Finally, data on sales by foreign affiliates are excluded. BOP conventions imply that, if factors of production move to another country for a period longer than one year, a change in residency status is considered to have occurred. The output generated by such factors that is sold in the host market will no longer be registered as trade in the balance of payments.

Source: Hoekman 1995.

attract FDI flows to the liberalising economy, which increases competition and the demand for inputs from both the host and home economies. However, a more general treatment of barriers to services trade could be developed within his model framework. This is outlined in more detail below.

All of these links should be incorporated when modelling the impacts of FDI liberalisation in the services sector. The inclusion of trans-border price and output coordination by multinationals, identified by Markusen et al. (1995), also needs to be considered. The relevance of multinational coordination will depend on the sectors and countries being analysed. It may be more likely to occur in the North American auto market (which Markusen et al. modelled) than for other types of FDI, such as that in service industries.

Petri notes a further interaction that is identified in the theory but not incorporated into his FDI model: the interaction between foreign affiliates and their host economy through various dynamic relationships, including externalities associated with scale or technological spillovers (see APEC 1996, and Blomström and Kokko 1997, for discussions of these effects). Also, Petri's model specification does not capture the benefits for consumers of increased product variety, which is likely to be an important outcome of FDI liberalisation. The possibility for including these effects should also be examined.

Developing a global modelling framework similar to Petri's is a large task. Such a framework would nevertheless address many of the problems associated with earlier modelling of barriers to services trade. It would recognise the services traded by commercial presence as well as those traded via other modes of delivery. If the model recognised the different cost structures of foreign affiliates and allowed for economies of scale and product differentiation, it would capture at least some of the motivations for FDI stressed in the literature. And as outlined shortly, it would provide a framework within which there could be comprehensive coverage of the different types of barriers to services trade. A first step in this direction is given in Dee and Hanslow (1999).

An alternative, smaller task may be to apply Petri's framework to a model of a single economy. This would allow the impact of FDI liberalisation in that economy to be examined without requiring information for other individual regions. The microeconomic distinctions between domestic and foreign firms made by Petri would still have to be incorporated, although only for the single economy. A major drawback of this approach is the limitations a single country model places on the liberalisation scenarios that can be examined. Using a model of a single economy means that only unilateral FDI liberalisation scenarios can be considered. While these scenarios will provide a starting point for examining FDI liberalisation, useful policy results will require modelling multilateral FDI liberalisation in the context of the GATS and other investment agreements.

Data

Limited FDI and services trade data continue to be major constraints on progress in modelling FDI liberalisation. To model the gains from multilateral liberalisation, data on bilateral investment stocks and flows are required, together with data on the value of services traded via FDI (as opposed to the other modes of supply, cross-border trade and the temporary movement of people), and data on the activities of foreign affiliates, so that their inputs and outputs can be distinguished from those of domestically owned firms.

Petri has made some progress in addressing these data constraints by constructing a database showing the role of FDI in six broad regions and three sectors (agriculture, manufacturing and services), drawing on the 1992 Global Trade Analysis Project (GTAP) database (Hertel 1997) and detailed survey data for Japan and the United States. In addition, the GTAP project itself is undertaking a major upgrade of its conventional services trade data. However, considerable extensions to Petri's approach, involving further assumptions and estimates, would be required if the model were to be extended to more sectors and regions.

If a single country model were used for unilateral liberalisation simulations, rather than building on Petri's existing global model, the required amount of information on FDI flows, stocks and activities would be reduced substantially. However, a more detailed industry disaggregation than Petri's could be adopted so that the impact of removing FDI barriers from individual service industries could be modelled.

INCORPORATING SERVICES TRADE BARRIERS INTO PETRI'S FRAMEWORK

A key characteristic of the Petri framework is that it expands the dimensionality of conventional multicountry, multiregion CGE models. For example, in a conventional model such as GTAP, household demands would have a commodity-region-region dimension and capital stocks would have an industry-region dimension:

$x_h(i,s,d)$ demand by households in region d for commodity i from source region s

$k(j,d)$ capital stock in industry j in region d

By contrast, in the Petri framework, household demands would have a commodity-region-region-region dimension and capital stocks would have an industry-region-region dimension:

$x_h(i,s,d,h)$ demand by households in region d for commodity i from production facility located in host region s but owned by home country h^2

$k(j,d,h)$ capital stock in production facility for industry j located in host region d but owned by home country h

Thus, capital located in a country might be domestic or foreign-owned, and would generate profit streams accruing to domestic and foreign owners. In principle, households in a country could purchase from purely domestic firms, from foreign affiliates located at home or, via cross-border trade, from firms located offshore (including possibly the offshore affiliates of local firms).

In practice, the nature of some services could make it hard to supply them via cross-border trade.

Household (as well as intermediate, investment and government) preferences among these different sources would be an important determinant of the ultimate mix of local provision, trade via commercial presence and trade via the other modes of supply. This would be captured through parameters specifying elasticities of substitution in demand between the various sources. The other key determinant would be the relative supply prices from these sources. These would be affected by transport costs and trade barriers. They would also be affected by the rates of return to capital required by investors in order to be willing to invest more in one location rather than another.

But each service flow, and each flow of profits, becomes a candidate for having a tax or tariff wedge attached to it to represent barriers to services trade.

The nature of barriers to services trade

How the barriers should be incorporated depends in part on how they have been estimated. The aim of many of the chapters in this volume has been to move beyond frequency-type measures of barriers to services trade, in order to obtain a price impact. Examples are the price estimates of the barriers to telecommunications trade in Chapter 7, and the price estimates of the barriers to trade in banking services in Chapter 13. In the case of banking services, the estimated impact was on banks' net interest margins, a specific measure of the markup of 'price' over 'costs' for banks. Thus, at least for banking, the estimated price impact is precisely an estimate of the height of the 'rent rectangle'. But where should the rent rectangles be put?

The barriers to services trade can be subdivided in two dimensions. First, it is possible to distinguish barriers to establishment from barriers to ongoing operation (see, for example, Chapters 11 and 13). This is not quite the same as distinguishing barriers to commercial presence from barriers to other modes of service supply, since, as noted in Chapter 4, the barriers to commercial presence can themselves apply to establishment or to ongoing operation. But the distinction between barriers to setting up and barriers to ongoing operation is akin to Baldwin's (1999) distinction between barriers that raise the fixed costs of operating and those that raise the marginal costs. Barriers to establishment can be modelled as barriers on the movement of capital, and barriers to ongoing operation can be modelled as barriers on the services provided once the capital is established.[3]

Second, it is possible to distinguish barriers that discriminate against foreign suppliers (be they locally based foreign affiliates or offshore suppliers) and those that affect domestic and foreign suppliers equally (e.g. Chapters 11 and 13). This is equivalent to the distinction between derogations from national treatment and restrictions on market access.

Now consider how this four-way classification of barriers can be incorporated into the Petri framework.

Restrictions on ongoing operation

Figures 16.1a and 16.1b show the restricted and unrestricted equilibriums in the market for a particular service in a particular region, indicating the impact of discriminatory and non-discriminatory barriers to ongoing operation. The panels distinguish three sources of supply: from domestic firms, from locally based offshore affiliates, and from offshore firms. Strictly speaking, in the Petri framework, these three sources of supply are imperfect substitutes in demand. However, the relevant elasticities of substitution are likely to be reasonably high, considering that they are capturing firm-level product differentiation (see Petri 1997 and also Francois and Shiells 1994). So, for the purpose of simplification, the diagram assumes perfect substitution on the demand side.

The left panel of Figure 16.1a shows total demand and the supply curve of domestic firms. The middle panel shows the resulting excess demand (the excess of total demand over the supply of domestic firms, taken from the left panel) and the supply curve of locally based foreign affiliates. The right panel traces the excess demand taken from the middle panel, along with offshore supply. In the unrestricted equilibrium, the economy buys Q_1 from domestic firms, Q_2 from locally based offshore affiliates, and Q_3 from offshore firms.

Figure 16.1b shows the corresponding restricted equilibrium, where discriminatory and non-discriminatory barriers to ongoing operation put a wedge between prices and costs of provision. Note that, because of the discriminatory restrictions, the wedge faced by locally based foreign affiliates and offshore suppliers is higher than the wedge faced by domestic firms.

The restricted equilibrium price P^R_e is higher than the unrestricted equilibrium price P_e (compare the third panels of Figures 16.1a and 16.1b), and both locally based foreign affiliates and offshore firms unambiguously supply less in restricted than in unrestricted equilibrium. In the absence of any non-discriminatory restriction on domestic firms, they would unambiguously supply more under the restricted than the unrestricted equilibrium. But, if they face non-discriminatory restrictions of their own, it depends whether the tax equivalent of these is sufficiently large to offset the advantage to domestic firms conferred by the discriminatory restrictions.

Thus, in a CGE context, the restrictions on ongoing operation faced by offshore firms selling in the local market can be modelled as a tariff equivalent. The restrictions faced by domestic firms and locally based foreign affiliates can be modelled as a production tax equivalent on their operations. Both tariffs and production taxes put a wedge between the domestic price and the domestic or foreign cost of production. Note that using production taxes rather than consumption taxes assumes that any restrictions on ongoing

Figure 16.1a Unrestricted equilibrium for a service

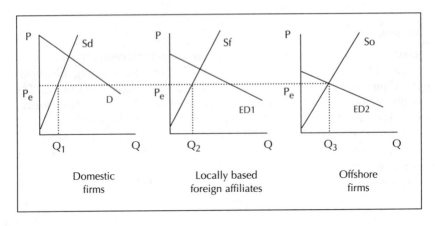

Figure 16.1b Restricted equilibrium for a service

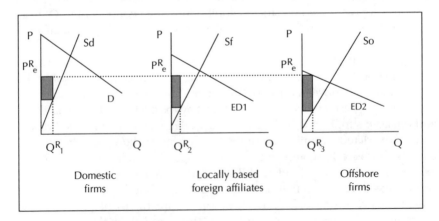

operation would affect any exports made by domestic firms and by locally based offshore affiliates, as well as their sales on the domestic market. Given the nature of the restrictions on ongoing operation in maritime, for example, this seems reasonable (see Chapter 10).

Restrictions on establishment

Figures 16.2a and 16.2b show the restricted and unrestricted equilibriums in the market for capital in a particular region, indicating the impact of discriminatory and non-discriminatory barriers to establishment. The left and

Figure 16.2a Unrestricted equilibrium for capital

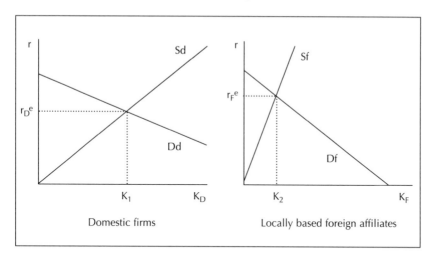

Figure 16.2b Restricted equilibrium for capital

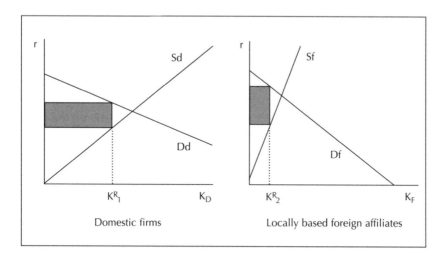

right panels show, respectively, the supply and demand for local capital by domestic firms, and the supply and demand for foreign-owned capital by locally based offshore affiliates. Since, in the Petri framework, these are two completely different types of firms, there is no necessary connection, at least in partial equilibrium, between demand for local and foreign capital. Similarly, domestic and foreign investors have preferences about the shares of their portfolios that they hold domestically and offshore, so there is no necessary connection, at least in partial equilibrium, between the supply of local and foreign capital (in contrast to perfect arbitrage models). Thus, in unrestricted equilibrium, there is no necessity for the rental prices of capital to equalise in the domestic firms and in the locally based offshore affiliates (Figure 16.2a).

Figure 16.2a shows the impact of discriminatory and non-discriminatory restrictions on establishment. Here the estimated impact of these restrictions on output prices has been converted (using capital–output ratios) to an equivalent impact on the rental price of capital. Because of discriminatory restrictions, the wedge faced by locally based offshore affiliates is larger than that faced by domestic firms.

It appears that the restrictions would lead unambiguously to less capital being used in both domestic firms and in locally based offshore affiliates. However, this need not be the case once the effect on the 'output' market for the service is taken into account. If, because of discriminatory restrictions, locally based offshore affiliates employ less capital and therefore offer fewer services, the demand faced by domestic firms would expand, moving their demand curve for capital to the right. Once these more general equilibrium effects are taken into account, the story is likely to be the same as it was in Figure 16.1 – the impact on locally based offshore affiliates is unambiguously negative, but the impact on local firms depends on whether the negative impact of non-discriminatory restrictions offsets the advantage conferred on them by discriminatory restrictions.

In a CGE context, the restrictions on establishment faced by domestic firms and locally based foreign affiliates can be modelled as the equivalent of an income tax on capital.

Who gets the rents?

Who gets the rents depends in part on where they are generated. If the price impact of the restrictions to services trade has been estimated empirically by looking at the effects on some markup of price over cost (as in Chapter 13), the empirical work itself answers the question of where the rents are generated. This is the basis on which Figures 16.1 and 16.2 have been drawn, where the shaded areas in Figures 16.1b and 16.2b show the rents that are generated by the restrictions.[4]

If the impact has been estimated by looking at prices alone, or costs alone, even the existence of rents is speculative – some restrictions may have raised prices by raising costs, with no clear impact on price–cost margins.

But rents can also be passed around, particularly by government mechanisms such as auctioning the rights to establish or operate, or by private mechanisms such as transfer pricing. The question of the ultimate beneficiary need not be the same question as the question of where the rents are generated. Casual observation suggests that governments typically do not sell the rights to establish or operate in restricted service markets. By selling the rights, the rents from the restrictions would have been passed to governments. But this issue requires further research.

If governments do not acquire the rents by auction mechanisms, it seems natural to assume that they are retained by the firms in which they are generated and are then passed on to their shareholders. But, to the extent that the rents show up in the taxable income of firms, governments may still acquire a portion. However, locally based foreign affiliates may have the option of transferring the rents shown in the middle panel of Figure 16.1b and the right panel of Figure 16.2b, along with other income, to their home country by transfer pricing – say, by inflating the price they pay their parent company for any intermediate inputs or headquarters services provided by the parent. A modelling decision would therefore still need to be made on which country, if any, the rents of foreign affiliates were taxed in. This question is also under-researched in a CGE context.

THE WELFARE IMPLICATIONS OF SERVICES TRADE LIBERALISATION

One of the truly great innovations introduced with the GTAP model framework was a mechanism for decomposing the welfare implications of trade liberalisation scenarios, which can be highly complex, into a series of intuitive components (Huff and Hertel 1996, based on Keller 1980). So, even without having built a large Petri-style CGE model along the lines outlined, one can nevertheless anticipate what the welfare decomposition in such a model would look like, using the GTAP techniques, and try to anticipate the welfare effects of the sort of quantity responses to trade liberalisation that were implicit in Figures 16.1 and 16.2.

GTAP welfare decomposition

The basic intuition of the GTAP decomposition is as follows. National utility depends on real household consumption C, real government consumption G, and real national saving S. It is determined by the following maximisation problem:

Max $U(C,G,S)$ subject to $P_c C + P_g G + P_s S$ = net national income

If U takes a Cobb-Douglas form, then the equivalent variation (EV), which is a money measure of absolute changes in national utility, takes a particularly simple form:

EV =   scale term * [nnp - p]

where nnp is the percentage change in net national income, and p is the percentage change in a price index that is itself a share weighted sum of percentage changes in P_c, P_g and P_s. In a model without FDI or other forms of international capital mobility, net national income is measured by total factor income (net of depreciation) and total indirect tax receipts.

It turns out that a number of the standard zero pure profit and market clearing equations of a GCE model can be substituted into this expression for net national income, to yield a particularly useful decomposition of the EV measure:

$$EV = \text{scale term} * [\ TAX_1{}^*q_1 + TAX_2{}^*q_2 + \ldots + TAX_N{}^*q_n$$

$$+ \text{'terms of trade' effect}$$
$$+ \text{'terms of saving and investment' effect}$$
$$+ \text{contribution from endowment growth}$$
$$+ \text{contribution from technical change}$$
$$+ \text{term arising from non-homotheticity of household preferences in GTAP]}$$

The first terms, involving the product of an initial tax rate (TAX_i) and the percentage change in the quantity moving across that tax wedge (q_i), spell out the efficiency effects of trade liberalisation. They measure the way in which the efficiency loss triangles, such as in Figures 16.1 and 16.2, would change as some or all of the trade taxes changed in a liberalisation scenario.

Imagine a commodity or service that has a high production tax to start with, so that TAX_i is large and positive for that commodity. Economic theory would tell us that production of that commodity would be smaller that it would be in an undistorted equilibrium. Thus, any trade liberalisation scenario that increased the quantity produced, so that q_i was positive, would move the economy closer to undistorted equilibrium and contribute positively to national welfare (because $TAX_i{}^*q_i$ would be positive). This could come about because this commodity was itself subject to liberalisation, and the initial TAX_i reduced as part of the scenario. But it could equally come about as an indirect result of liberalisation elsewhere. If so, it would still contribute positively to overall welfare.

Now imagine a commodity or service that had a production subsidy to start with, so that TAX_i was negative. Production would be larger than in undistorted equilibrium, and any liberalisation scenario that reduced the quantity produced (so that qi was negative) would also contribute positively to overall welfare (because $TAX_i{}^*q_i$ would still be positive).

But the welfare decomposition also highlights the possibility of perverse welfare implications from trade liberalisation scenarios. Suppose a commodity or service has a production tax in initial equilibrium, but that its quantity produced falls as a result of liberalisation elsewhere in the economy. This might happen if taxes on close substitutes were eliminated as part of the liberalisation scenario. This would contribute negatively to overall welfare (because $TAX_i{}^*q_i$ would be negative). Thus, the welfare decomposition highlights quite explicitly possible dangers associated with partial liberalisation, a topic that will be discussed further in the context of services trade liberalisation below. It remains to explain briefly the remaining terms in the welfare decomposition, before examining how it would change in the presence of FDI and other forms of international capital mobility.

The second term is a conventional 'terms of trade' effect, showing that when the price of something used to derive income (i.e. exports) rises relative to the price of something used to derive utility (i.e. imports), an economy enjoys a terms of trade improvement and this contributes positively to overall welfare. The 'terms of saving and investment' effect has a similar logic: when the price of something used to derive income (i.e. investment) rises relative to the price of something used to derive utility (i.e. saving), this also contributes positively to overall welfare.

The welfare decomposition also notes that, if capital stocks increase exogenously for some reason, this contributes directly to national utility. However, the normal non-static welfare decomposition for GTAP does not consider the question of how the increase in capital stocks comes about, or who finances it. This will be addressed shortly. The decomposition also notes that technical changes contribute directly to overall welfare. The final term in the decomposition arises because of the functional form of household preferences across commodities.

Incorporating FDI

Now consider how the welfare decomposition would change in the presence of FDI and other forms of international capital mobility. One way to view this would be to consider how the relevant definition of net national income would change. With international capital mobility, net national income would be the sum of total factor income (net of depreciation), total indirect tax receipts, net foreign dividend income from FDI, and net interest income from the issuing of bonds.

The last term would arise in a model that allowed each country to issue bonds internationally to finance its domestic investment and FDI. A model of international borrowing and lending was developed by McDougall (1993) and incorporated into the Salter (Jomini et al. 1994) and IC95 (Dee et al. 1996) models. A combined model of borrowing and FDI could have perfect international arbitrage in bond interest rates, while breaking the nexus between interest rates and rates of return on FDI, something that appears consistent with the empirical evidence (IC 1991).

With the definition of net national income altered in this way, the same derivations could be use to decompose the first two income terms. The amended definition would simply have the two additional income terms on the end:

$$EV = \text{scale term} * [\ TAX_1{}^*q_1 + TAX_2{}^*q_2 + \ldots + TAX_N{}^*q_n$$
$$+ \text{'terms of trade' effect}$$

+ 'terms of saving and investment' effect
+ contribution from endowment growth
+ contribution from technical change
+ term arising from non-homotheticity of household preferences in GTAP
+ contribution from net income from FDI (including rents)[5]
+ contribution from net interest income]

Thus, the analysis of efficiency effects – the efficiency with which resources are deployed within an economy – would be the same as before. But there would be an additional consideration that the income generated within a country need not all accrue to the residents of that country. Experience with models such as Salter and IC95 suggests that the impact of net foreign income payments can alter the welfare implications of trade liberalisation scenarios in important ways. This should not be surprising, since the rectangles in Figures 16.1 and 16.2 are typically larger than the triangles.

Principles of services trade liberalisation

On the efficiency side, the results of services trade liberalisation would depend again on the sizes and signs of the $TAX_i^*q_i$ terms. These terms suggest a number of possible principles of services trade liberalisation.

In general terms, the greatest gains are to be had from liberalising the most highly distorted sectors. These are the sectors where the TAX_i terms are the highest, and where the induced quantity responses q_i also tend to be the greatest.

In the context of services trade liberalisation, this suggests that the biggest gains would be achieved by removing discriminatory measures against foreign-based or foreign owned suppliers. Because of the way distortions compound, eliminating a 10 per cent tax equivalent of a discriminatory barrier levied on top of a non-discriminatory barrier would yield higher welfare gains than eliminating a 10 per cent tax equivalent levied on its own. This is because, in the first case, the relevant TAX_i term would include the sum of the initial discriminatory and non-discriminatory barriers, and could be much higher than 10 per cent.

In addition, reducing or eliminating the most highly distorted sectors usually helps to avoid the possibility of perverse second-best welfare effects. This has been explored by Dee et al. (1998) in the context of APEC's early voluntary sectoral liberalisation initiatives.

Consider the liberalisation of discriminatory barriers to services trade in the context of Figure 16.1b. The 'tax' wedge on locally based foreign affiliates and offshore firms would be reduced so as to equal the wedge on domestic firms. The equilibrium price P^R_e would fall slightly, and output of the locally based foreign affiliates and offshore firms would expand, contributing positively to welfare. But output of domestic firms would contract slightly (because of the fall in P^R_e), contributing negatively to welfare. Thus, the removal of discriminatory restrictions could lead to a 'perverse' contribution from domestic firms. Because domestic firms face a smaller 'tax' wedge to start with, this perverse effect is unlikely to dominate. However, its possibility suggests that, for services, an across-the-board approach to liberalisation may be better than a top-down approach.

The same principles can be used to consider which services sectors to liberalise first, as well as to consider the priority to be attached to services trade liberalisation as a whole, relative to liberalisation in other sectors.

The tax or tariff equivalents of barriers to trade in banking services appear to be as high as 60 per cent (Chapter 13). The tax or tariff equivalents of barriers to trade in telecommunications services are up to 50 per cent in developed countries (Chapter 6). These estimates are higher than most remaining tariffs in manufacturing, though lower than remaining protection in many areas of agriculture. This confirms the priority to be attached to the forthcoming GATS negotiations, along with further progress on agriculture. The relative sizes of the barriers among services sectors can also be used to prioritise negotiations within the GATS.

This discussion has been based primarily on efficiency effects. But there is still the question of the contributions to welfare of changes in the size of international income transfers, via the net returns to FDI and net interest income. This is difficult to assess without having built a CGE model of the type outlined in this chapter, to analyse empirically the impact of various services trade liberalisation scenarios.

NOTES

The authors were employed by the Australian Productivity Commission. The views expressed in this chapter are those of the staff involved and do not necessarily reflect those of the commission. The Productivity Commission is the Australian government's principal review and advisory body on microeconomic reform. It conducts public inquiries and research into a broad range of economic and social issues affecting the welfare of Australians. Information on the commission, its publications and its current work program can be found on the World Wide Web at <http://www.pc.gov.au>.

1   Petri's model does not capture product variety as a factor which affects consumer utility *per se*. However, increased choice is likely to be an important benefit of FDI liberalisation.
2   A complication to be grappled with at the level of both data and theory is that most foreign affiliates are not 100 per cent foreign owned. In many countries, the minimum level of foreign control required for investment to be counted as direct rather than portfolio investment is as low as 10 per cent. However, incorporating this distinction at the theoretical level could involve modelling issues of corporate control, such as the trade-off between having a local partner with local knowledge, versus diluting foreign corporate control, that could be peripheral to issues of services trade liberalisation.
3   In common with some other frameworks (e.g. Dee et al. 1996), Petri's framework does not explicitly identify the fixed costs that might account for

increasing returns to scale, even though it is broadly consistent with increasing returns and imperfect competition (see also Francois and Shiells 1994).

4   Note that, since in reality foreign affiliates are typically less than 100 per cent foreign owned (and restrictions apply to the entire affiliate), a model that isolates FDI stocks into 'wholly foreign owned' firms in its database and applies restrictions to those firms will understate the size of the rents generated by restrictions on foreign affiliates. Nevertheless, rescaling the size of the price wedge to generate the 'correct' level of rents would overstate the allocative efficiency effects of the restrictions. Arguably, given the uncertainties associated with rent allocation in any event, the former treatment is preferable to the latter.

5   One complication for the welfare decomposition is that, while a dollar may be a dollar as far as net interest income is concerned, investors in the Petri framework have a preference for diversity in their FDI portfolios. This could be handled by modifying this net foreign dividend income term by a term reflecting investors' preference for diversity.

17 A comparison of existing services trade arrangements within APEC

Sherry Stephenson

INTRODUCTION

This chapter provides a review of the provisions relating to trade in services in the five sub-regional agreements covering services within APEC. In alphabetical order, these are the following:

- the ASEAN Framework Agreement on Services (1995);
- the Closer Economic Relations (CER) Agreement between Australia and New Zealand (1989);
- the Free Trade Agreement between Chile and Canada (1997);
- the Free Trade Agreement between Chile and Mexico (1997); and
- the North American Free Trade Agreement (NAFTA) between Canada, Mexico, and the United States (1994).

The chapter contains information on the general rules and disciplines contained in these agreements set out against several pertinent elements and disciplines characterising services agreements. Table A17.1 contains information on the treatment of services in specific sectoral chapters within the above agreements, where relevant. The information in both parts is set out in a comparative format, to better facilitate comparison and analysis.

All of the agreements containing services provisions have the stated objective of constituting a free trade area. These free trade agreements contain substantial elements of integration and wide-ranging rules and disciplines covering many areas, including services. Only the provisions on services, however, are being examined in this chapter. The purpose of this chapter and the comparative information it contains is to assist those interested in the approaches adopted at the sub-regional level by various APEC members towards liberalising services trade, and to draw out the common elements in existing agreements.

SUMMARY OF THE PROVISIONS

With respect to the provisions on services in the five sub-regional agreements, a number of observations can be made.

All of the sub-regional agreements contain rules and disciplines covering trade in services as well as provisions for the liberalisation of such trade. However, the approach adopted by the various agreements towards liberalisation of traded services differs, as does the depth and coverage of the rules and disciplines governing such trade.

Four of the five agreements have adopted a negative-list approach towards the liberalisation of trade in services. This means effectively that all traded services transactions may take place freely, and services may be provided without restrictions by foreign suppliers of services in the markets of other members to the agreement, unless otherwise specified in lists of exemptions or non-conforming measures, set out in annexes. Such lists may include exemptions from most-favoured-nation (MFN) treatment, for the maintenance of quantitative restrictions, or for discrimination in treatment as between foreign and domestic suppliers of services. However, unless otherwise specified, all services transactions are to be allowed without conditions or restraints. This includes services provided through foreign direct investment, where such investment is the object of rules and explicit investor guarantees. This approach is followed by Australia and New Zealand in their CER protocol, by Chile in its free trade agreements with Canada and Mexico, and by the members of NAFTA.

In contrast, ASEAN members have opted for a positive-list approach to liberalisation of trade in services, similar to that followed under the Uruguay Round and now enshrined in the General Agreement on Trade in Services (GATS) of the World Trade Organisation (WTO). Liberalisation under this approach is carried out through the negotiation of specific commitments which accompany a framework of rules and principles. Such liberalisation applies, however, only to services activities that are listed in national schedules. The commitments in such schedules are set out by sector and specified according to the four defined modes of supply: cross border trade in services (similar to trade in goods); the establishment of commercial presence (corresponding to foreign direct investment); the movement of consumers (e.g. tourists); or via the temporary presence of foreign providers (through the movement of natural persons). Each specific commitment may also be subject to qualification as to MFN treatment, market access or national treatment.

The coverage of service sectors is comprehensive in the CER agreement and NAFTA, as well as in the treaties signed by Chile with Canada and Mexico. The CER agreement applies 'subject to the foreign investment policies of the Member States', while for the other three agreements, the chapter on trade in services relates specifically to cross-border trade, with a separate chapter containing specific disciplines and guarantees for foreign direct investment, such as the right of pre-establishment. The chapters on services and on investment are to be read together in these agreements, as they contain complementary disciplines. These three agreements do provide for the exclusion of air transport services (routing) and non-competitive government services. Under the ASEAN framework agreement, all services sectors are subject to the rules and disciplines, but only those sectors in which members have made market-access commitments are included in the scope of liberalisation. To date, ASEAN members have made commitments in seven of the twelve sectors.

All of the sub-regional agreements on services within APEC provide for MFN treatment and national treatment. In the case of the ASEAN framework agreement, this is through reference to incorporation of the definitions and other provisions of the GATS, in all areas where no other specific provisions exist in the agreement. In the CER agreement, the NAFTA, and the Chilean bilateral treaties, MFN and national treatment are set out as basic, unconditional principles of the agreements, whereas under the ASEAN framework agreement, the extension of national treatment to foreign suppliers of services is not automatic, and applies only to those sectors included in the national schedules of commitments, 'subject to any conditions and qualifications set out therein'. In the cases of the CER agreement, the NAFTA and the Chilean bilateral treaties, the wording of the MFN and national treatment articles is framed not in terms of 'like services and service suppliers', as under the GATS, but is defined as treatment no less favourable than that accorded 'in like circumstances' to its own services providers.

The possibility of non-conforming measures or lists of exemptions is found in the four agreements having adopted a negative-list approach to services liberalisation. All non-conforming measures or exemptions (i.e. those that constitute restrictions to services trade) are to be set out in annexes to the CER agreement, the NAFTA, and the Chilean bilateral free trade agreements. The latter three treaties specify that this is to cover measures at the federal, as well as the state or provincial and local levels. (However, this has not been put into application under any of these agreements and non-conforming measures actually found in the annexes are those at the federal level only). Liberalisation undertaken since the CER agreement came into force has meant that the list of exemptions has been reduced considerably over the past ten years, just as the scope of liberalisation has widened. Parties to the other three agreements have not as yet effected any changes to their lists of exemptions.

There are no provisions specific to quantitative restrictions in the ASEAN agreement on services or in the CER agreement. Specific provisions on quantitative restrictions (both discriminatory and non-discriminatory) do exist in the other three agreements. These provide for such restrictions to be set out in specific annexes. All non-discriminatory quantitative restrictions are to be the object of negotiation every two years, with a view to their liberalisation or removal. There is no similar requirement for discriminatory quantitative restrictions.

General requirements to ensure transparency are found in all of the sub-regional agreements. These include publication requirements, notification requirements, and the obligation to establish a contact point or to otherwise provide information on services. All parties to the various agreements are required to publish all laws, regulations, procedures and administrative rulings in their national markets pertaining to trade in services. However, only proposed measures or changes to existing measures are to be the object of notification to other parties. Four of the five agreements (i.e. not the ASEAN agreement) also include a provision that, 'to the extent possible', would allow interested parties to comment on any proposed measure that would affect trade in services, before it is enacted as a law, regulation or administrative ruling.

There is no article or provision in the sub-regional agreements under examination that is equivalent to Article VI on Domestic Regulation in the GATS (although the ASEAN agreement references this article *de facto*). There are provisions, however, on licensing and certification that are narrower than the broader scope of domestic regulation. These provisions require that licensing and certification procedures do not constitute unnecessary or disguised barriers to trade in services and are based on objective and transparent criteria. The same article in all four agreements also covers recognition (which is the object of a separate GATS article) and requires parties to give equal opportunity to members of the agreement to demonstrate that the qualifications of their services providers should be recognised on the same footing as others. The NAFTA treaty and the Chilean bilateral treaties go further, requiring that within two years of application of the agreements, any citizenship or permanent residency requirements that are maintained for the licensing or certification of professional service providers must be eliminated. The ASEAN framework agreement contains a separate article on mutual recognition that allows for the recognition of equivalency in educational requirements or experience in the granting of licences or certifications.

All of the sub-regional agreements covering services contain an article on monopolies. These provisions do not go further than monopoly practices, however, and do not extend to the full range of restrictive business practices. While this article is incorporated into the text of the services agreement itself in cases of the ASEAN and CER agreements, in the NAFTA and in the Chilean bilateral treaties with Canada and Mexico, such monopoly provisions form a separate chapter applying to both goods and services. The purpose of such provisions in all cases is to require that any monopoly supplier of services does not affect the market-access interests of service suppliers of an agreement's other members. This means that service suppliers who are monopolists should act solely in 'accordance with commercial considerations' in their activities as producers, buyers, or sellers of traded services.

The possibility for general safeguard action with respect to services is found only in the ASEAN agreement (through reference to the provisions of

GATS, where the possibility for such action is set out in Article X). Specific criteria for the undertaking of safeguard action have yet to be elaborated, however, in the WTO context. The CER protocol does not contain any safeguard provision whatsoever, while the other three agreements (and the ASEAN agreement as well), foresee the possibility of safeguard action in the case of balance-of-payments difficulties. In such cases, members may adopt measures that restrict financial transfers and payments. There is nothing in these three agreements that specifies (as is the case under Article XII of the GATS) that such restrictions must be carried out in a non-discriminatory manner, or that they must be temporary in nature.

Exceptions to the scope of liberalisation are provided for in all of the agreements, which conceive of these in a similar manner. Such exceptions are explicitly mentioned as those necessary to protect consumers, essential security interests, public morals, and health and safety. The CER agreement is broader in its list of possible exceptions and also includes the possibility of exceptions to prevent unfair, deceptive or misleading practices, and to secure compliance with laws and regulations relating to customs enforcement, tax avoidance or evasion, and foreign exchange control.

Future liberalisation of traded services also figures prominently in the five agreements, but with different forms and degrees of commitment. Under the ASEAN agreement, future liberalisation is to be a continuous process, carried out through a series of negotiations aimed at expanding the schedules of members' national commitments. Under the CER protocol, members are to try to liberalise the restrictions on services inscribed in the annexes, but no specific process is provided for this. Under the NAFTA and the Chilean treaties, a provision exists for the liberalisation of non-discriminatory quantitative restrictions, through periodic negotiations. Beyond this provision, the Chile/Mexico treaty goes even further to include a generally applicable requirement for future negotiations on the liberalisation of service sectors, with a view to achieving the elimination of the remaining restrictions.

Provisions for dispute settlement are present in all of the five agreements, again in various forms and depth. The ASEAN agreement references its Protocol on Dispute Settlement and states that a future mechanism for dealing with disputes will be established under this protocol. The other four agreements include provisions for consultations, and the NAFTA and Chilean bilateral treaties with Canada and Mexico also include detailed provisions for the establishment and functioning of a panel. In the latter three agreements, such provisions are part of separate chapters on dispute settlement. NAFTA has additional dispute settlement provisions for financial services, and the Canada/Chile treaty contains provisions on dispute settlement in the chapter on Temporary Entry for Business Persons.

The possibility for modification of schedules is found exclusively in the ASEAN framework agreement, as this is the only sub-regional agreement under which liberalisation is carried out on the basis of national schedules of commitments, as discussed above. This provision allows ASEAN members to modify or withdraw any commitment in their schedules at any time after three years from the date on which the commitment entered into force, under certain conditions. However, withdrawal of a commitment requires compensatory adjustment, which must be made on an MFN basis to all other members of the agreement.

Separate chapters setting out additional disciplines for specific service sectors (i.e. financial services and transport) are contained in NAFTA, while separate chapters on telecommunications and on the temporary entry of business persons are found in NAFTA and in the agreements signed by Chile with Canada and Mexico. Professional services are included in an annex to these three agreements. Neither the ASEAN framework agreement nor the CER agreement contains separate chapters on specific service sectors.

Table 17.1 outlines the general rules and disciplines of the five services trade agreements that exist within APEC.

CONCLUSION

Two broad approaches to services liberalisation are evident in these five sub-regional agreements that were entered into during the 1990s. One is based on the GATS (that of ASEAN) and the other is based on the approach first adopted in the CER and subsequently NAFTA (and the Chilean bilateral treaties). The key to this distinction is based on whether the approach to sectoral coverage is a negative (in the latter case) or positive-list approach.

Neither approach guarantees the full liberalisation of trade in services. In fact, both may theoretically provide the same degree of liberalisation, depending on the number of exemptions taken out on the NAFTA-type arrangement or the number of sectors not included in the GATS-type agreements. Also, neither type will necessarily specify a timeframe over which the remaining impediments will be removed, although they may specify commitments to further liberalisation.

It can be argued that there are significant benefits for the liberalisation process from the agreements that adopted a negative-list approach. NAFTA-type agreements provide a great deal of information on barriers to trade, whereas the GATS-type agreements provide less information of this type. The documentation of non-conforming measures under the CER and NAFTA-type agreements draws attention to such restrictions, leads to analysis of them and thus to greater appreciation of their costs. This sequence of events is more likely to bring pressure upon governments and lead to changes in policy. It could also be argued that this type of agreement leads to increased stability of rules and provisions for services activities.

While these points suggest that the negative-list approach has some advantages, comprehensiveness comes at a cost. A full negative list demands a large amount of detail about the policy instruments applying to international services transactions. If the costs of the documentation of policy are high, then an alternative is to tackle sectors in a specific order. If that approach is adopted, some choices of which sectors to tackle first will have to be made. These choices and the extent of commitments to be undertaken in chosen sectors might be determined by the negotiating processes in the development of the regional arrangements, or by the constraints imposed by the WTO on regional arrangements in the service sector. On efficiency grounds, it may be preferable to target highly protected areas first in a regional arrangement and then extend those commitments globally. However, identification of the sectors for priority treatment also requires substantial work of the type documented in other chapters in this volume.

A further issue is the membership of regional arrangements. It might be expected that a group of economies at a similar stage of development will gain less from a regional arrangement than a group of more diverse economies. This chapter has not reviewed the effects of various combinations of economies at different stages of development. The extent of gains from sub-regional reform, allowing for capital flows in the service sector, is an interesting empirical issue for further modelling work.

NOTES

The work on which this chapter was based was prepared on behalf of the Pacific Economic Cooperation Council (PECC) and presented to the September 1998 meeting of the APEC Group on Services. The author would like to acknowledge the assistance of Soonwha Yi and Anne-Lise Georges in the preparation of this document.

1   Neither the ASEAN Framework Agreement on Services nor the CER Agreement contain any chapters on specific service sectors.

Table 17.1 General provisions of the five treaties

I. Legal name and date

ASEAN	*Legal Name:* ASSOCIATION OF SOUTH EAST ASIAN NATIONS ASEAN FRAMEWORK AGREEMENT ON SERVICES *Effect:* 15 December 1995
CER	*Legal Name:* AUSTRALIA NEW ZEALAND CLOSER ECONOMIC RELATIONS-TRADE AGREEMENT *Effect:* 1 January 1989
CHILE/ CANADA	*Legal Name:* CHILE-CANADA FREE TRADE AGREEMENT *Effect:* 5 July 1997
CHILE/ MEXICO	*Legal Name:* FREE TRADE AGREEMENT BETWEEN CHILE AND MEXICO *Effect:* 1 August 1999
NAFTA	*Legal Name:* NORTH AMERICAN FREE TRADE AGREEMENT *Effect:* 1 January 1994

II. Objectives

ASEAN

Article I: Objectives:

The objectives of the Member States under the ASEAN Framework Agreement on Services are: to enhance cooperation in services amongst Member States in order to improve the efficiency and competitiveness, diversify capacity and supply and distribution of services of their service suppliers within and outside ASEAN; to eliminate substantially restrictions to trade in services amongst Member States; and to liberalise trade in services by expanding the depth and scope of liberalisation beyond those undertaken by Member States under the GATS with the aim to realising a free trade area in services.

CER

Article 1: Objectives:

The objectives of the Member States in concluding this Protocol to the Agreement are: (a) to strengthen the relationship between Australia and New Zealand; (b) to liberalise barriers to trade in services between the Member States; (c) to improve the efficiency and competitiveness of their service industry sectors and expand trade in services between the

Member States; (d) to establish a framework of transparent rules to govern trade in services between the Member States; and (e) to facilitate competition in trade in services.

CHILE/ CANADA

PART I, Chapter A

Article A-02: Objectives:

The objectives of this Agreement, as elaborated more specifically through its principles and rules, including national treatment, most-favoured-nation treatment and transparency, are to: a) eliminate barriers to trade in, and facilitate the cross-border movement of, goods and services between the territories of the Parties; b) promote conditions of fair competition in the free trade area; c) increase substantially investment opportunities in the territories of the Parties; d) create effective procedures for the implementation and application of this Agreement, for its joint administration and for the resolution of disputes; and e) establish a framework for further bilateral, regional and multilateral cooperation to expand and enhance the benefits of this Agreement.

Article A-01 Establishment of the Free Trade Area

The Parties to this Agreement, consistent with Article XXIV of the *General Agreement on Tariffs and Trade 1994* and Article V of the *General Agreement on Trade in Services* which are part of the *Marrakesh Agreement Establishing the World Trade Organisation*, hereby establish a free trade area.

CHILE/ MEXICO

Chapter 1, Article 1-02: Objectives:

The objectives of this Agreement, as elaborated more specifically through its principles and rules, including national treatment, most-favoured-nation treatment and transparency, are to: (a) stimulate the expansion and diversification of trade between the Parties; (b) eliminate barriers to trade in, and facilitate the cross-border movement of, goods and services between the territories of the Parties; (c) promote conditions of fair competition in the free trade area; (d) increase substantially investment opportunities in the territories of the Parties; (e) provide adequate and effective protection and enforcement of intellectual property rights in each Party's territory; (f) establish a framework for further bilateral, regional and multilateral cooperation to expand and enhance the benefits of this Agreement; and (g) create effective procedures for the implementation and application of this Agreement, for its joint administration and for the resolution of disputes.

Article 1-01: Establishment of the Free Trade Area

The Parties to this Agreement, consistent with Article XXIV of the General Agreement on Tariffs and Trade of 1994, Article V of the GATS, that are part of the WTO, and the 1980 Montevideo Treaty, hereby establish a free trade area.

NAFTA

Chapter 1, Article 102: Objectives:

The objectives of this Agreement, as elaborated more specifically through its principles and rules, including national treatment, most-favoured-nation treatment and transparency, are to: (a) eliminate barriers to trade in, and facilitate the

Table 17.1 (continued)

cross-border movement of, goods and services between the territories of the Parties; (b) promote conditions of fair competition in the free trade area; (c) increase substantially investment opportunities in the territories of the Parties; (d) provide adequate and effective protection and enforcement of intellectual property rights in each Party's territory; (e) create effective procedures for the implementation and application of this Agreement, for its joint administration and for the resolution of disputes; and (f) establish a framework for further trilateral, regional and multilateral cooperation to expand and enhance the benefits of this Agreement.

Article 101: Establishment of the Free Trade Area

The Parties to this Agreement, consistent with Article XXIV of the General Agreement on Tariffs and Trade, hereby establish a free trade area.

III. Sectoral coverage

ASEAN

A. Measures

Article IV: Negotiations of Specific Commitments:

Member States shall enter into negotiations on measures affecting trade in specific service sectors. Such negotiations shall be directed towards achieving commitments under the GATS and for which Member States shall accord preferential treatment to one another on a MFN basis. Each Member State shall set out in a schedule, the specific commitments it shall undertake under above.

B. Bodies

Article XIV: Final Provision:

The Terms and definitions and other provisions of the GATS shall be referred to and applied to matters arising under this Framework Agreement for which no specific provision had been made under it.

Relevant provision in GATS: Part I, Scope and Definitions - Article 1

For the purposes of this Agreement: 'measures by Members' means measures taken by: central, regional or local governments and authorities, and non-governmental bodies in the exercise of powers delegated by central, regional or local governments or authorities. In fulfilling its obligations and commitments under the Agreement, each member shall take such reasonable measures as may be available to it to ensure their observance by regional and local governments and authorities and non-governmental bodies within its territory.

C. Exclusions to Coverage

Article XIV: Final Provision:

The Terms and definitions and other provisions of the GATS shall be referred to and applied to matters arising under this Framework Agreement for which no specific provision had been made under it.

Relevant provision in GATS: Part I, scope and Definitions- Article 1
'services' include any service in any sector except services supplied in the exercise of governmental authority.

CER	A. Measures *Article 2: Scope of Protocol:* This Protocol shall apply to the provision of services in the Free Trade Area referred to in Article 2 of the Agreement. The provisions of this Protocol shall apply subject to the foreign investment policies of the Member States. This Protocol shall apply to any measure, in existence or proposed, of a Member State that relates to or affects the provision of a service by or on behalf of a person of the other Member State within or into the territory of the first Member State. B. Bodies Not specified C. Exclusions to Coverage *Article 2: Scope of Protocol:* Except as otherwise provided in particular Articles, this Protocol shall not apply to the provision within or into the territory of one Member State of the services inscribed by that Member State in the Annex until such time as such services inscribed by it have been removed from the Annex in accordance with Article 10 of this Protocol.
CHILE/ CANADA	A. Measures *PART III, Chapter H, Article H-01* Measures adopted or maintained by a Party relating to cross-border trade in services by service providers of the other Party, including measures respecting: a) the production, distribution, marketing, sale and delivery of a service; b) the purchase or use of, or payment for, a service; c) the access to and use of distribution and transportation systems in connection with the provision of a service; d) the presence in its territory of a service provider of another Party; and e) the provision of a bond or other form of financial security as a condition for the provision of a service. B. Bodies *Article H-12. Definitions* For purposes of this Chapter, a reference to a national or provincial government includes any non-governmental body in the exercise of any regulatory, administrative or other governmental authority delegated to it by that government. C. Exclusions to Coverage *PART III, Chapter H, Article H-01* Excluded from the Agreement: cross border trade in financial services; air services, including domestic and international air transportation services, whether scheduled or non-scheduled, and related services in support of air services, other than (i) aircraft repair and maintenance services during which an aircraft is withdrawn from service, and (ii) speciality air

Table 17.1 (continued)

	services; or subsidies or grants provided by a Party or by a state enterprise, including government-supported loans, guarantees and insurance.
CHILE/ MEXICO	A. Measures *Chapter 10, Article 10-02: Scope of Application:* Measures adopted or maintained by a Party relating to cross-border trade in services by service providers of the other Party, including measures respecting: (a) the production, distribution, marketing, sale and delivery of a service; (b) the purchase or use of, or payment for, a service; (c) the access to and use of distribution and transportation systems in connection with the provision of a service; (d) the presence in its territory of a service provider of the other Party; and (e) the provision of a bond or other form of financial security as a condition for the provision of a service. B. Bodies *Chapter 10, Article 10-02: Scope of Application:* Measures by a Party are measures adopted or maintained by: national, federal or state governments ; and non-governmental organisations exercising regulatory faculties, administrative, or other governmental characters delegated by national, federal or state governments. C. Exclusions to Coverage *Chapter 10, Article 10-02: Scope of Application:* Excluded from the Agreement: cross border trade in financial services; air services, including domestic and international air transportation services, whether scheduled or non-scheduled, and related services in support of air services, other than (i) aircraft repair and maintenance services during which an aircraft is withdrawn from service, and (ii) speciality air services; (iii) computerised system of reservation; procurement by a party or a state enterprise; or subsidies or grants provided by a Party or by a state enterprise, including government-supported loans, guarantees and insurance; government services.
NAFTA	A. Measures *Chapter 12, Article 1201: Scope and Coverage* Measures adopted or maintained by a Party relating to cross-border trade in services by service providers of another Party, including measures respecting: (a) the production, distribution, marketing, sale and delivery of a service; (b) the purchase or use of, or payment for, a service; (c) the access to and use of distribution and transportation systems in connection with the provision of a service; (d) the presence in its territory of a service provider of another Party; and (e) the provision of a bond or other form of financial security as a condition for the provision of a service.

B. Bodies

Article 1213: Definitions

For purposes of this Chapter, a reference to a federal, state or provincial government includes any non-governmental body in the exercise of any regulatory, administrative or other governmental authority delegated to it by that government.

C. Exclusions to Coverage

Chapter 12, Article 1201: Scope and Coverage

Excluded from the Agreement: financial services; air services, including domestic and international air transportation services, whether scheduled or non-scheduled, and related services in support of air services, other than (i) aircraft repair and maintenance services during which an aircraft is withdrawn from service, and (ii) speciality air services; subsidies or grants provided by a Party or by a state enterprise, including government-supported loans, guarantees and insurance; or procurement by a Party or a state enterprise.

IV. Definitions

ASEAN

Article XIV: Final Provision:

The Terms and definitions and other provisions of the GATS shall be referred to and applied to matters arising under this Framework Agreement for which no specific provision had been made under it.

GATS: Definitions contained in Article XXVIII.

CER

Article 3: Definitions:

Provision of services includes: (a) the production, distribution, marketing, sale and delivery of a service; and (b) for the purpose of the activities referred to in the previous sub-paragraph of this paragraph: (i) access to and use of domestic distribution systems; and (ii) rights of establishment.

Measure includes any law, regulation, or administrative practice.

Person of a Member State means: (a) a natural person who is a citizen of, or ordinarily resident in, that State; (b) a body corporate established under the law of that State; (c) an association comprising or controlled by: (i) persons described in one or both of sub-paragraphs (a) or (b); or (ii) persons described in one or both of sub-paragraphs (a) or (b) and persons so described in relation to the other Member State.

CHILE/
CANADA

Chapter H, Article H-12

Cross-border trade in services is defined as provision of a service: a) from the territory of one Party into the territory of the other Party; b) in the territory of one Party by a person of that Party to a person of the other Party; c) by a national of one Party in the territory of the other Party; but does not include the provision of a service in the territory of a Party by an investment, as defined in Article G-40 (Investment - Definitions), in that territory.

Table 17.1 (continued)

CHILE/ MEXICO	*Chapter 10, Article 10-01: Definitions:* Cross-border trade in services is defined as provision of a service: a) from the territory of one Party into the territory of the other Party; b) in the territory of one Party in the territory of the other Party, to a person of the other Party; or c) by a national of one Party in the territory of the other Party, but does not include the provision of a service in the territory of a Party by an investment, as defined in Article 9-01 (Investment-Definitions), in that territory.
NAFTA	*Chapter 12, Article 1213: Definitions* Cross-border provision of a service or cross-border trade in services means the provision of a service: (a) from the territory of a Party into the territory of another Party, (b) in the territory of a Party by a person of that Party to a person of another Party, or (c) by a national of a Party in the territory of another Party. Cross-border provision of a service or cross-border trade in services does not include the provision of a service in the territory by an investment, as defined in Article 1139 (Investment – Definitions), in that territory, which is set out in Chapter 11 on Investment.

V. Most-favoured-nation treatment

ASEAN	*Article XIV: Final Provision:* The terms and definitions and other provisions of the GATS shall be referred to and applied to matters arising under this Framework Agreement for which no specific provision has been made under it. *Relevant provision in GATS: PART II, Article II – Most-Favoured-Nation Treatment* Each Member shall accord immediately and unconditionally to services and service suppliers of any other Member, treatment no less favourable than that it accord to like services and service suppliers of any other country. A Member may maintain a measure inconsistent with paragraph 1 provided that such measure is listed in, and meets the conditions of, the Annex on Article II Exemptions. The provisions of this Agreement shall not be so construed as to prevent any Member from conferring or according advantages to adjacent countries in order to facilitate exchanges limited to contiguous frontier zones of services that are both locally produced and consumed.
CER	*Article 6: Most-Favoured-Nation Treatment:* In relation to the provision of services inscribed by it in the Annex, each Member State shall accord to persons of the other Member State and services provided by them treatment no less favourable than that accorded in like circumstances to persons of third states.

CHILE/ CANADA	*Chapter H, Article H-03:* Each Party shall accord to service providers of the other Party treatment no less favourable than that it accords, in like circumstances, to service providers of any non-Party.
CHILE/ MEXICO	*Chapter 10, Article 10-04: Most-Favoured-Nation Treatment* Each Party shall accord to service providers of the other Party treatment no less favourable than that it accords, in like circumstances, to service providers of any non-Party.
NAFTA	*Chapter 12, Article 1203: Most-Favoured-Nation Treatment* Each Party shall accord to service providers of another Party treatment no less favourable than that it accords, in like circumstances, to service providers of any other Party or of a non-Party.

VI. National treatment

ASEAN	*Article XIV: Final Provision:* The terms and definitions and other provisions of the GATS shall be referred to and applied to matters arising under this Framework Agreement for which no specific provision has been made under it. *Relevant provision in GATS: PART III, Article XVII - National Treatment* In the sectors inscribed in its schedule, and subject to any conditions and qualifications set out therein, each Member shall accord to services and service suppliers of any other Member, in respect of all measures affecting the supply of services, treatment no less favourable than that it accords to its own like services and service suppliers. A Member may meet the requirement of paragraph 1 by according to services and service suppliers of any other Member, either formally identical treatment or formally different treatment to that it accords to its own like services and service suppliers. Formally identical or formally different treatment shall be considered to be less favourable if it modifies the conditions of competition in favour of services or service suppliers of the Member compared to like services or services suppliers of any other Member.
CER	*Article 5: National Treatment:* Each Member State shall accord to persons of the other Member State and services provided by them treatment no less favourable than that accorded in like circumstances to its persons and services provided by them. Notwithstanding paragraph 1 of this Article, the treatment a Member State accords to persons of the other Member State may be different from the treatment the Member State accords to its persons, provided that: (a) the difference in treatment

Table 17.1 (continued)

	is no greater than that necessary for prudential, fiduciary, health and safety or consumer protection reasons; and (b) such different treatment is equivalent in effect to the treatment accorded by the Member State to its ordinary residents for such reasons. The Member State proposing or according different treatment under paragraph 2 of this Article shall have the burden of establishing that such treatment is consistent with that paragraph.
CHILE/ CANADA	*Chapter H, Article H-02: National Treatment* Each Party shall accord to service providers of the other Party treatment no less favourable than that it accords, in like circumstances, to its own service providers. The treatment accorded by a Party under the paragraph above means, with respect to a province, treatment no less favourable than the most favourable treatment accorded, in like circumstances, by that province to service providers of the Party of which it forms part.
CHILE/ MEXICO	*Chapter 10, Article 10–03: National Treatment* Each Party shall accord to service providers of the other Party treatment no less favourable than that it accords, in like circumstances, to its own service providers. The treatment accorded by a Party under the paragraph above means, with respect to a province, treatment no less favourable than the most favourable treatment accorded, in like circumstances, by that province to service providers of the Party of which it forms part.
NAFTA	*Chapter 12, Article 1202: National Treatment* Each Party shall accord to service providers of another Party treatment no less favourable than that it accords, in like circumstances, to its own service providers. The treatment accorded by a Party under the paragraph above means, with respect to a state or province, treatment no less favourable than the most favourable treatment accorded, in like circumstances, by that state or province to service providers of the Party of which it forms part.

VII. Treatment of non-conforming measures

ASEAN	Article XIV: Final Provision: The terms and definitions and other provisions of the GATS shall be referred to and applied to matters arising under this Framework of Agreement for which no specific provision has been made under it. Relevant provision in GATS: Annex

and Article II: Exemptions. This Annex specifies the conditions under which a Member, at the entry into force of this Agreement, is exempted from its obligations under paragraph 1 or Article II.

CER

Article 17: Inclusions in the Annex until March 31 1989

A Member State may inscribe a service in the Annex until March 31 1989. Before doing so, it shall provide written reasons for the proposed inscription to the other Member State and undertake consultations with a view to establishing whether any problems arising from the non-inscription of a service would be resolved by other means.

CHILE/
CANADA

Chapter H, Article H-06: Reservations

Articles H-02 (National Treatment), H-03 (MFN Treatment) and H-05 (Local Presence) do not apply to: (a) any existing non-conforming measure that is maintained by (i) a Party at the national or provincial level, as set out in its Schedule to Annex I, or (ii) a local government; (b) the continuation or prompt renewal of any non-conforming measure referred to in (a); or (c) an amendment to any non-conforming measure referred to in (a) to the extent that the amendment does not decrease the conformity of the measure, as it existed immediately before the amendment, with Articles H-02, H-03 and H-05.

Articles H-02, H-03 and H-05 do not apply to any measure that a Party adopts or maintains with respect to sectors, subsectors or activities, as set out in its Schedule to Annex II.

CHILE/
MEXICO

Chapter 10, Article 10-07: Reservations

Articles 10-03 (National Treatment), 10-04 (MFN Treatment), and 10-06 (Local Presence) do not apply to: (a) any existing non-conforming measure that is maintained by (i) a Party at the national, federal, or state level, as set out in its Schedule to Annex I, or (ii) a local government; (b) the continuation or prompt renewal of any non-conforming measure referred to in (a); or (c) an amendment to any non-conforming measure referred to in (a) to the extent that the amendment does not decrease the conformity of the measure, as it existed immediately before the amendment, with Articles 10-03, 10-04 and 10-06.

Articles 10-03, 10-04 and 10-06 do not apply to any measure that a Party adopts or maintains with respect to sectors, subsectors or activities, as set out in its Schedule to Annex II.

NAFTA

Chapter 12, Article 1206: Reservations

Articles 1202 (National Treatment), 1203 (MFN Treatment) and 1205 (Local Presence) do not apply to: (a) any existing non-conforming measure that is maintained by (i) a Party at the federal level, as set out in its Schedule to Annex I, (ii) a state or province, for two years after the date of entry into force of this Agreement, and thereafter as set out by a Party in its Schedule to Annex I in accordance with par. 2, or (iii) a local government; (b) the continuation or prompt renewal of any non-conforming measure referred to in (a); or (c) an amendment to any non-conforming measure referred to in (a) to the extent that the amendment does not decrease the conformity of the measure, as it existed immediately before the amendment, with Articles 1202, 1203 and 1205.

Table 17.1 (continued)

Each Party may set out in its Schedule to Annex I, within two years of the date of entry into force of this Agreement, any existing non-conforming measure maintained by a state or province, not including a local government. Articles 1202, 1203 and 1205 do not apply to any measure that a Party adopts or maintains with respect to sectors, subsectors or activities, as set out in its Schedule to Annex II.

VIII. Quantitative restrictions

ASEAN Not Specified

CER Not Specified

CHILE/ CANADA

Chapter H, Article H-12: Definitions

Quantitative restriction means a non-discriminatory measure that imposes limitations on: (a) the number of service providers, whether in the form of a quota, a monopoly or an economic needs test, or by any other quantitative means; or (b) the operations of any service provider, whether in the form of a quota or an economic needs test, or by any other quantitative means.

Chapter H, Article H-07: Quantitative Restrictions

Each Party shall set out in its Schedule to Annex IV any quantitative restriction that it maintains at the national or provincial level.

Each Party shall notify the other Party of any quantitative restriction that it adopts, other than at the local government level, after the date of entry into force of this Agreement and shall set out the restriction in its Schedule to Annex IV. The Parties shall periodically, but in any event at least every two years, endeavour to negotiate the liberalisation or removal of the quantitative restrictions set out in Annex IV pursuant to paragraphs 1 and 2.

CHILE/ MEXICO

Chapter 10, Article 10-01 Definitions

Quantitative restrictions: a non-discriminatory measure that imposes limitations on: (a) the number of service providers, whether in the form of a quota, a monopoly or an economic needs test, or by any other quantitative means; or (b) the operations of any service provider, whether in the form of a quota or an economic needs test, or by any other quantitative means.

Article 10-08: Quantitative Restrictions

1. Each Party shall set out in its Schedule to Annex V any quantitative restriction that it maintains at the national, federal, or state level.

2. Each Party shall notify the other Party of any quantitative restriction that it adopts, other than at the local government

NAFTA

level, after the date of entry into force of this Agreement and shall set out the restriction in its Schedule to Annex V.

3. The Parties shall periodically, but at least every two years, endeavour to negotiate the liberalisation or removal of the quantitative restrictions set out in Annex V pursuant to paragraphs 1 and 2.

Article 1213: Definitions

Quantitative restriction means a non-discriminatory measure that imposes limitations on: (a) the number of service providers, whether in the form of a quota, a monopoly or an economic needs test, or by any other quantitative means; or (b) the operations of any service provider, whether in the form of a quota or an economic needs test, or by any other quantitative means.

Article 1207: Quantitative Restrictions

Each Party shall set out in its Schedule to Annex V any quantitative restriction that it maintains at the federal level. Within one year of the date of entry into force of this Agreement, each Party shall set out in its Schedule to Annex V any quantitative restriction maintained by a state or province, not including a local government. Each Party shall notify the other Parties of any quantitative restriction that it adopts, other than at the local government level, after the date of entry into force of this Agreement and shall set out the restriction in its Schedule to Annex V. The Parties shall periodically, but in any event at least every two years, endeavour to negotiate the liberalisation or removal of the quantitative restrictions set out in Annex V pursuant to paragraphs 1 through 3.

IX. Transparency requirements

ASEAN

A. Publication

Article XIV: Final Provision

The terms and definitions and other provisions of the GATS shall be referred to and applied to matters arising under this Framework Agreement for which no specific provision has been made under it.

Relevant provision in GATS: Article III - Transparency

Each Member shall publish promptly all relevant measures of general application, which pertain to or affect the operation of the General Agreement on Trade in Services (GATS).

B. Notification requirements

Article XIV: Final Provision

The terms and definitions and other provisions of the GATS shall be referred to and applied to matters arising under this Framework Agreement for which no specific provision has been made under it.

Relevant provision in GATS: Article III - Transparency

Each Member shall promptly and at least annually inform the Council for Trade in Services of the introduction of any new, or any changes to existing, laws, regulations or administrative guidelines which significantly affect trade in services covered by its specific commitments under the GATS.

Table 17.1 (continued)

	C. Contact Points *Article XIV: Final Provision:* The terms and definitions and other provisions of the GATS shall be referred to and applied to matters arising under this Framework Agreement for which no specific provision has been made under it. *Relevant provision in GATS: Article III – Transparency* Each Member shall also establish one or more enquiry points to provide specific information to other Members. Such enquiry points shall be established within two years from the entry into force of the Agreement Establishing the WTO. Appropriate flexibility with respect to the time-limit within which such enquiry points are to be established may be agreed upon for individual developing countries.
CER	**A. Publication** *Article 13: Transparency* Each Member State shall make public promptly all laws, regulations, judicial decisions and administrative rulings pertaining to trade in services. Each Member State shall, to the extent possible, provide maximum possible opportunity for comment by interested parties on proposed laws, regulations, procedures and administrative rulings affecting trade in services. **B. Notification requirements** *Article 16: Notification* A Member State shall provide written notice to the other of any proposed or actual measure that it considers might materially affect the operation of this Protocol. The notice shall include the reasons for the measure. The written notice shall be given as far in advance as possible of implementation of the measure. If prior notice is not possible, the Member State implementing the measure shall provide written notice to the other Member State as soon as possible after implementation. **C. Contact Points** *Article 16: Notification* Upon request of the other Member State, information and response to questions pertaining to any actual or proposed measure, whether or not previously notified, shall be promptly provided.
CHILE/ CANADA	**A. Publication** *Chapter L, Article L-02: Publication* Each Party shall ensure its laws, regulations, procedures and administrative rulings of general application respecting any

matter covered by this Agreement are promptly published or otherwise made available in such a manner as to enable interested persons and the other Party to become acquainted with them.

To the extent possible, each Party shall: (a) publish in advance any such measure that it proposes to adopt; and (b) provide interested persons and the other Party a reasonable opportunity to comment on such proposed measures.

B. Notification requirements

Chapter H, Article H-09: Procedures

The Commission shall establish procedures for:

(a) a Party to notify and include in its relevant Schedule: (i) quantitative restrictions in accordance with Article H-07(2), (ii) commitments pursuant to Article H-08, and (iii) amendments of measures referred to in Article H-06(1)(c); and (b) consultations on reservations, quantitative restrictions or commitments with a view to further liberalisation.

Article H-07: Quantitative Restrictions

Each Party shall notify the other Party of any quantitative restriction that it adopts, other than at the local government level, after the date of entry into force of this Agreement and shall set out the restriction in its Schedule to Annex IV.

Chapter L, Article L-03: Notification and Provisions of Information

To the maximum extent possible, each Party shall notify the other Party of any proposed or actual measures that the Party considers might materially affect the operation of this Agreement or otherwise substantially affect the other Party's interests under this Agreement.

C. Contact Points

Part VII, Chapter L, Article L-01:

Each Party shall designate a contact point to facilitate communications between the Parties on any matter covered by this Agreement.

CHILE/ MEXICO

A. Publication

Chapter 16, Article 16-02: Publication:

Each Party shall ensure its laws, regulations, procedures and administrative rulings of general application respecting any matter covered by this Agreement are promptly published or otherwise made available in such a manner as to enable interested persons and the other Party to become acquainted with them.

To the extent possible, each Party shall: (a) publish in advance any such measure that it proposes to adopt; and (b) provide interested persons and the other Party a reasonable opportunity to comment on such proposed measures.

B. Notification requirements

Chapter 10, Article 10-11: Procedures

The Parties shall establish procedures for: (a) a Party to notify and include in its relevant Schedule: (i) commitments pursuant to Article 10-10, (ii) amendments of measures referred to in Article 10-07 (1) and (2), and (iii) quantitative

Table 17.1 (continued)

	restrictions in accordance with Article 10–08; and (b) consultations on reservations, quantitative restrictions or commitments with a view to further liberalisation.
	Article 10–08: Quantitative Restrictions
	Each Party shall notify the other Parties of any quantitative restriction that it adopts after the date of entry into force of this Agreement and shall set out the restriction in its Schedule to Annex V.
	Chapter 16, Article 16–04: Notification and Provisions of Information:
	To the maximum extent possible, each Party shall notify the other Party of any proposed or actual measures that the Party considers might materially affect the operation of this Agreement or otherwise substantially affect the other Party's interests under this Agreement.
	C. Contact Points
	Chapter 16, Article 16–02: Information Centre:
	Each Party shall designate a contact point to facilitate communications between the Parties on any matter covered by this Agreement.
NAFTA	A. Publication
	PART SEVEN, ADMINISTRATIVE AND INSTITUTIONAL PROVISIONS; Chapter 18: Publication, Notification and Administration of Laws
	Article 1802: Publication
	Each Party shall ensure that its laws, regulations, procedures and administrative rulings of general application respecting any matters covered by this Agreement are promptly published or otherwise made available in such a manner as to enable interested persons and Parties to become acquainted with them.
	To the extent possible, each Party shall: (a) publish in advance any such measure that it proposes to adopt; and (b) provide interested persons and Parties a reasonable opportunity to comment on such proposed measures.
	B. Notification requirements
	Chapter 12, Cross-Border Trade in Services, Article 1209: Procedures
	The Commission shall establish procedures for a Party to notify and include in its relevant Schedule: (i) state or provincial measures in accordance with Article 1206(2) (Reservations); (ii) quantitative restrictions in accordance with Article 1207(2) & (3) (Quantitative Restrictions); (iii) commitments pursuant to Article 1208 (Liberalisation of Non-Discriminatory Measures); and (iv) amendments of measures referred to in Article 1206(1)(c).
	Article 1207: Quantitative Restrictions
	Each Party shall notify the other Parties of any quantitative restriction that it adopts, other than at the local government

level, after the date of entry into force of this Agreement and shall set out the restriction in its Schedule to Annex V.

Article 1803: Notification and Provision of Information

To the maximum extent possible, each Party shall notify any other Party with an interest in the matter of any proposed or actual measure that the Party considers might materially affect the operation of this Agreement or otherwise substantially affect that other Party's interests under this Agreement.

On request of another Party, a Party shall promptly provide information and respond to questions pertaining to any actual or proposed measure, whether or not that other Party has been previously notified of that measure.

C. Contact Points

PART SEVEN: ADMINISTRATIVE AND INSTITUTIONAL PROVISIONS; Chapter 18: Publication, Notification and Administration of Laws

Article 1801: Contact Points

Each Party shall designate a contact point to facilitate communications between the Parties on any matter covered by this Agreement. On the request of another Party, the contact point shall identify the office or official responsible for the matter and assist, as necessary, in facilitating communication with the requesting Party.

X. Licensing and certification

ASEAN

Article XIV: Final Provision:

The terms and definitions and other provisions of the GATS shall be referred to and applied to matters arising under this Framework Agreement for which no specific provision has been made under it.

Relevant provision in GATS: Article VI: Domestic Regulation

Paragraph 4

With a view to ensuring that measures relating to qualification requirements and procedures, technical standards and licensing requirements do not constitute unnecessary barriers to trade in services, the Council for Trade in Services shall, through appropriate bodies it may establish, develop any necessary disciplines. Such disciplines shall aim to ensure that such requirements are, *inter alia*: based on objective and transparent criteria, such as competence and the ability to supply the service; not more burdensome than necessary to ensure the quality of the service; in the case of licensing procedures, not in themselves a restriction on the supply of the service.

CER

Article 9: Licensing and Certification

Paragraph 1

Each Member State shall endeavour to ensure that licensing and certification measures shall not have the purpose or effect of impairing or restraining, in a discriminatory manner, access of persons of the other Member State to such licensing or certification.

Table 17.1 (continued)

CHILE/ CANADA	*Chapter H, Article H-10: Licensing and Certification* With a view to ensuring that any measure adopted or maintained by a Party related to the licensing or certification of nationals of another Party does not constitute an unnecessary barrier to trade, each Party shall endeavour to ensure that any such measure: (a) is based on objective and transparent criteria, such as competence and the ability to provide a service; (b) is not more burdensome than necessary to ensure the quality of a service; and (c) does not constitute a disguised restriction on the cross-border provision of a service.
CHILE/ MEXICO	*Chapter 10, Article 10-12: Licensing and Certification* With a view to ensuring that any measure adopted or maintained by a Party related to the licensing or certification of nationals of the other Party does not constitute an unnecessary barrier to trade, each Party shall endeavour to ensure that any such measure: (a) is based on objective and transparent criteria, such as competence and the ability to provide a service; (b) is not more burdensome than necessary to ensure the quality of a service; and (c) does not constitute a disguised restriction on the cross-border provision of a service.
NAFTA	*Chapter 12, Article 1210: Licensing and Certification* With a view to ensuring that any measure adopted or maintained by a Party related to the licensing or certification of nationals of another Party does not constitute an unnecessary barrier to trade, each Party shall endeavour to ensure that any such measure: (a) is based on objective and transparent criteria, such as competence and the ability to provide a service; (b) is not more burdensome than necessary to ensure the quality of a service; and (c) does not constitute a disguised restriction on the cross-border provision of a service.

XI. Recognition

ASEAN	*Article V: Mutual Recognition:* Each Member State may recognise the education or experience obtained, requirements met, or licenses or certifications granted in another Member State, for the purpose of licensing or certification of service suppliers. Such recognition may be based upon an Agreement or arrangement with the Member State concerned or may be accorded autonomously. Nothing in the paragraph above shall be so construed as to require any Member State to accept or to enter into such mutual recognition agreements or arrangements.
CER	*Article 9: Licensing and Certification:* Paragraph 2 Each Member State shall encourage the recognition of the qualifications obtained in the other Member State, for the purpose of licensing and certification requirements for the provision of services.

CHILE/ CANADA

Chapter H, Article H-10:

Where a Party recognises, unilaterally or by agreement, education, experience, licences or certifications obtained in the territory of a non-Party: nothing in Article H-03 shall be construed to require the Party to accord such recognition to education, experience, licences or certifications obtained in the territory of the other Party; and the Party shall afford the other Party an adequate opportunity to demonstrate that education, experience, licences or certifications obtained in the other Party's territory should also be recognised or to conclude an agreement or arrangement of comparable effect.

Each Party shall, within two years of the date of entry into force of this Agreement, eliminate any citizenship or permanent residency requirement set out in its Schedule top Annex I that it maintains for the licensing or certification of professional service providers of the other Party. Where a Party does not comply with this obligation with respect to a particular sector, the other Party may, in the same sector and for such period as the non-complying Party maintains its requirement, solely have recourse to maintaining an equivalent requirement set out in its Schedule to Annex I or reinstating: a) any such requirement at the national level that it eliminated pursuant to this Article; or b) on notification to the non-complying Party, any such requirement at the provincial level existing on the date of entry into force of this Agreement.

MEXICO/ CHILE

Chapter 10, Article 10-12: Accordance of Licensing and Certifications:

Where a Party recognises, unilaterally or by agreement, education, experience, licences or certifications obtained in the territory of a non-Party: nothing in Article 10-04 shall be construed to require the Party to accord such recognition to education, experience, licences or certifications obtained in the territory of the other Party; and the Party shall afford the other Party an adequate opportunity to demonstrate that education, experience, licences or certifications obtained in the other Party's territory should also be recognised or to conclude an agreement or arrangement of comparable effect.

Each Party shall, within two years of the date of entry into force of this Agreement, eliminate any citizenship or permanent residency requirement set out in its Schedule top Annex I that it maintains for the licensing or certification of professional service providers of the other Party. Where a Party does not comply with this obligation with respect to a particular sector, the other Party may, in the same sector and for such period as the non-complying Party maintains its requirement, solely have recourse to adopting or maintaining an equivalent requirement

NAFTA

Chapter 12, Article 1210: Licensing and Certification

Where a Party recognises, unilaterally or by agreement, education, experience, licences or certifications obtained in the territory of another Party or of a non-Party: (a) nothing in Article 1203 (MFN Treatment) shall be construed to require the Party to accord such recognition to education, experience, licences or certifications obtained in the territory of another Party; and (b) the Party shall afford another Party an adequate opportunity to demonstrate that education, experience, licences or certifications obtained in that other Party's territory should also be recognised or to conclude an agreement or arrangement of comparable effect.

Table 17.1 (continued)

Each Party shall, within two years of the date of entry into force of this Agreement, eliminate any citizenship or permanent residency requirement set out in its Schedule to Annex I that it maintains for the licensing or certification of professional service providers of another Party. Where a Party does not comply with this obligation with respect to a particular sector, any other Party may, in the same sector and for such period as the non-complying Party maintains its requirement, solely have recourse to maintaining an equivalent requirement set out in its Schedule to Annex I or reinstating: (a) any such requirement at the federal level that it eliminated pursuant to this Article; or (b) on notification to the non-complying Party, any such requirement at the state or provincial level existing on the date of entry into force of this Agreement.

XII. Monopolies

ASEAN

Article XIV: Final Provision:
The terms and definitions and other provisions of the GATS shall be referred to and applied to matters arising under this Framework Agreement for which no specific provision has been made under it.
Relevant provision in GATS: PART II, Article VIII - Monopolies and Exclusive Service Suppliers
Each Member shall ensure that any monopoly supplier of a service in its territory does not, in the supply of the monopoly service in the relevant market, act in a manner inconsistent with that Member's obligations under Article II (MFN Treatment) and specific commitments.
The Council for Trade in Services may, at the request of a Member which has a reason to believe that a monopoly supplier of a service of any other Member is acting in a manner inconsistent with this Member's specific commitments or with paragraph above, request the Member establishing, maintaining or authorising such supplier to provide specific information concerning the relevant operations.
If, after the entry into force of the Agreement Establishing the WTO, a Member grants monopoly rights regarding the supply of a service covered by its specific commitments, that Member shall make such notification to the Council for Trade in Services no later than three months before the intended implementation of the grant of monopoly rights.
The provisions of this Article shall also apply to cases of exclusive service suppliers.

CER

Article 12. Monopolies:
Where a Member State maintains a monopoly for the provision of a service inscribed by it in the Annex, the services of such monopoly shall be made available to persons of the other Member State for normal business activities in respect of price, quality and quantity under transparent and non-discriminatory conditions.
Member States shall endeavour to prevent monopoly service providers under their direct control from using revenues

deriving from their monopoly activities for the purpose of subsidising services they may provide in competition with persons of the Member States.

CHILE/
CANADA

Chapter J, Article J-02:
Nothing in this Agreement shall be construed to prevent a Party from designating a monopoly.
Where a Party intends to designate a monopoly and the designation may affect the interests of persons of the other Party, the Party shall: (a) wherever possible, provide prior written notification to the other Party of the designation; and (b) endeavour to introduce at the time of the designation such conditions on the operation of the monopoly as will minimise or eliminate any nullification or impairment of benefits in the sense of Annex N-04 (Nullification or Impairment).
Each Party shall ensure, through regulatory control, administrative supervision or the application of other measures, that any privately-owned monopoly that it designates and any government monopoly that it maintains or designates: (a) acts in a manner that is not inconsistent with the Party's obligations under this Agreement wherever such a monopoly exercises any regulatory, administrative or other governmental authority that the Party has delegated to it in connection with the monopoly good or service, such as the power to grant import or export licenses, approve commercial transaction or impose quotas, fees or other charges; (b) except to comply with any terms of its designation that are not inconsistent with subparagraph (c) or (d), acts solely in accordance with commercial considerations in its purchase or sale of the monopoly good or service in the relevant market, including with regard to price, quality, availability, marketability, transportation and other terms and conditions of purchase or sale; (c) provides non-discriminatory treatment to investments of investors, to goods and to service providers of the other Party in its purchase or sale of the monopoly good or service in the relevant market; and (d) does not use its monopoly position to engage, either directly or indirectly, including through its dealings with its parent, its subsidiary or other enterprise with common ownership, in anticompetitive practices in a non-monopolised market in its territory that adversely affect an investment of an investor of the other Party, including through the discriminatory provision of the monopoly good or service, cross-subsidisation or predatory conduct.
The paragraph above does not apply to procurement by governmental agencies of goods or services for governmental purposes and not with a view to commercial resale or with a view to use in the production of goods or the provision of services for commercial sale.

CHILE/
MEXICO

Chapter 14, Article 14-03: Monopolies and State Enterprises:
Nothing in this Agreement shall be construed to prevent a Party from designating a monopoly.
Where a Party intends to designate a monopoly and the designation may affect the interests of persons of the other Party, the Party shall: (a) wherever possible, provide prior written notification to the other Party of the designation; and (b) endeavour to introduce at the time of the designation such conditions on the operation of the monopoly as will minimise or eliminate any nullification or impairment of benefits in the sense of Annex 18-02 (Each Party shall ensure, through

Table 17.1 (continued)

	regulatory control, administrative supervision or the application of other measures, that any privately-owned monopoly that it designates and any government monopoly that it maintains or designates: (a) acts in a manner that is not inconsistent with the Party's obligations under this Agreement wherever such a monopoly exercises any regulatory, administrative or other governmental authority that the Party has delegated to it in connection with the monopoly good or service, such as the power to grant import or export licences, approve commercial transaction or impose quotas, fees or other charges; (b) except to comply with any terms of its designation that are not inconsistent with subparagraph (c) or (d), acts solely in accordance with commercial considerations in its purchase or sale of the monopoly good or service in the relevant market, including with regard to price, quality, availability, marketability, transportation and other terms and conditions of purchase or sale; c) provides non-discriminatory treatment to investments of investors, to goods and to service providers of the other Party in its purchase or sale of the monopoly good or service in the relevant market; and (d) does not use its monopoly position to engage, either directly or indirectly, including through its dealings with its parent, its subsidiary or other enterprise with common ownership, in anticompetitive practices in a non-monopolised market in its territory that adversely affect an investment of an investor of the other Party, including through the discriminatory provision of the monopoly good or service, cross-subsidisation or predatory conduct. The paragraph above does not apply to procurement by governmental agencies of goods or services for governmental purposes and not with a view to commercial resale or with a view to use in the production of goods or the provision of services for commercial sale.
NAFTA	*Chapter 15, Competition Policy, Monopolies and State Enterprises* *Article 1502: Monopolies and State Enterprises* Nothing in this Agreement shall be construed to prevent a Party from designating a monopoly. Where a Party intends to designate a monopoly and the designation may affect the interests of persons of another Party, the Party shall: (a) wherever possible, provide prior written notification to the other Party of designation; and (b) endeavour to introduce at the time of the designation such conditions on the operation of the monopoly as will minimise or eliminate any nullification or impairment of benefits in the sense of Annex 2004 (Nullification and Impairment). Each Party shall ensure, through regulatory control, administrative supervision or the application of other measures, that any privately-owned monopoly that it designates and any government monopoly that it maintains or designates: (a) acts in a manner that is not inconsistent with the Party's obligations under this Agreement; (b) except to comply with any terms of its designation that are not inconsistent with subparagraph (c) or (d), acts solely in accordance with commercial considerations in the purchase or sale of the monopoly good or service in the relevant market, including with regard to price, quality, availability, marketability, transportation, and other terms and conditions of purchase or sale; c) provides non-discriminatory treatment to investments of investors, to goods and to service providers of another Party in its

purchase or sale of the monopoly good or service in the relevant market; and (d) does not use its monopoly position to engage, either directly or indirectly, in anticompetitive practices in a non-monopolised market in its territory that adversely affect an investment of an investor of another Party, including the discriminatory provision of the monopoly good or service, cross-subsidisation or predatory conduct.

The paragraph above does not apply to procurement by governmental agencies of goods or services for governmental purposes and not with a view to commercial resale or with a view to use in the production of goods or the provision of services for commercial sale.

XIII. Safeguards

ASEAN

Article XIV: Final Provision:

The terms and definitions and other provisions of the GATS shall be referred to and applied to matters arising under this Framework Agreement for which no specific provision has been made under it.

Relevant provision in GATS: PART II, Article X - Emergency Safeguards Measures

There shall be multilateral negotiations on the question of emergency safeguard measures based on the principle of non-discrimination. The results of such negotiations shall enter into effect on a date not later than three years from the entry into force of the Agreement Establishing the WTO.

Any Member may, notwithstanding the provisions of paragraph 1 of Article XXI (Modification of Schedules), notify the Council on Trade in Services of its intention to modify or withdraw a specific commitment after a period of one year from the date on which the commitment enters into force.

PART II, Article XII - Restrictions to Safeguard the Balance of Payments

In the event of serious balance-of-payments and external financial difficulties or threat thereof, a Member may adopt or maintain restrictions on trade in services on which it has undertaken specific commitments, including on payments or transfers for transactions related to such commitments.

The restrictions referred above: (a) shall not discriminate among Members; (b) shall be consistent with the Articles of Agreement of the International Monetary Fund; (c) shall avoid unnecessary damage to the commercial, economic and financial interests of any other Member; (d) shall not exceed those necessary to deal with the circumstances described above; (e) shall be temporary and be phased out progressively as the situation improves.

However, such restrictions shall not be adopted or maintained for the purpose of protecting a particular service sector.

CER

Not Specified.

Table 17.1 (continued)

CHILE/ CANADA	*Part Five - Other Provisions* *Chapter O, Exceptions, Article O-04:* Nothing in this Agreement shall be construed to prevent a Party from adopting or maintaining measures that restrict transfers where the Party experiences serious balance of payments difficulties, or the threat thereof, and such restrictions are consistent with this Article.
MEXICO/ CHILE	*Part Six: Administrative and Institutional Provisions* *Chapter 19, Exceptions, Article 19-06: Balance of Payments* Nothing in this Agreement shall be construed to prevent a Party from adopting or maintaining measures that restrict transfers where the Party experiences serious balance of payments difficulties, or the threat thereof, and such restrictions are consistent with this Article.
NAFTA	*Part Eight: Other Provisions* *Chapter 21, Exceptions* *Article 2104: Balance of Payments* Nothing in this Agreement shall be construed to prevent a Party from adopting or maintaining measures that restrict transfers where the Party experiences serious balance of payments difficulties, or the threat thereof, and such restrictions are consistent with paragraphs 2 through 4 and are: (a) consistent with paragraph 5 to the extent they are imposed on transfers other than Cross-Border trade in financial services; or (b) consistent with paragraphs 6 and 7 to the extent they are imposed on Cross-Border trade in financial services.

XIV. Exceptions

ASEAN	*Article XIV: Final Provision:* The terms and definitions and other provisions of the GATS shall be referred to and applied to matters arising under this Framework Agreement for which no specific provision has been made under it. *Relevant provision in GATS: PART II, Article XIV - General Exceptions* Nothing in this Agreement shall be construed to prevent the adoption or enforcement by any Member of measures: (a) necessary to protect public morals or to maintain public order; (b) necessary to protect human, animal or plant life or health; (c) necessary to secure compliance with laws or regulations which are not inconsistent with the provisions of this Agreement including those relating to: (i) the prevention of deceptive and fraudulent practices or to deal with the effects of a default on services contracts; (ii) the protection of the privacy of individuals; (iii) safety; (d) inconsistent with Article

XVII (National Treatment), provided that the difference in treatment is aimed at ensuring the equitable or effective imposition or collection of direct taxes in respect of services or service suppliers of other Members; (e) inconsistent with Article II (Most-Favoured-Nation Treatment), provided that the difference in treatment is the result of an agreement on the avoidance of double taxation or provisions on the avoidance of double taxation in any other international agreement or arrangement by which the Member is bound.

CER

Article 18: Exceptions:
Provided that such measures are not used as a means of arbitrary or unjustified discrimination against persons of the other Member State or as a disguised restriction on trade in services, nothing in this Protocol shall preclude the adoption by either Member State of measures necessary: (a) to protect its essential security interests; (b) to protect public morals and to prevent disorder or crime; (c) to protect human, animal or plant life or health; (d) to prevent unfair, deceptive, or misleading practices; (e) in pursuance of obligations under international agreements; or (f) to secure compliance with laws and regulations relating to customs enforcement, to tax avoidance or evasion, or to foreign exchange control.

CHILE/ CANADA

Part Five- Other Provisions
Chapter O, Exceptions, Article O-01: General Exceptions
Provided that such measures are not applied in a manner that would constitute a means of arbitrary or unjustifiable discrimination between countries where the same conditions prevail or a disguised restriction on trade between the Parties, nothing in: (c) Chapter I (Telecommunications), shall be construed to prevent the adoption or enforcement by either Party of measures necessary to secure compliance with laws or regulations that are not inconsistent with the provisions of this Agreement, including those relating to health and safety and consumer protection.

CHILE/ MEXICO

Part Six: Administrative and Institutional Provisions
Chapter 19, Exceptions, Article 19-02: General Exceptions
The paragraphs a), b) and c) of GATS Article XIV are incorporated to this Agreement and are an integral part of this Agreement, and will apply to: Part Two (Trade in Goods), to the extent that a provision of that Part applies to services, Part Three (Technical Barriers to Trade), Chapter 10 (Cross-Border Trade in Services), Chapter 11 (Air Transport Services), Chapter 12 (Telecommunications).

NAFTA

Part Eight: Other Provisions
Chapter 21, Exceptions
Article 2101: General Exceptions
Provided that such measures are not applied in a manner that would constitute a means of arbitrary or unjustifiable

Table 17.1 (continued)

discrimination between countries where the same conditions prevail or a disguised restriction on trade between the Parties, nothing in: (a) Part Two (Trade in Goods), to the extent that a provision of that Part applies to services, (b) Part Three (Technical Barriers to Trade), to the extent that a provision of that Part applies to services, (c) Chapter 12 (Cross-Border Trade in Services), and (d) Chapter 13 (Telecommunications), shall be construed to prevent the adoption or enforcement by any Party of measures necessary to secure compliance with laws or regulations that are not inconsistent with the provisions of this Agreement, including those relating to health and safety and consumer protection.

XV. Future liberalisation

ASEAN

Article IV: Negotiation of Specific Commitments:
Member States shall enter into negotiations on measures affecting trade in specific service sectors. Such negotiations shall be directed towards achieving commitments which are beyond those inscribed in each Member State's schedule of specific commitments under the GATS and for which Member States shall accord preferential treatment to one another on an MFN basis.
Each Member State shall set out in a schedule, the specific commitments it shall undertake under paragraph 1.

CER

Article 10: Liberalisation of Trade:
The Member States agree to review in accordance with Article 20 of this Protocol the status of services inscribed in the Annex with a view to the liberalisation of trade in such services and whether, and if so how, removal from the Annex could be achieved.
A Member State may, at any time, either upon request of the other Member State or unilaterally, remove in whole or in part services inscribed by it from the Annex by notifying the other Member State in writing of its intention to do so.

CHILE/ CANADA

Chapter H, Article H-07: Quantitative Restrictions
The Parties shall periodically, but in any event at least every two years endeavour to negotiate the liberalisation or removal of the quantitative restrictions set out in Annex IV pursuant to paragraphs 1 and 2.
Chapter H, Article H-08: Liberalisation of Non-Discriminatory Measures
Each Party shall set out in its Schedule to Annex V its commitments to liberalise quantitative restrictions, licensing requirements, performance requirements or other non-discriminatory measures.

CHILE/ MEXICO

Chapter 10, Article 10-08: Quantitative Restrictions
The Parties shall periodically, but at least every two years, endeavour to negotiate the liberalisation or removal of the quantitative restrictions set out in Annex V pursuant to paragraphs 1 and 2.

Chapter 10, Article 10-09: Future Liberalisation:

Through future negotiations summoned by the Commission, the Parties shall deepen the achieved liberalisation in the different service sectors, with a view to achieving the elimination of the remaining restrictions set out in conformity with Article 10-07 [Reservations] (1) and (2).

Chapter 10, Article 10-10: Liberalisation of Non-Discriminating Measures

Each Party shall set out in its Schedule Annex VI its commitments to liberalise quantitative restrictions, licensing requirements, performance requirements or other non-discriminatory measures.

Chapter 12, Article 10-11: Procedures

The Commission shall establish procedures for, *inter alia*, consultations on reservations, quantitative restrictions or commitments with a view to further liberalisation.

NAFTA

Chapter 12, Article 1207: Quantitative Restrictions

The Parties shall periodically, but in any event at least every two years, endeavour to negotiate the liberalisation or removal of the quantitative restrictions set out in Annex V [Quantitative Restrictions - Chapter 12] pursuant to paragraphs 1 through 3.

Chapter 12, Article 1208: Liberalisation of Non-Discriminatory Measures:

Each Party shall set out in its Schedule to Annex VI [Miscellaneous Commitments - Chapter 12] its commitments to liberalise quantitative restrictions, licensing requirements, performance requirements or other non-discriminatory measures.

Chapter 12, Article 1209: Procedures

The Commission shall establish procedures for, *inter alia*, consultations on reservations, quantitative restrictions or commitments with a view to further liberalisation.

XVI. Dispute settlement

ASEAN

A. Consultation

Article VII: Settlement of Disputes

The Protocol on Dispute Settlement for ASEAN shall generally be referred to and applied with respect to any disputes arising from, or any differences between Member States concerning the interpretation or application of this Framework Agreement or any arrangements arising therefrom.

A specific dispute settlement mechanism may be established for the purposes of this Framework Agreement which shall form an integral part of this Framework Agreement.

B. Panel Procedures. Not Specified.

Table 17.1 (continued)

CER

A. Consultation

Article 19: Consultation

The Member States shall, at the written request of either, promptly enter into consultations with a view to seeking an early, equitable and mutually satisfactory solution, if the Member State which requested the consultations considers that: an obligation under this Protocol had not been, is not being, or may not be fulfilled; or the achievement of any objective of this Protocol is being or may be frustrated.

For the purpose of this Protocol, consultations between the Member States shall be considered to have commenced on the day on which written notice requesting the consultations is given.

B. Panel Procedures. Not Specified.

CHILE/
CANADA

A. Consultation

Chapter N, Article N-06: Consultations

A Party may request in writing consultations with the other Party regarding any actual or proposed measure or any other matter that it considers might affect the operation of this Agreement.

The Parties shall make every attempt to arrive at a mutually satisfactory resolution of any matter through consultations under this Article or other consultative provisions of this Agreement. To this end, the Parties shall: (a) provide sufficient information to enable a full examination of how the actual or proposed measure or other matter might affect the operation of this Agreement; and (b) treat any confidential or proprietary information exchanged in the course of consultations on the same basis as the Party providing the information.

B. Panel Procedures

Article N-08: Request for an Arbitral Panel

If the Commission has convened pursuant to Article N-07(4), and the matter has not been resolved within: (a) 30 days thereafter; (b) 30 days after the Commission has convened in respect of the matter most recently referred to it, where proceedings have been consolidated pursuant to Article N-07(6); or (c) such other period as the Parties may agree, a Party may request in writing the establishment of an arbitral panel. The requesting Party shall deliver the request to its Section of the Secretariat and the other Party.

Article N-15: Initial Report

Unless the disputing Parties otherwise agree, the panel shall base its report on the submissions and arguments of the Parties and on any information before it pursuant to Article N-13 (Role of Experts) or N-14 (Scientific Review Boards).

Article N-16: Final Report

The panel shall present to the Parties a final report, including any separate opinions on matters not unanimously agreed, within 30 days of presentation of the initial report, unless the Parties otherwise agree.

CHILE/ MEXICO

A. Consultation

Chapter 18, Dispute Settlement

Article 18-04: Consultations

Any Party may request in writing consultations with any other Party regarding any actual or proposed measure or any other matter that it considers might affect the operation of this Agreement.

The Parties shall: (a) provide sufficient information to enable a full examination of how the actual or proposed measure or other matter might affect the operation of this Agreement; and (b) treat any confidential or proprietary information exchanged in the course of consultations on the same basis as the Party providing the information.

B. Panel Procedures

Article 18-06: Request for an Arbitral Panel

If the Commission has convened pursuant to Article 18-05(4), and the matter has not been resolved within: (a) 30 days thereafter, (b) 30 days after the Commission has convened in respect to the matter most recently referred to it, where proceedings have been consolidated pursuant to Article 2007(6), or (c) such other period as the consulting Parties may agree, any consulting Party may request in writing the establishment of an arbitral panel.

Article 18-13: Initial Report

Unless the disputing Parties otherwise agree, the panel shall base its report on the submissions and arguments of the Parties and on any information before it pursuant to Article 18-11 and 18-12.

Article 18-14: Final Report

The panel shall present to the disputing Parties a final report, including any separate opinions on matters not unanimously agreed, within 30 days of presentation of the initial report, unless the disputing Parties otherwise agree.

NAFTA

A. Consultation

Chapter 20, Institutional Arrangements and Dispute Settlement Procedures

Article 2006: Consultations

Any Party may request in writing consultations with any other Party regarding any actual or proposed measure or any other matter that it considers might affect the operation of this Agreement.

Unless the Commission otherwise provides in its rules and procedures established under Article 2001(4) (The Free Trade Commission), a third Party that considers it has a substantial interest in the matter shall be entitled to participate in the consultations on delivery of written notice to the other Parties and to its Section of the Secretariat.

The consulting Parties shall make every attempt to arrive at a mutually satisfactory resolution of any matter through consultations under this Article or other consultative provision of this Agreement.

B. Panel Procedures

Article 2008: Request for an Arbitral Panel

Table 17.1 (continued)

thereafter, (b) 30 days after the Commission has convened in respect to the matter most recently referred to it, where proceedings have been consolidated pursuant to Article 2007(6), or (c) such other period as the consulting Parties may agree, any consulting Party may request in writing the establishment of an arbitral panel.

Article 2016: Initial Report
Unless the disputing Parties otherwise agree, the panel shall base its report on the submissions and arguments of the Parties and on any information before it pursuant to Article 2014 (Role of Experts) and 2015 (Scientific Review Boards).

Article 2017: Final Report
The panel shall present to the disputing Parties a final report, including any separate opinions on matters not unanimously agreed, within 30 days of presentation of the initial report, unless the disputing Parties otherwise agree.

XVII. Modification of schedules

ASEAN	*Article X: Modification of Schedules of Specific Commitments:* A Member State may modify or withdraw any commitment in its schedule of specific commitments, at any time after three years from the date on which that commitment entered into force provided that it notifies other Member States and the ASEAN Secretariat of the intent to modify or withdraw a commitment three months before the intended date of implementation of the modification or withdrawal; and that it enters into negotiations with an affected Member State to agree to necessary compensatory adjustment. In achieving a compensatory adjustment, Member States shall ensure that the general level of mutually advantageous commitment is not less favourable to trade than that provided for in the schedules of specific commitments prior to such negotiations. Compensatory adjustment shall be made on a MFN basis to all other Member States. The Senior Economic Officials with the endorsement of the Asian Economic Ministers may draw up additional procedures to give effect to this Article.
CER	Not Applicable.
CHILE/ CANADA	Not Applicable.
CHILE/ MEXICO	Not Applicable.
NAFTA	Not Applicable.

Table A17.1 Sectoral coverage[1]

I. Financial services

CHILE/ CANADA	Not Specified.
CHILE/ MEXICO	Not Specified.
NAFTA	*Chapter 14: Financial Services* *Article 1401 : Scope and Definition* This Chapter applies to measures adopted or maintained by a Party relating to: (a) financial institutions of another Party; (b) investors of another Party, and investments of such investors, in financial institutions in the Party's territory; and (c) cross-border trade in financial services. *Future Liberalisation: Article 1404 (4)* The Parties shall consult on future liberalisation of cross-border trade in financial services as set out in Annex 1404.4. *Article 1405: National Treatment* Each Party shall accord to investors, financial institutions, and investments of investors of another Party in financial institutions treatment no less favourable than that it accords to its own investors, financial institutions and investment of its own investors in financial institutions, in like circumstances, with respect to the establishment, acquisition, expansion, management, conduct, operation, and sale or other disposition of financial institutions and investments in financial institutions in its territory. *Article 1406: Most-Favoured-Nation Treatment* Each Party shall accord to investors of another Party, financial institutions of another Party, investments of investors in financial institutions and cross-border financial service providers of another Party treatment no less favourable than that it accords to the investors, financial institutions, investments of investors in financial institutions and cross-border financial service providers of any other Party or of a non-Party, in like circumstances. *Recognition (in Article 1406: MFN Treatment)* A Party may recognise prudential measures of another Party or of a non-Party in the application of measures covered by this Chapter. Such recognition may be: (a) accorded unilaterally; (b) achieved through harmonisation or other means; or (c) based upon an agreement or arrangement with the other Party or non-Party. A Party according recognition of prudential measures under the paragraph above shall provide adequate opportunity to another party to demonstrate that circumstances exist in which there are or would be equivalent regulation, oversight,

Table A17.1 (continued)

implementation of regulation, and, if appropriate, procedures concerning the sharing of information between the Parties. Where a Party accords recognition of prudential measures under paragraph 1(c) and the circumstances set out in the second paragraph above exist, the Party shall provide adequate opportunity to another Party to negotiate accession to the agreement or arrangement, or to negotiate a comparable agreement or arrangement.

Article 1410: Exceptions

Nothing in this Part shall be construed to prevent a Party from adopting or maintaining reasonable measures for prudential reasons, such as: (a) the protection of investors, depositors, financial market participants, policy-holders, policy-claimants, or persons to whom a fiduciary duty is owed by a financial institution or cross-border financial service provider; (b) the maintenance of the safety, soundness, integrity or financial responsibility of financial institutions or cross-border financial service providers; and (c) ensuring the integrity and stability of a Party's financial system.

Article 1411: Transparency

Each Party shall, to the extent practicable, provide in advance to all interested persons any measure of general application that the Party proposes to adopt in order to allow an opportunity for such persons to comment on the measure. Such measure shall be provided: (a) by means of official publication; (b) in other written form; or (c) in such other form as permits an interested person to make informed comments on the proposed measure.

Article 1412: Financial Services Committee

The Parties hereby establish the Financial Services Committee.

II. Telecommunications

CHILE/
CANADA

Chapter I: Telecommunications

Article I-01: Scope and Coverage

This Chapter applies to: (a) measures adopted or maintained by a Party relating to access to and use of public telecommunications transport networks or services by persons of another Party, including access and use by such persons operating private networks; (b) measures adopted or maintained by a Party relating to the provision of enhanced or value-added services by persons of another Party in the territory, or across the borders, of a Party; and (c) standards-related measures relating to attachment of terminal or other equipment to public telecommunications transport networks.

Article I-02: Access to and Use of Public Telecommunications Transport Networks and Services

Each Party shall ensure that persons of another Party have access to and use of any public telecommunications transport network or service, including private leased circuits, offered in its territory or across its borders for the conduct of their business, on reasonable and non-discriminatory terms and conditions, including as set out in paragraphs 2 through 8 of this Article.

Article I-03: Conditions for the Provision of Enhanced or Value-Added Services

Each Party shall ensure that: (a) any licensing, permit, registration or notification procedure that it adopts or maintains relating to the provision of enhanced or value added services is transparent and non-discriminatory; and that applications filed hereunder are processed expeditiously; and information required under such procedures is limited to that necessary to demonstrate that the applicant has the financial solvency to begin providing services or to assess conformity of the applicant's terminal or other equipment with Party's applicable standards or technical regulations.

Article I-04: Standards-Related Measures

Further to the *Agreement on Technical Barriers to Trade* of the WTO Agreement each Party shall ensure that its standards-related measures relating to the attachment of terminal or other equipment to the public telecommunications transport networks, including those measures relating to the use of testing and measuring equipment for conformity assessment procedures, are adopted or maintained only to the extent necessary to: (a) prevent technical damage to public telecommunications transport networks; (b) prevent technical interference with, or degradation of, public telecommunications transport services; (c) prevent electromagnetic interference, and ensure compatibility, with other uses of the electromagnetic spectrum; (d) prevent billing equipment malfunction; or (e) ensure users' safety and access to public telecommunications transport networks or services.

Article I-05: Monopolies

Where a Party maintains or designates a monopoly to provide public telecommunications transport networks or services, and the monopoly, directly or through an affiliate, competes in the provision of enhanced or value-added services or other telecommunications-related services or goods, the Party shall ensure that the monopoly does not use its monopoly position to engage in anticompetitive conduct in those markets, either directly or through its dealings with its affiliates, in such a manner as to affect adversely a person of another Party.

Article I-06: Transparency

Further to Article L-02 (Publication), each Party shall make publicly available its measures relating to access to and use of public telecommunications transport networks or services, including measures relating to: (a) tariffs and other terms and conditions of service; (b) specifications of technical interfaces with the networks or services; (c) information on bodies responsible for the preparation and adoption of standards-related measures affecting such access and use; (d) conditions applying to attachment of terminal or other equipment to the networks; and (e) notification, permit, registration or licensing requirements.

Article I-07: Relation to Other Chapters

In the event of any inconsistency between this Chapter and another Chapter, this Chapter shall prevail to the extent of the inconsistency.

Article I-08: Relation to International Organisations and Arrangements

The Parties recognise the importance of international standards for global compatibility and interoperability of telecommunication networks or services and undertake to promote those standards through the work of relevant

Table A17.1 (continued)

international bodies, including the International Telecommunication Union and the International Organisation for Standardisation.

Article I-09: Technical Cooperation and Other Consultations

To encourage the development of interoperable telecommunications transport services infrastructure, the Parties shall cooperate in the exchange of technical information, the development of government-to-government training programs and other related activities. In implementing this obligation, the Parties shall give special emphasis to existing exchange programs.

The Parties shall consult with a view to determining the feasibility of further liberalising trade in all telecommunications services.

Article I-10: Definitions

Telecommunications: the transmission and reception of signals by any electromagnetic means.

Public telecommunications transport service: any telecommunications transport service required by a Party, explicitly or in effect, to be offered to the public generally.

Public telecommunications transport network: the public telecommunications infrastructure which permits telecommunications between and among defined network termination points.

Intra-corporate communications: telecommunications through which an enterprise communicates (a) internally or with or among its subsidiaries, branches and affiliates, as defined by each Party, or (b) on a non-commercial basis with other persons that are fundamental to the economic activity of the enterprise and that have a continuing contractual relationship with it.

Other definitions: authorised equipment, conformity assessment procedure, enhanced or value-added services, flat-rate pricing basis, network termination point, private network, protocol, standards-related measure, technical regulation, telecommunications service, terminal equipment.

CHILE/
MEXICO

Chapter 12: Telecommunications

Article 12-02: Scope and Coverage

This Chapter applies to: (a) measures adopted or maintained by a Party relating to access to and use of public telecommunications transport networks or services by persons of another Party, including access and use by such persons operating private networks; (b) measures adopted or maintained by a Party relating to the provision of enhanced or value-added services by persons of another Party in the territory, or across the borders, of a Party; and (c) standards-related measures relating to attachment of terminal or other equipment to public telecommunications transport networks.

Article 12-03: Access to and Use of Public Telecommunications Transport Networks and Services

Each Party shall ensure that persons of another Party have access to and use of any public telecommunications transport network or service, including private leased circuits, offered in its territory or across its borders for the conduct of their business, on reasonable and non-discriminatory terms and conditions, including as set out in paragraphs 2 through 8 of this Article.

Article 12-04: Conditions for the Provision of Enhanced or Value-Added Services

Each Party shall ensure that: (a) any licensing, permit, registration or notification procedure that it adopts or maintains relating to the provision of enhanced or value added services is transparent and non-discriminatory, and that applications filed hereunder are processed expeditiously; and (b) information required under such procedures is limited to that necessary to demonstrate that the applicant has the financial solvency to begin providing services or to assess conformity of the applicant's terminal or other equipment with Party's applicable standards or technical regulations.

Article 12-05: Standards-Related Measures

Further to the *Agreement on Technical Barriers to Trade* of the WTO Agreement each Party shall ensure that its standards-related measures relating to the attachment of terminal or other equipment to the public telecommunications transport networks, including those measures relating to the use of testing and measuring equipment for conformity assessment procedures, are adopted or maintained only to the extent necessary to: (a) prevent technical damage to public telecommunications transport networks; (b) prevent technical interference with, or degradation of, public telecommunications transport services; (c) prevent electromagnetic interference, and ensure compatibility, with other uses of the electromagnetic spectrum; (d) prevent billing equipment malfunction; or (e) ensure users' safety and access to public telecommunications transport networks or services; or (f) assure efficient use of the electromagnetic spectrum.

Article 12-06: Monopolies

Where a Party maintains or designates a monopoly to provide public telecommunications transport networks or services, and the monopoly, directly or through an affiliate, competes in the provision of enhanced or value-added services or other telecommunications-related services or goods, the Party shall ensure that the monopoly does not use its monopoly position to engage in anticompetitive conduct in those markets, either directly or through its dealings with its affiliates, in such a manner as to affect adversely a person of another Party.

Article 12-07: Transparency

Further to Article L-02 (Publication), each Party shall make publicly available its measures relating to access to and use of public telecommunications transport networks or services, including measures relating to: (a) tariffs and other terms and conditions of service; (b) specifications of technical interfaces with the networks or services; (c) information on bodies responsible for the preparation and adoption of standards-related measures affecting such access and use; (d) conditions applying to attachment of terminal or other equipment to the networks; and (e) notification, permit, registration or licensing requirements.

Article 12-08: Relation to Other Chapters

In the event of any inconsistency between a provision of this Chapter and one in another Chapter, the provision of this Chapter shall prevail to the extent of the inconsistency.

Table A17.1 (continued)

Article 12-09: Relation to International Organisations and Arrangements

The Parties recognise the importance of international standards for global compatibility and interoperability of telecommunication networks or services and undertake to promote those standards through the work of relevant international bodies, including the International Telecommunication Union and the International Organisation for Standardisation.

Article 12-10: Technical Cooperation and Other Consultations

To encourage the development of interoperable telecommunications transport services infrastructure, the Parties shall cooperate in the exchange of technical information, the development of government-to-government training programs and other related activities. In implementing this obligation, the Parties shall give special emphasis to existing exchange programs.

The Parties shall consult with a view to determining the feasibility of further liberalising trade in all telecommunications services.

Article 12-01: Definitions

Telecommunications: any transmission or reception of signals.

Public telecommunications transport service: any telecommunications transport service required by a Party, explicitly or in effect, to be offered to the public generally.

Public telecommunications transport network: the public telecommunications infrastructure which permits telecommunications between and among defined network termination points.

Intra-corporate communications: telecommunications through which an enterprise communicates (a) internally or with or among its subsidiaries, branches and affiliates, as defined by each Party, or (b) on a non-commercial basis with other persons that are fundamental to the economic activity of the enterprise and that have a continuing contractual relationship with it.

Other definitions: authorised equipment, conformity assessment procedure, enhanced or value-added services, flat-rate pricing basis, network termination point, private network, protocol, standards-related measure, technical regulation, telecommunications service, terminal equipment.

NAFTA

Chapter 13: Telecommunications
Article 1301: Scope

This Chapter applies to: (a) measures adopted or maintained by a Party relating to access to and use of public telecommunications transport networks or services by persons of another Party, including access and use by such persons operating private networks; (b) measures adopted or maintained by a Party relating to the provision of enhanced or value-added services by persons of another Party in the territory, or across the borders, of a Party; and (c) standards-related measures relating to attachment of terminal or other equipment to public telecommunications transport networks.

Article 1302: Access to and Use of Public Telecommunications Transport Networks and Services

Each Party shall ensure that persons of another Party have access to and use of any public telecommunications transport network or service, including private leased circuits, offered in its territory or across its borders for the conduct of their business, on reasonable and non-discriminatory terms and conditions, including as set out in paragraphs 2 through 8 of this Article.

Article 1303: Conditions for the Provision of Enhanced or Value-Added Services

Each Party shall ensure that: (a) any licensing, permit, registration or notification procedure that it adopts or maintains relating to the provision of enhanced or value added services is transparent and non-discriminatory, and that applications filed hereunder are processed expeditiously; and (b) information required under such procedures is limited to that necessary to demonstrate that the applicant has the financial solvency to begin providing services or to assess conformity of the applicant's terminal or other equipment with Party's applicable standards or technical regulations.

Article 1304: Standards-Related Measures

Each Party shall ensure that its standards-related measures relating to the attachment of terminal or other equipment to the public telecommunications transport networks, including those measures relating to the use of testing and measuring equipment for conformity assessment procedures, are adopted or maintained only to the extent necessary to: (a) prevent technical damage to public telecommunications transport networks; (b) prevent technical interference with, or degradation of, public telecommunications transport services; (c) prevent electromagnetic interference, and ensure compatibility, with other uses of the electromagnetic spectrum; (d) prevent billing equipment malfunction; or (e) ensure users' safety and access to public telecommunications transport networks or services.

Article 1304-7: The *Telecommunications Standards Subcommittee* established under Article 913(5) shall perform the functions set out in Annex 913.5.a-2.

Article 1305: Monopolies

Where a Party maintains or designates a monopoly to provide public telecommunications transport networks or services, and the monopoly, directly or through an affiliate, competes in the provision of enhanced or value-added services or other telecommunications-related services or goods, the Party shall ensure that the monopoly does not use its monopoly position to engage in anticompetitive conduct in those markets, either directly or through its dealings with its affiliates, in such a manner as to affect adversely a person of another Party.

Article 1306: Transparency

Each Party shall make publicly available its measures relating to access to and use of public telecommunications transport networks or services, including measures relating to: (a) tariffs and other terms and conditions of service; (b) specifications of technical interfaces with the networks or services; (c) information on bodies responsible for the preparation and adoption of standards-related measures affecting such access and use; (d) conditions applying to

Table A17.1 (continued)

attachment of terminal or other equipment to the networks; and (e) notification, permit, registration or licensing requirements.

Article 1307: Relation to Other Chapters

In the event of any inconsistency between this Chapter and another Chapter, this Chapter shall prevail to the extent of the inconsistency.

Artice 1308: Relation to International Organisations and Arrangements

The Parties recognise the importance of international standards for global compatibility and interoperability of telecommunication networks or services and undertake to promote those standards through the work of relevant international bodies, including the International Telecommunication Union and the International Organisation for Standardisation.

Article 1309: Technical Cooperation and Other Consultations

To encourage the development of interoperable telecommunications transport services infrastructure, the Parties shall cooperate in the exchange of technical information, the development of government-to-government training programs and other related activities. In implementing this obligation, the Parties shall give special emphasis to existing exchange programs.

The Parties shall consult with a view to determining the feasibility of further liberalising trade in all telecommunications services.

Article 1310: Definitions

Telecommunications: the transmission and reception of signals by any electromagnetic means.

Public telecommunications transport service: any telecommunications transport service required by a Party, explicitly or in effect, to be offered to the public generally.

Public telecommunications transport network: the public telecommunications infrastructure which permits telecommunications between and among defined network termination points.

Intra-corporate communications: telecommunications through which an enterprise communicates (a) internally or with or among its subsidiaries, branches and affiliates, as defined by each Party, or (b) on a non-commercial basis with other persons that are fundamental to the economic activity of the enterprise and that have a continuing contractual relationship with it.

Other definitions: authorised equipment, conformity assessment procedure, enhanced or value-added services, flat-rate pricing basis, network termination point, private network, protocol, standards-related measure, terminal equipment.

III. Transport

CHILE/CANADA

A. Air Transport Services

The Agreement excludes the following from its coverage: air services, including domestic and international air transportation services, whether scheduled or non-scheduled, and related services in support of air services, other than (i) aircraft repair and maintenance services during which an aircraft is withdrawn from service, and (ii) specialised air services.

B. Land Maritime Transportation Not Specified

CHILE/MEXICO

A. Air Transport Services

Chapter 10: Article 10-02: Scope of application:

This chapter does not apply to: air services, including domestic and international air transportation services, whether scheduled or non-scheduled, and related services in support of air services, other than (i) aircraft repair and maintenance services during which an aircraft is withdrawn from service, and (ii) speciality air services; and (iii) computerised system of reservation.

Chapter 11: Air Transport Services

Article 11-01: Definitions: For the effect of this Chapter, it shall make understood by the Air Transport Committee between the Government of Republic of Chile and the Government of United States of Mexico, signed on January 14, 1997 and their successor.

Article 11-02: Application scope: Except for the provisions in this Chapter, Chapter 17 (Administration of the Treaty), Chapter 19 (Exceptions), and Chapter 20 (Final Dispositions), this Treaty shall not be applied to the air transport services and the Parties shall be to the provision of the Committee.

B. Land Maritime Transportation Not Specified

NAFTA

A. Air Transport Services

Chapter 12: Cross-Border Trade in Services

Article 1202: Scope and Coverage

NAFTA provisions on services apply to: (i) aircraft repair and maintenance services during which an aircraft is withdrawn from service, and (ii) speciality air services.

They do not apply to: air services, including domestic and international air transportation services, whether scheduled or non-scheduled, and related services in support of air services, other than the ones specified above.

B. Land Maritime Transportation

Chapter 12, Annex 1212: Land Transportation

Contact Points

Table A17.1 (continued)

Each Party shall designate by January 1, 1994 contact points to provide information published by that Party relating to land transportation services regarding operating authority, safety requirements, taxation, data, studies and technology, and to provide assistance in contacting its relevant government agencies.

Review Process

The Commission shall, during the fifth year after the date of entry into force of this Agreement and during every second year thereafter until the liberalisation for bus and truck transportation set out in the Parties' Schedules to Annex I is complete, receive and consider a report from the Parties that assesses progress respecting liberalisation, including: (a) the effectiveness of the liberalisation; (b) specific problems for, or unanticipated effects on, each Party's bus and truck transportation industries arising from liberalisation; and (c) modifications to the period of liberalisation.

The Parties shall consult, no later than seven years after the date of entry into force of this Agreement, to consider further liberalisation commitments.

Article 913.5.a.i Committee on Standards-Related Measures

The Committee shall establish a *Land Transportation Standards Subcommittee*, in accordance with Annex 913.5.a1. [The Subcommittee is responsible for making compatible relevant standards-related measures for bus, truck and rail operations.]

IV. Professional services

CHILE/ CANADA	A. General Provisions

Annex H-10.5: Professional Services

Section I: General Provisions

Processing of Applications for Licences and Certifications

1. Each Party shall ensure that its competent authorities, within a reasonable time after the submission by a national of the other Party of an application for a licence or certification: (a) where the application is complete, make a determination on the application and inform the applicant of that determination; or (b) where the application is not complete, inform the applicant without undue delay of the status of the application and the additional information that is required under the Party's law.

B. Development of Professional Standards

2. The Parties shall encourage the relevant bodies in their respective territories to develop mutually acceptable standards and criteria for licensing and certification of professional service providers and to provide recommendations on mutual recognition to the Commission.

3. The standards and criteria referred to in paragraph 2 may be developed with regard to the following matters: (a) education - accreditation of schools or academic programs; (b) examinations - qualifying examinations for licensing,

including alternative methods of assessment such as oral examinations and interviews; (c) experience - length and nature of experience required for licensing; (d) conduct and ethics - standards of professional conduct and the nature of disciplinary action for non-conformity with those standards; (e) professional development and re-certification - continuing education and ongoing requirements to maintain professional certification; (f) scope of practice - extent of, or limitations on, permissible activities; (g) local knowledge - requirements for knowledge of such matters as local laws, regulations, language, geography or climate; and (h) consumer protection - alternatives to residency requirements, including bonding, professional liability insurance and client restitution funds, to provide for the protection of consumers.

4. On receipt of a recommendation referred to in paragraph 2, the Commission shall review the recommendation within a reasonable time to determine whether it is consistent with this Agreement. Based on the Commission's review, each Party shall encourage its respective competent authorities, where appropriate, to implement the recommendation within a mutually agreed time.

C. Temporary Licensing

5. Where the Parties agree, each Party shall encourage the relevant bodies in its territory to develop procedures for the temporary licensing of professional service providers of the other Party.

Review

6. The Commission shall periodically, and at least once every three years, review the implementation of this Section.

D. Foreign Legal Consultants

1. Each Party shall, in implementing its obligations and commitments regarding foreign legal consultants as set out in its relevant Schedules and subject to any reservations therein, ensure that a national of the other Party is permitted to practice or advise on the law of any country in which that national is authorised to practice as a lawyer.

E. Consultations With Professional Bodies

2. Each Party shall consult with its relevant professional bodies to obtain their recommendations on:

(a) the form of association or partnership between lawyers authorised to practice in its territory and foreign legal consultants; (b) the development of standards and criteria for the authorisation of foreign legal consultants in conformity with Article H-10; and (c) other matters relating to the provision of foreign legal consultancy services.

3. Prior to initiation of consultations under paragraph 7, each Party shall encourage its relevant professional bodies to consult with the relevant professional bodies designated by the other Party regarding the development of joint recommendations on the matters referred to in paragraph 2.

F. Future Liberalisation

4. Each Party shall establish a work program to develop common procedures throughout its territory for the authorisation of foreign legal consultants.

5. Each Party shall promptly review any recommendation referred to in paragraphs 2 and 3 to ensure its consistency with this Agreement. If the recommendation is consistent with this Agreement, each Party shall encourage its competent authorities to implement the recommendation within one year.

Table A17.1 (continued)

6. Each Party shall report to the Commission within one year of the date of entry into force of this Agreement, and each year thereafter, on its progress in implementing the work program referred to in paragraph 4.

7. The Parties shall meet within one year of the date of entry into force of this Agreement with a view to: (a) assessing the implementation of paragraphs 2 through 5; (b) amending or removing, where appropriate, reservations on foreign legal consultancy services; and (c) assessing further work that may be appropriate regarding foreign legal consultancy services.

G. Temporary Licensing of Engineers

Section III: Temporary Licensing of Engineers

1. The Parties shall meet within one year of the date of entry into force of this Agreement to establish a work program to be undertaken by each Party, in conjunction with its relevant professional bodies, to provide for the temporary licensing in its territory of nationals of the other Party who are licensed as engineers in the territory of the other Party.

2. To this end, each Party shall consult with its relevant professional bodies to obtain their recommendations on: (a) the development of procedures for the temporary licensing of such engineers to permit them to practice their engineering specialities in each jurisdiction in its territory; (b) the development of model procedures for adoption by the competent authorities throughout its territory to facilitate the temporary licensing of such engineers; (c) the engineering specialities to which priority should be given in developing temporary licensing procedures; and (d) other matters relating to the temporary licensing of engineers identified by the Party in such consultations.

3. Each Party shall request its relevant professional bodies to make recommendations on the matters referred to in paragraph 2 within two years of the date of entry into force of this Agreement.

4. Each Party shall encourage its relevant professional bodies to meet at the earliest opportunity with the relevant professional bodies of the other Party with a view to cooperating in the development of joint recommendations on the matters referred to in paragraph 2 within two years of the date of entry into force of this Agreement. Each Party shall request an annual report from its relevant professional bodies on the progress achieved in developing those recommendations.

5. The Parties shall promptly review any recommendation referred to in paragraph 3 or 4 to ensure its consistency with this Agreement. If the recommendation is consistent with this Agreement, each Party shall encourage its competent authorities to implement the recommendation within one year.

6. The Commission shall review the implementation of this Section within two years of the date of entry into force of this Section.

CHILE/
MEXICO

A. General Provisions
Chapter 10, Annex 10-12: Professional Services
Objective

1. The purpose of this annex is to establish rules that the Parties will have to follow in order to reduce and eliminate gradually, in their territories, the barriers to the supply of professional services.

Processing of Applications for Licences and Certifications

2. Each Party shall ensure that its competent authorities, within a reasonable time after the submission by a national of the other Party of an application for a licence or certification: (a) where the application is complete, make a determination on the application and inform the applicant of that determination; or (b) where the application is not complete, inform the applicant without undue delay of the status of the application and the additional information that is required under the Party's law.

B. Development of Professional Standards

3. The Parties shall encourage the relevant bodies in their respective territories to develop mutually acceptable standards and criteria for licensing and certification of professional service providers and to provide recommendations on mutual recognition to the Commission.

4. The standards and criteria referred to in paragraph 3 may be developed with regard to the following matters: (a) education - accreditation of schools or academic programs; (b) examinations - qualifying examinations for licensing, including alternative methods of assessment such as oral examinations and interviews; (c) experience - length and nature of experience required for licensing; (d) conduct and ethics - standards of professional conduct and the nature of disciplinary action for non-conformity with those standards; (e) professional development and re-certification - continuing education and ongoing requirements to maintain professional certification; (f) scope of practice - extent of, or limitations on, permissible activities; (g) local knowledge - requirements for knowledge of such matters as local laws, regulations, language, geography or climate; and (h) consumer protection - alternatives to residency requirements, including bonding, professional liability insurance and client restitution funds, to provide for the protection of consumers.

5. On receipt of a recommendation referred to in paragraph 3, the Commission shall review the recommendation within a reasonable time to determine whether it is consistent with this Agreement. Based on the Commission's review, each Party shall encourage its respective competent authorities, where appropriate, to implement the recommendation within a mutually agreed time.

C. Temporary Licensing

6. Where the Parties agree, each Party shall encourage the relevant bodies in its territory to develop procedures for the temporary licensing of professional service providers of the other Party.

Review

7. The Commission shall periodically, and at least once every three years, review the implementation of the provisions of this Annex.

D. Foreign Legal Consultants Not specified.

E. Consultations With Professional Bodies Not specified.

Table A17.1 (continued)

F. Future Liberalisation Not specified.

G. Temporary Licensing of Engineers Not specified.

NAFTA

A. General Provisions

Chapter 12, Annex 1210.5: Professional Services

Section A - General Provisions

Processing of Applications for Licences and Certifications

1. Each Party shall ensure that its competent authorities, within a reasonable time after the submission by a national of another Party of an application for a licence or certification: (a) where the application is complete, make a determination on the application and inform the applicant of that determination; or (b) where the application is not complete, inform the applicant without undue delay of the status of the application and the additional information that is required under the Party's law.

B. Development of Professional Standards

2. The Parties shall encourage the relevant bodies in their respective territories to develop mutually acceptable standards and criteria for licensing and certification of professional service providers and to provide recommendations on mutual recognition to the Commission.

3. The standards and criteria referred to in paragraph 2 may be developed with regard to the following matters: (a) education - accreditation of schools or academic programs; (b) examinations - qualifying examinations for licensing, including alternative methods of assessment such as oral examinations and interviews; (c) experience length and nature of experience required for licensing; (d) conduct and ethics - standards of professional conduct and the nature of disciplinary action for non-conformity with those standards; (e) professional development and re-certification - continuing education and ongoing requirements to maintain professional certification; (f) scope of practice - extent of, or limitations on, permissible activities; (g) local knowledge - requirements for knowledge of such matters as local laws, regulations, language, geography or climate; and (h) consumer protection - alternatives to residency requirements, including bonding, professional liability insurance and client restitution funds, to provide for the protection of consumers.

C. Temporary Licensing

5. Where the Parties agree, each Party shall encourage the relevant bodies in its territory to develop procedures for the temporary licensing of professional service providers of another Party.

Review

6. The Commission shall periodically, and at least once every three years, review the implementation of this Section.

D. Foreign Legal Consultants

Section B Foreign Legal Consultants

1. Each Party shall, in implementing its obligations and commitments regarding foreign legal consultants as set out in its

relevant Schedules and subject to any reservations therein, ensure that a national of another Party is permitted to practice or advise on the law of any country in which that national is authorised to practice as a lawyer.

E. Consultations With Professional Bodies

2. Each Party shall consult with its relevant professional bodies to obtain their recommendations on: (a) the form of association or partnership between lawyers authorised to practice in its territory and foreign legal consultants; (b) the development of standards and criteria for the authorisation of foreign legal consultants in conformity with Article 1210; and (c) other matters relating to the provision of foreign legal consultancy services.

3. Prior to initiation of consultations under paragraph 7, each Party shall encourage its relevant professional bodies to consult with the relevant professional bodies designated by each of the other Parties regarding the development of joint recommendations on the matters referred to in paragraph 2.

F. Future Liberalisation

4. Each Party shall establish a work program to develop common procedures throughout its territory for the authorisation of foreign legal consultants.

5. Each Party shall promptly review any recommendation referred to in paragraphs 2 and 3 to ensure its consistency with this Agreement. If the recommendation is consistent with this Agreement, each Party shall encourage its competent authorities to implement the recommendation within one year.

6. Each Party shall report to the Commission within one year of the date of entry into force of this Agreement, and each year thereafter, on its progress in implementing the work program referred to in paragraph 4.

7. The Parties shall meet within one year of the date of entry into force of this Agreement with a view to: (a) assessing the implementation of paragraphs 2 through 5; (b) amending or removing, where appropriate, reservations on foreign legal consultancy services; and (c) assessing further work that may be appropriate regarding foreign legal consultancy services.

G. Temporary Licensing of Engineers

Section C Temporary Licensing of Engineers

1. The Parties shall meet within one year of the date of entry into force of this Agreement to establish a work program to be undertaken by each Party, in conjunction with its relevant professional bodies, to provide for the temporary licensing in its territory of nationals of another Party who are licensed as engineers in the territory of that other Party.

2. To this end, each Party shall consult with its relevant professional bodies to obtain their recommendations on: (a) the development of procedures for the temporary licensing of such engineers to permit them to practice their engineering specialities in each jurisdiction in its territory; (b) the development of model procedures for adoption by the competent authorities throughout its territory to facilitate the temporary licensing of such engineers; (c) the engineering specialities to which priority should be given in developing temporary licensing procedures; and (d) other matters relating to the temporary licensing of engineers identified by the Party in such consultations.

Table A17.1 (continued)

3. Each Party shall request its relevant professional bodies to make recommendations on the matters referred to in paragraph 2 within two years of the date of entry into force of this Agreement.

4. Each Party shall encourage its relevant professional bodies to meet at the earliest opportunity with the relevant professional bodies of the other Parties with a view to cooperating in the development of joint recommendations on the matters referred to in paragraph 2 within two years of the date of entry into force of this Agreement. Each Party shall request an annual report from its relevant professional bodies on the progress achieved in developing those recommendations.

5. The Parties shall promptly review any recommendation referred to in paragraphs 3 or 4 to ensure its consistency with this Agreement. If the recommendation is consistent with this Agreement, each Party shall encourage its competent authorities to implement the recommendation within one year.

6. The Commission shall review the implementation of this Section within two years of the date of entry into force of this Section.

7. Appendix 1210.5C applies to the Parties specified therein.

Appendix 1210.5-C: Civil Engineers

The rights and obligations of Section C of Annex 1210.5 apply to Mexico with respect to civil engineers 'ingenieros civile') and to such other engineering specialities that Mexico may designate.

V. Movement of natural persons supplying services under the agreement

ASEAN	Not specified.
CER	*Article 2: Scope of Protocol* This protocol shall apply to any measure, in existence or proposed, of a Member State that relates to or affects the provision of a service by or on behalf of a person of the other Member State within or into the territory of the first Member State. *Article 3: Definitions* Person of a Member State means: a natural person who is a citizen of, or ordinarily resident in, that State; etc. *Article 4: Market Access:* Each Member State shall grant to persons of the other Member State and services provided by them access rights in its market no less favourable than those allowed to its own persons and services provided by them.

CHILE/ CANADA	*Chapter K: Temporary Entry of Business Persons* *Article K-08: Definitions* business person means a citizen of a Party who is engaged in trade in goods, the provisions of services or the conduct of investment activities; and temporary entry means entry into the territory of a Party by a business person of the other Party without the intent to establish permanent residence. *Article K-01: General Principles* Further to Article A-02 (Objectives), this Chapter reflects the preferential trading relationship between the Parties, the desirability of facilitating temporary entry on a reciprocal basis and of establishing transparent criteria and procedures for temporary entry, and the need to ensure border security and to protect the domestic labour force and permanent employment in their respective territories. *Article K-02: General Obligations* Each Party shall apply its measures relating to the provisions of this Chapter in accordance with Article K-01 and, in particular, shall apply expeditiously those measures so as to avoid unduly impairing or delaying trade in goods or services or conduct of investment activities under this Agreement. *Article K-05: Working Group* The Parties hereby establish a Temporary Entry Working Group, comprising representatives of each Party, including immigration officials, to consider the implementation and administration of this Chapter and any measures of mutual interest.
CHILE/ MEXICO	*Chapter 10, Article 10-02: Application Scope (Paragraph 4)* Nothing in this Chapter (General Principles on Trade in Services) shall be construed to impose any obligation on a Party with respect to a national of another Party seeking access to its employment market, or employed on a permanent basis in its territory, or to confer any right on that national with respect to that access or employment. *Chapter 13: Temporary Entry for Business Persons* *Article 13-02: General Principles* The provisions of this Chapter reflect the preferential trading relationship between the Parties, the desirability of facilitating temporary entry on a reciprocal basis and of establishing transparent criteria and procedures for temporary entry. Also the provisions reflect the need to ensure border security and to protect the domestic labour force and permanent employment in their respective territories. *Article 13-03: General Obligations* Each Party shall apply its measures relating to the provisions of this Chapter in accordance with Article 13-02 and, in particular, shall apply expeditiously those measures so as to avoid unduly impairing or delaying trade in goods or services or conduct of investment activities under this Agreement.

Table A17.1 (continued)

	The Parties shall endeavour to develop and adopt common criteria, definitions and interpretations for the implementation of this Chapter. *Article 13-06: Working Group* The Parties hereby establish a Temporary Entry Working Group, comprising representatives of each Party, including immigration officials, in order to consider the implementation and administration of this Chapter and of any measure mutually interested. The Working Group shall meet at least once a year.
NAFTA	*Chapter 12, Article 1201: Scope and Coverage (Paragraph 3)* Nothing in this Chapter (Cross-Border Trade in Services) shall be construed to impose any obligation on a Party with respect to a national of another Party seeking access to its employment market, or employed on a permanent basis in its territory, or to confer any right on that national with respect to that access or employment. *Chapter 16: Temporary Entry for Business Persons* *Article 1601: General Principles* Further to Article 102 (Objectives), this Chapter reflects the preferential trading relationship between the Parties, the desirability of facilitating temporary entry on a reciprocal basis and of establishing transparent criteria and procedures for temporary entry, and the need to ensure border security and to protect the domestic labour force and permanent employment in their respective territories. *Article 1602: General Obligations* Each Party shall apply its measures relating to the provisions of this Chapter in accordance with Article 1601 and, in particular, shall apply expeditiously those measures so as to avoid unduly impairing or delaying trade in goods or services or conduct of investment activities under this Agreement. The Parties shall endeavour to develop and adopt common criteria, definitions and interpretations for the implementation of this Chapter. *Article 1605: Working Group* The Parties hereby establish a Temporary Entry Working Group, comprising representatives of each Party, including immigration officials. The Working Group shall meet at least once a year.

18 Services issues in APEC

Christopher Findlay and Tony Warren

INTRODUCTION

Trade and cross-border investments in services have grown rapidly, particularly in those economies with high rates of growth. Yet significant impediments to trade and investment flows in this sector remain. The multilateral system has made significant progress on reforming the services sector, but the extent of the barriers remaining suggests that the services sector provides a special challenge. This chapter argues that the liberalisation process is constrained, not just by the usual resistances to reform, but by other factors which arise because of the nature of impediments to services transactions. While, as usual, there are substantial gains from unilateral action, there also is the opportunity for groups of like-minded countries to promote the liberalisation of the services sector, as long as the consequence is a genuinely liberalising one.

This chapter makes specific suggestions with respect to the Asia Pacific Economic Cooperation (APEC) process as it relates to the services sector. APEC offers an opportunity for progress, particularly in the context of the challenges to regional cooperation posed by the financial crisis in some East Asian economies, and the inbuilt work program on services which is a feature of the World Trade Organisation (WTO) process. APEC, we suggest, can complement unilateral initiatives. Its members could consider some regional initiatives, in the style of the 'open club' approach to liberalisation. Finally, APEC members could support the global liberalisation process by working towards a position on some of the issues being discussed globally and by promoting outcomes from the global process.

SERVICES LIBERALISATION IN APEC

The APEC Leaders in their 'Declaration of Common Resolve' in Osaka in November 1995 observed that: 'Reflecting the diverse character of APEC and the broad scope of our activities, we will achieve the long-term goal of free and open trade and investment in several ways. We will:

- encourage and concert the evolving efforts of voluntary liberalisation in the region;
- take collective action to advance our liberalisation and facilitation objectives; and
- stimulate and contribute to further momentum for global liberalisation'.[1]

Also in Osaka on 19 November 1995, APEC economic leaders adopted the Osaka Action Agenda (OAA), which is described as a 'blueprint for implementing their commitment to free and open trade and investment, business facilitation, and economic and technical cooperation'. Part I of the OAA deals with trade and investment liberalisation and facilitation. Part II deals with economic and technical cooperation in areas such as energy and transportation, infrastructure, small and medium-sized enterprises, and agricultural technology.[2]

With respect to services, the OAA specifies the following objectives and guidelines. The objective is that: 'APEC economies will achieve free and open trade and investment in the Asia–Pacific region by:

a   progressively reducing restrictions on market access for trade in services; and
b   progressively providing for, inter-alia, most-favoured-nation (MFN) treatment and national treatment for trade in services'.

The guidelines are that 'each APEC economy will:

a   contribute positively to the WTO negotiations on trade in services;
b   expand commitments under the General Agreement on Trade in Services (GATS) on market access and national treatment; and
c   consider undertaking further actions to facilitate supply of services'.

The OAA also says that 'APEC economies will take ... Collective Actions with regard to services in the telecommunications, transportation, energy and tourism sectors, and continue to seek Collective Actions in other sectors'. The details of these collective actions are summarised in Appendix 18.1.

Commitments to liberalise are implemented by individual economies, according to the schedules and sequences that they determine and that they spell out in their Individual Action Plans (IAPs). Their performance in meeting the commitments is made public and available for peer review. This process of an international commitment followed by peer review becomes a critical element in domestic policymaking.

In addition to the OAA objectives and guidelines, also important are the format guidelines of the IAPs. These state that, for services:[3]

Members could include in the Heading Statement for the issue area inter alia a report on any regulatory measures (e.g. investment, movement of natural persons) which have a general horizontal effect across services sectors, and any steps proposed to change or remove them. They could also include a report on any actions being taken to facilitate or improve the supply of services. In their detailed reports, members could report by exception against the GATS Services Sectoral Classification List ... with respect to:

a exceptions or restrictions by sector with respect to market access, MFN or National Treatment as defined by GATS standards, and any steps proposed to reduce or eliminate them;
b exceptions or restrictions by sector at levels below that of central governments (e.g. regional and local governments), and any steps proposed to reduce or eliminate them; and
c GATS commitments by sector, and an indication of any measures in the IAP which exceed GATS commitments, including through accelerated implementation.

These objectives and guidelines (both those of the OAA and those for the presentation of IAPs) are significant for two reasons. First, they highlight the aim of APEC members in applying GATS' principles (including MFN), in contributing to the WTO negotiations and in extending GATS' commitments. Second, they are extremely ambitious. They amount to a complete specification of a negative list for services in all sectors. The GATS adopted a different approach of pursing a positive list with respect to sectors and a negative list with respect to impediments within nominated sectors.

An examination of the commitments made in the 1998 IAPs illustrates the extent to which these guidelines are being followed.

Services commitments in the IAPs

PECC's 1995 *Survey of Impediments to Trade and Investment in the APEC Region* found that most APEC economies imposed few regulatory barriers on foreign providers of computer services, value-added telecommunications services and tourism services. However, many barriers were identified throughout the region in postal services, education, and transport services. Analysis of the IAPs of APEC member economies highlights how many of these remaining barriers continue to be removed unilaterally within the APEC process. The analysis by the chair of the Senior Officials Meeting (SOM) in APEC of new services and investment commitments and activities in 1998 is summarised in Appendix 18.2. The SOM chair highlighted commitments and activities in financial services, telecommunications, energy, professional services and transportation. The prominence of the transport sector is interesting, as it suggests that action in APEC is not dependent on precedent set in the WTO. The prominence of financial services is also timely in the context of the Asian financial crisis.

Apart from those sectors listed in the SOM chair's summary, infrastructure (e.g. water, gas) and tourism are also mentioned frequently in the IAPs for 1998. Less often mentioned are distribution, education, health and postal services. Education and health were two sectors that PECC's 1995 report identified as locations where impediments were frequently observed.

Despite the significant commitments observed, an examination of the IAPs for 1998 and those of the earlier years quickly indicates that the OAA and IAP guidelines are not being met. Some economies, as we noted above, are making substantial commitments but, not surprisingly, given their scope, the extent of reporting still does not meet the targets. The consequence is a lack of consistency which makes it more difficult to assess commitments relative to starting points and to assess the comparability of effort being made by member economies. There are some economies that have made no commitments and there are also activities reported which are not related to earlier commitments to reform. Overall, a lot of detail of activity is reported, but detail does not necessarily contribute to the degree of transparency that helps mobilise the domestic interests in reform in each member economy.

One option to strengthen the IAPs is to develop a new set of collective actions in APEC.[4] The APEC members could follow a WTO process. They could work together on the specification of impediments in a particular sector and come up with a framework for reporting impediments and commitments to change in that sector. This has already been done in the WTO for financial services and also for maritime services. APEC might therefore extend that approach to other sectors. The voluntary approach of APEC means that not all members can be expected to complete the templates immediately but they might all be involved in their construction.

The APEC approach to liberalisation could therefore be strengthened by further collective action to develop and disseminate methodologies that policymakers could draw on as they design reform strategies. The techniques reported in this volume can help specify priorities and systems for documenting both impediments and commitments to policy change.

FURTHER APEC CONTRIBUTIONS

Apart from strengthening the IAPs in relation to services, how else might APEC contribute to services sector liberalisation? Contributions can be classified into two areas:

1) constructing liberalising regional initiatives, and
2) complementing action at the global level.

Box 18.1 Selecting priorities for liberalisation

The top-down approach is based on the proposition that it is better to have uniform levels of protection than to have great disparities between sectors. Hence the optimal strategy for early sectoral liberalisation is to focus on those industries where protection is highest. Reducing the peaks will flatten the pattern of protection and lead to the greatest gains. The problem with the top-down approach is the political pressure that highly protected service industries are generally able to bring to bear on negotiations.[5] One problem for member economies trying to apply a top-down approach to sectoral selection is the relative lack of data on impediments to trade in services. This problem, however, may be less of a hurdle when the negative-list approach is adopted and when there is supplementary work done on the economic significance of various impediments.

Taking an easier route and selecting less protected sectors for early liberalisation – a bottom-down approach – is likely to thwart the benefits of trade reform for individual APEC members. It would advantage inefficient industries and penalise efficient sectors by imposing additional costs upon them and the rest of the economy. It may even have the effect of increasing resistance to reform.

An alternative criterion for sectoral selection that incorporates some of these political constraints is the producer-service approach. Producer services are primarily used as inputs into the productive processes of other industries. Major examples include freight services, business services and the more value-added financial and telecommunications services. On the other hand, some services are purchased primarily by final consumers – for example, media, education and health services. The literature on the political economy of protection indicates that coalitions of support for liberalisation are significantly easier to build in industries where consumers are concentrated and/or consumers expend a considerable proportion of their income on the service produced by that industry. This is more likely to be a characteristic of producer services than of consumer services.

A final possible method for selecting priority sectors is the use of intra-APEC trade intensities. By selecting industries that are primarily traded within the APEC region, it is possible to maximise the coalitions of support necessary to achieve liberalisation and hence produce immediate successes for APEC. There are several problems with using trade intensities as a criteria for selecting priority sectors. Trade intensities are, in part, a function of existing trade impediments. Industries with high trade intensities may have low barriers and some industries might have low intensities that would increase if the barriers to trade were removed. The use of trade intensities may lead to the selection of relatively lightly protected industries for early liberalisation, which would result in the distortionary effects detailed above. A further problem with the use of trade intensities for selecting priority industries is the general absence of bilateral trade data on services.

These criteria need not be mutually exclusive. For example, the top-down approach is likely to yield the greatest economic benefits and, within that group, selecting producer services is more likely to produce the political coalitions required for reform to succeed. In addition, selecting a bundle of services in which there is a high degree of actual or potential intraregional trade, and in which other members are taking similar action, will make it easier to mobilise domestic support by pointing to complementary commitments made in other economies belonging to the same regional organisation.

Regional initiatives

Sequencing reform

In some cases APEC members could decide to take some concerted action consistent with the principles of the APEC process. One is to comment on the appropriate sequencing of reform – for example on which sectors could be chosen as a priority for liberalisation. A number of criteria could be considered for the selection of such sectors. PECC, in a report for APEC, has reviewed the relevance of the top-down, bottom-down, producer-services and regional-trade-intensities approaches. These are summarised in Box 18.1, where it is argued that combinations of these principles might be used to develop liberalisation strategies.[6]

Open club model

Another approach which could be relevant to the service sector is to choose sectors that the global processes have had little success in liberalising.

A number of authors have suggested the use of a 'club' approach to services sector liberalisation. The idea was first discussed by Snape (1996), commenting on the GATS approach to standards. The criteria are that these clubs should be open in not seeking to disadvantage outsiders, in defining explicit criteria for including new members and in actively promoting wider membership. These conditions make it more likely that regional services agreements will be liberalising.[7]

These principles suggest that any agreements on services sector liberalisation would be automatically extended to all members that meet the criteria. This idea has a couple of implications. It could, for example, mean that not all members of a regional arrangement have to sign on to services sector agreements immediately; in the case of APEC, this is the 21-x solution, although the economies among the x would ideally commit to a timetable for adopting a services agreement. It also means that 21+x is possible.

One issue is whether open club principles are consistent with GATS rules on regional approaches to liberalisation. GATS members are required to extend to all signatories the benefits of any special treatment they negotiate with a particular member. The GATS will accept regional arrangements in services trade, although any regional agreement should:

- attain substantial sectoral coverage;
- eliminate existing discriminatory measures and/or prohibit new measures; and
- not raise barriers to services trade against countries which are not parties to the regional agreement.

A regional services agreement that covers only a few sectors will not meet these criteria.[8] Of more significance may be the adoption of regional arrangements to deal with issues which are complementary to the GATS. One example is mutual recognition arrangements on standards relevant to services transactions.

The open club principle of not seeking to disadvantage outsiders appears to be consistent with the rules of the GATS. However, it is sometimes argued that the foundation members of a club will always try to negotiate arrangements that best suit themselves. Countries that join later will always be at a disadvantage. The important contribution that higher level organisations, such as APEC, could make to AFTA and CER could be to vet agreements negotiated by subgroups. Non-members could comment on the conditions of membership even if they did not plan to join immediately. In the process, non-members could be invited to offer a schedule for joining the club.

The application of this approach has been illustrated by reference to air transport[9] and to shipping services (Choi, Kim and Findlay 1997).

Economic and technical cooperation

We have noted already the scope to apply the processes of collective action in APEC to the reporting process in the IAPs as it applies to services. A further feature of APEC is its program of economic and technical cooperation.[10] Briefly, this program can be interpreted as a series of collective activities in APEC designed to promote the implementation of the commitments that lead to the liberalisation and facilitation goals. It includes activities to help reduce the costs of implementation of new policy arrangements and avoid bottlenecks to future growth, which might also impede the process of liberalisation. It also includes the development of new institutions which complement the liberalisation process. Examples include systems of competition policy or prudential control.

Prudential control will be important in dealing with issues that arise as financial markets are opened to foreign banks or other foreign-owned institutions. This form of domestic regulation is designed to achieve particular levels of safety or service quality in the services sector. According to Article VI of the GATS, forms of domestic regulation should be operated in a transparent manner and should not be an impediment to market access.[11] There is considerable work to be done to implement Article VI, and collective action in APEC can make a contribution to the goals of the GATS with respect to domestic regulation.

A further set of issues relate to competition policy. Warren, Tamms and Findlay (1999) observe that reform of air transport regulation will not necessarily deal with all the issues associated with market access. Entrants face another set of barriers to essential inputs, for example airport services, and to marketing arrangements. The implication is that liberalisation, even when organised in a multilateral fashion, should be supplemented with the instruments of competition policy in order to be more likely to lead to a competitive outcome. They argue that a two-pronged approach to reform is valuable. It should deal with both market access issues and with the competition policy issues that also arise in relation to other essential inputs into the production process.

These sorts of issues are not unique to air transport. They also arise, for example, in telecommunications.[12] APEC's program of collective action can contribute to the design of new domestic competition policy instruments for these sectors and, where necessary, can develop cooperation over competition policy issues.[13]

Complementing the global programs

The members of APEC can clearly contribute to issues in the WTO process, by:

- reducing the confusion in scheduling by advocating a move towards a more clearly defined distinction between market access and national treatment;
- increasing the likelihood that all countries benefit from the GATS by pushing for the development of negotiating clusters (as already mentioned with respect to the transport sector); and
- implementing Article VI on domestic regulation (as noted above).

These structural issues in the WTO process are discussed in Chapter 19. A more specific contribution that APEC members could make relates to the development of rules on trade in professional services.

APEC professionals

There is scope for regional cooperation to develop complementary structures to the GATS for professional services.[14] The main barriers to trade in professional services relate to citizenship or nationality requirements, commercial establishment requirements and the lack of recognition of professional qualifications. Rules on establishment and nationality requirements are highlighted under the GATS by the application of principles of market access and national treatment. However, issues remain about the recognition of qualifications. At the end of May 1997, the WTO Council for Trade in Services adopted guidelines for mutual recognition agreements in the accountancy sector.

Typically, mutual recognition agreements are negotiated bilaterally. The GATS permits this exception from the non-discrimination principle. It also specifies that this approach could be applied more widely in terms of the open club model. As Snape (1996) points out, professional services is the area in which the precedent for the club approach to the liberalisation of the services sector was set in the GATS. Article VII of the GATS provides that members can recognise the qualifications of suppliers from other countries and that this might be the result of negotiation or of autonomous action. But once recognised in this way, members are obliged to allow other interested members to negotiate accession or to demonstrate that they meet the criteria. Members are also required to report their negotiations or decisions to the WTO Council for Trade in Services. Members are urged to use existing international standards or to work towards such standards.

The Accountancy Guidelines spell out how Article VII might be implemented. For example, they explain what might be included in a mutual recognition agreement and the procedure by which it might be negotiated. These guidelines are not binding and are presented to facilitate the negotiation of mutual recognition agreements by members and to facilitate the accession by non-members to such arrangements. The guidelines are not specific to accountancy and could be applied to any profession.

Strategies for APEC to accelerate the liberalisation of professional services are:

- to reiterate the relevance of the Accountancy Guidelines for its members and for all professional services;
- to endorse negotiations among members or groups of members on professional services, for example negotiations which might take place between AFTA and CER members, by accepting that the outcomes of those negotiations are part of a member's Individual Action Plan;
- to monitor the application of the accession principle to agreements already established; and
- to actively encourage parties to a mutual recognition agreement to accept new participants through the monitoring process in APEC.

CONCLUSION

This chapter has argued that significant progress in liberalising the services sector appears to be possible through the APEC process. Inspection of the IAPs of member economies reveals that significant commitments to free up the sector (including those beyond WTO commitments) are being made. Assessing the significance of these new commitments, and those already made, is a topic for further research. Implementation is yet another issue.

APEC's contributions can be classified into three areas:

1 strengthening the capacity to design and implement unilateral action;
2 constructing liberalising regional initiatives; and
3 complementing action at the global level.

APEC's approach to unilateral liberalisation can be strengthened by further cooperative action, such as developing and disseminating methodologies for adding to the information base that policymakers can use as they design reform strategies. A more comprehensive approach to listing barriers to trade in services is one way that cooperative action could facilitate liberalisation in each member economy. Another example of cooperative action suggested here is to provide support for reform in terms of building the capacity to deal with policy issues that arise during liberalisation. This is especially relevant in the financial sector but other topical examples also arise in the telecommunications sector.

In some cases APEC members could decide to take some concerted action consistent with the principles of the APEC process. One such action is to comment on the appropriate sequencing of reform, for example on which sectors could be chosen as a priority for liberalisation. A number of criteria could be considered for the selection of such sectors. This chapter outlines the top-down, bottom-down, producer-services and regional-trade-intensities approaches and argues that combinations of these principles might be used develop liberalisation strategies.

Another approach that would be particularly useful is to choose sectors with which the global processes have had some difficulty in achieving reform and in which a regional initiative can make a contribution to longer term liberalisation. In these sectors a club approach to services sector liberalisation is relevant: these clubs should be open in that they would not seek to disadvantage outsiders, would define explicit criteria for including new members and would actively promote wider membership. This chapter illustrated how this approach might be applied in two transport sectors.

There are a number of other initiatives which can strengthen the global arrangements that apply to services. One of these is the specification of GATS' commitments in a negative list format, as discussed above. Other initiatives where preliminary discussion in APEC prior to taking a position to the WTO processes would be helpful include the following:

- reducing the confusion in scheduling by advocating a move towards a more clearly defined distinction between market access and national treatment; and
- increasing the likelihood that all countries will benefit from the GATS by pushing for the development of negotiating clusters.

This chapter also noted the scope in APEC to make progress on the implementation of GATS processes and procedures which could be applied to professional services.

APPENDIX 18.1: SUMMARY OF THE KEY FEATURES IN SELECTED SECTORS OF THE SERVICES AND INVESTMENT COMPONENTS OF THE 1998 INDIVIDUAL ACTION PLANS[15]

Services

Financial Services

Australia introduced a new regulatory system for the financial services industry.

Canada will develop a new framework for the entry of foreign banks into Canada, which will allow direct branching by foreign banks.

Hong Kong, China conducted a review and implemented improvements to its monetary, futures and securities markets.

Indonesia made a commitment to relax limitations on branching of foreign banks.

Japan substantially improved commitments from the 1995 level including developments such as the Foreign Exchange and Foreign Trade Control Law. It enacted a reform bill that will see greater liberalisation in the securities and asset management industries and the completion of its financial reform by 2001.

Malaysia is allowing an increase in foreign equity participation in the insurance sector and will issue six new licences for life reinsurance business by 2005.

The ***Philippines*** increased foreign participation in investment houses and finance companies to 60 per cent.

Singapore set up two committees to review its policies for the financial sector, with the objective of ensuring its long-term competitiveness. This includes an examination of policies towards regulating and developing the sector, so as to foster new growth areas.

Chinese Taipei is raising foreign equity in securities company to 25 per cent and is permitting foreign investment in foreign exchange brokerage firms.

Thailand allowed foreign shareholdings of 100 per cent in financial institutions for ten years.

The ***United States*** will eliminate existing reservations against new entrants or expansion of existing foreign companies in its financial sector.

Telecommunications

Australia sold one-third of Telstra Corporation (its national telecommunications carrier).

Brunei has implemented its commitments under its schedule for the WTO Agreement on Basic Telecommunications Services.

Canada has started the elimination of the remaining monopolies and the liberalisation of the provision of international services and satellite services, including measures with regard to foreign ownership, under the Terms of the WTO Agreement on Basic Telecommunications Services.

Chile signed the Fourth Protocol to the GATS on Telecommunication Services.

Hong Kong, China implemented GATS commitments to open up the market for, and accorded national treatment to, foreign suppliers of local basic and various international telecommunications services and also advanced the end date of the exclusive licence in certain external telecommunications services and circuits.

Japan abolished the limitations on foreign capital participation in all Type 1 telecommunications carriers (except for NTT), including the ones for radio licences.

Korea raised the limit on foreign ownership of wire and wireless facility-based basic telecom service providers to 49 per cent from 33 per cent in 1998.

Malaysia increased foreign equity in basic telecommunications companies to 61 per cent for a period of five years.

Papua New Guinea corporatised the telecommunication sector with the establishment of three separate corporate entities.

The *Philippines* privatised Luzon telecommunications and eighteen public calling sites.

Singapore gave out one more PBTS licence and one more PCMTS licence in April 1998. These are to commence operations on 1 April 2000. Singapore will grant more public basic telecommunications services (PBTS) licences from 1 April 2002 as demand allows.

Chinese Taipei opened licence applications for satellite communication services and is raising foreign investment in basic telecommunications companies (except Chung Hwa Telekom) up to 60 per cent, with direct investment not exceeding 20 per cent.

Thailand approved the Telecommunications Master Plan, and is focusing on liberalisation, the establishment of a regulatory body, and the privatisation of the two state enterprises.

Energy

In *Australia* agreement was reached in November 1997 on a national industry-specific regulatory framework for third-party access to natural gas pipelines.

China approved an additional seven foreign-funded power projects by the end of 1997, and will encourage greater foreign participation in power generation, coal, drilling and exploration of oil and natural gas.

Japan abolished the certification system of gasoline suppliers in January 1998.

In *Korea* foreign participation in individual power producer (IPP) operations was allowed as of 1 January 1998. This will allow large-scale consumers to import natural gas for their own use from 2001. Korea will privatise the Korean Gas Corporation in 2001.

The **Philippines** will restructure the entire electricity supply and privatise the National Power Corporation.

Thailand is promoting competition in the generation of electricity by promoting private investment under the IPP program, the SPP program and the privatisation of government-owned power.

Transportation

Australia sold 99-year leases for fourteen airports and also sold Federal Government-owned rail operations (the Australian National Railways Commission). It abolished cabotage on Christmas Island trade and most cruise shipping.

Brunei concluded an open skies agreement with the United States and an air services agreement with New Zealand. The number of representative offices, branches and joint-venture foreign transport enterprises has increased.

Korea raised the limit on foreign equity holdings for aviation services from 20 per cent to not more than 50 per cent.

New Zealand and the **United States** concluded open bilateral air services agreements with APEC economies.

Chinese Taipei is planning to lift the one-half ratio limitation on foreign equity holdings and increase the number of foreign directors on the boards of airfreight forwarding and off-airport air cargo terminal services companies.

Thailand will remove MFN exemptions in maritime transport under the GATS by 2005 and consider removal of limitations on market access in maritime transport. It will also allow foreign operators to operate non-scheduled air services as well as aircraft and maintenance services.

Professional Services

Japan relaxed regulations on 'gaikokuho-jimu-bengoshi' (foreign lawyers qualified by Japanese law) relating to requirements on practicing experience and lifted the ban on practicing third-country law.

Korea is considering amending regulations regarding the admission of foreign certified practising accountants (CPAs) and easing other regulations in order to enhance transparency of accounting practices.

Singapore removed the requirement that at least two-thirds of the shares in limited liability architectural and engineering corporations be held by registered architects and engineers respectively.

Chinese Taipei allowed foreign lawyers to be attorneys of foreign legal affairs and to independently practice the law of their home jurisdiction or international law.

Other Services

Other areas where specific liberalisation measures are mentioned include distribution services in **Korea** and **China,** audio-visual services in **Hong Kong, China**, tourism services in **China**, environmental services in **China** and **Japan,** and construction and education services in **Korea.**

Investment

Australia has removed the prohibitions on takeovers by foreign interests of the four major domestic banks.

Indonesia reduced to sixteen the number of business sectors in the 'Negative Investment List' that are totally closed for investment and to nine the sectors that are closed to foreign investment.

Korea liberalised thirteen business sectors in 1998 and reduced the number of businesses restricted to foreign investment to 31 out of 1,148 sectors. Restrictions on foreign ownership of land were abolished.

Malaysia allowed foreign equity ownership of 100 per cent in manufacturing projects from July 1998 till the end of 2000, without any export requirements imposed.

The *Philippines* has delisted private domestic construction contracts from the negative list, effectively increasing foreign equity participation from 40 per cent to 100 per cent.

Singapore acceded to the Multilateral Investment Guarantee Agency (MIGA) Convention and is putting in place a more disclosure-based regulatory system.

Thailand has allowed majority foreign ownership in promoted projects subject to the agreement of shareholders.

APPENDIX 18.2: ACTIONS IN SPECIFIC AREAS – SERVICES: EXTRACT FROM THE OSAKA ACTION AGENDA

Telecommunications

APEC economies will:

a conform, where appropriate, to the Guidelines for Trade in International Value-Added Network Services (IVANS) by 1998;
b generally conform, where appropriate, to the Guidelines for Harmonisation of Equipment Certification in the immediate term;
c continue to work jointly to harmonise administrative procedures governing certification of customer telecommunications equipment; and
d develop and begin to implement on an elective basis a model Mutual Recognition Arrangement on conformity assessment by the end of 1997.

Transportation

APEC economies will:

a promote the implementation of International Civil Aviation Organisation and International Maritime Organisation standards, regulations and safety measures;

b complete the Transportation Road Transport Harmonisation Project and encourage the development of mutual recognition arrangements for road vehicles;

c encourage involvement in dialogue with the United Nations Economic Commission for Europe and strive to move towards harmonisation of road vehicle regulations within an appropriate international forum;

d examine the possibility of taking appropriate steps to facilitate privatisation or corporatisation of transportation infrastructure projects;

e after completing, in 1995, Phase II of the Transportation Electronic Data Interchange Study identifying barriers to transportation industry use of Electronic Data Interchange, initiate a pilot Electronic Data Interchange trial program, and determine the future direction of the adoption of Electronic Data Interchange as widely as possible throughout the transport sector in the region; and

f seek to eliminate, as soon as practicable within the next ten years, the requirement for paper documents (both regulatory and institutional) for the key messages relevant to international transport and trade.

Energy

APEC economies will facilitate investment in the energy sector by:

a identifying, by the end of 1996, institutional, regulatory and procedural impediments that affect investment in electricity infrastructure;

b developing, by the end of 1996, a guidance framework to facilitate investment;

c developing, by the end of 1999, coordinated solutions to more complex issues based on the outcomes of the above activities, and extending these activities to other aspects of the energy supply chain where appropriate; and

d considering, in the long-term, issues associated with facilitating transborder infrastructure and the financing thereof;

APEC economies will accept equivalence in accreditation and increase harmonisation of energy standards by:

a establishing, by the end of 1996, the basis for the mutual recognition of testing protocols and the accreditation of laboratories, and the acceptance of the test results arising from them;

b reaching, by the end of 1999, agreement on the mutual recognition of testing protocols and the accreditation of laboratories, and the acceptance of the test results arising from them; and

c extending, in the long-term, work on energy standards to specific products starting from domestic appliances and going on to selected items of industrial and commercial equipment.

Tourism

APEC economies will identify impediments to tourism growth and formulate strategies that will improve tourism movements and investment in the Asia-Pacific region.

NOTES

Some sections of this paper are updates from Findlay and Warren (1998). An earlier version was presented at the Kobe University and Australian National University joint seminar, 'Australia, Japan and APEC', 19 January 1999.

1   Quoted from material on <http://www.apecsec.org.sg/virtualib/econlead/osaka.html> (accessed 30 May 1999).
2   More detail is available at the APEC Secretariat Website from which this text was extracted. See <www.apecsec.org.sg/97brochure.html#Osaka> (accessed 30 May 1999).
3   These guidelines are found at <http://www.apecsec.org.sg/apec_organization/policy_procedure/iap/iap_format_guide.html> (accessed 5 August 1999).
4   Each year the collective actions in each of the areas of the Osaka Action Agenda are summarised and reported to ministers. For more details, see <http://www.apecsec. org.sg/cti98/1998cit.html> (accessed 30 May 1999).
5   There is also a qualification to the significance of this criteria where protection is provided in the form of volume constraints. See Vousden (1990) for a review of literature on the sequencing of reform in the presence of quantitative trade restrictions. For example, there are no offsets to the welfare gains to reform within the services sector when all impediments take the form of quantitative restrictions and where all the substitutes for the reforming sectors are also protected by quantitative restrictions.
6   Implementation of these strategies is a separate question. Attempts in the Early Voluntary Sectoral Liberalisation initiative to take concerted action in a number of merchandise sectors (on an MFN basis) in APEC did not produce specific commitments from a sufficient number of members but instead led to the sectors chosen to be referred to the WTO.
7   A set of generally applicable criteria for open clubs to facilitate trade or investment among groups of economies was first proposed by Drysdale, Elek and Soesastro (1998).
8   However, air transport, which we discuss below, may be a special case because of its current exclusion from the GATS.
9   See Findlay, Chia and Singh (1997). The specification of the open club approach was elaborated by Andrew Elek, Christopher Findlay, Paul Hooper and Tony Warren in a submission to the Productivity Commission. Subsequently, at least in its draft report, the Commission endorsed this approach as one of a portfolio of measures for liberalisation in this sector.
10 According to a summary statement on economic and technical cooperation at the APEC Internet site, APEC Economic Leaders committed in Osaka to 'promote action-oriented economic and technical cooperation in a wide range of areas' towards realising the APEC goals of promoting trade and investment liberalisation in the region, narrowing disparities in the region, and achieving growth and prosperity of the region as a whole. To achieve this, member economies will 'work through policy dialogues and joint activities to broaden and deepen intra-regional cooperation' in the various areas of economic and technical cooperation.

APEC's Economic and Technical Cooperation Agenda provides the avenues by which economies can cooperate in the formulation and conduct of joint activities in the areas of research, data and information sharing, surveys, training programs, seminars, technical demonstrations, exchange of experts, technology sharing and transfer, establishment of research and business networks, and many other undertakings that promote the effective use of the region's resources and increase the effectiveness of policy measures. See <(http://www.apecsec.org.sg/virtualib/history/mapa/vol4/ vol4int.html> (accessed 30 May 1999).

11 For details of the text of this article, see the text of the GATS at <http://www.wto.org/wto/ services/2-obdis.htm> (accessed 30 May 1999). Issues of prudential control are dealt with explicitly in the annex on financial services (see <http://www.wto.org/wto/services/10-anfin.htm>, accessed 30 May 1999).

12 Issues involved in the liberalisation of telecommunications are examined in Chua (1998).

13 The collective work on services in APEC is coordinated by the Group on Services (GOS) whose work plan can be inspected at <http://www.apecsec.org.sg/cti/cti97/iva2-2.html> (accessed 30 May 1999). Collective actions by this group at the time of writing included ongoing work on exchanging information on arrangements for services trade and investment, analysis of services commitments in the IAPs, compilation of data on services trade, work to understand the impact of liberalisation, development and adoption of common professional standards, and monitoring of the WTO's work on services.

14 The following paragraphs are based on discussions in Warren and Findlay (1997).

15 Edited from the SOM Chair's summary report of the 1998 IAPs (dated 13/11/98), <http://www.apecsec.org.sg/iap/98/iap98.html> (APEC Internet site, accessed 30 May 1999). These are the SOM Chair's views on the highlights of the services and investment commitments.

19 The WTO agenda: next steps

Richard Snape

INTRODUCTION

That a General Agreement on Trade in Services (GATS) was secured in the Uruguay Round of multilateral trade negotiations was a major achievement. There was considerable opposition from several key developing countries to including services trade in these negotiations at all. Agreement to include them was secured only by having the services negotiations on a different track from the GATT-based negotiations, with the negotiations strictly not being between contracting parties to the GATT, but between trade ministers representing their governments. The negotiations were serviced by the GATT Secretariat following GATT procedures and practices. The distinction between the two tracks became blurred over time, particularly after the midterm review (Croome 1995).

While the GATT essentially concentrates on cross-border trade of goods, the GATS extends its coverage to all forms of trading services, or of obtaining access to foreign markets. It also explicitly encompasses regulations relating to access that do not discriminate against (or for) foreigners as such.

The question then arises as to whether trade liberalisation under the GATS would be more successful if its coverage were limited to that of the GATT – cross-border trade and measures that discriminate between domestic and foreign suppliers (between 'us' and 'them'). This would then leave measures that regulate access but do not discriminate between us and them – other aspects of competition policy, investment, and movement of people – to separate negotiations. In all these areas the negotiations could cover both goods and services; the relevant principles generally apply to both.

This chapter addresses with respect to both the GATT and the GATS the question of gaining access to foreign markets, the barriers to this access, the principles of product coverage and the extent of actual coverage, and the lessons that may be drawn.

Gaining access to foreign markets

Access to foreign markets can be achieved in many ways: by trade across frontiers, production in the foreign market, licensing foreign production, and franchising.

The point has been made many times that, while most goods can be traded at arm's length so that there is no need for the producer and consumer of the good to be in physical proximity, this is not the case for many services (Bhagwati 1984; Sampson and Snape 1985). Of course, some goods do not travel: ready-mixed concrete and soufflés are two examples. And many services can be traded when the parties to the transaction are at a considerable distance from each other: all those services that can be traded through the electronic media and post, and the 'servicing' of goods are examples.[1] Nevertheless, the option of arm's-length trading between the parties to a transaction is much more commonly available in goods trade than in services trade.

Because of this, those governments that were pressing for GATT-type rules to be developed for services pressed for all modes of supply to be covered by services agreement: not only cross-border trade but also 'commercial presence' and the movement of service consumers and of people to supply services.[2] The GATT itself has very little direct relevance to commercial presence or investment.[3] The one relevant provision relates to trade-related investment measures – that is, investment requirements tied to the cross-border trade in goods. These provisions received modest attention in the trade-related investment measures (TRIMs) agreement of the Uruguay Round. The GATT has no provisions relating to the movement of people whether as consumers or producers.

Barriers to foreign markets

Barriers to market access by foreigners can be imposed in many ways. First, they can be imposed at the frontier – tariff and non-tariff barriers, regulations relating to establishing a foreign commercial presence and foreign investment (and to disestablishment and disinvestment), exchange controls and other restrictions on the transfer of funds, restrictions on the movement of people and their ability to visit or work in foreign countries, and so on. Second, barriers can be imposed internally, in the form of differential regulations or taxes imposed on foreign producers or products. Both these forms of barriers discriminate against foreigners, and in many cases the distinction between frontier and internal is quite blurred, for example in some services such as beamed transmissions from abroad.

Third, foreign access can also be impeded in ways that do not in themselves discriminate against foreigners, but that impede all access whether it be by local or by foreign suppliers. These non-discriminatory barriers – non-discriminatory with respect to the nationality or the residence of the suppliers – fall under the heading of national competition policy where this term is interpreted broadly to embrace not only restrictive trade practices by firms but legislated barriers to entry to an activity as well as government regulation of access to essential facilities where 'natural monopoly' elements are present.

Table 19.1 summarises the broad coverage of the GATT and the GATS with respect to rules constraining the imposition of barriers to access, encompassing the modes by which access to markets may be secured, and the point and manner at which access may be denied for each mode. As in

Table 19.1 Coverage of GATT and GATS

Access barrier	Form of market access		
	Cross-border	Investment/commercial presence	Movement of people
GATT			
Discrimination against foreigners			
Frontier	(1) Main focus of GATT: MFN, proscription of quotas, etc.	(4) Covered by GATT only when related to cross-border trade	(7) No
Internal	(2) GATT national treatment	(5) No	(8) No
Barrier to both nationals and foreigners	(3) Little in GATT[a]	(6) No	(9) No
GATS			
Discrimination against foreigners			
Frontier	(1) Yes (including MFN, etc., and national treatment)	(4) Yes (including MFN, etc., and national treatment)	(7) Yes (including MFN, etc., and national treatment)
Internal	(2) Yes (including national treatment, market access and business practices)	(5) Yes (including national treatment, market access and business practices)	(8) Yes (including national treatment, market access and business practices)
Barriers to both nationals and foreigners	(3) Yes Market-access monopoly and business practices	(6) Yes Market-access monopoly and business practices	(9) Yes Market-access monopoly and business practices

Note:
a Non-violation nullification or impairment (Article XXIII) has relevance.

the previous two paragraphs, a distinction is made between measures that discriminate between domestic and foreign supplies and those that limit supplies or suppliers from all sources. In the former category a distinction is also made between those measures that are applied at the frontier and those that are applied internally. Both the GATT and the GATS also have provisions that apply to discrimination among foreign suppliers (MFN and exceptions to it), but this form of discrimination is not included in the table. The first part of Table 19.1 applies this taxonomy to goods trade and to the GATT. The first two cells are of primary importance in the GATT. Thus in cell 1, the GATT proscribes all non-tariff frontier barriers as a general rule, with exceptions in certain circumstances. For cell 2, the national treatment article of the GATT is of primary relevance. There is little relevance to cell 3 in the GATT, though the non-violation provisions of the nullification or impairment article (see Hoekman and Mavroidis 1994) are at least of potential application. For cell 4, provisions relating to investment are covered by the GATT only to the extent that regulations governing international trade are tied to investment, as noted above. The GATT is not directly relevant to the other cells of the table.

As mentioned above, the distinction between a frontier and non-frontier barrier is often quite unclear for services trade. In part reflecting this, the GATS concept of national treatment does not draw on a distinction between frontier and internal but embraces all policies that might discriminate between domestic and foreign suppliers (by all means of supply). (In contrast, the national treatment article of the GATT is headed 'National Treatment on Internal Taxation and Regulation'.) National treatment in the GATS requires that 'each Member shall accord to services and service suppliers of any other Member, in respect of all measures affecting the supply of services, treatment no less favourable than it accords its own like services and services suppliers' (Article XVII: 1). If left at that, it would imply no discrimination at all against foreigners in all services – unlike national treatment in the GATT with respect to goods. But this liberality is conditioned by the first part of the same sentence in the article: 'in the sectors inscribed in its schedule, and subject to any conditions and qualifications set out therein'. Thus any form of discrimination against foreigners is in fact allowable, provided it is scheduled and does not discriminate among foreign sources of supply.

But that is not the end of the matter, for the principal demandeurs in the services negotiations were concerned with barriers to access that would apply to all suppliers whether they discriminated against foreigners or not. These barriers may be imposed by governments (e.g. legislated barriers to entry to an activity) or by the owners of 'natural monopolies' (whether they be government owners or not) or may be caused by other restrictive trade practices engaged in by enterprises. To address these other forms of barriers to market access, there is a 'market-access' article (Article XVI), and articles covering monopolies and exclusive service suppliers (Article VIII) and business practices (Article IX).

The market-access article provides that '[w]ith respect to market access through … [all] modes of supply … each Member shall accord services and service suppliers of another Member treatment no less favourable than that provided for under the terms, limitations and conditions agreed and specified in its schedule'. This article then partly overlaps the national treatment provisions, for national treatment covers any form of discrimination against foreign supplies. This overlap is a source of some confusion (Hoekman 1995: 347). But the provisions of the market-access article extend beyond those of national treatment to measures that restrict access but that do not discriminate against foreigners as such (Hoekman 1995: 334; Snape and Bosworth 1996). In this regard they extend into what, on a broad definition of the term, is part of competition policy – that part which relates to government regulation of competition in specific service sectors. The article relating to monopolies and exclusive service suppliers provides that monopoly suppliers (or exclusive service suppliers) should not be allowed by a member to 'act in a manner inconsistent with that Member's obligations' under the agreement, and that where a monopoly supplier is competing outside the scope of its monopoly, the member should ensure that the monopoly 'does not abuse its monopoly position to act in its territory in a manner inconsistent' with the member's obligations under the GATS. The 'business practices' article contains very weak provisions – consultation and information – regarding business practices that may restrict competition and trade.

Like national treatment, the market-access and monopoly provisions apply only to the service sectors for which specific obligations have been undertaken. (The monopoly provisions also relate to non-discrimination among foreigners.) The market-access article also contains provisions that constrain the use of a number of quantitative restrictions on supply for all service sectors for which specific commitments are undertaken, and which, with one exception (this relating to foreign capital), appear to apply equally to national and foreign suppliers.[4]

Thus these three articles (and particularly the market-access and monopolies articles) take the GATS well beyond the provisions of the GATT with respect to barriers to supply that do not discriminate against foreign suppliers as such. The GATT is almost entirely concerned with relations between us and them; these provisions of the GATS are not concerned with us and them but between 'some of us' on the one hand and 'the rest of us and them' on the other.

Barriers to access can be applied directly – that is, on the product or service itself – or through the means of transacting, or through the means of payment for the transaction. For cross-border trade in goods, air, sea, rail, or road transport is essential. Means to pay for the products is also essential. In the above discussion, I have focused on direct rather than indirect barriers. Barriers to means of transport or means of payment are indirect barriers to trade in goods. Similarly, barriers to these forms of transport, and to payment, also provide indirect barriers to trade in services as well as being direct barriers to the trade in transport or financial services in themselves. In addition, barriers to access to electronic transmission facilities also provide barriers to the cross-frontier 'transport' of services as well as being barriers to telecommunications and other services in themselves. Viewed in this way telecommunications is just another form of transportation, though one that is particularly important for cross-border trade in services.

Transport services receive little attention in the GATT, apart from the national treatment provisions requiring that internal transportation charges should not discriminate against foreigners (Article III: 4), and provisions requiring freedom of transit for goods. Transport by air, sea, and basic telecommunications has proved to be a particularly difficult area for negotiation under the GATS and within regional trade agreements also, as have financial services.

PRODUCT COVERAGE

As Table 19.1 illustrates, the coverage of the GATS is in principle very much broader than the GATT. In this sense it is a more general agreement. But this breadth of coverage has been secured at a cost in terms of the ease by which particular service sectors can be excluded from the major provisions of the GATS. Under the GATT all products are covered by the general provisions, and exclusion of products from such coverage occurs only in special circumstances (e.g. the waivers for many agricultural products that were secured by the United States and European countries). Under the GATS, however, many of the most important provisions apply only to the service sectors specified in the schedules of members and, unlike the GATT, even the MFN principle can be implemented, in the first instance, on a conditional rather than an unconditional basis for specific measures. From this perspective the GATS is a much less general agreement than the GATT.

For the purpose of scheduled commitments for 'products' under the GATS, services have been divided into 161 sectors, for example legal, data-processing, research and development on natural sciences, real estate on a fee or contract basis, advertising, photographic, postal, rail transport, cargohandling, and so on. Specific commitments are recorded in members' schedules for these sectors; if a sector is not scheduled, there are no restrictions on the forms or extent of the barriers to market access that can be maintained or imposed on that sector.

Any measure restricting access to service markets must be non-discriminatory between foreign member suppliers unless it was listed as an exemption to non-discrimination at the time the agreement came into force. This date was 1 January 1995 but, because negotiations were extended beyond that date for many key sectors, the date was extended for these sectors. Such exemptions from unconditional MFN treatment do not exist under the GATT.[5] Under the GATS they are to be reviewed after no more than five years and 'in principle' are to continue for no more than ten years.

Thus as far as MFN is concerned, the GATS applies a negative-listing approach; all measures for all sectors are covered unless specifically exempted, and then in principle only for a limited time. On the other hand the national treatment and market-access provisions are on a positive list basis with respect to sectoral coverage; sectors are not covered unless they are listed. Once listed, however, a mainly negative-listing approach is adopted with respect to national treatment. Under the national treatment provisions there can be no discrimination against foreign supplies except in the manners specified for the scheduled sectors.

Under the market-access article, access (for each mode of supply) is to be no less favourable than specified in members' schedules – a positive-listing approach. And for those sectors for which market-access commitments are undertaken (positive listing), a number of quantitative restrictions are prohibited unless scheduled (negative listing). The list of quantitative restrictions is not exhaustive (Hoekman 1995: 339); any other restrictions on access would have to be constrained on a positive-list basis.

The positive-listing approach to any constraint on restrictions on barriers is in part the price for the coverage of all modes of delivery. It is also due to the complexity of regulations in some service sectors – for example, telecommunications and financial services – and the protection of turf by regulators. But it greatly inhibits the transparency of the barriers that exist for services trade; this may be contrasted with the North American Free Trade Agreement (NAFTA) and the Closer Economic Relations (CER) agreement between Australia and New Zealand, both of which adopt a negative-listing approach. (In regard to positive and negative listing of sectors, the experience of the Canada–US Free Trade Agreement, which had positive listing, as well as the GATS negotiations, influenced the negotiations for NAFTA (Hoekman and Sauvé 1994; Snape and Bosworth 1996).) If a sector or a part of a sector is not scheduled, then there is no disclosure at all with respect to the barriers to trade in that sector or sub-sector.

The possibility of MFN exemptions together with the positive listing of sectors and the practice of scheduling commitments by mode of supply for each sector (which, as Sauvé 1995b and Hoekman 1995: 351 state, is not actually required by the GATS) introduces a very strong sectoral bias to the negotiations under the GATS. Sector-specific reciprocity, and even mode-of-supply sector-specific reciprocity is encouraged. The sectoral trade-offs which can remove major stumbling blocks are particularly difficult to secure when negotiations are sector-specific. Sector-specific negotiations are highly susceptible to being blocked or distorted (e.g. to favour one mode of delivery over another) by vested interests (including regulators) who are able to mount effective campaigns designed to focus attention on the costs to the particular sector or mode of trade liberalisation, rather than the gains to other sectors, and to the economy in general, of such reforms. The difficulties here have been accentuated by the stand-alone sector-specific negotiations that have extended into 1997.

On the other hand, the inclusion of particularly difficult sectors in cross-sectoral negotiations can impede liberalisation in other sectors – the exclusion of much of agriculture, and textiles and clothing from general GATT coverage and negotiations facilitated progress in liberalisation in other areas. The difficult nuts of agriculture, and textiles and clothing were only cracked in the context of negotiations much broader than those previously undertaken under GATT auspices, in the Uruguay Round. The optimum bundling of issues for successful negotiations – providing opportunities for trade-offs on the one hand and avoiding stumbling blocks on the other – is touched on by Goldstein (1997).

Quite apart from the sector-specific nature of the negotiations, trade-offs are inherently more difficult to negotiate in services than goods (Hoekman 1995). First, tariffs on goods provide a continuum for negotiation – a 60 per cent tariff is negotiable to all levels between 60 and 0. But barriers to trade in services, which are seldom in a price-based form comparable to tariffs on goods, are less quantifiable and are often subject to significant bureaucratic interpretation. They are frequently embedded in domestic regulations that restrict domestic as well as foreign access and often are justified on grounds such as consumer rather than producer protection. A second, and related point, is that some demandeurs in services are addressing negotiated reciprocity not in terms of the extent of market opening, as has been the tradition in GATT negotiations, but in terms of market openness. This interpretation of reciprocity places a particularly heavy political-economy burden on countries with closed service markets.

NEGOTIATIONS AND COMMITMENTS

While securing a services agreement was an achievement, the progress in actually liberalising services trade under the auspices of the GATS has been very limited to date.[6] Little more than limited standstill commitments within sectors already open has been achieved even by those countries making significant commitments, though for some countries the telecommunications agreement, which was concluded in February 1997, involved significant commitments to market opening.

Most developed countries have made sectoral commitments in more than 70 sectors while the United States, members of the European Union (EU), Japan, Switzerland, and Austria have made commitments for more than 100 sectors, as compared with a maximum of around 150.[7] Transition economies made commitments in about half of all sectors, with developing countries only 16 per cent (Low 1995; Altinger and Enders 1996, Tables 19.2, 19.3). (These data and those in the next paragraph predate the conclusions of the telecommunications and financial services agreements.)

These overall sectoral commitment numbers are poor indicators of the coverage of services production. To illustrate the limited extent of the coverage of commitments, reference can be made to Australia, not because it is out of step in its commitments, but simply because calculations have been made at the Productivity Commission of the production coverage of its commitments.

Australia has made commitments in more than 80 sectors. But it has been estimated that prior to the telecommunications agreement only one-fifth of its total production of services was covered by liberalising obligations – bound commitments not to maintain non-conforming measures – and these commitments are biased heavily toward services already relatively open (IC 1995b: 189–214).[8] Major sectors – at least some of which are known to have highly restrictive trade measures – were excluded from Australia's schedule, or subject to unbound commitments. Other countries' schedules have similar characteristics.

Analysis of GATS schedules for the combined economies of the Asia-Pacific Economic Cooperation (APEC) grouping indicates that well over two-thirds of possible service markets – defined as each mode of supply in each service sector in each APEC economy – may be impeded (APEC 1995: 72). Cross-border supply is the least restricted mode of supply within APEC economies as a group, while the presence of natural persons is the most constrained mode of supply.

When the WTO and hence the GATS came into operation on 1 January 1995, negotiations were largely incomplete in the key areas of telecommunications, financial services, maritime transport and the movement of natural persons.[9] A timetable was established for extending these negotiations.

The results of the financial services agreement – concluded on 28 July 1995 with an interim agreement and then only after a one-month extension – were unsatisfactory. The United States insisted that offers from other countries were inadequate, and invoked an MFN exemption for the entire financial services sector, refusing to join the interim agreement, though leaving its offer on the table. Twenty-nine countries (counting the EU as one) of the 76 WTO members that made commitments in the financial services sector improved their offers during the extended negotiations and became members of the interim agreement.[10] Although some concessions were made to relax foreign equity participation and operational restrictions, these remain well below those needed to open financial markets significantly. Most developing countries still have not scheduled all their financial services sectors, and thus many elements of financial services remain completely unbound.

Negotiations on the movement of natural persons, aimed at achieving better temporary entry of senior executives and professionals supplying services, also concluded unsatisfactorily on 28 July 1995. There are no plans to resume them.

Negotiations on basic telecommunications, initially due to conclude on 30 April 1996, were suspended in June of that year but then were brought to a successful conclusion in February 1997. The suspension occurred when the United States claimed that only ten out of the thirty-four country offers presented were acceptable, the United States being particularly concerned with 'one-way bypass' or the ability of a monopoly supplier in another country to exploit the competitive conditions in the US market to secure monopoly returns on the traffic between the United States and its own country (Hoekman, Low and Mavroidis 1996). But with some significantly improved offers, 69 countries, embracing over 90 per cent of the basic telecommunications business of WTO members, reached an agreement, which was implemented in 1998.

A set of regulatory principles (including the establishment of independent regulators, terms for interconnection, and promises not to engage in anticompetitive cross-subsidisation) were agreed, as were commitments to significant market opening by many countries. For some countries, including those of the EU, the United States and Australia, the commitments largely involved the locking in of competition reforms that had already been implemented or announced. But others, including the Philippines, Thailand and Singapore, made significant new commitments. Several developing countries and the United States lodged exceptions to MFN, the latter with respect to direct-to-home transmission and digital broadcasting by satellite.

No agreement on maritime transport services was achieved by the deadline of 30 June 1996. Negotiations were suspended until 2000 when a further round of comprehensive negotiations on trade in services was scheduled to commence. Of the 42 governments participating in the negotiations, only 24 (including the EU as a single entity) tabled offers. The United States refused to make an offer in the negotiations.

LESSONS?

It is arguable that the GATS is too general in one dimension – modes of delivery and forms of barrier to access – and not general enough in another – obligations. It is arguable also that reducing the former dimension of generality could increase what could be achieved in the latter.

Breadth of coverage: investment, competition policy and people

International investment and competition policy (including under this latter heading government-legislated barriers to entry, provision of access to essential facilities, and regulation of restrictive trade practices) have proved to be particularly difficult areas for multilateral negotiation of binding commitments, and even difficult within the relative homogeneity of the Organisation for Economic Cooperation and Development (OECD). Yet both of these subjects are embraced by the GATS. In many respects the problems to be addressed in investment and competition policies are not specific to services trade but are as applicable to goods trade as to services trade. Probably they are both more amenable to negotiation as separate agreements under the WTO, covering goods as well as services trade, rather than as parts of goods or services agreements. The movement of people also is probably best left to separate negotiations, involving as it does much broader social and political questions than are generally addressed in trade negotiations.

These excisions would then leave for services trade negotiations the same topics that are covered by the GATT – cross-border trade and measures that discriminate between domestic and foreign suppliers (between us and them). Thus referring to the lower panel in Table 19.1, the GATS would cover cells 1, 2, and, to the same extent as the GATT, cell 4; an investment agreement would cover cells 4 and 5 in both parts of the table, the movement of people would cover cells 7 and 8, while a competition policy agreement (covering government regulations and enterprise behaviour) would embrace cells 3, 6 and 9.

The reduction of coverage to measures that discriminate between domestic and foreign suppliers (and among foreign suppliers) would imply the removal of the market-access and other competition policy articles from the GATS. (The introduction of a nullification and impairment article similar to Article XXIII of the GATT could be introduced to cope with government actions intended to frustrate liberalisation commitments.) The market-access article does not appear to add anything to the provisions of the national treatment article insofar as discrimination between foreign and domestic supplies is concerned, and removing it would remove an overlap and confusion with respect to these discriminatory measures.

Breadth of coverage: difficult sectors

As noted, there are two major areas in which the obligations under the GATS are less general and binding than under the GATT: MFN and national treatment. MFN exceptions can be taken, and have been taken, for measures applying to major service sectors – in particular financial services, basic telecommunications, shipping and audiovisual. (The main part of air transport services is effectively excluded by an annex to the GATS itself.) Removing investment from the coverage of the GATS should facilitate multilateral agreement on those financial services that would still remain under its coverage, but for the other areas major difficulties would remain. As mentioned above, under the GATT, much of agricultural, and clothing and textiles effectively remained out of the coverage of the general rules for decades, and they returned to the fold (though this has yet to be fully tested) only in the context of the very broad trade-offs that were achieved in the Uruguay Round. So under the GATS it may take considerable time, and possibly very broad trade-offs, to secure the application of MFN to the service sectors for which broad exceptions from MFN have been taken.

This implies that financial services, telecommunications, maritime and air transport, and perhaps audiovisual services, may indeed best be negotiated separately from other services, being brought into cross-sectoral negotiations and trade-offs as part of a much broader set of negotiations than can occur under the GATS.

Cross-border trade

Perhaps more tractable, and important, is the lack of generality of national treatment and the positive listing of sectors for which specific commitments are made. As mentioned above, the lack of distinction between frontier measures and internal measures that discriminate between national and foreign supplies of services implies that full national treatment would imply free trade in services. Under the GATT, internal measures that so discriminate are proscribed; so also are all frontier measures apart from tariffs, except in stated circumstances. The effect of these proscriptions is that there is only one form of generally sanctioned discrimination against foreign suppliers – import tariffs – which then is the object of specific commitments (bindings) and negotiations. To secure national treatment as a general obligation under the GATS, a small set of sanctioned forms of discrimination against foreigners could be necessary, these being the subject of specific obligations, with national treatment as a general obligation for all other measures that would discriminate between domestic and foreign service supplies (Snape 1994; Hoekman 1995: 349–50). National treatment could then be addressed as a general obligation on a negative-list basis – all sectors would be covered and all measures that lay outside the 'sanctioned' list could be applied only if they were explicitly listed (and accepted in negotiations) as exceptions. With respect to the sanctioned exceptions, they could be addressed in the same way as tariffs under the GATT – on a positive-list basis when bindings are negotiated. This approach would be greatly facilitated if the breadth of coverage of the GATS were to be reduced as suggested above.

The key question is what these sanctioned barriers should be. For cross-border trade in many if not most services, tariff-like charges would be quite feasible (Deardorff 1994; Hoekman 1995: 349–50). Examples would be taxes on foreign television programs transmitted locally (rather than quantitative limitations), taxes on life or health insurance placed abroad (rather than prohibition), taxes on data processing undertaken abroad, and so on. Of course there may be many implementation difficulties, but generally these would be no more difficult to police than quantitative restrictions or prohibitions on cross-border trade (UNCTAD and World Bank 1994, Ch. 6).[11] But even if practical, the idea of converting all non-price measures into price measures may be too bold for all cross-border service transactions. Thus the possibility of a limited number of sanctioned non-price measures perhaps should be entertained, if that is what is required to secure negative listing for the coverage of service sectors and of non-sanctioned barriers and the advantages of relative liberalisation and transparency that would accompany such listing.

NAFTA as a model

Much of what has been suggested – other than the legitimisation of a restricted number of frontier measures – is close to what has been adopted in NAFTA.

In that agreement there are separate chapters for investment and competition policy (including monopolies and state enterprises), which cover both goods and services, for temporary movement of business persons, for telecommunications and financial services, and for cross-border trade in services. Special provisions also apply to air and maritime services. As noted above, the general approach in NAFTA to cross-border trade in services is one of negative listing, in contrast to the earlier Canada–US Free Trade Agreement. NAFTA could provide the model for a substantial recasting of the GATS when it comes up for review. What has been achieved in telecommunications and financial services could stand as separate agreements; what has been achieved in investment commitments in services could provide the basis for more general investment agreement covering goods and services. And an agreement on competition policy would provide the basis for removing the market-access article from a services agreement – there is no market-access article in NAFTA.

POSTSCRIPT: JUNE 1999

A couple of years have passed since this paper was completed. Two matters need to be addressed.

In commenting on the paper at the conference at which it was presented, Bob Baldwin made the point that a major driving force for services negotiations in the Uruguay Round was concern by potential exporters of services regarding barriers to establishment and protected local monopolies – that is, concern about foreign investment and competition policy. To take these matters out of GATS could lose the main constituency for services liberalisation in GATS.

I agree with Baldwin that this would indeed be a risk and that without an effective bundling of issues, momentum for liberalisation in a GATS context could be lost. Such a bundling would be necessary in the design of negotiations for further liberalisation.

The other matter is the failure of proposals for a multilateral agreement on investment. Not only is this proposal dead, but in many political circles it has a bad odour. Now would not be the appropriate time to unpack investment from the GATS and to attempt to negotiate an investment agreement covering both goods and services.

In view of this, it would appear better to press ahead with investment liberalisation for services as a stepping stone to a broader agreement. When investment in services production is liberalised on a broad front this could be the appropriate time for a relatively painless extension of the principles to other forms of investment.

NOTES

This chapter draws in part on Snape and Bosworth (1996). The author is grateful to Malcolm Bosworth for discussions and his contributions. He is also grateful for comments from the appointed discussants of the paper, Robert Baldwin and Ron McKinnon, and other participants at the conference it was presented at, particularly Ambassador Kesavapany, Geza Feketekuty, Frieder Roessler, Jaroslaw Pietras, David Vines, and Gary Sampson. Nothing in the chapter or in the postscript should be taken as reflecting the views of the Productivity Commission or the Australian Government. This chapter originally appeared in *The WTO as an International Organization*, edited by Anne O. Krueger with the assistance of Chonira Aturupane, and is published here with the kind permission of Chicago University Press.

1   The distinction between what is trade in a good and trade in a service is not always clear. How much transformation in a good has to occur before it becomes a new good? How long does the rental of a movie have to be before the transaction becomes one in a good rather than in a service? And so on.
2   Commercial presence and investment are not identical, and regulations distinguish between them. But a substantial commercial presence will usually require investment, and the two are treated together in this chapter.
3   Of course it has indirect relevance in so far as the existence of trade barriers influences investment-location decisions.
4   These apply to limitations on the number of service suppliers, on the value of service transactions or assets, on the total number of service operations or the quantity of service output, on the number of people employed, and on foreign capital or shareholding, and on requirements for specific types of legal entity or joint venture.
5   GATT exemptions from MFN were not possible (apart from free trade areas, customs unions, grandfathered preferences and for and between developing countries, and the non-application provisions of Article XXXV) until the Uruguay Round, when limited selectivity for Article XIX on safeguard measures was introduced.
6   This section in particular draws on Snape and Bosworth (1996).
7   This figure is less than the previously mentioned 161, as several financial sectors were combined.
8   A quarter of Australia's services production, including coastal shipping, was excluded outright from its specific GATS commitments, while those sectors scheduled for which no obligations were made to provide market access or national treatment – thereby allowing existing restrictions to continue and new ones to be introduced – represented a further 55 per cent of Australian services production. Under the telecommunications agreement, Australia committed itself to significant liberalisation policies that had already been implemented or announced.
9   The EU, largely at the insistence of the French government, excluded the audiovisual sector from MFN treatment. The EU (along with some other members) thus made no sectoral commitment in this sector, and may impose discriminating or non-discriminating measures in the entire audiovisual sector. However, it will be the subject of future negotiations.
10 These offers were implemented until 1 November 1997, after which time members had 60 days to negotiate further amendments to specific offers on financial services, or to take MFN exemptions.
11 While it is difficult to think of cross-border service transactions in which the difficulties of implementation of non-price measures are not as great as price measures, it may be easier, for example, to detect the existence of equipment that can receive foreign transmissions, and restrict or tax its installation, than it is to monitor the receipt of transmissions themselves.

References

ACA (Australian Communications Authority) (1998), *Telecommunications Performance Report 1997–98*, Melbourne: ACA.

Aigner, D.J., C.A.K. Lovell and P. Schmidt (1977) 'Formulation and estimation of stochastic frontier production function models', *Journal of Econometrics*, 6: 21–37.

Altinger, L. and A. Enders (1996) 'The scope and depth of GATS commitments', *World Economy*, 19(3), 307–32.

Angbazo, L. (1997) 'Commercial bank net interest margins, default risk, interest-rate risk, and off-balance sheet banking', *Journal of Banking and Finance*, 21: 55–87.

APEC (Asia Pacific Economic Cooperation) (1996) *Guide to the Investment Regimes of Member Economies*, Singapore: APEC Committee on Trade and Investment.

—— (1997a) *The Impact of Investment Liberalisation in APEC*, Singapore: APEC Economic Committee, November.

—— (1997b) 1997 Individual Action Plan Submissions, <http://www.apecsec.org>, Singapore.

—— (1997c) *1997 Annual Report to Ministers*, Singapore: APEC Secretariat.

—— (1998a) *Guide to the Investment Regimes of Member Economies*, Singapore: APEC Committee on Trade and Investment.

—— (1998b) 1998 Individual Action Plan submissions, Singapore, <http://www.apecsec.org>.

Areeda, P., H. Hovenkamp and J. Solow (1995) *Antitrust Law: An Analysis of Antitrust Principles and their Application*, Boston: Little, Brown and Company.

Australian International Education Foundation (AIEF) (1998) *Overseas Student Statistics 1997*, Canberra: Australian Government Publishing Service.

Baldwin, R. (1999) 'Frictional trade barriers, developing nations and a two tiered world trading system', draft paper (12 February) prepared for a Centre for Economic Policy Research conference, London.

Barth, J.R., D.E. Nolle, and T.N. Rice (1997) 'Commercial banking structure, regulation and performance: an international comparison', *Office of the Controller of the Currency (OCC) Working Paper 97–6*, March, Washington DC: OCC.

Baumol, W., J. Panzar and R. Willig (1982) *Contestable Markets and the Theory of Industry Structure*, New York: Harcourt Brace Jovanovich.

Bhagwati, J. (1984) 'Splintering and disembodiment of services and developing countries', *The World Economy*, 7(2): 133–44.

BIS (Bank for International Settlements) (1997) *Core Principles for Effective Banking Supervision*, Basle: BIS.

—— (1998) 'Tenth International Conference of Banking Supervisors', media release, 22 October.

Blomström, M. and A. Kokko (1997) 'How foreign investment affects host economies', *Policy Research Working Paper 1745*, Washington DC: World Bank, March.

Boles de Boer, D. and L. Evans (1996) 'The economic efficiency of telecommunications in a deregulated market: the case of New Zealand', *Economic Record*, 72(216): 24–35.

Bora, B. and S. Guisinger (1997) 'Impact of investment liberalisation in APEC', mimeo, Adelaide: School of Economics, Flinders University.

Bora, B., C. Findlay and T. Warren (1997) 'Potential for services and investment liberalisation between AFTA and CER', paper prepared for AFTA–CER Linkage: The Way Forward conference, Singapore: ISEAS, September.

Bosworth, M., C. Findlay, R. Trewin and T. Warren (1997) 'Measuring trade impediments to services within APEC', *The Economic Implications of Liberalizing APEC Tariff and Nontariff Barriers to Trade*, Washington DC: International Trade Commission, Publication 3101.

Bowles, D. and R. Maddock (1998) 'The supply of direct exchange lines in developing countries' in S. Macdonald and G. Madden (eds) *Telecommunications and Socio-Economic Development*, Amsterdam: Elsevier, 25–37.

Brown, D., A. Deardorff and R. Stern (1996) 'Modelling multilateral trade liberalisation in services', *Asia Pacific Economic Review*, 2(1), April, 21–34.

Brown, D., A. Deardorff, A. Fox and R. Stern (1995) 'Computational analysis of goods and services trade liberalisation in the Uruguay Round', in W. Martin and L.A. Winters (eds) *The Uruguay Round and the Developing Economies*, Discussion Paper 307, Washington DC: World Bank, 365–80.

—— (1996) 'Computational analysis of goods and services liberalisation in the Uruguay Round' in W. Martin and A. Winters (eds) *The Uruguay Round and Developing Economies*, Cambridge: Cambridge University Press.

Brueckner, J.K. and P.T. Spiller (1994) 'Economies of traffic density in the deregulated airline industry', *Journal of Law and Economics*, 87(2): 379–415.

BTCE (Bureau of Transport and Communications Economics) (1992) 'Quality of service: conceptual issues and telecommunications case study', *Report 75*, Canberra: Australian Government Publishing Service.

—— (1997) *Aerocost2 User Guide and Reference Manual,* Appendix B, Canberra: Australian Government Publishing Service.

Butz, D.A. (1993) 'Ocean shipping economics: free trade and antitrust implications', *Contemporary Policy Issue*, 11(July), 69–80.

Castle, L.V. and C. Findlay (1988) 'Introduction', in L. Castle and C. Findlay (eds) *Pacific Trade in Services*, Sydney: Allen and Unwin, 1–15.

Choi, D.-H., J. Kim and C. Findlay (1997) 'Transport services liberalisation in APEC', *Asia Pacific Economic Review*, 3(2).

Chua, J. (1998) 'Telecommunications industry in the Philippines', a paper in the series *The Impact of Liberalisation: communicating with APEC communities*, published for APEC by PECC and the APEC Study Centres Consortium, November.

Claessens, S. and T. Glaessner (1998) *The Internationalization of Financial Services in Asia*, Washington DC: World Bank.

Coelli, T. (1996) 'A Guide to FRONTIER Version 4.1: a computer program for stochastic frontier production and cost function estimation', Centre for Efficiency and Productivity Analysis Working Paper 96/07, Armidale: University of New England.

Corden, W.M. (1994) 'Comment' in J. Williamson (ed.) *The Political Economy of Policy Reform*, Washington DC: Institute for International Economics, 111–13.

Costello, P. (Treasurer) (1997) 'Release of the report of the financial system inquiry and initial government response on mergers policy', media release, 9 April.

Croome, J. (1995) *Reshaping the World Trading System: A History of the Uruguay Round,* Geneva: World Trade Organisation, 113–14.

Davis, T.M. (1998) *Open Doors 1997–98: Report on International Education Exchange,* New York: Institute of International Education.

Deardorff, A.V. (1994) 'Market access' in *The New World Trading System: Readings,* Paris: OECD.

Deardorff, A.V. and R.M. Stern (1985) *Methods of Measurement of Non-Tariff Barriers,* Geneva: UNCTAD.

—— (1997) 'Measurement of non-tariff barriers', *OECD Economics Department Working Paper 179,* Paris: OECD.

Dee, P. and Hanslow, K. 1999, Multilateral Liberalisation of Services Trade, Productivity Commission Staff Research Paper, Canberra: Ausinfo.

Dee, P., A. Hardin and M. Schuele (1998) 'APEC early voluntary sectoral liberalisation', Productivity Commission Staff Research Paper, Canberra: AusInfo.

Dee, P., C. Geisler and G. Watts (1996) 'The impact of APEC's free trade commitment', Industry Commission Staff Information Paper, Canberra: Australian Government Publishing Service, February.

Destler, I.M. (1995) *American Trade Politics* (3rd Edition), Washington DC: Institute for International Economics, 304–5.

Dick, H. (1996) 'International airlines and container shipping: a comparison of long-run competitive dynamics', in H. Dick (ed.) *Airline Deregulation in the Asia-Pacific: Towards Open Skies?,* University of Sydney: Institute of Transport Studies, 17–32.

Dick, H. and P. Rimmer (1993) 'The transpacific economy: a network approach to spatial structure', *Asian Geographer,* 12(1&2): 5–17.

Dick, H. and S. Kentwell (1991) *Sold East: Traders, Tramps and Tugs of Chinese Waters,* Melbourne: Nautical Association.

Disclosure (1999) *Global Researcher – Worldscope database,* January, United States: Disclosure.

Donovan, D. and Y.H. Mai (1996) 'APEC trade liberalisation: the impact of increased capital mobility', *Australian Commodities,* 3(4), December, Canberra: ABARE, 520–6.

Drake, W. and K. Nicholäidis (1992) 'Ideas, interests and institutionalization: trade in services and the Uruguay Round, *International Organization,* 46(1), 37–100.

Drysdale, P., A. Elek and H. Soesastro (1998) 'Open regionalism: the nature of Asia Pacific integration', in P. Drysdale (ed.) *Europe, East Asia and APEC: A Shared Agenda,* Cambridge: Cambridge University Press.

DTRD (Department of Transport and Regional Development) (1998) Avstats database, Canberra.

EC (European Commission) (1996) 'Report of United States Barriers to Trade and Investment', Directorate General for External Relations.

ECLAC (Economic Commission for Latin America and the Caribbean) (1998) *Concentration in Liner Shipping: Its Causes and Impacts for Ports and Shipping Services in Developing Regions,* Document LC/G.2027, Santiago: United Nations ECLAC, 20 May.

Elek, A. (1996) 'APEC: An open economics association in the Asia–Pacific region', in B. Bora and C. Findlay (eds) *Regional Integration and the Asia–Pacific,* Melbourne: Oxford University Press, 223–34.

Elek, A., C. Findlay, P. Hooper and T. Warren (1999) 'Open skies or open clubs?: New issues for Asia Pacific Economic Cooperation', *Journal of Air Transport Management,* June.

Ergas, H. (1996) 'Telecommunications across the Tasman: a comparison of regulatory approaches and economic outcomes in Australia and New Zealand', Centre for

Research in Network Economics and Communications, Working Paper Series, University of Auckland.

—— (1998) 'Telecommunications following deregulation' in *Industry Commission, 1997 Industry Economics Conference Proceedings*, Canberra: Industry Commission.

Ergas, H., and P. Paterson (1991) 'International telecommunications settlement arrangements: an unstable inheritance?', *Telecommunications Policy*, 15(1): 29–48.

Ergas, H., E. Ralph and J. Small (1998) 'Declaration of GSM roaming: an economic analysis' (mimeo).

Findlay, C. and T. Warren (1998) 'The General Agreement on Trade in Services in the Asia Pacific and developing countries', a report prepared for the United Nations Economic and Social Commission for Asia and the Pacific, May.

Findlay, C., L.S. Chia and K. Singh (1997) *Asia Pacific Air Transport: challenges and policy reforms*, Singapore: Institute of Southeast Asian Studies.

FLG (WTO Financial Leaders Group) (1997) *Common List of Barriers to Financial Services Trade*, 11 April.

Francois, J.F. and C.R. Shiells (1994) 'AGE models of North American free trade', in J.F. Francois and C.R. Shiells (eds) *Modelling Trade Policy: Applied General Equilibrium Assessments of North American Free Trade*, Cambridge University Press, 3–44.

Francois, J.F. and I. Wooton (1999) 'Trade in international transport services: the role of competition', Centre for Economic Policy Research Discussion Paper (forthcoming), Amsterdam and Rotterdam: Tinbergen Institute, (Internet publication at <http:// www.intereconomics. com/francois/>, August).

Francois, J.F. and K. Reinert (1996) 'The role of services in the structure of production and trade: stylised facts from a cross-country analysis', *Asia-Pacific Economic Review*, 2(1), 35–43.

Frank, B. and J.C. Bunel (1991) 'Contestability, competition and regulation – the case of liner shipping', *International Journal of Industrial Organisation*, 9: 141–59.

Frieden, R. (1996) *International Telecommunications Handbook*, London: Artech House.

Garbacz, C. and H. Thompson (1997) 'Assessing the impact of FCC lifeline and link-up programs on telephone penetration', *Journal of Regulatory Economics*, 11: 67–78.

Gardner, B. (1997) 'EU competition policy and liner shipping conferences', *Journal of Transport Economics and Policy*, 31(3), September, 317–24.

Garnaut, R. (1994) 'Australia' in J. Williamson (ed.) *The Political Economy of Policy Reform*, Washington DC: Institute for International Economics, 51–72.

Gehlhar, M. (1998) 'Bilateral Transport Margins', in McDougall, R.A., A. Elbehri, and T.P. Truong (eds) *Global Trade Assistance and Protection: The GTAP 4 Data Base*, Center for Global Trade Analysis, Purdue University.

Gehlhar, M., D. Gary, T.W. Hertel, K.M. Huff, E. Ianchovichina, B.J. McDonald, R.A. McDougall, M.E. Tsigas and R. Wigle (1997) 'Overview of the GTAP Data Base', in T. W. Hertel (ed.) *Global Trade Analysis: Modeling and Applications*, New York: Cambridge University Press.

Ghang, J.H., D.H. Choi and K.S. Cho (1998) *Emerging New International Shipping Regime and Korean Shipping Policy towards the 21st Century*, Seoul: Korea Maritime Institute.

Gillen, D.W., R. Harris and T.H. Oum (1997) *Assessing the Benefits and Costs of International Air Transport Liberalization*, Draft Report to Transport Canada, July.

Goldstein, M. and P. Turner (1996) 'Banking crises in emerging economies: origins and policy options', *BIS Economic Papers*, 36, October, Basle: BIS.

Government of Indonesia (1998a) *Memorandum of Economic and Financial Policies*, memorandum to IMF, <http://www.imf.org/external/np/LOI/011598.htm>, 15 January.

—— (1998b) *Letter of Intent: Supplementary Memorandum on Economic Policies*, letter and memorandum to IMF, <http://www.imf.org/external/np/loi/041098.htm>, 10 April.

—— (1998c) *Letter of Intent: Second Supplementary Memorandum on Economic Policies*, letter and memorandum to IMF, <http://www.imf.org/external/np/loi/062498.htm>, 24 June.

Government of South Korea (1997a) *Letter of Intent and Memorandum on Economic Program*, letter and memorandum to IMF, <http://www.imf.org/external/np/loi/120397.htm>, 3 December.

—— (1997b) *Summary of Economic Program*, letter and memorandum to IMF, <http://www.imf.org/external/np/oth/korea.htm>, 5 December.

—— (1997c) *Letter of Intent and Memorandum on Economic Program*, letter and memorandum to IMF, <http://www.imf.org/external/np/loi/122497.htm>, 24 December.

—— (1998a) *Letter of Intent and Memorandum on Economic Program*, letter and memorandum to IMF, <http://www.imf.org/external/np/loi/020798.htm>, 7 February.

—— (1998b) *Letter of Intent and Memorandum on Economic Program*, letter and memorandum to IMF, <http://www.imf.org/external/np/loi/050298.htm>, 2 May.

—— (1998c) *Letter of Intent and Memorandum on Economic Program*, letter and memorandum to IMF, <http://www.imf.org/external/np/loi/072498.htm>, 24 July.

Government of Thailand (1997) *Memorandum on Economic Policies of the Royal Thai Government*, letter and memorandum to IMF, <http://www.imf.org/external/np/loi/112597.htm>, 25 November.

—— (1998a) *Memorandum on Economic Policies of the Royal Thai Government*, letter and memorandum to IMF, <http://www.imf.org/external/np/loi/022498.htm>, 24 February.

—— (1998b) *Letter of Intent: Memorandum on Economic Policies of the Royal Thai Government*, letter and memorandum to IMF, <http://www.imf.org/external/np/loi/052698.htm>, 26 May.

—— (1998c) *Letter of Intent: Memorandum on Economic Policies of the Royal Thai Government*, letter and memorandum to IMF, <http://www.imf.org/external/np/loi/082598.htm>, 25 August.

Greene, W.H. (1990) *Econometric Analysis*, New York: Macmillan Press.

Hardin, A. and L. Holmes (1997) 'Services trade and foreign direct investment', Industry Commission Staff Research Paper, Canberra: Australian Government Publishing Service, November.

Hendricks, K., M. Piccione and G. Tan (1995) 'The economics of hubs: the case of monopoly', *Review of Economic Studies*, 62: 83–99.

Hertel, T. (1997) *Global Trade Analysis: Modelling and applications*, Cambridge: Cambridge University Press.

Higher Education Statistics Agency (HESA) (1998) *Students in Higher Education Institutions*, HESA: Cheltenham.

Hill, T. (1977) 'On goods and services', *Review of Income and Wealth*, 24(4): 315–38.

Hirsch, S. (1989) 'Services and service intensity in international trade', *Weltwirtschaftliches Archiv*, 125: 45–60.

Ho, T.S.Y. and A. Saunders (1981) 'The determinants of bank interest margins: theory and empirical evidence', *Journal of Financial and Quantitative Analysis*, 4: 581–600.

Hoekman B. (1995) 'Assessing the General Agreement on Trade in Services', in W. Martin and L.A. Winters (eds) *The Uruguay Round and the Developing Economies*, World Bank Discussion Paper 307, Washington DC: World Bank, pp. 327–64.

Hoekman, B. and C. Braga (1997) 'Protection and trade in services', *Policy Research Working Paper 1747*, Washington DC: World Bank.

Hoekman, B. and M. Kostecki (1995) *The Political Economy of the World Trading System: From GATT to the WTO*, Oxford: Oxford University Press, 68.

Hoekman, B. and P. Mavroidis (1994) 'Competition, competition policy, and the GATT', *World Economy*, 17(2), 121–50.

Hoekman, B. and P. Sauvé (1994) 'Liberalizing trade in services', Discussion Paper 243, Washington DC: World Bank.

Hoekman, B., P. Low and P. Mavroidis (1996) 'Antitrust disciplines and market access negotiations: lessons from the telecommunications sector', paper presented at the Oslo Competition Conference, 13–14 June, Oslo.

Hufbauer, G.C. (1996) 'Surveying the costs of protection: a partial equilibrium approach', in J.J. Schott (ed.) *The World Trading System – Challenges Ahead*, Washington DC: Institute for International Economics, December.

Huff, K.M. and T.W. Hertel (1996) 'Decomposing welfare changes in the GTAP model', *GTAP Technical Paper 5*, West Lafayette, Indiana: Department of Agricultural Economics, Purdue University. Also available from the GTAP website at <http://www.agecon.purdue.edu/gtap/>, dated July 1996.

IC (Industry Commission) (1991) *Availability of Capital*, Report No. 18, Canberra: Australian Government Publishing Service.

—— (1995a) 'The growth and revenue implications of Hilmer and related reforms', a Report by the Industry Commission to the Council of Australian Governments, Canberra.

—— (1995b) Annual Report, 1994–1995, Appendix G, Canberra: Australian Government Publishing Service.

—— (1997) *Trade and Assistance Review 1996–97*, Canberra: Australian Government Publishing Service.

ICAO (International Civil Aviation Organisation) (1996) *Civil Aviation Statistics of the World 1995*, Montreal.

IMF (International Monetary Fund) (1993) *Balance of Payments Manual*, Fifth Edition, Washington DC: IMF.

—— (1995) *International Financial Statistics*, 11, August, Washington DC: IMF.

—— (1996) *International Financial Statistics*, 23, August, Washington DC: IMF.

—— (1997) *International Financial Statistics*, 35, August, Washington DC: IMF.

—— (1998) *International Capital Markets: Developments, Prospects and Key Policy Issues*, September, Washington DC: IMF.

ITU (International Telecommunications Union) (1994) *World Telecommunication Development Report*, Geneva: ITU.

—— (1997) *World Telecommunications Development Report 1996–97*, Geneva: ITU.

—— (1998) *Telecommunications Reform*, 1998, June, Geneva: ITU.

—— (1999) *Telecommunication Reform, 1998 Volumes I–V*, Geneva: ITU.

Jomini, P., R. McDougall G. Watts and P.S. Dee (1994) *The Salter Model of the World Economy: Model Structure, Database and Parameters*, Canberra: Industry Commission.

Kang, J., C. Findlay and D. Choi (1998) 'Prospects for liberalisation in shipping services', paper presented at SEAPOL conference on APEC Ocean Economy and Sustainable Governance, Xiamen, China, 29–30 October.

Karsenty, G. (1999) 'Just how big are the stakes?: An assessment of trade in services by mode of supply', paper presented at the Services 2000: New Directions in Services Trade Liberalization conference, 1–2 June, Washington DC.

Keller, W. (1980) *A General Equilibrium Approach*, Amsterdam: North-Holland.

Kirby, M.G. (1986) 'Airline economics of "scale" and Australian domestic air transport policy', *Journal of Transport Economics and Policy*, 20: 339–52.

KMI (Korea Maritime Institute) (1998) *KMI Research Materials 1998*, Seoul: Korea Maritime Institute (in Korean).

Landes, W. and R. Posner (1981) 'Market Power in Antitrust Cases', Harvard Law Review, 94.

Lederer, P.J. (1993) 'A competitive network design problem with pricing', *Transportation Science*, 27(1): 25–38.

Lerner, A. (1934) 'The concept of monopoly and the measurement of monopoly power', 1 *Review of Economic Studies* 157.

Levine, R. (1996) 'Foreign banks, financial development and economic growth', in C.E. Barfield (ed.) *International Financial Markets: Harmonization versus Competition*, Washington DC: American Enterprise Institute Press.

Low, P. (1995) 'Impact of the Uruguay Round on Asia: trade in services and Trade Related Investment Measures', paper presented at the Asian Development Bank conference, Emerging Global Environment and Developing Asia, Manila, 29–30 May.

Marko, M. (1998a) 'An evaluation of the Basic Telecommunications Services Agreement', paper presented to Measuring Impediments to Trade in Service workshop, Productivity Commission, Canberra, 30 April–1 May.

—— (1998b) 'An evaluation of the Basic Telecommunications Services Agreement', CIES Policy Discussion Paper 98/09, Centre for International Economic Studies, University of Adelaide.

Markusen, J.R. (1995) 'The boundaries of multinational enterprises and the theory of international trade', *Journal of Economic Perspectives*, 9(2), 169–89.

Markusen, J.R., T.F. Rutherford and L. Hunter (1995) 'Trade liberalisation in a multinational dominated industry', *Journal of International Economics*, 38(1–2), February, 95–117.

Mattoo, A. (1996) *National Treatment in the GATS: Corner-stone or Pandora's Box?*, Geneva: WTO.

—— (1998) 'Financial Services and the WTO: Liberalization in the developing and transition economies', paper presented at the Measuring Impediments to Trade in Services workshop, Productivity Commission, Canberra, 30 April–1 May.

McAvoy, P. (1995) 'Tacit collusion under regulation in the pricing of interstate long-distance telephone service', *Journal of Economics and Management Strategy*, 4(2): 147–85.

McDougall, R.A. (1993) 'Incorporating international capital mobility into Salter', *Salter Working Paper 21*, Canberra: Industry Commission.

McDougall, R.A., A. Elbehri, and T.P. Truong (1998) *Global Trade Assistance and Protection: The GTAP 4 Data Base*, Center for Global Trade Analysis, Purdue University.

McGuire, G. (1998) *Australia's Restrictions on Trade in Financial Services*, Staff Research Paper, Canberra: Productivity Commission, November.

McGuire, G. and M. Schuele (1999) 'Asia Pacific restrictions on trade in financial services', paper presented at APEC Business Advisory Council meeting, Brunei Darussalam, 5–7 February.

McKibbin, W.J. and P.J. Wilcoxen (1996) 'The role of services in modelling the global economy', *Asia Pacific Economic Review*, 2(2), August, 3–13.

Meeusen, W. and J. van den Broeck (1977) 'Efficiency estimation from Cobb-Douglas production functions with composed error', *International Economic Review*, 18(2), 435–44.

MITI (Ministry of International Trade and Industry) (1996) *Report on the WTO Consistency of Trade Policies by Major Trading Partners*, Industrial Structure Council of Japan.

Moulton, B.R. (1986) 'Random group effects and the precision of regression estimates', *Journal of Econometrics*, 32: 385–97.

Mueller, J. (1974) 'On sources of measured technical efficiency: the impact of information', *American Journal of Agricultural Economics*, 56: 730–38.

Mukherjee, N. (1996) 'Exporting labour services and market access commitments under GATS in the World Trade Organisation. An analysis from the perspective of developing countries', *Journal of World Trade*, 30(5), October, 21–42.

Mulgan, G. (1991) *Communication and Control: Networks and New Economics of Communication*, New York: Guildford Press.

Nau, H. (1987) 'Bargaining in the Uruguay Round', in J. Finger and A. Olechowski (eds) *The Uruguay Round: A Handbook on Multilateral Trade Negotiations*, Washington DC: The World Bank, 75–80.

NBER (National Bureau of Economic Research) (1998) 'Do we still need commercial banks?', NBER Reporter, Fall, 14–18, Massachusetts: NBER.

NGMTS (Negotiating Group on Maritime Transport Services) (1994) Questionnaire on maritime transport services – Note by the Secretariat: S/NGMTS/W/2, 21 October.

Noll, R. (1995) 'The role of antitrust in telecommunications', *Antitrust Bulletin*, 40(3): 501–28.

OECD (Organisation for Economic Cooperation and Development) (1990) 'Performance indicators for public telecommunications', *Information, Computer and Communications Policy* 22, Paris: OECD.

—— (1994) *The General Agreement on Trade in Services (GATS): An Analysis*, OECD/ GD(94)123, Paris: OECD.

—— (1996) Trade Directorate (TD)/Trade Committee (TC)/Working Party of the Trade Committee Paper No. 50 (WP(96)50), Paris: OECD.

—— (1997a) *Indicators of Tariff and Non-tariff Trade Barriers*, Paris: OECD.

—— (1997b) *Assessing Barriers to Trade in Services: Pilot Study Applications to the Accountancy and Telecommunications Sectors*, TD/TC/WP(97)26, Paris: OECD.

—— (1997c) *Existing Impediments to Maritime and Multimodal Trade in Selected Non-OECD Countries*, DSTI/SI/MTC(97)20, Paris: OECD.

—— (1997d) 'Replies by OECD member countries to the questionnaires for the workshop. Working document for the Third OECD Workshop on Professional Services', 20–21 February, Paris: OECD, 1–353.

—— (1998) *Open Markets Matter: The Benefits of Trade and Investment Liberalisation*, Paris: OECD, April.

Olechowski, A. (1987) 'Nontariff barriers to trade' in J. Finger and A. Olechowski (eds) *The Uruguay Round: A Handbook on Multilateral Trade Negotiations*, Washington DC: The World Bank, 121–6.

Oum, T H. and C. Yu (1995) 'A productivity comparison of the world's major airlines', *Journal of Air Transport Management*, 2: 181–95.

Pangestu, M., C. Findlay, P. Intal and S. Parker (eds) (1996*) Perspectives on the Manila Action Plan for APEC*, Manila: PECC, Asia Foundation and PIDS.

PC (Productivity Commission) (1998a) *Impacts of Competition Enhancing Air Services Agreements: A Network Modelling Approach*, Research Report, Melbourne.

—— (1998b) 'International Air Services Draft Report', June, Melbourne.

PC (Productivity Commission) (1998c) 'International Benchmarking of the Australian Waterfront', Research Report, Canberra: AusInfo, April.

—— (1999) 'International benchmarking of Australian telecommunications services', Research Report, Melbourne: AusInfo, March.

PECC (Pacific Economic Cooperation Council) (1995) *Survey of Impediments to Trade and Investment in the APEC Region*, Singapore: PECC.

Petri, P.A. (1997) 'Foreign direct investment in a computable general equilibrium framework', paper presented at the Making APEC Work: Economic Challenges and Policy Alternatives conference, Keio University, Tokyo, 13–14 March.

Piggott, R. (1996) 'Proposals on advancing liberalisation through regulatory reform', in *OECD, International Trade in Professional Services: Assessing Barriers and Encouraging Reform*, Paris: OECD, 101–7.

PSA (Prices Surveillance Authority) (1993) 'Implications for Australia of shipping conference pricing behaviour', Discussion Paper, Canberra: Australian Government Publishing Service, September.

Ralph, E. and J. Ludwig (1997) 'Competition and telephone penetration: an international statistical comparison', presentation to the TPRC, 27–29 September, Alexandria VA.

RBA (Reserve Bank of Australia) (1994) *Annual Report – 1994 Report and Financial Statements*, RBA, Sydney.

—— (1996) *Prudential Supervision of Banks – Prudential Statements*, Sydney: RBA, March.

Sampson, G. and R. Snape (1985) 'Identifying issues in trade in services', *The World Economy* 8(2): 171–82.

Sargan, J.D. (1964) 'Wages and prices in the United Kingdom: a study in econometric methodology', (with discussion) in *Econometric Analysis for National Economic Planning*, P. E. Hart, G. Mills and J. K. Whitaker (eds.) Butterworths, London, 25–63.

Saunders, A. and L. Schumacher (1997a) *The Determinants of Bank Interest Rate Margins: An International Study*, Washington DC: George Washington University.

—— (1997b) *The Determinants of Bank Interest Margins in Mexico's Post-Privatization Period*, Washington DC: George Washington University.

Sauvé, P. (1995a) 'Designing trade rules for the professions', in *OECD, Liberalisation of Trade in Professional Services*, Paris: OECD, 37–42.

—— (1995b) 'The General Agreement on Trade in Services: much ado about what?', in D.A. Schwanen (ed.) *Trains, Grains, and Automobiles: Canadian Perspectives on the Uruguay Round*, Toronto: C.D. Howe Institute.

Scanlan, M. (1994) 'Introducing competition into the telecommunications network: is competition law rather than regulation the answer?', *Telecommunications Policy*, 18(6): 432–4.

Scherer, F.M. (1987) 'Antitrust, efficiency and progress', *New York University Law Review*, 62(5): 998–1019.

Snape, R.H. (1994) 'Services and the Uruguay Round', in *The New World Trading System: Readings*, Paris: OECD.

—— (1996) 'Which regional trade agreement' in B. Bora and C. Findlay (eds) *Regional Integration and the Asia-Pacific*, Melbourne: Oxford University Press.

Snape, R.H. and M. Bosworth (1996) 'Advancing Service Negotiations', in J. Schott (ed.) *The World Trading System: Challenges Ahead*, Washington DC: Institute for International Economics, 185–203.

Sorsa, P. (1997) *The GATS Agreement on Financial Services – A Modest Start to Multilateral Liberalization*, Geneva: IMF.

Spiller, P. and C. Cardelli (1997) 'The frontier of telecommunications deregulation: small countries leading the pack', *Journal of Economic Perspectives*, 11(4), 127–38.

Stern, R.M. and B.M. Hoekman (1987) 'Issues and data needs for GATT negotiations on services', *The World Economy,* 10(1): 39–60.

—— (1988) 'The services sector in economic structure and in international transactions', in L. Castle and C. Findlay (eds) *Pacific Trade in Services*, Sydney: Allen and Unwin, 19–63.

Taylor, L. (1980) *Telecommunications Demand: A Survey and Critique*, Cambridge, MA: Ballinger Publishing Company.

Terrell, H.S. (1986) The role of foreign banks in domestic banking markets, in H. Cheng (ed.) *Financial Policy and Reform in Pacific-Basin Countries*, Lexington: Lexington Books.

TradePort (1998) Country Library – Market Research Reports, <http://www.tradeport.org/cgi-bin/banner.pl/ts/countries/index.html> (accessed December 1998).

Trewin, R. (1998) 'Applying frontier analysis to measure performance in telecommunications', paper presented to Measuring Impediments to Trade in Services workshop, Productivity Commission, Canberra, 30 April–1 May 1998.

Trewin, R., L. Weiguo, Erwidodo and S. Bahri (1995) 'Analysis of the technical efficiency over time of West Javanese rice farms', *Australian Journal of Agricultural Economics* 39(2), August, 143–63.

UNCTAD (United Nations Conference on Trade and Development) (1996) *World Investment Report 1996: Investment, Trade and International Policy Arrangements*, New York and Geneva: United Nations.

—— (1998a) *World Investment Report 1998: Trends and Determinants*, United Nations Conference on Trade and Development, New York and Geneva: United Nations.

—— (1998b) *Review of Maritime Transport 1998*, UNCTAD/RTM(98)/1, New York and Geneva: United Nations.

UNCTAD and World Bank 1994 *Liberalising International Transactions in Services: A Handbook*, United Nations: New York.

UNESCO (United Nations Educational, Scientific and Cultural Organisation) (1997) *UNESCO Statistical Yearbook*, Paris: UNESCO.

USDT (United States Department of Transportation) (1993) *Maritime Subsidies*, Washington DC: Maritime Administration, US Department of Transportation, September.

USITC (United States International Trade Commission) (1995) 'General Agreement on Trade in Services: examination of major trading partners' schedules of commitments', Publication No. 2940, December.

USTR (United States Trade Representative) (1995) *National Trade Estimate Report on Foreign Trade Barriers*, US Government Printing Office.

—— (1998) *National Trade Estimate Report on Foreign Trade Barriers*, Washington DC, <http://www.ustr.gov> (accessed December 1998).

Vousden, N. (1990) *The Economics of Trade Protection*, Cambridge: Cambridge University Press, 216–18.

Wallenstein, G. (1990) *Setting Global Telecommunication Standards: The Stakes, the Players and the Process*, Norwood MA: Artech House.

Wallis, S., B. Beerworth, J. Carmichael, I. Harper and L. Nicholls (1997) *Financial System Inquiry Discussion Paper*, Canberra: Australian Government Publishing Service.

Warren, T. (1995) 'Trade in telecommunications services', Economics Division Working Paper No. 95/3, Canberra: Research School of Pacific and Asian Studies, Australian National University.

Warren, T. (1996) *The Political Economy of Services Trade and Investment Policy: Australia, Japan and the United States,* doctoral dissertation, Research School of Pacific and Asian Studies, The Australian National University.

—— (1997) 'The political economy of reform of Japanese service industries', *Pacific Economic Papers,* 270.

—— (1998) 'The political economy of telecommunications trade and investment policy' in S. Macdonald and G. Madden (eds) *Telecommunications and Socio-Economic Development,* Oxford: Elsevier.

—— (1999) 'A quantity-impact measure of impediments to trade in telecommunications services', paper presented to the Impediments to Trade in Services: Telecommunications seminar, ANU, Canberra, 19 March 1999.

Warren, T. and C. Findlay (1997) 'Potential for services liberalisation between AFTA and CER', paper presented at the AFTA-CER Linkage: The Way Forward conference, Singapore, 5–6 September.

—— (1999) 'How significant are the barriers? Measuring impediments to trade in services', paper presented at the Service 2000: New Directions in Service Trade Liberalisation Conference at the University Club in Washington DC, 1–2 June.

Warren, T., V. Tamms and C. Findlay (1999) 'Beyond the bilateral system: competition policy and trade in international aviation services', paper presented at the American Economic Association annual meeting and meeting of the Transportation and Public Utilities Group, Network, 3 January.

White, L.J. (1988) *International Trade in Ocean Shipping Services,* Massachusetts: Harper and Row.

World Bank (1998) *World Bank Atlas,* Washington DC: World Bank.

WTO (World Trade Organisation) (1994) *General Agreement on Trade in Services and Related Instruments,* Geneva: WTO, April.

—— (1995) *Trade Policy Review* (for relevant WTO members), Geneva: WTO.

—— (1996) *Trade Policy Review* (for relevant WTO members), Geneva: WTO.

—— (1997a) *Trade Policy Review* (for relevant WTO members), Geneva: WTO.

—— (1997b) *Annual Report 1997,* Geneva: WTO.

—— (1997c) 'Synthesis of the responses to the questionnaire on the accountancy sector', Working Party on Professional Services, S/WPPS/W/11, 5 May, Geneva: WTO.

—— (1998a) *Maritime Transport Services,* background note by the Secretariat, S/C/W/62, 16 November.

—— (1998b) 'Schedules of specific commitments on financial services' (for relevant WTO members), 26 February.

—— (1998c) 'The results of the financial services negotiations under the General Agreement on Trade in Services (GATS)', media release, 4 March.

—— (1998d) *Trade Policy Review* (for relevant WTO members), Geneva: WTO.

—— (1998e), *Education Services,* background note by the Secretariat, September, 98-3691, Geneva: WTO.

WTO/NGMTS (World Trade Organisation/Negotiating Group on Maritime Transport Services) (1994) *Compilation of Specific Commitments: Maritime Transport Services,* Geneva: WTO, 24 June.

Yong, J.S. (1996) 'Excluding capacity-constrained entrants through exclusive dealing: theory and an application to ocean shipping', *Journal of Industrial Economics,* 44(2): 115–29.

Index